"Scott Aniol's *Changed from Glory into Glory* is an excell[...] y and practice of worship in the Old Testament and the Ch[...] estament to the present. Though writing from the [...] -handed approach points out the positive featu[...] reas in which they might have gone astray. He [...] iblical and historical study, that how we worshi[...] learned a lot from it—and you will too. This is a fine res[...] layperson alike, and it deserves careful and prayerful reading."

David W. Music
Professor of Church Music
Baylor University

"The reasons that I am enthusiastic about this book are many, but I will condense them to these five. One, it gives a narrative and doctrinal interaction with the history of Christian worship from Adam to the present. Two, it shows the revealed manner of worship from Genesis to Revelation isolating the principles that govern God's message of how he is to be approached. Three, it shows how these principles were implemented and followed in large part throughout the history of the church while indicating how culture and populism began to reshape the cultus and even pollute this biblical pattern. Four, the author unashamedly, and in harmony with the necessity of Christian witness and conviction, encourages sound biblical thinking about the preeminent element of human life, worship. Five, he sets forth a specific manner of ordering worship that he believes is in accord with biblical principles and the best elements of liturgical development in the church—Gospel-shaped worship. This book is a work of Christian scholarship, thoroughly engaging to the mind, challenging to the heart, and is aimed at edification in a way equivalent to its information."

Tom J. Nettles
Senior Professor of Historical Theology
Southern Baptist Theological Seminary

"Like many of the deepest realities of Christianity, worship itself involves a both/and proposition. As Scott Aniol helpfully points out in *Changed from Glory into Glory*, what happens when Christians gather to adore God both expresses what they believe as well as forms that belief. With a bold historical trajectory that stretches from the Bible to today, Aniol explores that critical two-fold dynamic for Christians past and present."

Lester Ruth
Research Professor of Christian Worship
Duke Divinity School

"Anybody who wants to live responsibly should understand the symbiotic relationship between worldview and worship, which shapes us all. Actually, understanding it should be *obligatory* for Christian leaders, and I know of no better guide than this book. It's a brief but comprehensive survey of how Christians have answered the second most important question in our lives: what are we saved for? Here you will encounter voices from the past, yet the argument looks forward, and the prose is clear. There's something for every curious reader."

Paul Munson
Professor of Music
Grove City College

"Scott Aniol is absolutely correct that worship practices shape our lives, our beliefs, and our history far more than we often realize. Therefore, if we want to disciple ourselves and others, we need to pay careful attention to and give significant thought to our worship practices. However, we have tended to be uninformed of how the church across the ages has thought and worked in terms of worship, leaving us captive to the whims of our current settings. Aniol has done us a great service in this book by giving us a thorough history of the church in terms of worship, which can help us think along with the church across the ages about how we can faithfully worship the Lord and cultivate godliness. This is a rich treasure, and I warmly commend it to all."

Ray Van Neste
Dean, School of Theology & Missions
Union University

"*Changed from Glory into Glory: The Liturgical Story of the Christian Faith* is a book I've been hoping someone would write for a long time, and I can't think of a more qualified person to write it than Scott Aniol. He masterfully synthesizes historical, cultural, theological, and biblical tributaries that converge in the ocean of Christian worship—an ocean that ultimately shapes and forms the devotional lives of every believer. The accessible and engagingly written content in Dr. Aniol's book fits beautifully in the minds and hearts of students in a seminary classroom, a church Bible study, or the lay person simply wanting to explore the liturgical history of the Christian faith and how worship has formed our religion and how our religion has formed our worship. I have already used several portions of this book as significant resource material for the class I teach on the theology of worship, and it will be required reading for my future classes on this subject. Both the church and the academy have been given a wonderful gift in *Changed from Glory into Glory*."

Joseph R. Crider
Dean, School of Church Music and Worship
Southwestern Baptist Theological Seminary

"The worship of God is a field that demands careful biblical study, thoughtful historical appraisal, and pastoral care. Aniol writes with a clear commitment to honor the Lord in truth, affection, and obedience. This work instructs us to consider liturgical studies in order that our worship practices might please the Lord, edify the church in our mission of making disciples, and faithfully proclaim the completed work of Christ."

Matt Boswell
Hymnwriter
Assistant Professor of Church Music and Worship
The Southern Baptist Theological Seminary

"In this book, Scott Aniol leads us on a fascinating, guided tour of worship from ancient Israel to the contemporary church. This book carefully examines a vast variety of approaches to liturgy through the ages. Aniol has provided a very helpful resource for both students of the history of worship and those charged to lead worship today."

Joel R. Beeke
President
Puritan Reformed Theological Seminary

"In my twenty years of teaching worship, I have never seen a book that so skillfully narrates the history of Christian worship in the context of pastoral and broadly Reformed commitments. This book will be eminently useful in introductory worship courses as well as courses in the history or theology of worship. Lay and scholarly readers across denominational lines—and regardless of their approach to the practice of Christian worship—will benefit greatly from this volume, which effectively weds careful historical synthesis with practical liturgical awareness and concern. I highly recommend it."

Matthew Pinson
President, Welch College

"This new work on the entire history of Christian worship and liturgy (the latter always present whether acknowledged or not) is indeed ambitious, yet so needed. In a single compass, Prof. Aniol capably traverses two millennia of Christian worship. In such a large survey, it is no surprise to find places here and there where a knowledgeable reader might have expressed things differently. Nonetheless, Prof. Aniol has put all who discuss this vital area of the Christian world in his debt: we have here a trustworthy guide to the form of Christian worship as it has been developed since the Apostolic era as well as incisive analysis as to the why and wherefore of this development. Ideal for personal study or as a course text."

Michael A.G. Haykin
Chair & professor of church history,
The Southern Baptist Theological Seminary.

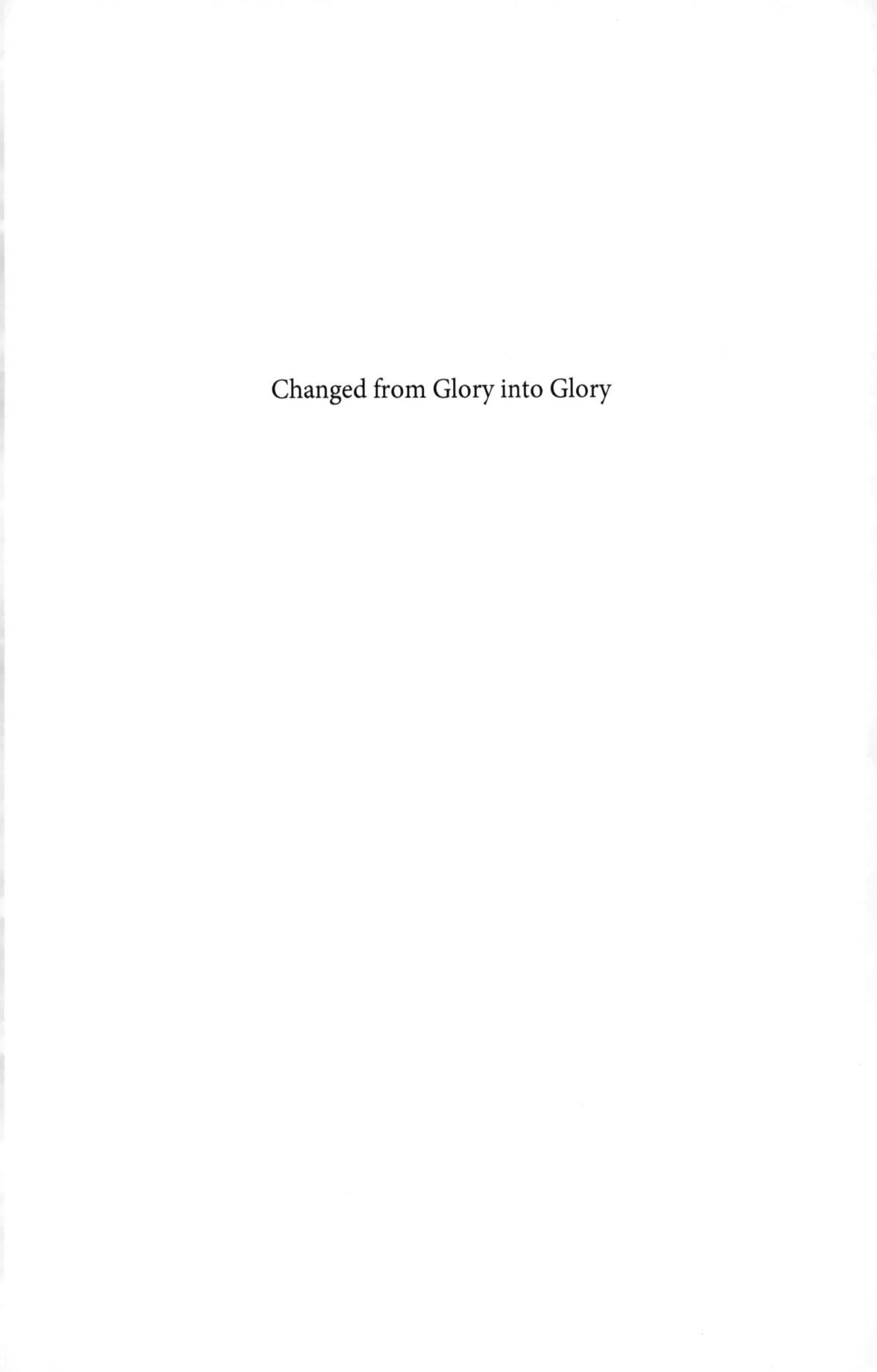

Changed from Glory into Glory

Scott Aniol

Changed from Glory into Glory

The Liturgical Story of The Christian Faith

Changed from Glory into Glory
Copyright © Scott Aniol 2022

All rights reserved. This book or any portion thereof may not be reproduced or used in any manner whatsoever without the express written permission of the publisher except for the use of brief quotations in a book review.

Published by: Joshua Press, Peterborough, Ontario
www.JoshuaPress.com

Cover design by Corey M.K. Hughes

Hardcover ISBN: 978-1-77484-048-1
Paperback ISBN: 978-1-77484-049-8
Ebook ISBN: 978-1-77484-050-4

Contents

Foreword by David S. Dockery	xi
What Is a Liturgical History?	1
Chapter 1: Worldview-Forming Worship	7

PART ONE: THE OLD TESTAMENT

Chapter 2: Foundations of Worship	21
Chapter 3: The Golden Age of Hebrew Worship	37
Chapter 4: Exile and Return	53
Conclusion to Part One	65

PART TWO: THE NEW TESTAMENT

Chapter 5: Jesus Christ	73
Chapter 6: New Testament Worship	87
Chapter 7: A Theology of Christian Worship	103
Conclusion to Part Two	115

PART THREE: CATHOLIC CHRISTIANITY

Chapter 8: The Early Church	123
Chapter 9: The Expansion of Worship	139
Chapter 10: The Unification of Worship	151
Conclusion to Part Three	165

PART FOUR: REFORMATION

Chapter 11: The German Reformation	173
Chapter 12: Worship Regulated by Scripture	187
Chapter 13: The English Reformation	201
Conclusion to Part Four	215

PART FIVE: SHIFTING SANDS

Chapter 14: A New Worldview Emerges	223
Chapter 15: The Rise of Evangelical Worship	237
Chapter 16: Contemporary Worship	251
Conclusion to Part Five	267

PART SIX: LOOKING FORWARD
    Chapter 17: By the Waters of Babylon: Worship in a Post-Christian Culture   275
    Chapter 18: How Corporate Worship Makes Disciples   289

Appendices
    Appendix 1 Planning a Gospel-Shaped Worship Service   303
    Appendix 2 Glossary   315
    Appendix 3 Timeline   321
    Appendix 4 For Further Study   327

Index   331
Scripture Index   339

Foreword

Changed from Glory into Glory, by Scott Aniol, tells the story of the worship and beliefs of the people of God in a thoughtful and insightful way since the days of the Old Testament saints. Aniol rightly contends that most followers of Christ, including church leaders, need to think afresh about the Trinitarian God, Scripture, creeds, confessional beliefs, hymns, and worship practices. This engaging book that you hold in your hands serves as a splendid resource to guide Christians in our beliefs and practices as well as in the worship of our majestic God.

The apostle Paul, writing to the church at Thessalonica, urged the followers of Jesus Christ to "stand firm and hold to the traditions you were taught, either by our message or by our letter" (2 Thess 2:15). Similarly, the apostle exhorted Timothy, his apostolic legate, to "hold on to the pattern of sound teaching that you have heard from me" (2 Tim 1:13a). The history of Christianity shows us wonderful examples of where the church has stood firm and held faithfully to the pattern of Christian teaching and the best of the Christian tradition. The interpretive historical overview found in this volume also enables us to see where the church has lost its compass along the way. Aniol skillfully guides his readers to see the strength and weaknesses in each epoch of the church's story.

Often those who study the history of doctrine fail to take into consideration the close connection between the church's teachings and the worship practices of the church. Others, who study the history of liturgy often do so by divorcing these practices from theology. The great church historian Jaroslav Pelikan, in his voluminous writings about the church's tradition, often reminded us that faithful doctrinal understanding must include a comprehensive understanding of what the church has believed, taught, and confessed on the basis of the Word of God. Aniol brings together belief, teaching, and confession as he enables readers to connect worldview and worship, doctrine and liturgy, Christian thought and Christian practice, doing so in an edifying manner. Given the variety of practices in contemporary Christian worship and the accompanying challenges represented in the historical tradition, *Changed from Glory into Glory* is as timely as it is informative.

The challenges to traditional forms of worship in recent decades have created an uneasiness for many. Renewal in our worship will require time, patience, and careful instruction. Aniol's work points to an understanding of worship as the active response to God the Father through the Son as enabled by the Holy Spirit. Praise, prayer, preaching, the celebration of the ordinances/sacraments, confession, and giving are all Christ-centered, scripturally informed actions. The focus of the church's worship on the exalted Christ provides a Spirit-enabled and much needed depth for our lives and our practice. We see through the pages of history that the worship of God through the Son has taken place in and by the Holy Spirit. Thus, we see that fitting and acceptable worship for our day can only be offered by and through the enabling ministry of the Holy Spirit.

While using history as the window to think carefully and wisely about Christian worship, Aniol is not hesitant to ground worship in the teaching of Holy Scripture. In Acts 2, the early church experienced formal celebration in the temple and informal gatherings in the homes. The theme of this book reminds us not to neglect the whole counsel of God

(Acts 20:27) when thinking about worship and the renewal of worship. Our priority is to create worship services that touch lives, edify the people of God, and exalt the Trinitarian God. Anything less will fail to be faithful to Scripture and the best of Christian tradition.

In Romans 15:5, the apostle Paul asks God to grant the gift of unity to the church, resulting in a unity of praise, so that with one mind and one mouth we may glorify God (Rom. 15:6). Not only does Christian unity help to encourage faithful worship, but our shared worship promotes a common unity. With discerning hearts as to how such an observation is applied today, we note that in the life of the early church it was affirmed that the *lex orandi* is the *lex credendi*; that is, the law of praying and worship is the law of believing. Believers are called to come together regularly (Heb 10:25) to offer praise, adoration, and worship to our great and gracious God. We come to worship as redeemed men and women in need of ongoing and sanctifying grace.

After working our way through Aniol's insightful historical survey, we recognize that the ultimate purpose for believers in every age and every context is the worship and praise of the one who called us unto himself (Eph 1:3-14). To worship God is to ascribe to him the supreme worth which he alone is worthy to receive. Worship is desired by God and made possible by his grace. To worship God includes reverence and adoration; it also involves a corporate confession of faith as well as Spirit-prompted service expressed in prayer and singing, which points toward an indissoluble relationship between worship and a life of service, resulting in lives of discipleship that are pleasing to God. *Changed from Glory into Glory* calls for us to reprioritize the worship and praise of almighty God in the life of the twenty-first century church. As we come together to worship, we will seek to provide opportunities where tradition and creativity can serve as sources of renewal and reform for our worship.

Aniol encourages us to see that Christian worship needs renewal because our church services tend to be pragmatic, experience oriented, and human centered. The biblical view of worship tells us that worship is to be focused on God, as we exalt his name and recognize his glory. Renewal in our worship will be characterized by an emphasis on faithful preaching as well as reading and hearing the Word of God, a high degree of congregational involvement in praise, prayer, singing, giving, and confession, and a view of the ordinances/sacraments which affirms their mystery and value for spiritual formation.

As Aniol has shown, several sectors of contemporary church life tend to be confused about the nature and mission of the church, evidence a minimal use of the Bible, especially its public reading, to manifest a variety of understandings about the purpose and practice of worship and have an inadequate view of the church's ordinances/sacraments. Moreover, Aniol has given us examples throughout history when the church has seemingly lost its way and the Spirit of God has intervened to bring about reform and renewal. One of the first steps toward rediscovering the importance of worship in our day is to point the people of God toward the reprioritizing of worship. We must help people learn afresh that worship is not passive but active. We gather on the Lord's Day to acknowledge and offer heartfelt thanks for what God has done for us and is doing in us.

Changed from Glory into Glory guides us toward appreciating anew that Christian worship is primarily rooted in an event, the Christ-event in which God has revealed himself as our loving and compassionate Creator and Redeemer. Indeed, worship serves as a response to the birth, ministry, death, resurrection, and exaltation of Jesus Christ. Authentic worship is possible only as the Spirit of God enables this response and prompts our love and

Foreword

praise of God. Moreover, this volume points us to resources and lessons found in the history of the church that should not be ignored. We learn that much which is often easily dismissed as tradition can be rebaptized by the Holy Spirit to shape our congregational worship. Our author's purpose in tracing the various paths of the liturgical tradition is not necessarily to help us become expert church historians, but to help us retrieve and recapture the best aspects of this tradition as life-giving resources of renewal

As Aniol has emphasized in his other writings, the church needs to rediscover the significance and importance of Christian communion. If the central act of worship in the New Testament is the corporate celebration of the Lord's Supper, then we should seek to give it renewed focus. The regular observance of the Supper will enhance our love for the Lord, reminding us regularly of what he has done for us in the redemptive work on the cross while granting us hope as we look toward and long for his promised return. Another important aspect of Christian practice to recover is the need to prepare for worship. Church leaders need to step back and take a fresh look at what is involved in Scripture-guided worship as well as in structuring services to have coherent movement that is theologically, biblically, and thematically informed. When this begins to take place, worshipers will start to gather not just to listen and observe, but to exalt God and to affirm their faith.

Renewal in our worship will refocus an emphasis on the importance of all things being done for the glory of God (1 Cor 10:31). The church will begin to turn away from the secularly influenced and individualistic emphases that so easily find their way into our practice. Instead, believers will seek to prioritize those things which will bring about mutual edification in the body of Christ (1 Cor 14:26). This mutual upbuilding through the development of mutual relationships will take place as members carry out their various ministries in the power of the Spirit.

When genuine worship takes place, not only will the entire body be enhanced and built up but also the mission and outreach of the church will be strengthened. Notice that in Isaiah 6:1-8, after the prophet had authentically encountered God high and lifted up, three things resulted: (1) a renewed recognition of who God is; (2) a fresh realization of the need for repentance and forgiveness; and (3) a new desire for mission. The people of God who have worshiped their God and who have been mutually strengthened will be prepared to enter the world for a life of God-honoring service, outreach, and mission. Exalting God and reaching people are hardly in conflict. As a matter of fact, real outreach, evangelism, and missions are prefaced on genuine worship as we see time and again in both the Old Testament and the New (Is 6:1–8; Matt 28: 16–20; John 4; and Acts 13).

As you work your way through this excellent book, I want to invite you to join me in praying for the Spirit of God to use this volume to bring renewal to our worship and in the lives of congregations around the globe. As we learn from history, let us thoughtfully reflect on the positive lessons worthy of emulation while seeking to avoid repeating the errors of previous generations. I know that when you have finished reading *Changed from Glory into Glory,* you will join with me in giving thanks for Scott Aniol and this gift he has provided for us. May God enable Christ followers to recover the significance and vitality of authentic biblical worship for our individual lives, for our families, and for our churches.

Soli Deo Gloria

David S. Dockery
President, International Alliance for Christian Education and Distinguished Professor of Theology,
Southwestern Baptist Theological Seminary

What Is a Liturgical History?

This book is a history of the Christian faith, but it's not your typical church history—it is a *liturgical* history of the Christian faith. Allow me to explain what I mean.

There are many valuable ways to study the history of the church; church historians often trace the development of creedal theology, recount the lives of key theologians and church leaders, or study significant events in the life of the church. Each of these is a valuable way to understand how we arrived where we are today. Some of the most helpful examples of general church histories of this kind include Justo L. González's *The Story of Christianity* (HarperOne, 2010), Zondervan's two volume *Church History* by Ferguson, Woodbridge, and James III (2013), and Mark A. Noll's *Decisive Moments in the History of Christianity* (Baker, 2012).

I am convinced, however, for reasons that will become apparent throughout the book, that one of the best ways to truly understand what lies at the core of the Christian faith is by studying its worship. As I will show in Chapter 1, the Christian religion is more than its theology; in fact, very often what truly constitutes the central commitments of Christianity in various stages of history actually differs from the prominent creeds of the period. Rather, one of the most accurate indicators of the central convictions of a church or movement is the way that it worships.

The Problem
Yet, I think it's safe to say that most evangelical Christians don't realize this about their worship. Worship is what we do when we gather for church on Sunday—we sing some songs and listen to a sermon that hopefully will give us some practical advice for the week. Worship for most evangelicals tends to focus on methodology: How many songs will we sing? What instrumentation will we use? In what order will we organize the service? How we worship is based on cultural conventions, preferences of the people, or tradition. What matters is what we believe and the sincerity of our hearts; how we worship is simply the authentic overflow of our hearts toward God.

The Solution
My goal in this book is to demonstrate that corporate worship does something far more significant than many Christians recognize—liturgy forms our religion. But as I will show, the reverse is equally true—religion forms our liturgy. It's the age-old chicken-and-egg question: which comes first? The answer depends on from which perspective we're looking. From the perspective of leaders among God's people who

have given intentional considerations to these matters, religion forms liturgy. But for most Christians who have not thought much about it—leaders and laity alike—liturgy has formed their religion without them even knowing it. I am convinced that a central solution to problems we face today in evangelical Christianity is to recover a lost understanding that worship involves more than simply expressing devotion to God through songs we enjoy; rather, worship forms the very core of who we are as Christians.

The Story
This is where the liturgical story will help us. Most of this book traces biblical and church history with a specific focus upon the worship of God's people. The study of what has come before us teaches us what we would not otherwise understand if we limited our focus to the present time only, and it can teach us in at least three ways. First, it can help us to recognize error and understand how it develops. A reason Christians may resist studying the history of Christian worship is the immediately apparent errors that crept into Christian worship very early in its development. This fact may cause some to wonder about the value of such study. Yet the study of error is always valuable since it helps us to avoid those same errors today. Edmund Burke's oft-repeated axiom, "Those who don't know history are doomed to repeat it," is as true for worship as it is for any other sphere. Studying where people have gone wrong will help us prevent those same mistakes.

Another way we are taught through the study of history is by recognizing the common successes that we should emulate. God's people have certainly made many mistakes in their understanding and practice of worship along the way, but they have often succeeded as well. By studying those successes, we can observe how God-pleasing worship has formed God-pleasing Christians so that we can achieve the same purpose with our worship today.

It is common for well-meaning Christians to piously proclaim that in order to worship God rightly, all they need is to study the Bible's principles and apply them to contemporary settings. Yet this perspective is dangerously naïve. Yes, our primary focus is the ministry of worship today, but the study of what happened yesterday is profoundly important for us to be able to understand today. The prophet Isaiah recognized this when he said, "Listen to me, you who pursue righteousness, you who seek the Lord: look to the rock from which you were hewn, and to the quarry from which you were dug" (Isa. 51:11). As we shall see, where we are today is not by random chance; the problems we face in worship, as well as the good that we see, find deep roots in what has happened between the early church and today. If we want to understand where we are today, we must "look to the rock from which [we] were hewn."

What Is a Liturgical Worship?

Finally, the study of the development of worship through history will help us understand and prepare for tomorrow. Ecclesiastes 1:9 observes, "What has been is what will be, and what has been done is what will be done, and there is nothing new under the sun." What is the best way for us to prepare for the years ahead when we have no idea what new philosophical, cultural, sociological, and ecclesiastical problems will arise? The best way is to study what has happened before, because it is sure to happen again.

A Roadmap

The first and last chapters of this book provide its central argument; everything in between—the liturgical story itself—supports and illustrates my thesis that religion forms our liturgy, and liturgy forms our religion. Chapter 1 constructs the framework upon which I will tell the liturgical story of the Christian faith. I unpack the two core elements of my thesis—religion and liturgy—to explain what I mean by these terms so that we can better observe them and how they interact in the story. Chapters 2 through 16 tell the story:

Part One: The Old Testament
    Chapter 2: Foundations of Worship
    Chapter 3: The Golden Age of Hebrew Worship
    Chapter 4: Exile and Return
Part Two: The New Testament
    Chapter 5: Jesus Christ
    Chapter 6: New Testament Worship
    Chapter 7: A Theology of Christian Worship
Part Three: Catholic Christianity
    Chapter 8: The Early Church
    Chapter 9: The Expansion of Worship
    Chapter 10: The Unification of Worship
Part Four: Reformation
    Chapter 11: The Reformation of Worship
    Chapter 12: Worship Regulated by Scripture
    Chapter 13: English Reformations
Part Five: Divergence
    Chapter 14: A New Worldview Emerges
    Chapter 15: The Rise of Evangelical Worship
    Chapter 16: Contemporary Worship
Part Six: Looking Forward
    Chapter 17: By the Waters of Babylon: Worship in a Post-Christian Culture

Throughout the story, I have made it a point as much as possible to quote the words of the important theologians and church leaders themselves, including their poetry and prayers, and outline their worship services so that you can immerse yourself in the story, experiencing for yourself how these various worship practices have formed the religion of God's people.

The final chapter provides an interpretation of the story through the framework set forth in Chapter 1, highlighting how throughout the story, religion has formed liturgy, and liturgy has formed religion. I conclude with some suggestions for how this might impact evangelical worship today.

How to Use this Book
Throughout the book, I have provided tools to make this a helpful resource for individuals, church small groups, or introductory worship courses at the undergraduate and graduate levels. Every Part in the book concludes with a **Study Guide** that can help support comprehension, discussion, reflection, and further study in each of the eras of liturgical history under consideration.

People and Terms
At the end of each Part, I have included a list of important people and terms that appeared in the section. This can provide a helpful review of what was covered in the section as well as a reference list for those wishing to commit the information to memory.

Recommended Resources
Since this book covers an incredible vast period of time—the entire history of the world!—I certainly have not gone into considerable depth on every topic. Other helpful books cover periods of liturgical history in more detail, and I have included a list of some of them at the end of each Part for those who wish to study a particular era more.

Questions for Study and Reflection
Each Study Guide includes several questions based on the information in the section. These questions could be used by an individual for personal reflection, by small groups to stimulate discussion based on the material in that part, or professors could use these as essay questions in a course using this book as its text.

What Is a Liturgical Worship?

Glossary
I have included a glossary at the end of the book that provides succinct definitions of people and terms found in the history.

Timeline
Finally, I have provided a timeline of the events covered in the book as a ready reference.

The Goal
It is my prayer that by experiencing the liturgical story of the Christian faith, you will better grasp the central significance of corporate worship in the formation of God's people. If you are a church leader, my intent is to help you consider how the practices you employ week by week in your corporate worship *have been formed* by certain religious commitments and *are forming* the people in your congregation because of the commitments those practices embody. If you are a Christian church member, my purpose is to help you think intentionally about what values the worship practices you perform each week embody and how those are forming you.

Chapter 1
Worldview-Forming Worship

Imagine a dense forest separating two cities. In order to engage in commerce between these cities, merchants must pass through the forest. For the earliest of these merchants, this was a very difficult task, wrought with many mistakes and casualties. Eventually, though, over time and with experience, the merchants discovered the safest, quickest route through the forest. Once they did, they began to carefully mark the path so that they would remember the best way to go. Even then, each of these early journeys required careful attention to the markers so that they would not stray from the best way. Over time, however, their regular trips along that same route began to form a much more visible path to the degree that years later merchants hardly pay attention; they doze peacefully as their horses casually follow the heavily trod road. Here now is a well-worn path cut through the wood upon which travelers mindlessly pass from one city to the other. This path may seem mundane, but in reality, it is embedded with values such as desire for safety, protection from the dangers of the forest, and conviction that this is the quickest way through. The snoozing merchants do not give thought to these values any longer, but the values are there nonetheless, and whether they know it or not, their journey has been shaped by those values. Those values are, as it were, worn into the shape of the path itself.

This fictional story represents the liturgical story of the Christian faith, well-illustrating the dynamic, formative nature of the relationship between religion and liturgy. Christian religion is like a path through the forest that was formed long ago, but along which God's people travel through life every day. Sometimes this formation occurs consciously, but most of the time the journey of God's people has been shaped by values imbedded in their liturgies in ways Christian pilgrims rarely recognize.

It is for the purpose of understanding the formative relationship between religion and liturgy that I tell the liturgical story of Christian religion. But before I do, I need to further clarify what I mean by both *religion* and *liturgy*.

What Is the Nature of Religion?
Worldview
Religion is composed of two parts, the first of which is worldview. A worldview consists of a set of assumptions a person holds about reality; it is a lens through which he understands and interprets everything around him. James Sire has provided a helpful and influential definition of worldview:

A worldview is a commitment, a fundamental orientation of the heart, that can be expressed as a story or in a set of presuppositions (assumptions which may be true, partially true, or entirely false) that we hold (consciously or subconsciously, consistently or inconsistently) about the basic constitution of reality, and that provides the foundation on which we live and move and have our being.[1]

Several elements of this definition are important to recognize. First, central to this definition of worldview is that it is "*a fundamental orientation of the heart.*" In fact, David Naugle has suggested that what philosophers today call "worldview" is essentially equivalent to the biblical concept of the "heart." He argues, "As the image and likeness of God, people are animated subjectively from the core and throughout their being by that primary faculty of thought, affection, and will which the Bible calls the 'heart.'"[2] In both the Old and New Testaments, the idea of heart refers to "the central defining element of the human person."[3] Naugle observes,

> In Hebraic thought the heart is comprehensive in its operations as the seat of the intellectual (e.g., Prov. 2:10a; 14:33; Dan. 10:12), affective (e.g., Exod. 4:14; Ps. 13:2; Jer. 15:16), volitional (e.g., Judg. 5:15; 1 Chr. 29:18; Prov. 16:1), and religious life of a human being (e.g., Deut. 6:5; 2 Chr. 16:9; Ezek. 6:9; 14:3).[4]

Likewise in the New Testament, "the heart is the psychic center of human affections (Matt. 22:37–39; John 14:1, 27; 2 Cor. 2:4), the source of the spiritual life (Acts 8:21; Rom. 2:29; 2 Cor. 3:3), and the seat of the intellect and the will (Rom. 1:21; 2 Cor. 9:7; Heb. 4:12)."[5] Thus, while the philosophical concept of worldview is a relatively recent philosophical development, "what the heart is and does in a biblical way is what the philosophers were getting at unconsciously in coining the term 'world-view.'"[6] A worldview is not primarily a set of ideas or beliefs; rather, it involves the innate inclinations at our core.

This leads to a second important characteristic of worldview: a worldview is *a set of assumptions about the basic constitution of reality*. Since worldview is not primarily stated beliefs but rather an orientation of the heart, these assumptions about reality are not usually stated or held explicitly; rather, they become formed within us often without any conscious intention. Another word for this is what philosophers have called

---

[1] James W. Sire, *Naming the Elephant: Worldview as a Concept*, 2nd edition (Downers Grove: IVP Academic, 2015), 141.
[2] David K. Naugle, *Worldview: The History of a Concept* (Grand Rapids: Eerdmans, 2002), 267.
[3] Naugle, *Worldview*, 266.
[4] Naugle, *Worldview*, 268.
[5] Naugle, *Worldview*, 268–269.
[6] Naugle, *Worldview*, 270.

the moral imagination—an inner image of the world. Everything we encounter filters through and is interpreted by this inner image. Sire provides eight helpful questions that form the presuppositions that lie at the core of our worldview:

1. What is prime reality—the really real?
2. What is the nature of external reality, that is, the world around us?
3. What is a human being?
4. What happens to a person at death?
5. Why is it possible to know anything at all?
6. How do we know what is right and wrong?
7. What is the meaning of human history?
8. What personal, life-orienting core commitments are consistent with this worldview?[7]

Now, in evaluating a worldview, these assumptions can be stated, and as we shall see, we can consciously and intentionally assess and even change our assumptions—we can reorient our hearts. But in the normal course of life, most people do not give careful reflection on these questions or evaluate their worldview; rather, these innermost assumptions about reality, assumptions that orient the core of our being, are naturally formed very early in life based on what we experience in the environments in which we grow; thus, a worldview often develops subconsciously, unless we intentionally reshape our worldview based on other factors.

Third, it is the heart orientation of a worldview that *"provides the foundation on which we live and move and have our being."* The inner image of the world formed within us—our moral imagination—interprets reality and thus affects how we evaluate and respond to what we encounter. It is what motivates and moves us to act in certain ways within the various circumstances of life. This is why the Bible commands, "Keep your heart with all vigilance, for from it flow the springs of life" (Prov. 4:23). As Naugle suggests,

> From a scriptural point of view, therefore, the heart is responsible for how a man or woman sees the world. Indeed, what goes into the heart from the outside world eventually shapes its fundamental dispositions and determines what comes out of it as the springs of life. Consequently, the heart establishes the basic presuppositions of life and, because of its life-determining influence, must always be carefully guarded.[8]

---

[7] Sire, *Naming the Elephant*, 20–21
[8] Naugle, *Worldview*, 272.

This is all the case for individuals, but it is also characteristic of entire societies. Because a worldview is a heart orientation formed in an environment, individuals within particular communities tend to develop similar assumptions about reality and thus a collective worldview. It is also important to recognize at this point the possibility that certain worldview assumptions of non-believers can often be very similar to that of a biblical worldview. This is true for two biblical reasons: first, all people are made in the image of God (Gen. 1:27); second, God's creation provides a general revelation that reveals to all people God's "invisible attributes, namely, his eternal power and divine nature" (Rom. 1:20). Unbelievers suppress this truth about God, but nevertheless their assumptions about reality emerge from that suppressed knowledge—they borrow the biblical worldview without even knowing it, and they operate in the world as if God exists while at the same time rejecting him. For example, throughout most of the course of human history, even unbelieving people have assumed the existence of an immaterial reality that cannot be perceived merely with the physical senses, and therefore they have sought to interpret what happened in the world around them on the basis of transcendent reality, just like God's people do. Yet while God's people share worldview assumptions like this with some unbelievers, ultimately their heart orientation is different, and this is due to a fundamental difference of the second component of religion—theology.

Theology
Broadly speaking, theology is how we intentionally answer the questions Sire provided above that form the assumptions at the core of our worldview. What we believe about the nature of reality, the purpose and meaning of life, the basis of right and wrong, and most importantly God form our theology. Theology and worldview are, therefore, very closely related—they both involve answers to the same sorts of questions, and they both fundamentally influence the way we live. The difference I am drawing between them is that the assumptions that form worldview are fundamentally subconscious and unsated, while the beliefs that form theology are consciously affirmed. Theology is fundamentally propositional, while worldview is affective. Theology is usually more deliberately developed than worldview, often explicitly taught and based on sacred documents. For Judaism and Christianity, of course, theology is based on the divine revelation found in Scripture.

Worldview and theology interact dynamically. On the one hand, our fundamental assumptions about the nature of reality affect the kind of theology we are willing to accept; sometimes the worldview a person has inculcated early in life will make accepting certain theological propositions more difficult unless he is willing to adjust his worldview. On the other hand, as we consciously develop a theology, that theology can

Worldview-Forming Worship

begin to reform our worldview, especially if we are aware of conflict between our worldview and theology. This lies at the root of Jesus' command, "Let not your hearts be troubled. Believe in God; believe also in me" (John 15:1); he was commanding his disciples to change the orientation of the hearts through a change in belief.

Like worldview, our theology fundamentally affects how we live. As A. W. Tozer famously stated, "What comes into our minds when we think about God is the most important thing about us."[9] However, if a conflict does exist between our worldview and our theology, and we are unaware of that conflict, at the end of the day our worldview is more fundamental. In other words, we may consciously say we believe certain things, but if we have not worked to change the orientation of our hearts to reflect our stated beliefs, our heart's orientation is what will ultimately determine how we live.

Religion

Everyone has an implicit worldview—a fundamental orientation of the heart expressed in assumptions about reality, and most people have an explicit theology—conscious beliefs expressed in stated propositions. The combination of worldview and theology is what constitutes a religion. Expressed in this way, all people have a religion, whether they acknowledge it or not. Even atheists have a religion; their worldview consists of an assumption that only matter is real, combined with a theology that denies the existence of God. This produces an atheist religion that affects everything about how they live and interact in society.

Thus, while believers and unbelievers may sometimes hold to similar assumptions about the nature of reality, since their theologies are fundamentally different, biblical religion and non-biblical religion are always antithetical to one another. The Bible teaches that stark enmity exists between God and the world, between belief and unbelief. There is no neutrality between God and the world, a disparity articulated clearly in passages such as James 4:4 and 1 John 2:25:

> Do you not know that friendship with the world is enmity with God? Therefore, whoever wishes to be a friend of the world makes himself an enemy of God.
> Do not love the world or the things in the world. If anyone loves the world, the love of the Father is not in him.

This biblical concept of "the world" refers to the religion—a combination of worldview and theology—of this present sinful age that is ruled by Satan. It is a value system that is actively hostile to God and alienated from God. The world around us is not neutral;

---

[9] A. W Tozer, *The Knowledge of the Holy* (New York: HarperCollins, 1961), 1.

it is ruled by "the prince of the power of the air" (Eph. 2:2) who is the "god of this world" (2 Cor. 4:4). It is human environment left to itself.

Biblical religion, on the other hand, involves the formation of a worldview and theology in accordance with the Word of God. Conscious belief in the truths of Scripture—most importantly what it teaches about God's purpose for his creation, the reality of sin and judgment, and forgiveness found in the atonement of Jesus Christ—reorients the believer's heart toward God, motivating him to live in accordance with God's will for his glory.

Discussions of worldview, theology, and religion can often seem abstract and irrelevant to the practical issues of life, but nothing could be further from the truth. Our underlying assumptions combined with our beliefs concerning God and the purpose of life—our religion—affects everything about us: what we value, where we find meaning and purpose, how we interact with others—everything concerning our life in this world.

What Is the Nature of Liturgy?
This all brings us to the second part of my central thesis—liturgy. Liturgy is a word that I am using to describe the way we "live and move and have our being." Our English word comes from the Greek term *leitourgia*, which is simply a compound word comprised of *laos*—"people" and *ergon*—"work." Historically, the term was used to describe various works done in public as a member of community, such as military or political service, or even vocational labor, relationship between friends or family members, and care for the ill. In other words, in its oldest and broad usage, liturgy referred to the common customs and routines of life within a community, what in more recent times we might commonly call "culture."

Culture
The English word "culture" finds its Latin roots in discussions of the cultivation and care of livestock and crops. It was first used metaphorically to describe differences between groups of people, similarly to how we use it today, no earlier than 1776.[10] The idea progressed through several different uses over time. It first narrowly denoted what

---

[10] Johann Gottfried Herder; *Reflections on the Philosophy of the History of Mankind*, 1776.

Matthew Arnold would call "the best which has been thought and said in the world,"[11] what we today might call "high culture." But as early as the mid-nineteenth century, anthropologists began to use the idea to designate all forms of human behavior within society, not limited to high culture, including what we might today call "folk culture" or "pop culture." British anthropologist Edward Tylor is credited for the first influential use of the term in this way when in 1871 he defined culture as "that complex whole which includes knowledge, belief, art, morals, law, custom, and any other capabilities and habits acquired as a member of society."[12]

In other words, as it is used most commonly today, "culture" refers to the common behavioral patterns of a group of people—their "liturgy"—including their arts, language, customs, and rituals. It is this anthropological understanding of culture as the totality of human practices in a society that has become the predominant use of the idea among Christians and non-Christians alike. Adopting the anthropologist's definition of culture is not a problem for Christians—indeed, it may be a helpful category in studying the way humans behave as members of their society, but we must make sure that Scripture informs that understanding. The parallel idea in Scripture to anthropological notions of culture is that of social behavior, something about which the Bible has much to say. For example, when addressing the matter of behavior, New Testament authors admonish Christians to "be holy in all your conduct" in contrast to the "futile ways inherited from your forefathers" (1 Pet. 1:15, 18). They also identify human labor—both the act and what it produces—as the object of God's judgment (Rom. 2:6) and as an honorable endeavor that can lead unbelievers to "glorify God" (1 Pet. 2:12).

It is just this understanding of culture as the behavior of people in society that ties in to our foregoing discussion of religion. As we have seen, our religion—worldview combined with theology—determines the patterns of our behavior—culture. As Roger Scruton notes, culture is "a shared spiritual force which is manifest in all the customs, beliefs and practices of a people;" it is "a demonstration of a belief system."[13] This follows closely T. S. Elliot's classic argument that "no culture can appear or develop except in relation to a religion."[14] Culture flows out of and reflects the religious commitments, beliefs, and values of a people group, and it does so as it is cultivated over long spans of time. The very term "culture" illustrates the long-term, progressive cultivation

---

[11] Matthew Arnold, *Culture and Anarchy: An Essay in Political and Social Criticism* (London: Smith, Elder, and Co, 1869), viii.

[12] Edward B. Tylor, *Primitive Culture: Researches into the Development of Mythology, Philosophy, Religion, Art, and Custom* (London: John Murray, 1871), 1.

[13] Roger Scruton, *Modern Culture*, Continuum Compacts (London; New York: Continuum, 2005), 1, 286.

[14] T. S. Eliot, *Christianity and Culture: The Idea of a Christian Society and Notes Towards the Definition of Culture* (New York: Harcourt, Brace, 1949), 100.

of something over time, influenced and nurtured by the environment in which it grows. Cultural forms are natural products of the environment in which they were nurtured. All cultural forms, then, are expressions of value systems, and thus culture is not neutral—it is fundamentally religious. And like worldview, the development of cultures occurs usually not deliberately or consciously. We simply go about our lives, interacting with other members of society, producing practical tools and creating art, unaware of how our worldview is affecting everything that we do.

Conversely, just as religion is what forms culture, so cultures influence the formation of religion, especially for people or societies that do not intentionally shape their religion and its underlying worldview based on conscious theological beliefs. In fact, as I noted earlier, most people's worldviews are formed without intentional reflection, and the dominant influence for the formation of a people's worldview is their cultural environment. The implicit assumptions embedded in the core of cultural behaviors form and shape the worldview of the people in that culture, typically without intentionality or even awareness. Thus, as James K. A. Smith has emphasized in recent years,[15] culture is liturgical, being comprised of rhythms and routines that embody religious values and have power to form those values into those who participate in them.

Cultus

Yet there is a second element within the broader concept of liturgy, which is actually the more common use of the term, and the one that centers on the primary focus of this book—worship. While the Greek term *leitourgia* was originally used to describe all sorts of social works, what I have called "culture," it later came to refer specifically to public works of worship to God, primarily due to its use in the Greek translation of the Old Testament, the Septuagint (LXX).[16] The LXX translators deliberately chose this term to uniquely denote the formal service of the priests on behalf of the people of God, and they used it almost exclusively for that kind of work in contrast to other public patterns of behavior. This use of the term set the standard for the years to come, and this is how we typically use the word liturgy today, to refer to corporate worship.

Here, too, there is a relationship to the Latin root for the word "culture," which originally denoted the cultivation of plants and animals. The term "cultus" grew from this original Latin source alongside "culture," and referred to the public acts of worship

---

[15] See James K. A. Smith, *Desiring the Kingdom: Worship, Worldview, and Cultural Formation* (Grand Rapids: Baker Academic, 2009); James K. A. Smith, *You Are What You Love: The Spiritual Power of Habit* (Grand Rapids: Brazos Press, 2016).

[16] H. Strathman, "λειτουργία, *Theological Dictionary of the New Testament* (Grand Rapids: Wm. B. Eerdmans, 1985), 4:219.

Worldview-Forming Worship

performed by a religious community. Sigmund Mowinckel provided this helpful definition of the original meaning of the word:

> Cult ... may be defined as the socially established and regulated holy acts and words in which the encounter and communion of the Deity with the congregation is established, developed, and brought to its ultimate goal ... a relation in which a religion becomes a vitalizing function as a communion of God and congregation, and of the members of the congregation among themselves ... the visible and audible expression of the relation between the congregation and the deity.[17]

In other words, "cultus" is rituals and expressions of communal worship.

Like theology, cultus is more deliberately formed. Religious communities establish rituals, ceremonies, artistic expressions, and other sacred acts in ways that express and nurture their religion. Yet here, too, there is often an unconscious interplay between cultus and culture. Often people's worship becomes shaped and molded by the common culture around them. Likewise, the cultic acts of a dominant religious community within a society can have a significant impact upon the cultural behaviors of that society.

Liturgy

Both of these behavioral patterns, culture—the general patterns of a society's behavior, and cultus—the patterns of a religious community's worship, are encompassed under the category of liturgy. These are practices that have formed over time within a community that both reflect and form underlying religion (worldview + theology).

Lex Orandi, Lex Credendi

What we have seen, then, is a dynamic interplay between four realities: worldview, theology, culture, and cultus. Worldview and theology affect one another and constitute religion; culture and cultus affect one another as liturgy. But this kind of mutual formation occurs at a macro level as well, *between* religion and liturgy, impacting and shaping one another at both conscious and subconscious levels.

---

[17] Sigmund Mowinckel, *The Psalms in Israel's Worship* (Grand Rapids: Wm. B. Eerdmans, 2004), 15–16.

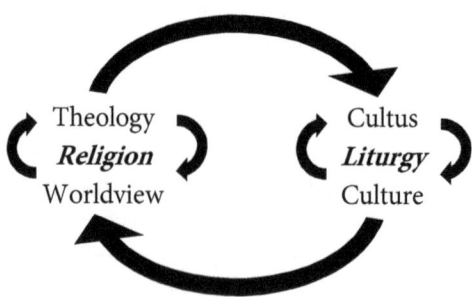

This interaction characterizes the central purpose and premise of this book, captured in the Latin phrase, *lex orandi, lex credendi*—"the law of prayer, the law of belief." This ancient concept recognized the fundamental relationship between acts of worship and belief. *Lex credendi* is another way to describe religion, the combination of worldview and theology. *Lex orandi* designates liturgy, the behavioral patterns of both culture and cultus. The relationship between the two, as we have already seen, involves both reflection and formation. In other words, public worship both *reveals* belief and *forms* belief. How a community worships—its content, its liturgy, and its forms of expression—reveals the underlying religious commitments (worldview + theology) of those who plan and lead the worship. As Frank Senn has noted, "as a ritual system, liturgy expresses nothing less than a worldview."[18] This may not always be intentional, either. Often church leadership inherits certain ways of worshiping and employs them without ascertaining exactly what kinds of beliefs the worship practices embody, sometimes resulting in worship that does not reflect the church's stated theological convictions.

This is significant exactly because of the second half of the premise—corporate worship *forms* the beliefs of the worshipers. Public worship is not simply about authentic expression of the worshipers; rather, how a church worships week after week progressively shapes their beliefs since those worship practices were cultivated by and embody certain beliefs. This happens whether or not the worshipers consciously recognize it, and therefore if church leadership has not given consideration to how the way they worship is shaping the theology of the congregation, it is quite possible that worshipers are being formed in ways the leadership does not intend.

This is why it is so important for church leaders, and indeed all Christians, to carefully identify what kinds of beliefs have shaped their various worship practices so that they will choose to worship in ways that best form their minds and hearts in ways consistent with their theological convictions. That is the goal of this book: studying worship in the Old and New Testaments will reveal how God deliberately prescribed

---

[18] Frank C. Senn, *New Creation: A Liturgical Worldview* (Minneapolis: Fortress Press, 2000), xi.

Worldview-Forming Worship

worship that would form his people as he desires, and tracing the evolution of Christian worship from after the close of the New Testament to the present day will help elucidate how theological beliefs affected the worship practices we have inherited.

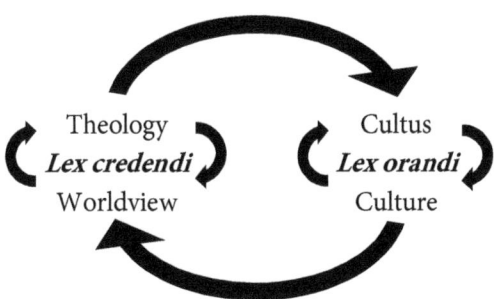

Study Guide for Chapter 1
People and Terms

culture
cultus
heart
leitourgia
lex orandi, lex credendi
liturgy
moral imagination
religion
theology
worldview
worship

Recommended Resources

Aniol, Scott. *Worship in Song: A Biblical Approach to Music and Worship.* Winona Lake, IL: BMH Books, 2009.

Castleman, Robbie F. *Story-Shaped Worship: Following Patterns from the Bible and History.* Downers Grove, IL: InterVarsity Press, 2013.

Faulkner, Quentin. *Wiser Than Despair: The Evolution of Ideas in the Relationship of Music and the Christian Church.* 2nd ed. Simpsonville, SC: Religious Affections Ministries, 2012.

Ross, Allen P. *Recalling the Hope of Glory: Biblical Worship from the Garden to the New Creation.* Grand Rapids: Kregel, 2006.

Sire, James W. *Naming the Elephant: Worldview as a Concept.* 2nd edition. Downers Grove: IVP Academic, 2015.

Smith, James K. A. *You Are What You Love: The Spiritual Power of Habit.* Grand Rapids: Brazos Press, 2016.

Tozer, A. W. *Whatever Happened to Worship.* Fort Lauderdale, FL: Christian Publications, 1985.

Westermeyer, Paul. *Te Deum: The Church and Music.* Minneapolis: Fortress Press, 1998.

Questions for Discussion and Reflection

1. Define "worldview." How does the concept of worldview relate to the biblical idea of "heart"?
2. Explain how worldview and theology combine to form a religion.
3. Define "liturgy." In what ways do both cultus and culture have liturgical essence?
4. Explain the dynamic relationship between religion (worldview + theology) and liturgy (culture + cultus).

PART ONE: THE OLD TESTAMENT

Oh sing to the Lord a new song;
sing to the Lord, all the earth!
Sing to the Lord, bless his name;
tell of his salvation from day to day.
Declare his glory among the nations,
his marvelous works among all the peoples!

For great is the Lord, and greatly to be praised;
he is to be feared above all gods.
For all the gods of the peoples are worthless idols,
but the Lord made the heavens.
Splendor and majesty are before him;
strength and beauty are in his sanctuary.

Ascribe to the Lord, O families of the peoples,
ascribe to the Lord glory and strength!
Ascribe to the Lord the glory due his name;
bring an offering, and come into his courts!
Worship the Lord in the splendor of holiness;
tremble before him, all the earth!

Say among the nations, "The Lord reigns!
Yes, the world is established; it shall never be moved;
he will judge the peoples with equity."

Let the heavens be glad, and let the earth rejoice;
let the sea roar, and all that fills it;
let the field exult, and everything in it!
Then shall all the trees of the forest sing for joy before the Lord,
for he comes, for he comes to judge the earth.
He will judge the world in righteousness,
and the peoples in his faithfulness.

—King David, c. 1025 B.C.

Chapter 2
Foundations of Worship

"In the beginning, God."

With those opening words of the book of Genesis, we find the very foundation for all biblical religion. God's self-existence, creative power, and divine providence over all things provides the basis for a Christian worldview and theology, which should flow into how Christians worship (cultus) and, indeed, the entirety of how they live (culture).

As Christians, we might be tempted to bypass the Old Testament as we seek to understand the relationship between what we believe and how we worship, but that would be a grave mistake. The historical record, poetry, and prophecy contained in the Old Testament were "written for our instruction," Paul said (Rom. 15:4; 1 Cor. 10:11). Although, as we will see, the coming of Christ does fundamentally change some aspects of how we relate to God as his people, the core and essence of biblical Christianity finds its center in the worldview and theology of the Old Testament. Therefore, careful study of worship in these ancient books will help us as Christians to properly shape our theology and practice of worship in a way that is founded upon transcendent principles.

Creation
Creation is the very basis of and foundation for worship. The central principle of biblical worship is the fact that it is God-initiated and based upon his self-revelation. God's speaking the world into existence was in its very essence an act to create worship. God created the universe *ex nihilo* through his spoken word for the express purpose of displaying his own glory (Ps. 19:1), and he created Adam in his image in order that Adam might witness that glory and respond in worship. God's chief end is to glorify himself, and he calls all people everywhere to fulfill their purpose in life of doing the same (Isa. 43:6–7).

Yet this desire to be worshiped did not stop with speaking the world into existence; creation certainly displays the glory of God, but creation alone is not enough to reveal the God to be worshiped. Adam would not have known whom he was to worship except that God said something to him. God revealed himself to Adam and told him of his purpose in Genesis 2:15: "The Lord God took the man and put him in the garden of Eden to work it and keep it." The phrase "work it and keep it" seems to imply that man's purpose was to garden, yet the work of gardening would not have been necessary prior to the Fall. Rather, the two verbs in this phrase have a deeper significance.

The first verb is *avid*, which, according to Allen Ross, is "used frequently for spiritual service, specifically serving the LORD (Deut. 4:19) and for the duties of the Levites (see Num. 3:7–8; 4:23–24, 26)."[1] The second verb is *shamar*; and Ross notes that "its religious use is that of observing spiritual duties or keeping the commands (Lev. 18:5)."[2] He explains,

> In places where these two verbs are found together, they often refer to the duties of the Levites (cf. Num. 3:7–8; 8:26; 18:5–6), keeping the laws of God (especially in the sanctuary service) and offering spiritual service in the form of the sacrifices and all the related duties—serving the LORD, safeguarding his commands, and guarding the sanctuary from the intrusion of anything profane or evil.[3]

God placed Adam in the Garden of Eden—the perfect sanctuary of God—to literally "worship and obey." This purpose for humankind is expressed elsewhere in Scripture (e.g., Isa. 43:7). God created Adam and Even in order that they might serve as priests in his holy sanctuary.

Worship Components

What did this worship entail? Several clues give us early indication of what worship is all about. The early chapters of Genesis demonstrate the nature of the relationship between God and his image-bearers in the Garden. Each day God "walked" with them in the cool of the garden (Gen. 3:8). The garden God had made for Adam and Eve served as a sanctuary where God was present with his people. His desire was to fellowship with them, to commune with them, not as equals, but as the Creator with his creation. Notably, the verb for "walked" in Genesis 3:8 is used later to describe God's presence in the sanctuary (Lev. 26:12; 2 Sam. 7:6–7). This idea of communion with God in his sanctuary as revealed by him distills the essence of worship as it is developed through the entirety of Scripture.

But this notion of communion with God was not of the casual nature of two equal friends. Rather, this communion with God was on his terms. He set specific boundaries and limits to what that communion would entail, and disobedience of his instructions would result in death—separation from this communion in his very presence. In other words, this communion was covenantal in nature; it was a formal relationship between God and his people in which both parties had a part to play, God as creator and provider, and humankind as servant with particular commands to obey. This

---

[1] Allen P. Ross, *Recalling the Hope of Glory: Biblical Worship from the Garden to the New Creation* (Grand Rapids: Kregel, 2006), 105.
[2] Ross, *Recalling the Hope of Glory*, 105.
[3] Ross, *Recalling the Hope of Glory*, 106.

formal relationship does not diminish the personal essence of communion with God, any more than a formal wedding covenant prevents intimacy between husband and wife. Nevertheless, communion with God was instituted by and regulated by God such that he received ultimate glory and his people would receive the greatest good.

But, of course, Adam and Eve disobeyed. Their sin broke the perfect communion they had enjoyed with him in his holy sanctuary, and thus God expelled them from his presence, placing cherubim with a flaming sword to guard entrance into God's presence (Gen. 3:24). Before he did, however, God himself provided the solution to that broken communion. By slaying an innocent animal and covering Adam's and Eve's nakedness with the animal's skin, God was already picturing the means by which he would restore the broken communion. He made a promise to Adam and Eve in the form of a *protoevangelium*—a "pre-gospel" in Genesis 3:15 when he promised the serpent, "I will put enmity between you and the woman, and between your offspring and her offspring; he shall bruise your head, and you shall bruise his heal." In this way, two key elements of worship that would be developed later appear in the creation/fall narrative, namely, atonement and covenant.

Thus all the elements that later describe biblical worship are already available to us in these early pages of Scripture: worship entails drawing near to communion with God himself in his holy sanctuary. This communion is on his terms and it is initiated by his revelation to his people. Sin breaks this communion, however, and erects barriers that prevent people from drawing near to God's presence. God responds to this terrible situation by establishing a unilateral covenant with his people and providing atonement by which they can draw near to (for now) imperfect fellowship with him.

The First Worship War

The very first conflict following the Fall was a conflict over worship. Genesis 4:3–8 relates how Abel's offering to the Lord was accepted, while Cain's was not. These offerings were important because they were God's means for at least temporarily and partially restoring communion with his people. Yet for some reason that is not explicit in the text, "the Lord had regard for Abel and his offering, but for Cain and his offering he had no regard" (vv. 4–5). At this point in Genesis, we do not have any clear revelation as to the content of acceptable worship. It is at least possible that God had demanded an animal sacrifice, and since Cain brought a food offering instead, that is why God rejected him. There is no way to determine this with absolute certainty, however. On the other hand, some assume that the offering wasn't the problem; Cain's heart attitude or motivation were deficient, and that is why God rejected him. This conclusion, too, is based on speculation since the text does not fully explain why God rejected Cain.

Revelation in the New Testament, however, does give a clearer picture. The author of Hebrews explains that Abel proved that he was "righteous" through his sacrifice (Heb. 11:4), while Jude 1:1 describes Cain as one who "abandoned himself for the sake of gain," and John 3:12 says that Cain's deeds were "evil." These descriptions relate most specifically to the inward spiritual condition of the men, yet Hebrews also notes that Abel's *sacrifice* itself was "more excellent" than Cain's and that his righteousness was determined by "his gifts." Perhaps the fact that Abel brought the "fat portions" of "the firstborn of his flock" (Gen. 4:4) was evidence that he brought his best in order to please God.

Taken together, this information reveals a two-fold emphasis in evaluating worship, an emphasis that appears often in biblical discussions of worship. First, the inward heart motivation is of utmost importance in true worship. At least part of what led to Cain's rejection was an evil heart. But a heart of worship will manifest itself in excellent, obedient offerings to God. Good heart motivation alone does not justify disobedience of God's clear instructions or worshiping in flippant, casual ways. On the other hand, doing exactly what God has commanded without a heart that desires to please and glorify him is equally deficient. Both are important.

Called by God

The first Patriarch of Israel, Abraham, was not originally a worshiper of the true God; he dwelt in the land of Ur, worshiping many false gods (Josh. 24:2). God initiated his contact with Abraham (Gen. 12:1), once again reaffirming the principle that all true worship begins with the God who reveals himself to his people. Each specific act of worship during what is known as the patriarchal period of Abraham, Isaac, and Jacob is a response to God's revelation to his people. For example, Abraham built an altar to the Lord after God commanded him to leave his land (Gen. 12:7). He also worshiped Yahweh when he expressed his willingness to sacrifice his son (Gen. 22:1–14). Likewise, Isaac built an altar to the Lord (Gen. 26:24–25), and Jacob set up a stone altar after his vision of the ladder to heaven (Gen. 28:18). During this time of the nation of Israel's beginnings, the worship of God's people came naturally as they responded in faith to God's self-revelation. Worship practices, traditions, and liturgies were apparently passed on by tradition and took place in the family setting. The book of Genesis does not record God giving his people clear directions concerning how he was to be worshiped (that wouldn't happen until Sinai), yet they observed standard practices of sacrifice, offering, and meal in worship to the Lord, just as had Adam's sons and Noah (Gen. 8:20–21).

Two events in Abraham's life are worth noting for their descriptions of patriarchal worship. The first occurred when Abram encountered the king of Salem (the future location of Jerusalem), Melchizedek, who Moses calls a "priest of God Most High" (Gen. 14:18). Not much is known about this mysterious king-priest, but God must have revealed himself to Melchizedek since he worshiped the same God as Abram (v. 22). This holy man pronounced a blessing from God upon Abram:

> Blessed be Abram by God Most High,
>   Possessor of heaven and earth;
> and blessed be God Most High,
>   who has delivered your enemies into your hand!

Melchizedek gave this blessing in the context of a meal, which signified the communion these men shared with one another and with their common God. In response, Abram performed an act of worship that would later become part of Israel's worship: "Abram gave him a tenth of everything," a "tithe" that would later be used to fund worship in the tabernacle and temple. Importantly, Melchizedek prefigures Christ as king-priest (Ps. 110:4; Heb. 7:17, 21), and it is no coincidence that in this context, God establishes a covenant with Abraham in which he promised Abraham (Gen. 17:5) a posterity (Gen. 15:5), a land (Gen. 15:18), and blessing to other nations through his family (Gen. 12:3).

The second event is God's command for Abraham to offer his son, Isaac, upon an altar (Gen. 22:1–19). God had finally given Abraham and Sarah the son he had promised them, only to command Abraham, "Take your son, your only son Isaac, whom you love, and go to the land of Moriah, and offer him there as a burnt offering on one of the mountains of which I shall tell you" (v. 2). Confident that "God will provide for himself the lamb for a burnt offering" (v. 8), Abraham followed God's command, obeying even to the point of binding Isaac upon the altar and raising his knife to kill him. God did, indeed, provide a ram as a substitutionary sacrifice (v. 13) and reaffirmed his promises to Abraham (vv. 15–18). Again, no coincidence, this same mountain is where Solomon will later build the temple (2 Chr. 3:1), and the concept of a substitutionary sacrifice continued to be central in Israel's later worship theology.

Redeemed by God

Moses' encounter with God is, like with Adam and the patriarchs, initiated by God. It was in this encounter at the burning bush in the wilderness of Midian at Mt. Horeb (another name for Sinai) that God emphasized his unique covenant name, "Yahweh"—"I Am" (Exod. 3:14). This title highlighted the eternality of God, and, unlike some of the other generic names for God that were shared with other false gods (such as "El"), this name distinguished the true God from all others. God also stressed the need for holiness when drawing near to his presence, commanding Moses, "Do not come near; take your sandals off your feet, for the place on which you are standing is holy ground" (Exod. 3:5). The holiness of God does not allow sin in his presence, a reality God would reemphasize later when he establishes his sanctuary.

This period of Moses' leadership is the time in which the worship of Yahweh by a specific people he has called out becomes clearly his plan. The very reason Moses demanded for Pharaoh to let the people go was that they might form a worshiping community (Exod. 3:18; 5:3). The plagues of Egypt, while also presenting potent incentive for Pharaoh to free the people, clearly proclaimed Yahweh's superiority over the false gods of Egypt. The Passover event (Exod. 12) further emphasized the idea of atonement that was already in the people's consciousness since when God covered Adam and Eve's nakedness in the Garden.

Worship at Sinai
Fifty days after the exodus from Egypt, the people arrived at the foot of Mt. Sinai, where God specifically set apart the worshiping community and gave instructions for how he desired to be worshiped, serving as the "formative era of Israelite worship and history."[4] Again, this encounter is on God's initiative. The people don't come on their own attempting to get their God's attention. Rather, "The Lord called out to [Moses] out of the mountain" (Exod. 19:5)—God himself called them to draw near to his presence. After giving Moses the Law, God called Moses, Aaron and his sons, the elders, and all the people to draw near to worship him (Exod. 24:1). The people had to remain at a distance, however (v. 2), once again emphasizing the fact that sin cannot come fully into the presence of God. For this very reason, this worship service continued with necessary consecration of the people. Moses presented God's "rules" to the people as a way to reemphasize their own sinfulness and then offered the necessary sacrifices of atonement so that they would be accepted (vv. 3–8). God communicated his approval and acceptance of them based on the atoning sacrifice when the leaders of the people "saw the God of Israel, ... and he did not lay his hand" against them (vv. 9–11). Following this period of God's revelation of himself, the people's sacrifices, and God's affirmation of acceptance before him, the people listened to the Book of the Covenant as Moses read it in their hearing (Exod. 24:7). They responded with "All that the Lord has spoken we will do, and we will be obedient." The ultimate expression of the fact that they were now welcome in his presence for communion with him was that "they beheld God, and ate and drank" (v. 11). In the ancient near east, eating at someone's table signified that you were welcome and accepted; to eat and drink before the

---
[4] Andrew Hill, *Enter His Courts with Praise: Old Testament Worship for the New Testament Church* (Grand Rapids: Baker, 1996), 35.

presence of God was a powerful statement that the people had gained acceptance with God, not through their own work, but through the means that he had established.

Later, after building the tabernacle and consecration of the priests, the nation celebrated a similar worship service, characterized by the fact that they "drew near and stood before the Lord" (Lev. 9:5). This gathering in God's presence was based on God's invitation and dependent upon obedience to his directives (v. 6). It began with a general call to worship in verse 7, followed by a period in which Aaron and the priests offer atoning sacrifices on behalf of themselves and the people. Verses 23–24 demonstrate the amazing revelation that God accepted their sacrifices, and he revealed this to them by displaying his glory and consuming the sacrifice with fire from heaven. The people now knew that they were accepted by God because of the sacrifice. Following the consecration, the people celebrated the Passover feast (Num. 9). The worship encounter climaxed with an expression of the very essence of worship—communion with God at the table.

These services of worship, most frequently described as "solemn assemblies" in the Old Testament, follow a progression that became standard for the worship of God's people from that time forward: God desired communion with the people he had set apart, but because of their sinfulness, they could not draw near to his presence. Yet he called them to come and provided the means for them to be able to at least partially draw near through a sacrifice of atonement. Once the people obeyed his commands for sacrifice, God accepted them, albeit partially, and spoke to them. The people responded with commitment and a visible celebration of their acceptance in God's presence in the form of a feast. This "Sinai liturgy" could be summarized this way:

God reveals himself and calls his people to worship
God's people acknowledge and confess their need for forgiveness
God provides atonement
God speaks his Word
God's people respond with commitment
God hosts a celebratory feast

The Decalogue
The Law itself, summarized in the Ten Commandments (Exod. 20:1–17; Deut. 5:4–21) established the basis upon which the people of God could maintain their communion with him. The first four commandments directly relate to worship. The first commandment prohibits God's people from worshiping any other god. The second commandment is often interpreted as reiterating the first, but it is actually an entirely different command. While the first commandment addresses *who* we are to worship, the second commandment identifies *how* we are to worship—or at least how we are *not* to

worship; we may not worship the true God by means of a visual aid meant to symbolize him. Taking God's name in vain, forbidden in the third commandment, involves invoking God in word or deed—such as worship—without a heart sincerely focused upon him in a duly honoring manner. The fourth commandment codified instructions regarding Sabbath observance, but the Sabbath principle itself had been established all the way back as part of creation.

If the first four commandments provided instructions regarding the cultus of Israel, the remaining six govern their culture. Honoring parents was to characterize their civilization, stressing the importance of honoring the received heritage. In contrast to the pagan nations around them, God commanded that Israel's culture would be such that murder, adultery, theft, and even deceit and covetousness would be unacceptable. A society cultivated with the commands of the decalogue at their core would flourish (Deut. 6:1–3).

The Greatest Commandment

In the context of giving the Law at Mt. Sinai and the promise that if they follow God's commands as a nation, God will bless them, we find a statement that stands at the core of biblical religion: "Hear, O Israel: The Lord our God, the Lord is one. You shall love the Lord your God with all your heart and with all your soul and with all your might" (Deut. 6:4–5). While the Ten Commandments were themselves a summary of the Law, this declaration was an even more concise summary of the first four commandments regarding their worship; Jesus would later indicate this when he named this as "the great commandment in the Law" and summarized the rest of the commandments with, "You shall love your neighbor as yourself." He indicated, "On these two commandments depend all the Law and the Prophets" (Matt. 22:36–40).

Several characteristics of this statement, known as the "*Shema*" (from the first word, "Hear" in Hebrew), connect directly with the central thesis of this book. First, the statement is a concise statement of Israel's theology: The Lord is one. This doctrine separated Israel's worship from the worship of all other pagan nations that were either polytheistic (worship of many gods) or henotheistic (worship of one god among many). Israel's theology was explicitly monotheistic, unique among all the religions of the world to this day.[5] Second, notice that the central command of this statement addresses a heart orientation, what I have characterized as worldview. In other words, according to the *Shema*, biblical religion consists of *both* right theology and right worldview—explicitly believing right things about God and then having the heart rightly oriented toward God.

---

[5] The only other monotheistic religions of any significance are Christianity and Islam, both of which derive from Judaism.

Foundations of Worship

Immediately following the *Shema*, God instructs the people concerning how they can cultivate this proper religion (theology + worldview):

> And these words that I command you today shall be on your heart. You shall teach them diligently to your children, and shall talk of them when you sit in your house, and when you walk by the way, and when you lie down, and when you rise. You shall bind them as a sign on your hand, and they shall be as frontlets between your eyes. You shall write them on the doorposts of your house and on your gates. (Deut. 6:6–9)

Cultivating biblical religion involved more than just an intellectual exercise; it required structuring a cultural environment, both in the family and the community at large, that would over time orient their hearts properly. This meant establishing practices, routines, and rituals that kept God regularly before them and embodied a sensibility toward him that would form both their theology and worldview. Every aspect of what they did in both everyday cultural activities and in their dedicated solemn assemblies of worship was to be directed toward the end of truly knowing and loving God.

The Sanctuary

At Mt. Sinai, God established standardized practices of worship—the "cultus"—for his people. First, God commanded that the people build a sanctuary for him. They built the tabernacle of God—and later the temple—according to God's specific instructions (Exod. 25:8–9, 40; 27:8; Num. 8:4; cf. Acts 7:44; Heb. 8:5). This sanctuary of his presence was not for his benefit—Solomon would acknowledge later that God had no need for a house (1 Kgs. 8:27). Rather, the tabernacle was for the people's benefit; it provided a place where sinners were given the means necessary to draw near to the holy presence of God for communion with him, and the very layout and structure represented the core necessities for such communion to be possible. Furthermore, Exodus 25 explains that God gave Moses the exact pattern for the tabernacle, and Hebrews 8:5 confirms that this pattern was based upon the heavenly tabernacle. Thus, the instructions for the earthly sanctuary of God were not arbitrary; they reflect and picture the heavenly realities of God's dwelling place. This implies that the specific details of the tabernacle are not unimportant even for the church today. Since they image spiritual, heavenly realities, they have direct application to our theology of worship and even our liturgies and practice.

The various parts of the tabernacle represent the biblical understanding of worship that has already begun to emerge in the early pages of Scripture. God's presence dwelt in the Holy of Holies, and worship entailed drawing near to that presence. Various barriers prevented the people from drawing near, however, because of their sinfulness and unworthiness. Images of cherubim in several places harkened back to cherubim guarding the Eden sanctuary—they were embroidered on the veil that hid the Holy of Holies (1 Kgs. 6:23–28) and on the ceiling and walls of the tabernacle (Exod. 26:31; 1 Kgs. 6:29), and two golden cherubim guarded the ark of God's presence (Exod. 25:18–22). Therefore, God provided a means by which his people could approach communion with him. Upon entering through the gate of the tabernacle courtyard, a worshiper would have first encountered the high altar, made of wood and covered with bronze (Exod. 27:1–8; 38:1–8), which symbolized the atonement necessary for drawing near to the holy presence of God. Next came the bronze laver (Exod. 30:17–21), which pictured cleansing, purification, and regeneration. Rituals performed at these places provided the temporary and partial access to God. Interestingly, there is no mention of music as part of the tabernacle worship. Not until David do we find explicit descriptions or instructions about corporate worship music. The people of Israel certainly had music as part of their culture and even used it to praise the Lord, but it is not part of the Mosaic Law.

To direct the building of the tabernacle and all of its accoutrements, God called out Bezalel and Oholiab, men "filled with the Spirit of God, with ability and intelligence, with knowledge and all craftsmanship, to devise artistic designs, to work in gold, silver, and bronze, in cutting stones for setting, and in carving wood, to work in every craft" (Exod. 31:1–11). The Holy Spirit of God actively worked through the craftsmanship of these men to bring beauty and order in the midst of God's people, what he had intended for his people in the Garden sanctuary of Eden.

Only Levites were allowed into the tabernacle itself, and even then, only those who were assigned for the day's duties. Inside the first room of the tabernacle, the "Holy Place," the priest would encounter three pieces of furniture. First was the lamp stand, symbolizing the light of God and often associated with his revelation (Exod. 25:31–40; 37:17–24). Next was the wooden table overlaid with gold, upon which lay the showbread (Exod. 25:23–30; 37:10–16). As we've seen before, a table symbolized the communion with God to which the worshiper was drawing near. Finally, the priest would tend to the altar of incense just outside the veil to the Most Holy Place (Exod. 30:1–10; 37:25–29), which symbolized the intercessory prayers of the people into the presence of God, another symbol of the free and open access they had to him because of the sacrifice of atonement. Only the High Priest himself was permitted into the Holy of Holies, and that only once a year on the Day of Atonement. In this most sacred of rooms stood the ark of the covenant (Exod. 25:10–22; 37:1–9), upon which the very presence of God dwelt and where the blood of the atoning sacrifice was sprinkled each year. This was a picture of the place of God's presence and the ultimate apex of Yahweh worship.

Yet the ark was not simply a *representation* of God's presence in the Holy of Holies—Scripture indicates that the Spirit of God descended and actually dwelt there in their midst. After the tabernacle was built, "the glory of the LORD filled the tabernacle," and the visible manifestations of his presence—a cloud by day and fire by night—remained there "in the sight of all the house of Israel" (Exod. 40:35, 38). It was from above the mercy seat on the ark that God spoke to Moses and the people (Num. 7:89). Nehemiah later identifies the Holy Spirit as the person of God who instructed his people there (Neh. 9:20), remaining in their midst (Hag. 2:5) until he leaves during Ezekiel's prophetic ministry (Ezek. 9:3; 10:18; 11:23).

Thus, the very structure and layout of the tabernacle pictured the biblical theology of worship. Worship involves drawing near to communion with God, but since our sin prevents that, God establishes means of atonement and cleansing by which we are enabled to draw near to hear his Word, to eat with him, and to bring our prayers before his throne.

Sacrifices

Even the order of the sacrifices pictures this. God gave specific instructions concerning sacrifices to him:

> An altar of earth you shall make for me and sacrifice on it your burnt offerings and your peace offerings, your sheep and your oxen. In every place where I cause my name to be remembered I will come to you and bless you. If you make me an altar of stone, you shall not build it of hewn stones, for if you wield your tool on it you profane it. And you shall not go up by steps to my altar, that your nakedness be not exposed on it. (Exod. 20:24–26)

Worshipers would begin with the Sin Offering (Lev. 4:1–5:13; 6:24–30), symbolizing the substitution necessary for atonement. When a sin offering was made, the worshiper would place one hand on the head of the animal and make confession of his sin while he killed the animal with his other hand. Part of the blood from that animal would be sprinkled on the veil and on the altar of incense in the Holy Place. Worshipers would progress next to the Guilt Offering (Lev. 5:15–6:7; 7:1–6), by which their communion with others against whom they had sinned would be restored through some sort of reparation before the offering was made. They would next offer a Burnt Offering (Lev. 1; 6:8–13), which would be wholly consumed, symbolizing the totality of dedication of one's life to God's service. These three offerings provided atonement by which sinners were enabled to enter restored communion with God. A worshiper may also voluntarily offer a Grain Offering of flour (Lev. 2) as an expression of thanksgiving for what God had done. After a handful of this offering was burnt on the altar, the rest would be given to the priests for food. Finally, would be the Peace Offering (Lev. 3; 7:11–36), which did not *gain* the worshiper peace—that had already been gained through the atoning sacrifices. Rather, the Peace Offering was a celebration of peace already established, and it would often conclude with the worshiper eating part of what had been offered, again picturing free and open communion with God.

Thus, the order of worship in the temple could be summarized this way:

God reveals himself and calls his people to worship (Temple entrance)
God's people acknowledge and confess their need for forgiveness (Sin, Guilt, and Burnt Offerings)
God provides atonement
God speaks his Word (reading of the Law)
God's people respond with commitment (Grain Offering)
God hosts a celebratory feast (Peace Offering)

God set apart priests for service in the sanctuary, including performing the sacrifices and tending to the various needs of the tabernacle. He gave Moses instructions concerning the priests, including their garments (Exod. 28) and consecration (Exod. 29; Lev. 8). Priests were to come from Moses' tribe, the Levites, under the leadership of his brother Aaron and his descendants (Exod. 4:4–17). A priest's robe was to be all blue, with pomegranates of blue, purple, and red embroidered into the hem, with gold bells interspersed.

Worship Time
Although individuals could worship whenever they wished, God prescribed regular times of worship, including daily worship in which a burnt offering was made each morning and evening (Exod. 29:38–42; 30:7–8; Num. 28:2–8), the weekly Sabbath during which more offerings were performed, special sacrifices at the beginning of each month (Num. 28:11–15), and three harvest festival periods, Unleavened Bread, Harvest, and Ingathering (Exod. 23:14–17).

The religious year began in the spring with the Passover and the Feast of Unleavened Bread, which began on Nisan 14. This celebration coincided with the beginning of harvest season, and other subsequent festivals marked important junctures in the harvest process in addition to their spiritual significance. Passover commemorated Israel's deliverance from Egypt and God's passing over the homes whose doorposts were sprinkled with blood and so symbolized redemption and atonement. It began a three-day festival composed of three feasts, the first of which was technically Passover, but sometimes the term describes the three days in unity. The same is true of the second day Feast of Unleavened Bread; this title technically refers to the second day but sometimes describes the whole celebration. The Feast of Unleavened Bread continued the remembrance of deliverance and atonement by commemorating the command God gave his people on that fateful night to eat unleavened bread. The third day of the festival was known as the Feast of Firstfruits, which took place on the day after Sabbath following Passover (Sunday morning). This was a day specifically tied to the harvest season in which the people would rejoice in the early signs of fruitfulness and anticipate a great harvest to come. They would take the firstfruit of the barley harvest and offer it to the Lord in the sanctuary. The harvesting of crops began fifty days after the Feast of Firstfruits with the Feast of Weeks, which celebrated the ripening of the firstfruits and beginning of the wheat harvest. This was also often combined with a commemoration of the giving of the Law of Moses at Mt. Sinai, which took place fifty days after the Exodus.

The autumn festivals began at the Hebrew New Year with the Feast of Trumpets, which announced a time to celebrate the end of one year and the beginning of the next. It also marked a time of national repentance, pardon, and covenant renewal. Ten days later came the holiest day of the year, the Day of Atonement. On this day the High Priest performed sacrifices to atone for the sins of the nation, and it was on this day only that he was permitted inside the Holy of Holies to sprinkle blood on the mercy seat of the Ark of the Covenant. The final festival of the liturgical year came five days later with the Feast of Tabernacles (also called "Booths"). This day celebrated the final harvest of the year and also commemorated the wilderness wanderings. The people would often construct tents and live in them for a week to reenact the earlier Israelites' experience.

Syncretism and Idolatry

Along with many other commands that concerned just about every aspect of Hebrew life, God gave his people very specific instructions about how they were to relate to the people around them, including in their culture and worship practices.

Deuteronomy 12:2–8 reveals important principles in this regard. God commanded that the people destroy the *places* where pagans worshiped, including their *altars*, their *pillars*, their *images*, and even the *names* of the places. This is clearly more than simply insisting that they worship Yahweh rather than false gods; this is also stark evidence that God rejects worship that imitates pagan worship in any way. Everything in pagan culture embodies religious commitments, and those elements that are imbibed with pagan religious meaning must be rejected for use in worship. One might ask why they had to destroy, for example, the altars and pillars; wouldn't these be useful even for the worship of the true God? Yet God commanded that they be destroyed. He summarized his desires with the words, "You shall not worship the LORD your God in that way"

(v. 4). Instead, they were to listen to his instructions and find a place of his choosing for their worship.

Yet the people disobeyed these principles even as they waited at the foot of the mountain for Moses to return from receiving the law tablets. The golden calf incident is a terrible failure for this newly formed worship community, but unfortunately one that foreshadows many other failures in the days and years ahead. Fearing that Moses would never come back, the people demanded a physical representation of deity, just like the pagan nations had. Aaron complied, forming a golden calf, similar to the practice of both Egypt and Canaan, and the people celebrated with an orgiastic festival (Exod. 32:6) so noisy that sounded to Joshua's ears from a distance like "a noise of war in the camp" (Exod. 32:17).

Most people likely assume that the Israelites' problem here was one of worshiping a false god. Yet a closer look at what happened reveals something different. The common assumption is usually based upon the fact that most English translations use the term "gods" in Exodus 32:4–6 to describe what they desired to worship—"These are your gods, O Israel," the people said. This is a legitimate translation of the Hebrew term *Elohim* in this text, a plural reference to deity common in the ancient near east. However, that very term (in its plural form) is also used elsewhere to unquestionably refer to the true God, and other clues in the text indicate that the people were actually trying to worship the true God. One clear example is what Aaron says in verse 5: "Tomorrow shall be a feast to *Yahweh*." Clearly, the attempt here was to worship the true God through the golden calf. Moses made this fact explicit when he related this event at the end of his life in Deuteronomy 9:16: "And I looked, and behold, you had sinned against *Yahweh Elohim* (the LORD your God). You had made yourselves a golden calf. You had turned aside quickly from the way that the Lord had commanded you." His final statement describes exactly what was so wrong with what they did—they did not follow God's commands regarding worship. Their motivation may indeed have been noble. They may truly have been attempting to show honor to the true God by erecting a symbol of strength and nobility in his name. Yet what this event makes clear is that God rejects worship of him in improper forms. He has the right to tell his people how he wants to be worshiped, and his people must follow those instructions to the letter. This event is also an illustration of a problem that will plague Hebrew worship for a long time—syncretism. They mixed true worship with false. They were attempting to worship the right object, but they were doing so not only through means that God had not prescribed, but also through means they copied from the pagan nations around them. God always rejects this kind of worship.

Another example of this principle is found in Leviticus 10:1–3, after the tabernacle was completed. Here Aaron's sons, Nadab and Abihu are severely punished by God for their worship. What was their problem? Their failure was not in that they attempted to worship a false god or that they attempted to worship the true God in a manner he had forbidden. Their sin was that, as the text says, they "offered unauthorized fire to the Lord, *which he commanded them not*" (emphasis mine). This account further emphasizes that God is concerned not only with heart motive—although that is certainly central—nor is he simply concerned that people worship him alone—although that is, of course, true. He is also concerned that his people worship him in the right way, which includes not worshiping in ways that he has forbidden or inventing new ways to worship that he has not commanded. Again, God alone has the authority to establish worship practices.

Memorial

The requirement of specific times and rituals for worship, both weekly and annually, established a fundamental principle for God's people that did not end with Israel. God's creation of these worship days and festivals was not arbitrary; rather, in establishing these days, God clearly articulated their purpose. For example, when God founded the annual Passover observance, he proclaimed, "This day shall be for you a memorial day, and you shall keep it as a feast to the Lord; throughout your generations, as a statue forever, you shall keep it as a feast" (Exod. 12:14). In calling this feast a "memorial," God meant more than simple a passive remembrance of the first event of Passover; this is clear by the fact that the Hebrews were meant, not merely to recount the event of the first Passover, but to actually *reenact* the event. In so doing, the people of Israel for generations to come would not only remember the facts of the Exodus from Egypt, but they would also be formed by the event as if they had been there themselves as a means to renew their covenant with God. God explains this later in verse 24 of Exodus 12:

> You shall observe this rite as a statute for you and for your sons forever. And when you come to the land that the Lord will give you, as he has promised, you shall keep this service. And when your children say to you, 'What do you mean by this service?' you shall say, 'It is the sacrifice of the Lord's Passover, for he passed over the houses of the people of Israel in Egypt, when he struck the Egyptians but spared our houses.' And the people bowed their heads and worshiped.

God uses the same root word when he commands, "*Remember* the Sabbath day, to keep it holy. Six days you shall labor, and do all your work, but the seventh day is a Sabbath to the Lord your God" (Exod. 20:8-9 emphasis mine). God intended this weekly "memorial" to reenact his own rest on the seventh day of creation: "For in six days the Lord made the heaven and earth, the sea, and all that is in them, and rested on the seventh day. Therefore the LORD blessed the Sabbath day and made it holy" (v. 11). "Rest" for God at the end of creation week did not indicate a ceasing from work, for he continually "upholds the universe by the word of his power" (Heb. 1:3). Rather, God ceased his active creative work *ex nihilo* and took pleasure in the good things he had made. In the same way, God wanted his people to "rest" in him, communing with him as he had always intended. By establishing this weekly routine for his people, God was ensuring that they would regularly renew their covenant with him (Exod. 31:12–17), enjoy communion with him, and be set apart for him alone.

This principle of memorial applied to every Sabbath and to each of the holy days, festivals, and solemn assemblies of worship in Israel, revealing the power of corporate worship to form both the people's theology and their worldview—their religion. As we shall see later, this principle applies equally to Christian worship as well.

Chapter 3
The Golden Age of Hebrew Worship

After Israel entered the promised land, the periods of the Judges and King Saul were almost entirely characterized by religious syncretism. God had commanded the people to completely destroy all those who inhabited the land; however, Scripture seems to indicate that although under Joshua much land was conquered, after his death Israel failed to obey this command (Josh. 13:1). Instead, they established treaties with the people and began a process that led to intermarriage, syncretism, and ultimately full idolatry. Even the ark of the covenant became seen as a magical talisman they would bring to battle with them for good luck (1 Sam. 4:3), which led to its eventual capture by the Philistines. Worship at the tabernacle in Shiloh, where Joshua had erected it shortly before his death (Josh. 18:1) had become so corrupt, that God "forsook his dwelling at Shiloh, the tent where he dwelt among mankind, and delivered his power to captivity, his glory to the hand of the foe" (Ps. 78:60–61). Shiloh was completely destroyed, but apparently the tabernacle survived, and Samuel later relocated it to Gilgal (1 Sam. 11:15). God also rejected the tribe of Ephraim, where Shiloh was located, as the heir to Joseph's birthright, and passed it on to Judah (Ps. 78:67–68), the new royal tribe that would produce Israel's kings.

With the rise of the Davidic monarchy, however, came a sort of "golden age" in Hebrew worship. This did not happen right away. Although David was a man after God's own heart, he nevertheless initially failed to follow God's clear instructions for worship. This is perhaps no clearer than in his attempt to bring the ark of the covenant back to Gibeon, where the tabernacle had apparently been erected after King Saul massacred the entire priesthood he suspected were loyal to David (1 Sam. 22:9–23).

Bringing the Ark to Jerusalem
The ark had been captured by the Philistines prior to the reign of King Saul (1 Sam. 4:11). Israel had gone to battle against the Philistines and had adopted the pagan practice of carrying with them a "magical talisman," something God had never commanded of them. Consequently, when the Philistines won the battle, they captured the ark, and the glory of the Lord departed from Israel. The ark remained in Philistine hands for several months (1 Sam. 6:1). Even then, God demonstrated his superiority over all other false gods—when the Philistines placed the ark before the image of their god, Dagon, God caused the idol to topple over one day, and then the next day it broke into pieces. He then sent tumors upon the people wherever the ark remained, and consequently, the Philistines sent the ark back to Israel, where it rested at Beth

Shemesh briefly (1 Sam. 6:13–15) and at Kiriath Jearim for over one hundred years, until some years into David's reign, which began at Jerusalem. Remarkably, Saul never recovered the ark to place it back in the tabernacle during the entirety of his reign. This indifference is reflected in Saul's daughter, Mikal, who married David but despised David for bringing the ark into Jerusalem (1 Chr. 15), accomplishing what her father never managed to do.

Thus, after David consolidated his rule in Jerusalem, he determined to bring the ark to its proper place. David desired a good thing, but nevertheless, while he "consulted with the commanders" and "with every leader" concerning how to recover the ark (1 Chr. 13:1), he did not consult the Lord or his Law. Instead, "All the assembly agreed to do so, for the thing was right in the eyes of all the people" (v. 4). God had given clear instructions concerning the handling of the sacred ark (Exod. 25:13–14; cf. 1 Chr. 15:2, 13, 15). When the ark was not in its place in the Holy of Holies, it was to be covered with animal skins and cloth so that no one could see it. It was to be transported only by priests by inserting two poles through the rings on the side of the ark. No one was to touch the ark or look upon it, except for the High Priest on the Day of Atonement, when he would enter the Holy of Holies to sprinkle blood on the mercy seat for the sins of the people.

Though David and the people's motivation were right, their failure to transport the ark in the manner that God had prescribed resulted in death. Instead of carrying the ark as instructed in the Law, they put the ark on a new cart led by oxen. This was certainly intended to be a sign of respect, but it was not what God had commanded and was, in fact, the same manner of transport the Philistines had devised earlier. Consequently, when Uzzah, one of the men charged with driving the cart, took hold of the ark to keep it from falling when the oxen stumbled, God killed him. Again, Uzzah's motivation was certainly noble, but right motivation alone is insufficient to please God; God also demands that his people obey his commands. Initially David was angry at God for killing Uzzah, but that anger soon turned to fear as David recognized the holiness and justice of God.

The ark remained in the house of Obed-edom for three months, at which time David determined to attempt to bring the ark to Jerusalem a second time (1 Chr. 15). This time, however, David approached the task far differently, and the contrast between these two attempts reveals important principles for biblical worship. While the first attempt to recover the ark was primarily a socio-political feat done merely in consultation with the leaders of Israel, the second attempt was performed with reverence in accordance with the Law's demands. Instead of gathering political and military leaders, David gathered Levitical leaders. In this second attempt, David clearly recognized his initial problem: "Because you did not carry it the first time, the Lord our God broke out against us, because we did not seek him *according to the rule*" (v. 13 emphasis mine). This time, "the priests and the Levites consecrated themselves to bring up the ark of the Lord, the God of Israel. And the Levites carried the ark of God on their shoulders with the poles, *as Moses had commanded according to the word of the Lord*" (vv. 14–15 emphasis mine). And this time, David and the people were able to bring the ark successfully to Jerusalem.

Contrasting these two attempts to bring the ark to Jerusalem reveals important worship principles that had already been established in the Old Testament. While God desires sincere hearts in worship, right motives alone are not enough. God has given clear instructions concerning how he is to be worshiped, and any deviation from such instruction renders worship vain. Furthermore, God does not want his people to approach him in manners that mimic pagan forms of worship. God desires worship with true hearts and in the ways he has commanded. He alone has the prerogative to determine how he is to be worshiped.

The Jerusalem Temple
Because David successfully defeated Israel's enemies during his reign, Israel enjoyed peace and prosperity. This allowed David to establish his rule in Jerusalem, building for himself an elaborate palace. He also desired to build a house for the worship of God on the land he purchased from Araunah at God's command (2 Sam. 24:16–25; 2 Chr. 6:6). This same location was where Abraham had offered Isaac (2 Chr. 3:1) and where the king-priest Melchizedek had reigned (Gen. 14). David brought the ark of the covenant there to a tabernacle he built, but because David had shed so much blood during his campaigns to establish peace in Israel, God told him that he would not be the one to build the temple; rather, his son Solomon would do so (1 Chr. 22:6–8).

God did allow David to make the plans for the temple, purchase all of the building materials, and organize the temple worship. Only Levite men thirty years or older were permitted to serve in the temple in various functions such as offering sacrifices, keeping the gates, and various other duties. At the time of David's organization, 38,000 men qualified to serve, and of those, 24,000 were to serve in the temple, 6,000 would be officers and judges, 4,000 were gatekeepers, and 4,000 were set apart to praise the Lord through music (1 Chr. 23:2–5).

After David's death, Solomon followed his father's instructions and built the temple, which had been given to David by inspiration from the Spirit of God; David had told Solomon, "All this [the Lord] made clear to me in writing from the hand of the Lord, all the work to be done according to the plan" (1 Chr. 28:19). The architecture and furniture of the temple were simply more elaborate and permanent versions of the tabernacle. The sanctuary was ninety feet long, thirty feet wide, and forty-five feet tall, with two twenty-seven feet tall free-standing pillars in front (2 Chr. 3:3; Jer. 52:21). It was adorned with precious jewels and gold (2 Chr. 3:6–7), the altar was made of bronze, thirty feet by thirty feet wide and fifteen feet high, and the laver was also made of bronze and enlarged to a circumference of forty-five feet and eight feet high standing on twelve bronze oxen (2 Chr. 4:1–5). All of the furniture and vessels to be used in the temple were made of pure gold (2 Chr. 4:7–22).

Construction of the temple took seven years (1 Kgs. 7:1; 9:10), after which Solomon arranged for the ark and all of the sacred elements to be brought from the tabernacle in Gibeon into their new home in the Jerusalem temple. Musicians appointed by David (more below), Asaph, Heman, and Jeduthun, led the Levitical singers using cymbals and accompanied by lyres, along with priests who played the silver trumpets "to make themselves heard in unison in praise and thanksgiving to the Lord" (2 Chr. 5:12–13).

Solomon's Dedication of the Temple
The dedication of the temple in 2 Chronicles 5–7 is instructive since it demonstrates a liturgical ordering that had already been practiced at Mt. Sinai and that would characterize public assemblies of worship in Israel and even later in the church. The service began with bringing the ark and the sacred implements to the temple according to the command of the Lord. In so doing, the people witnessed the presence of the Lord taking residence in their midst. This resulted in their recognition of their unworthiness to be in God's presence, manifested in their sacrifice of "so many sheep and oxen that they could not be counted or numbered" (2 Chr. 5:6). God demonstrated his acceptance of the sacrifices that he required by filling the temple with his visible glory (vv. 13–14), and the people responded with a song of thanksgiving:

> For he is good,
> for his steadfast love endures forever.

Solomon then expressed thanks and praise to the Lord for dwelling in their presence (2 Chr. 6:1–11) and offered the prayer of dedication for the temple, including a recounting of the law of God for the people (vv. 12–42):

> O Lord, God of Israel, there is no God like you, in heaven or on earth, keeping covenant and showing steadfast love to your servants who walk before you with all their heart, who have kept with your servant David my father what you declared to him. You spoke with your mouth, and with your hand have fulfilled it this day. Now therefore, O Lord, God of Israel, keep for your servant David my father what you have promised him, saying, "You shall not lack a man to sit before me on the throne of Israel, if only your sons pay close attention to their way, to walk in my law as you have walked before me." Now therefore, O Lord,

God of Israel, let your word be confirmed, which you have spoken to your servant David.

But will God indeed dwell with man on the earth? Behold, heaven and the highest heaven cannot contain you, how much less this house that I have built! Yet have regard to the prayer of your servant and to his plea, O Lord my God, listening to the cry and to the prayer that your servant prays before you, that your eyes may be open day and night toward this house, the place where you have promised to set your name, that you may listen to the prayer that your servant offers toward this place. And listen to the pleas of your servant and of your people Israel, when they pray toward this place. And listen from heaven your dwelling place, and when you hear, forgive. "If a man sins against his neighbor and is made to take an oath and comes and swears his oath before your altar in this house, then hear from heaven and act and judge your servants, repaying the guilty by bringing his conduct on his own head, and vindicating the righteous by rewarding him according to his righteousness."

Now, O my God, let your eyes be open and your ears attentive to the prayer of this place. And now arise, O Lord God, and go to your resting place, you and the ark of your might. Let your priests, O Lord God, be clothed with salvation, and let your saints rejoice in your goodness. O Lord God, do not turn away the face of your anointed one! Remember your steadfast love for David your servant. (vv. 14–23)

The people responded by consecrating the temple with more sacrifices, committing to follow the Lord in whatever he commanded (2 Chr. 7:1–7). The ceremony climaxed with a seven-day feast (vv. 8–9), which demonstrated the fellowship they now enjoyed in the presence of God, after which Solomon dismissed the people back to their homes (v. 10).

The liturgy of Solomon's dedication service resembles that of Israel's worship at Mt. Sinai years earlier: God had instructed his people to worship in this fashion, and all that Solomon did was in obedience to God's commands. Because of their sin, the people were required to offer atoning sacrifices, and God displayed his pardon by sending fire from heaven, for which the people praised and thanked him. God spoke his Word to the people, and they responded with commitment to obey him. The service climaxed with a visible picture of fellowship in God's presence in the form of a feast. The liturgy could be summarized this way:

God reveals himself and calls his people to worship
God's people acknowledge and confess their need for forgiveness
God provides atonement
God speaks his Word
God's people respond with commitment
God hosts a celebratory feast

Music in Hebrew Worship

Both descriptions of singing in the Old Testament as well as the Psalms themselves present a fairly clear picture of music in Hebrew worship. We must be careful not to transplant our perception of Jewish music today and simply assume that ancient Hebrew music sounded exactly the same. Hebrew music in Old Testament times was very different than what we know as modern Jewish music. Jewish music today is a complex mix of Western influences (because Jews were scattered all over the world until the early 1900s), Arabic traditions, and certainly some traditional folk influences. Further, our perception of Jewish music is usually filtered through pop culture and Hollywood. Therefore, our conception of what Hebrew worship music was like must come from the biblical accounts, and secondarily from archeological evidence from ancient times.

The other important factor in our consideration of Hebrew worship music that we must remember is that Israel was a theocracy; that is, their religion, politics, and social life were all intertwined, unlike our separation of church and state today. This is important because not all of the music recorded for us in the Old Testament was intended for corporate worship. Music is used for all sorts of purposes in the Bible: The Hebrews sang as they worked in the vineyards (Jer. 25:30; 48:33) and dug wells (Num. 21:17–18). They expressed themselves through music at social and political events such as coronations (1 Kings 1:39–40), family festivities (Gen. 31:27), funerals (2 Sam. 1:18–27), and military victories (Judg. 5:1ff; 1 Sam. 18:6–7; 2 Chr. 20:28). Since Israel was a theocracy, the content of even folk songs contained expressions of thanks and praise to God. Since cultus and culture were intertwined in Hebrew life, the Old Testament relates many common uses of music in everyday life. So, as we evaluate the music of Hebrew worship, we are limiting ourselves to those songs intended to be sung as part of corporate worship.

Temple Music

Music in the Temple consisted of choirs, often singing antiphonally (Pss. 136; 118:1–4), accompanied by lyres and cymbals (1 Chr. 16:42; 25:1, 6; 2 Chr. 5:12). Interestingly, David had established preliminary organization of Levitical musicians during his second attempt to recover the ark. During the first attempt the people had celebrated with music, but without any organization (1 Chr. 13:8); the second time however, David gave special care to the musicians just as he did to all aspects of the event. David appointed three chief musicians—Asaph, Heman, and Jeduthun (1 Chr. 15:17), each of whom played *tseltselim* (v. 19), two metal plates struck together to produce a clanging sound; as leaders of the singers, these men likely played these cymbals as a means to "conduct" the group, indicating the beginning of musical phrases.[1] David also

---

[1] Alfred Sendrey, *Music in Ancient Israel* (New York: Philosophical Library, 1969), 365–377.

appointed musicians to play the *kinnor* (often translated "lyre" or "harp"), a trapezoid-shaped instrument made of wood with strings of equal length, used to accompany singing, and the *nebel* (often translated "harp," "psaltery," "viol," or "lute"), a larger form of lyre.[2] Finally, musicians played two forms of trumpet, the *khatsotserot*, a straight horn made of silver that God had instructed Moses to make (Num. 10:2), and the *shofar*, a turned up animal horn. These trumpets were likely used to signal events rather than to accompany singing or play melodies since they had no valves or finger holes and therefore could play only a limited number of pitches.[3] Leading all of the musicians was Chenaniah (1 Chr. 15:22). These particular leaders and instruments that David prescribed during the second attempt to recover the ark were carried over directly into his organization of the temple musicians.

Since the music was unmetered, cymbals likely were used to indicate the beginnings of musical phrases rather than to keep a steady beat,[4] and trumpets signaled changes of events rather than accompanying the singing. The kinds of soft accompanying instruments used in the temple indicate that singing in worship would have been modest and restrained.[5] Melodies were likely simple, following the natural syllabic stress of the lyrics and lacking the regular even meter of modern music.[6] While the sound would have been relatively loud when vast numbers of singers participated, as was sometimes the case (e.g., 2 Chr. 15:12–14), this would have been due to the number of performers rather than to the character of singing itself. As Alfred Sendrey notes, "the outstanding feature of art-singing in Ancient Israel has been euphony and refinement. The preponderance of soft instruments, harps and lyres, as accompaniment in the culture, may serve as the most eloquent proof to this effect." Most descriptions of singing in the Old Testament indicates that Hebrew worship music was characteristically of a "quiet, solemn, and dignified quality."[7]

Shall We Dance?
One Hebrew cultural expression that naturally arises in discussion of worship is dance, especially in relation to both the character of their worship and its relationship to the surrounding pagan culture. Several terms in the Old Testament have been translated "dance" by various English translations. Of them, only the term *machowl* clearly signified artistic movement to music—what we would call "dancing" today. It likely

---

[2] John Stainer, *The Music of the Bible: With Some Account of the Development of Modern Musical Instruments from Ancient Types*, Revised ed. (London: Novello, Ewer, and Co., 1970), 25–28.
[3] Ovid R. Sellers, "Musical Instruments of Israel," *The Biblical Archaeologist* 4, no. 3 (n.d.): 43.
[4] Sendrey, *Music in Ancient Israel*, 365–377.
[5] Peter Gradenwitz, *The Music of Israel: From the Biblical Era to Modern Times* (Portland, OR: Amadeus Press, 1996), 34, 36.
[6] Sendrey, *Music in Ancient Israel*, 377.
[7] Sendrey, *Music in Ancient Israel*, 255–256.

described a kind of Jewish folk dance, always connected in the Old Testament with joyful civil celebrations. This dancing would have communicated joy and exuberance and certainly not any kind of immorality or sexuality. This term is used when Miriam and the Hebrew women celebrate the crossing of the Red Sea (Exod. 15:20), during the national celebration after David defeated Goliath (1 Sam. 18:6), and to describe Israel's future celebration in the Messianic kingdom (Jer. 31:4).

Only two times does *machowl* appear in the psalms:

Let them praise his name with dancing,
making melody to him with tambourine and lyre! (Ps. 149:3)

Praise him with tambourine and dance;
praise him with strings and pipe! (Ps. 150:4)

Some suggest that these two commands indicate the appropriateness of dance for corporate worship, particularly because, they argue, both psalms begin with statements indicating the context of corporate worship:

Praise the Lord!
Sing to the Lord a new song,
his praise in *the assembly of the godly*! (Ps. 149:1 emphasis mine)

Praise the Lord!
Praise God in *his sanctuary*! (Ps. 150:1 emphasis mine)

However, examining the rest of both of these psalms makes clear that not everything commanded in them refers to corporate worship; rather, their emphasis is the command to praise the Lord in all circumstances of life. They do indeed command believers to praise God in corporate worship—"the assembly of the godly" and "his sanctuary," but they also admonish, "let them sing for joy *on their beds*" (Ps. 149:5 emphasis mine) and "let the high praises of God be in their throats and *two-edged swords in their hands*, to execute vengeance on the nations and punishments on the peoples" (Ps. 149:6–7 emphasis mine). Surely these are not mandates to include beds and swords in corporate worship. In other words, the point of the final psalms of the Old Testament are to encourage believers to praise the Lord in every aspect of life, whether they are participating in corporate worship, enjoying a social event that includes dancing and making melody on the tambourine, sleeping, or executing God's justice through war. As the final verse proclaims, "Let everything that has breath praise the Lord! Praise the Lord" (Ps. 150:6)!

Other terms often translated "dance" are forms of *karar* and *raqad*, words that simply refer to joyful spinning, leaping, and jumping for joy. These could be translated "dance," but they are not as clear as *machowl*. Interestingly, the KJV is the most liberal in translating these other two terms as "dance." Newer translations usually render them as "jump" or "spin." Even so, there are only eleven occurrences of "dance" in the KJV and far fewer in newer translations.

In 2 Samuel 6, when David brought the ark to Jerusalem, "leaping and dancing before the Lord," *machowl* is not used; only *karar* and *raqad* appear to describe David's expressive act. Since the context is God punishing the people (specifically Uzzah) for not following his prescribed instructions for carrying the ark, what David was doing was certainly not an imitation of pagan dance. There is nothing in the text, outside of Michal's condemnation of David's act (more on this below), that indicates David's dance was orgiastic or otherwise pagan in character. Contextually, this seems to be more of a spontaneous leaping for joy because of the safe return of the ark. Further, even if this is some kind of choreographed, artistic dance, it is the only record of a king, priest, or prophet ever dancing. Michal's reaction to what David was doing was likely a response to the fact that the victory of bringing the ark to Jerusalem signified everything that was wrong with her father's rule—it is no coincidence that the author calls her "the daughter of Saul" (2 Sam. 6:16) here instead of "the wife of David"—and everything that was right with David's rule. This occasion officially marked the transition of rule from Saul's line to David's, which displeased Saul's daughter Michal.

Therefore, dance in the Old Testament appears to be non-sexual, exuberant celebration typically during a national celebration of victory. It never appears in the solemn assemblies of Israel's worship.

Psalms
The Book of Psalms provides us with the best picture of what Israel sang in its worship. The word "psalm" is derived from the Greek word *psalmoi*, which originally meant "music of the lyre," since the predominant instrument in Hebrew worship was the lyre. The title of the book in Hebrew is *tehillîm*, "Praises." The collection as we now have it was likely compiled by scribes after the Hebrews returned from exile, when it was grouped into five books:

Book I: Psalm 1–41
Book II: Psalms 42–72
Book III: Psalms 73–89
Book IV: Psalms 90–106

Book V: Psalms 107–150[8]

Scholars also recognize several literary forms and functions within the collection:
Hymn – songs of praise to God (92, 96, 103)
Lament – songs that cry out to God in time of need (22, 42)
Royal songs – songs that focus on the reign of God or the king (20, 45)
Historical litanies – songs that recount the works of God in the past (77, 136)
Penitential songs – songs of personal or national repentance (6, 51, 130)
Wisdom songs – songs that focus on practical living (1, 19)[9]

As previously mentioned, not all of the psalms were necessarily intended for use in the solemn assemblies of Hebrew worship. Some psalms are war songs (24), love songs (45), historical litanies (78, 105), and songs of personal or national lament (69). Many psalms were, however, specifically intended for worship, some of which were designated for particular services or other liturgical functions. For example, later Jewish tradition holds that designated psalms were sung on specific days during the daily service: Psalm 24 (Sunday), Psalm 48 (Monday), Psalm 82 (Tuesday), Psalm 94 (Wednesday), Psalm 81 (Thursday), Psalm 93 (Friday), Psalm 92 (Saturday).[10] Other psalms were sung during pilgrimages to Jerusalem, often designated as "Songs of Ascent" (120–134), or during the high festivals, such as the *Hallel* ("Praise") psalms (113–118). Headings in the collection were not necessarily original, but probably represent traditional authorship or include musical references.

As poems meant to be set to music, psalms employ various poetic devices, some of which have been successfully translated in English:

> *acrostic* – the first letter of each line or stanza forms a recognizable pattern.
>> Example: In Psalm 119, each stanza has eight lines that begin with the same letter of the alphabet, progression through all twenty-one stanzas. This is not usually translated in English.

> *anaphora* – repeating the same word in successive lines, developing the idea further with each line
>> Example:
>> "O sing to the Lord a new song;
>> sing to the Lord, all the earth!
>> Sing to the Lord, bless his name." (96:1–2)

---

[8] Allen Ross, *A Commentary on the Psalms: 1-41* (Grand Rapids: Kregel Academic, 2012), 50.
[9] Tremper Longman III., *How to Read the Psalms* (Downers Grove: IVP Academic, 1988), 19–36; Ross, *A Commentary on the Psalms*, 111–145.
[10] J. H. Hayes, *Understanding the Psalms* (Valley Forge: Judson, 1976), 16.

The Golden Age

apostrophe – directly addressing inanimate objects
> Example:
> "Tremble, O earth, at the presence of the Lord." (114:7)

chiasm – crossing lines or clauses
> Example:
> "For the Lord knows the way of the righteous,
> but the way of the wicked will perish." (1:6)

hyperbole – using exaggeration for emphasis
> Example:
> "My eyes shed streams of tears,
> because people do not keep your law." (119:136)

metaphor – using one idea to represent another because of similarities between them
> Example:
> "The Lord is my shepherd." (23:1)

personification – ascribing human qualities to an inanimate object or abstraction
> Example:
> "The sea looked and fled;
> Jordan turned back." (114:3)

The most common poetic device in Hebrew poetry is parallelism, which refers to correspondence that occurs between two (called a "bicolon") or three (called a "tricolon") phrases in a poetic line. In Hebrew parallelism, the second phrase (and third, if one exists) carries forward the thought found in the first line and develops it in some way. Often translators attempt to capture the parallelism, but not always. This development can take a couple different forms:

> With *synonymous parallelism*, the phrases repeat the same thought using different, but closely related, words.
> Example:
> "Why do the nations conspire
>   and the peoples plot in vain?
> The kings of the earth take their stand
>   and the rulers gather together
> against the Lord
>   and against his Anointed One.
> 'Let us break their chains,' they say,
>   'and throw off their fetters.'" (2:1–3)

With *antithetic parallelism*, the same thought is expressed, but in two different and often opposite perspectives.
Example:
"For the Lord knows the way of the righteous,
        but the way of the wicked will perish." (1:6)

Emblematic parallelism explicitly draws an analogy, usually using like or as.
Example:
"As the dear pants for flowing streams,
    so pants my soul for you, O God." (42:1)

Climactic parallelism uses repetition, often in the form of anaphora, to build each phrase in succession.
Example:
"Ascribe to the Lord, O heavenly beings,
    ascribe to the Lord glory and strength.
        Ascribe to the Lord the glory due his name;
worship the Lord in the splendor of holiness." (29:1–2)

Finally, with *pivot parallelism*, a word or clause stands in the middle of the poetic line, linking the two phrases on either side.
Example:
Give attention to the sound of my cry,
    my King and my God,
for to you do I pray." (5:2)

Poetic devices in the psalms served a number of different purposes, as they do in all songs. Some devices, such as acrostic and even the parallelism, aid memory, and all poetic devices help to make the poetry more singable, However, poetry also communicates the truths and ideas of the content in powerful ways not possible with mere prose. The poet uses aesthetic devices to create a world into which the singers and listeners enter and experience more than simply transmission of information to form their theology, but also formation of imagination and affections—their worldview. In this way poems, including songs like the psalms, both express *and* form biblical religion.

A brief survey of one psalm will help demonstrate the purpose and power of Hebrew singing:

Oh sing to the LORD a new song;
    sing to the LORD, all the earth!
[2] Sing to the LORD, bless his name;
    tell of his salvation from day to day.

The Golden Age

³ Declare his glory among the nations,
   his marvelous works among all the peoples!
⁴ For great is the LORD, and greatly to be praised;
   he is to be feared above all gods.
⁵ For all the gods of the peoples are worthless idols,
   but the LORD made the heavens.
⁶ Splendor and majesty are before him;
   strength and beauty are in his sanctuary.
⁷ Ascribe to the LORD, O families of the peoples,
   ascribe to the LORD glory and strength!
⁸ Ascribe to the LORD the glory due his name;
   bring an offering, and come into his courts!
⁹ Worship the LORD in the splendor of holiness;
   tremble before him, all the earth!
¹⁰ Say among the nations, "The LORD reigns!
      Yes, the world is established; it shall never be moved;
   he will judge the peoples with equity."
¹¹ Let the heavens be glad,
      and let the earth rejoice;
   let the sea roar, and all that fills it;
      ¹² let the field exult, and everything in it!
Then shall all the trees of the forest sing for joy ¹³ before the LORD,
   for he comes,
   for he comes to judge the earth.
   He will judge the world in righteousness,
      and the peoples in his faithfulness.

Psalm 96 was placed by the editors of the psalms in a series that are unified by a common poetic genre and theme. Psalms 93–100 are often referred to as "Enthronement Psalms," since their central message is affirmation of God's kingly reign over all things. This psalm in particular is an Enthronement Psalm directly connected to corporate worship. It was originally written by King David on the occasion of bringing the Ark of the Covenant to Jerusalem. First Chronicles 16:7 records, "Then on that day David first appointed that thanksgiving be sung to the LORD by Asaph and his brothers," and the following verses record the song. After this dedication service, David apparently took the song he had written and rearranged it into a couple different songs that Israel then regularly used in its worship. Portions of the song in 1 Chronicles 16 appear, almost verbatim, in Psalms 105 and 106, and verses 23–33 of 1 Chronicles 16 are almost exactly Psalm 96. What also makes this psalm particularly helpful for our purposes is that the Greek translation of the psalm indicates that it was also used at the dedication of the rebuilt temple after the Hebrews returned from Babylonian exile, which we will discuss in the next chapter. The context of both of these events, the dedication of David's tabernacle after the ark had been returned to Jerusalem, and the dedication of the Second Temple after return from exile seem fitting for a psalm expressing praise to God and affirmation of his sovereign reign over all things, particularly over the pagan nations and their gods.

Psalm 96 would be classified as a hymn in terms of genre. As noted above, a hymn is a song of praise in response to the nature and works of God, and we can clearly see this in the structure of the psalm. Verses 1–3 are calls to worship the Lord, and verses 4–6 describe the reasons for worship. That marks the first stanza of this hymn. A similar pattern follows in the second stanza beginning in verse 7, and in the third stanza beginning in verse 11. In each case, this song is an expression of worship in response to understanding truth about God.

Understanding this structure helps reinforce the purpose of singing in Hebrew worship. There is no question that Psalm 96 is a call to sing; in fact, David emphasizes this fact by repeating the call to sing three times right at the beginning. David further communicates something of the nature of singing very clearly in how he develops the idea in the psalm. The psalm opens with three commands to sing, followed by three verbs set in parallel with the three commands: Bless, Tell, Declare. David is developing what it means to sing with these three verbs—to sing is to bless the Lord, it is to tell of his salvation, it is to declare his glory. In fact, David uses verbs grouped in threes in this psalm a few more times to develop what it means to sing to the Lord, the next occurrence beginning in verse 7 with a threefold repetition of "Ascribe." To sing to the Lord is to ascribe to him something he deserves, namely, glory and strength, the glory due his name. Verse 8 commences another grouping of three verbs: Bring an offering, worship the Lord, tremble before him—further characterization of the nature of singing in worship. The next grouping of three verbs begins in verse 11 with three imperatives indicated with the word "Let" (the second "let" in English at the beginning of verse 11 isn't actually there in Hebrew), continuing the explanation of the nature of singing: be glad and rejoice, roar, exult. David intentionally used these groupings of three verbs to expand and explore the nature of singing to the Lord. His use of parallel groupings of three reveals that these are not separate ideas; he does not command the people to sing and then separately command them to bless, tell, declare, ascribe, and so forth as if these are just lists of things the people should do. Rather, in expressing these commands in parallel groups of threes, David developed one central thread of interconnected ideas. When we sing, we bless the Lord; when we sing, we tell of his salvation; when we sing, we declare his glory, we ascribe to him the glory and strength due his name, we rejoice, we express, and we exult.

In other words, singing in worship is not *just* making music; the verbs in these groupings reveal that profound things are taking place while singing in worship. We are expressing profound affections from our hearts like joy and exultation; we are magnifying God's glory and strength; we are proclaiming what he has done. And there are other kinds of expression that are not in this psalm but are described elsewhere. Singing helps us express thanksgiving, lament, contrition, praise, confession, grief, love, and so much more. In fact, singing helps us express those things to the Lord in ways that would not be possible if we didn't have song. Singing gives us a language for the expression of our hearts when words alone would be inadequate. God's people can and should certainly bless the Lord with simple words, telling of his salvation, declaring his glory, and exulting him with just words alone. But singing helps us to do all of that in nuanced and expansive ways that words alone cannot.

Yet heart expression through singing is not for its own sake in worship. Rather, singing to the Lord is a response to who God is and what he has done. We can see this just in the structure of Psalm 96. The calls to express through singing are repeatedly followed by reasons for those expressions. In fact, in two of the three stanzas, this is clearly evident with another grouping of three. For example, after the threefold call to sing and the threefold development of what that means, David presents three reasons to sing: for great is the Lord, for all the gods of the people are worthless, and splendor and majesty are before him. The same things occur in verse 13; after the threefold call for the earth, the sea, and the field to sing, David gives three reasons: for he comes, for he comes to judge the earth, he will judge the world. A good hymn is not simply an expression of emotion toward God, a recitation of facts about God, or a collection of correct theological statements. A good hymn contains both expressions of appropriate affections directed toward the Lord and theological reasons for those expressions, expressing both the theology and heart orientation of God's people.

But there is a second purpose for singing in worship that Psalm 96 models, and this purpose is apparent in the development of thought through the psalm. The psalm progresses in the first stanza from singing among the nations and among all the peoples into the second stanza where the command to ascribe glory to the Lord is given to all "the families of the peoples." There is an expansion from the people of God alone singing to him among the nations to all the nations ascribing glory to him, unveiling the tremendous evangelistic power of faithfully reciting the works of the Lord in worship and responding right heart expression. Yet even though the psalm describes all the peoples of the earth ascribing glory to the Lord, that was certainly not a reality when David wrote the psalm. Likewise, when David progresses in the third stanza to the earth itself praising God, that also is not a present reality as described in the song. The realities of all the families of the peoples and all creation ascribing glory to the Lord are future; they will not take place until the Lord comes again to judge the world. So why would David prescribe singing in response to things that have not yet taken place as if they have already happened?

The answer to that question reveals the second reason we sing in worship. The first reason we sing is expression—our hearts respond to past and present realities about God's nature and works, and singing gives us voice to express our hearts toward God in response. But the second reason we sing, which is highlighted when we respond to something that has not yet taken place, is that singing forms us. In other words, when we sing in response to something that has not yet happened, we are in a sense acting out that future reality and, in so doing, we are formed by it. By singing about all the families of the people and creation praising God when the Lord comes to judge the earth in righteousness and faithfulness, our hearts are shaped as if we are really experiencing those realities right now. It is more than just an expression of hope that these things will indeed happen; through art, we are making the future momentarily present such that it can form us. This is actually true for past and even present realities as well. Israel at the time of David hadn't experienced for themselves the Exodus, for example, and yet there are many psalms that artistically recreate the Exodus so that as people sang of that experience, they could be shaped by it as if they had been there. This is also why good songs don't just express things like joy, praise, thanksgiving, and adoration, they also recount the reasons for those responses, because by also singing the reasons, we are further formed by them as we experience them over and over through the art.

Chapter 4
Exile and Return

The golden age of Israel during the reigns of David and Solomon resulted in worship that followed God's instructions and was performed with sincerity and desire to commune with God. However, despite the fact that Solomon was the wisest man alive (1 Kgs. 4:30), he "loved many foreign women" who "turned away his heart" (11:1, 3). These foreign wives brought with them their gods, leading Solomon to build high places for these gods and to forsake the pure worship of God. God punished Solomon by raising adversaries against him and ultimately by dividing the kingdom after his death. One of those who opposed Solomon was Jeroboam, to whom God initially promised ten tribes and ultimately all Israel as long as Jeroboam would "listen to all that I command you, and will walk in my ways, and do what is right in my eyes by keeping my statutes and all my commandments, as David my servant did" (1 Kgs. 11:38). After Solomon's death, his son Rehoboam foolishly oppressed the people, leading to a division of the kingdom. Only Judah and the Levites remained loyal to Rehoboam while the other tribes united under Jeroboam, who established his reign in Shechem.

Yet in spite of God's promise of blessing, Jeroboam took a pragmatic approach to worship. He feared that if he allowed his people to travel to the temple in Jerusalem for worship, which was located in Judah, his people would turn back to follow Rehoboam. In order to avoid this, Jeroboam established new centers of worship, conveniently located at both ends of the kingdom, new means of worship through representing Yahweh with calves of gold, and a new priesthood (1 Kgs. 12:25–33). He did not encourage his people to worship other deities; he simply formed new ways to worship Yahweh through other means God had not prescribed.

Because of this, God cursed Jeroboam and his kingdom: "After this thing Jeroboam did not turn from his evil way, but made priests for the high places again from among all the people. Any who would, he ordained to be priests of the high places. And this thing became sin to the house of Jeroboam, so as to cut it off and to destroy it from the face of the earth" (1 Kgs. 13:33–34). Inevitably, the syncretism of Jeroboam led to complete idolatry. The northern kings following Jeroboam continued the syncretism that he had established until King Omri arranged the marriage of his son Ahab to Jezebel, princess of the neighboring kingdom of Phoenicia, who brought with her to the marriage her unbreakable devotion to the worship of Baal. No longer was the northern kingdom of Israel characterized by mere syncretism, as terrible as that is. Now, King Ahab instituted full Baal worship, for the first time actually erecting a temple and altars to the pagan deity. Consequently, although the southern kingdom of Judah enjoyed an occasional king who followed the Law of God, no king in the north worshiped Yahweh as he commanded.

The situation was not much better in the southern kingdom, either. Rehoboam, too, led the people to build high places and worship pagan gods (1 Kgs. 14:22–24). A few kings and priests attempted to return Judah back to the worship of Yahweh, some successfully for a time. For example, the priest Jehoiada led in the destruction of Baal's idols and temple and the restoration of the temple (2 Kgs. 12). Likewise, king Hezekiah cleansed the temple and restored its worship, reinstituting the Passover celebration that had been long neglected (2 Chr. 29–31), and the young king Josiah also returned to pure worship according to the Book of the Law (2 Kgs. 22–23; 2 Chr. 34). However, most of the southern kings were just as corrupt as those in the north, such as Ahaz (2 Kgs. 16) and Manasseh (2 Kgs. 21:1–18).

Other kings were mixed, such as Uzziah. Second Chronicles 26 records the fact that for the most part, Uzziah was a noble king who did what was right in the sight of the Lord, and therefore God rewarded him by giving him many military victories. However, "when he was strong, he grew proud, to his destruction. For he was unfaithful to the Lord his God and entered the temple of the Lord to burn incense of the altar of incense" (v. 16). The priests ran in after him and confronted him, insisting that he had no right to enter the temple: "It is not for you, Uzziah, to burn incense to the Lord, but for the priests, the sons of Aaron, who are consecrated to burn incense. Go out from the sanctuary, for you have done wrong, and it will bring you no honor from the Lord God" (v. 18). But Uzziah was angry and continued, and while he stood in the sanctuary and before the altar of incense, leprosy suddenly began to break out on his forehead. The priest saw it and quickly took him from the sanctuary. It was clear that the Lord had struck him for having dared to draw near to the Holy Place in such a presumptuous way: "And King Uzziah was a leper to the day of his death, and being a leper lived in a separate house, for he was excluded from the house of the Lord" (v. 21).

Reminder of the Heavenly Pattern of Worship

It is no coincidence that the death of Uzziah is the very context for the prophet Isaiah's vision of heavenly worship (Isa. 6:1–13). In a way, this was God reminding Isaiah of the pattern upon which pure earthly worship was supposed to be based. God called Isaiah up into the heavenly temple itself, where he "saw the Lord sitting upon a throne, high and lifted up" (v. 1). Surrounding God were seraphim singing what has come to be called the *Trisagion* ("thrice holy"),

> Holy, holy, holy is the Lord of hosts;
> The whole earth is full of his glory!

The sight of God in all of his holiness and splendor caused Isaiah to recognize his own sin and unworthiness to draw near to the presence of God in his temple, what Uzziah should have known before entering the earthly temple as he did. Thus, Isaiah confessed his sin before the Lord: "Woe is me! For I am lost; for I am a man of unclean lips, and I dwell in the midst of a people of unclean lips; for my eyes have seen the King, the Lord of hosts" (v. 5)! Yet God did not simply expel Isaiah from the temple due to his impurity; rather, God provided means of atonement. One of the seraphim took a burning coal from the altar and placed it on Isaiah's lips, proclaiming, "Behold, this has touched your lips; your guilt is taken away, and your sin atoned for." (v.7) Now Isaiah was welcome in the presence of God by the means God himself had provided. Standing accepted in God's presence, Isaiah heard the voice of the Lord giving him a message, to which Isaiah willingly offered obedience, and God sent Isaiah forth with that message of both instruction and blessing to the nation of Israel. This pattern of heavenly worship was the same basic order that the people of Israel had followed when they worshiped God at Mt. Sinai, after the construction of the tabernacle, and at the dedication of the temple:

God reveals himself and calls his people to worship
God's people acknowledge and confess their need for forgiveness
God provides atonement
God speaks his Word
God's people respond with commitment
(No feast in Isaiah 6)

Exile
Yet for the most part, the people of Israel and Judah did not heed the warnings of God's prophets. Because of their persistent syncretism and idolatry, both the northern and southern kingdoms were plagued with turmoil and war. God does not tolerate false worship; because the people did not keep his commandments, God allowed the northern kingdom to be defeated by Assyria in a series of invasions until finally, in 722 BC, Assyria completely defeated them and took the people captive. The southern kingdom did not fare much better. Because of their increasing idolatry, God raised up the nation of Babylon to invade the nation, and finally in 586 BC the city of Jerusalem along with the Temple were utterly destroyed, and in a series of deportations the people were taken captive to Babylon.

Two of the most well-known stories from the Old Testament are specifically meant to highlight how difficult it would have been for the Hebrews to worship God as he commanded while they were in exile—Daniel and the lion's den and the three Hebrews in the fiery furnace. In both cases, the matter in view is whether or not God's people in exile would worship him as he commanded or whether they would give into the pressure of their pagan captors and bow to false gods. Shadrach, Meshach, and Abednego refused to worship pagan gods, proclaiming, "Be it known to you, O king, that we will not serve your gods or worship the golden image that you have set up" (Dan. 3:18), and Daniel refused to stop worshiping as God required, kneeling "three times a day and prayed and gave thanks before his God, as he had done previously" (Dan. 6:10). However, in both cases, a vast *minority* actually followed God's commands; most of the nation continued to forsake the true worship of God.

The psalmist in Psalm 137 expressed vividly the cry of a faithful worshiper in the midst of such a bleak experience:

> By the waters of Babylon,
> > there we sat down and wept,
> > when we remembered Zion.
> On the willows there
> > we hung up our lyres.
> For there our captors
> > required of us songs,
> and our tormentors, mirth, saying,
> > "Sing us one of the songs of Zion!"
> How shall we sing the LORD's song
> > in a foreign land?
> If I forget you, O Jerusalem,
> > let my right hand forget its skill!
> Let my tongue stick to the roof of my mouth,
> > if I do not remember you,
> > if I do not set Jerusalem
> > above my highest joy!

We do not know for sure who wrote this psalm, but it was most certainly written by someone who had experienced for himself the Babylonian captivity, either shortly after the captivity ended or possibly some time into the captivity. It was customary for Jews to gather for worship by a river due to the necessity of ceremonial washings, so it is very likely that the setting of this psalm—"by the waters of Babylon"—refers to their attempt to gather for worship in exile. And yet instead, they sat down and wept; they hung up their lyres, the predominate instrument of accompaniment for temple worship. Their captors mocked them, but the captive Hebrews could not sing. They were God's people in a strange land with no homes and no place for worship.

Second Kings 17 succinctly diagnoses the cause of Israel's downfall as one of false worship: "And this occurred because the people of Israel had sinned against the Lord their God, who had brought them up out of the land of Egypt from under the hand of Pharaoh king of Egypt, and had feared other gods and walked in the customs of the nations whom the Lord drove out before the people of Israel, and in the customs that the kings of Israel had practiced" (2 Kgs. 17:7–8).

Restoration and Reform

Yet God had established an unconditional covenant with David that his royal line would be established forever, and the prophet Jeremiah promised the people that God would one day bring them back to their land (Jer. 30:3). And God always keeps his promises. After seventy years in exile, God moved in the heart of Persian king Cyrus, who had conquered Babylon, to send Hebrew exiles back to Jerusalem the following year, led by Zerubbabel (Ezra 1:1–11). This initiated a time of significant rebuilding and reform in Israel; most of the returning exiles had learned their lesson and desired to restore the temple and pure worship. The temple was successfully rebuilt in 515 BC, albeit at a fraction of its former glory. Yet the people labored to restore temple worship "according to the directions of David king of Israel" and "as it is written in the Book of Moses" (Ezra 3:10; 6:18). The priest Ezra led a second group of exiles back to the land in 467 BC, at which time he continued to encourage repentance and spiritual reform among the people (Ezra 7:1–10). In 454 BC a third wave of exile returned under the leadership of Nehemiah and the restoration continued (Neh. 2:1–10). As a necessary component of the reform of true worship, the Word of God was restored to a prominent position: "So Ezra the priest brought the Law before the assembly, both men and women and all who could understand what they heard ... And he read from it facing the square before the Water Gate from early morning until midday, in the presence of the men and the women and those who could understand. And the ears of all the people were attentive to the Book of the Law" (Neh. 8:2–3).

Hypocritical Worship

The people of Israel appear to have learned their lesson concerning syncretistic and idolatrous worship—there are no indications that the nation fell into those kinds of sin again. However, this does not mean they continued to worship God purely. As this study of worship in the Old Testament has revealed already several times, God cares both that his instructions concerning worship be followed and that worshipers approach him with sincere hearts of faith. While Israel began to follow the first of these requirements for fear of another exile, it is the second of these—sincere hearts—that becomes their dominant problem.

The final prophet of the Old Testament confronted this problem in particular. Malachi condemned the people for despising the Lord's name in worship by offering polluted food upon the alter (Mal. 1:6–7). They followed the strict commands concerning worship—they neither disobeyed a clear command nor added to what God had required, but they did so with hypocritical hearts, resulting in polluted offerings:

> But you say, "What a weariness this is," and you snort at it, says the Lord of hosts. You bring what has been taken by violence or is lame or sick, and this you bring as your offering! Shall I accept that from your hand? says the Lord. Cursed be the cheat who has a male in his flock, and vows it, and yet sacrifices to the Lord what is blemished. For I am a great King, says the Lord of hosts, and my name will be feared among the nations. (Mal. 1:13–14)

Yet God does not desire to simply be honored with his people's lips while their hearts are far from him (Isa. 29:13). He desires that his people truly know him out of sincere longing to fellowship with him rather than merely offering sacrifices out of habit and duty (Hos. 6:6). Therefore, although the people were not worshiping false gods or attempting to mix true and pagan worship, God nevertheless rejected their worship: "Oh that there were one among you who would shut the doors, that you might not kindle fire on my altar in vain! I have no pleasure in you, says the Lord of hosts, and I will not accept an offering from your hand" (Mal. 1:10). This time, however, instead of punishing the people by sending them out of his presence in the temple and the promised land, he simply removed his presence from the temple and from the land (Ezek. 9:3; 10:18; 11:23).

Similarities and Differences Between Hebrew and Pagan Worship
Similarities

There is no doubt that some of the practices of ancient Hebrew worship bear remarkable resemblance to the religions and worship practices of the pagan nations around them. One of the most significant recent archaeological discoveries concerns documents uncovered in 1929 from the Syrian coastal town of Ugarit dating from 1300–120 BC. Scholars believe this group of people to be the biblical "Canaanites," and thus study of these discoveries provides a wealth of information about Israel's neighbors.[1] Documents discovered include literary, ritual, and liturgical texts,[2] several of which non-theists use to prove that Israel's worship was essentially Canaanite in origin.[3] For

---

[1] Edward L. Greenstein, "Texts from Ugarit Solve Biblical Puzzles," *Biblical Archaeology Review* 36, no. 6 (December 2010): 48.

[2] N. Wyatt, *Religious Texts from Ugarit: The Words of Ilimilku and His Colleagues*, 2nd Edition (Sheffield, England: Sheffield Academic Press, 1998); John C. Gibson, *Canaanite Myths and Legends*, 2nd Edition (New York: T & T Clark, 1978); Dennis Pardee, *Ritual and Cult at Ugarit* (Atlanta: Society of Biblical Literature, 2002); Simon B. Parker, *Ugaritic Narrative Poetry* (Atlanta: Scholars Press, 1997).

[3] "The Baal cycle expresses the heart of the West Semitic religion from which Israelite religion largely developed" (Mark S. Smith, *The Ugaritic Baal Cycle*, vol. 1 [Leiden: Brill, 1994], xxvii).

example, the common Canaanite name for the highest deity of the pantheon of gods, El, was a title used throughout the Pentateuch for Israel's God as well. Indeed, even Israel's name contains this reference to deity, and in a particularly poignant passage, God himself tells Moses, "I am the LORD ['Yahweh']. I appeared to Abraham, to Isaac, and to Jacob, as God Almighty ['El Shaddai'], but by my name the LORD ['Yahweh'] I did not make myself known to them" (Exod. 6:2–3). Furthermore, the temples of Israel and of other religions often had comparable structures and purpose.[4] Not only did most nations share in common the practice of sacrificial rites,[5] Canaanite religion shared even essentially identical rituals such as the "scapegoat" (Lev. 16) and other purification rituals.[6] Finally, some argue direct borrowing between Israelite worship materials and their neighbors. For example, Psalm 104 appears to evidence close parallels with the Canaanite Baal worship cycle.[7] Even more significantly, some scholars have argued that Psalm 29 is actually directly borrowed from Canaanite poetry.[8]

Explaining the Similarities

There are at least three possible ways to explain similarities between Hebrew worship and pagan worship. First, secular scholars claim that the correspondences "point to a larger religious tradition shared broadly by West Semitic peoples, including the Israelites."[9] Therefore the worship of Israel—a nation that emerged relatively late[10]—must have evolved from the worship of these other older nations. To "claim that religion during the period of the state of Judah is accurately reflected in the final form of the text can be dismissed as naïve,"[11] they insist. Some argue that internal evidence within the Bible itself supports the claim that early Israel was polytheistic. For example, citing Genesis 6:1–4, which refers to "the sons of God," Christopher Rollston argues that the Hebrew term "is semantically and etymologically cognate to the Ugaritic term *bn 'ilm*,

---

[4] Mark S. Smith, *The Origins of Biblical Monotheism: Israel's Polytheistic Background and the Ugaritic Texts* (New York: Oxford University Press, 2003), 136.

[5] John Gray, *The Legacy of Canaan: The Ras Shamra Texts and Their Relevance to the OT* (Leiden: Brill, 1965), 192.

[6] David P. Wright, *The Disposal of Impurity: Elimination Rites in the Bible and in the Hittite and Mesopotamian Literature* (Atlanta: Scholars, 1987), 46.

[7] Peter Craigie, "The Comparison of Hebrew Poetry: Psalm 104 in Light of Egyptian and Ugaritic Poetry," *Semitics* 4 (1974): 10–21.

[8] Frank M. Cross, "Notes on a Canaanite Psalm in the Old Testament," *Bulletin of the American Schools of Oriental Research*, no. 117 (1950): 19–21.

[9] Smith, *The Origins of Biblical Monotheism*, 17.

[10] This is true even by the Bible's own account.

[11] Diana Vikander Edelman, ed., *The Triumph of Elohim: From Yahwisms to Judaisms* (Grand Rapids: Eerdmans, 1996), 17–18. Secular scholars almost unanimously reject the so-called "conquest theory" of Israel's origins in favor of two alternatives: the "peaceful settlement theory," which suggests a gradual immigration of nomadic tribes into Canaan, or the "peasant revolt theory," which claims that the Israelites were Canaanite peasants who eventually overthrew a more powerful clan. See John J. Bimson, "The Origins of Israel in Canaan: An Examination of Recent Theories," *Themelios* 15, no. 1 (October 1989): 4–15.

as well as to the various terms in Akkadian"[12] and refers to Israel's early belief in a pantheon of gods. This leads to the claim that later Israelites understood a hierarchy within the pantheon. The Canaanites believed in an "Assembled Body" of gods who operated under El's rule.[13] Rollston uses Job 1:6 (cf. also 2:1) to argue that Israel, like its neighbors, believed that Yahweh was the head of the pantheon when it states, "Now there was a day when the sons of God came to present themselves before the Lord."[14] This reasoning leads to certain conclusions among scholars who, with some variation, generally agree in their chronology of the evolution of Hebrew worship: Israel's worship was initially polytheistic, although once Israel is established in the land, "Yahweh is considered the national deity." [15] Later, "Yahweh becomes the head of the Israelite pantheon, but without a denial of the existence of other deities." [16] Israel believed that "Yahweh was king of a whole heavenly host that included lesser deities who did his bidding, having various degrees of autonomy depending upon their status within the larger hierarchy."[17] It is only later that "Israelite religion affirms the veracity of monotheism, with Yahweh as the sole deity, and with explicit denials of the existence of other deities."[18] Of course, a conviction in the truthfulness of Scripture would discount this view, and the differences between Hebrew and pagan worship discussed below further discredit it.

The second possibility, one that accounts for the fact that the people's worship came by way of divine revelation, argues that when God instituted worship forms for Israel, he "contextualized" worship in cultural forms and practices they would understand. Andrew Hill argues this for example, saying that the institution of sacrifices "demonstrates God's willingness to accommodate his revelation to cultural conventions. Human sacrifice was practiced in ancient Mesopotamia, and Abraham was no doubt familiar with the ritual since he came from Ur of the Chaldees (Gen. 11:21)." However, as we have already seen, God clearly says that Israel's worship is patterned after the worship of heaven (Exod. 25:8–9), not after the worship of the other nations, and he explicitly forbad borrowing worship practices from the other nations (Deut. 12:2–8). In fact, any time in Israel's history when they did disobey God and copy their neighbors, it always led to idolatry.

---

[12] Christopher A. Rollston, "The Rise of Monotheism in Ancient Israel: Biblical and Epigraphic Evidence," *Stone-Campbell Journal* 6 (Spring 2003): 102.

[13] James B. Pritchard, ed., *Ancient Near Eastern Texts Relating to the Old Testament* (Princeton, NJ: Princeton University Press, 1955), 130.

[14] Rollston, "Rise of Monotheism," 106.

[15] Rollston, "Rise of Monotheism," 114.

[16] Rollston, "Rise of Monotheism," 114.

[17] Edelman, *The Triumph of Elohim*, 20.

[18] Rollston, "Rise of Monotheism," 114.

The best explanation argues that unquestionable similarities between many primary characteristics of Hebrew worship and other nations is evidence, not for the fact that Israel's worship evolved from other nations, but rather that the worship of other nations evolved (or, better, *devolved*) from elements of worship that God instituted at creation. If one posits the truthfulness of the Old Testament, then it would make sense for all nations to share similar conceptions of deity and of the way to approach deity in worship, including similar language. The key elements of worship that appear in most religions were instituted in the first few chapters of Genesis. God placed Adam and Eve in his sanctuary as priests who serve him and commune with him. After they disobeyed him, God instituted the idea of substitutionary sacrifice and atonement, establishing a covenant with them. Each of these elements characterizes the worship of all religions since they are part of the religious heritage of all children of Adam. Romans 1:19–20 testifies to this when it says that God has revealed himself to all people through "the things that have been made." It is the pagans, then, who already operate on the basis of God's revelation, and this is further proven by the fact that all religions of the world—not just those of the ancient near east—share many of the essential similarities mentioned above.

Differences

Similarities do exist, but the differences are far greater. First, the Old Testament's theology and that of other ancient near eastern religions is starkly different. While the Old Testament God had no beginning (Ps. 90:2), the gods of both Canaanite and Egyptian religions had origins.[19] Furthermore, pagan gods were part of the natural world, not above it.[20] While the deities of other nations were manifested in nature itself, the God of the Old Testament transcended the creation he made and revealed himself in his works. This is why the record and study of history is far more significant for Israel than for any other ancient religion.[21] Third, while pagan worship had no central moral standard, Israel believed in moral absolutes rooted in God and revealed to them in his Law.[22] Israel's God, in contrast to the spiteful, immoral manner of pagan gods, is reliable and trustworthy. Fourth, Israel's monotheism stands in stark contrast to the polytheism of other nations. If monotheism were merely the natural evolution of religion from Israel's earlier polytheism, one wonders why no other nation in the ancient near

---

[19] John H. Walton, *Ancient Near Eastern Thought and the Old Testament: Introducing the Conceptual World of the Hebrew Bible* (Grand Rapids: Baker Academic, 2006), 87.

[20] Walton, *Ancient Near Eastern Thought and the Old Testament*, 87, 97; John D Currid, *Against the Gods: The Polemical Theology of the Old Testament* (Wheaton, IL: Crossway, 2013), 40; G. Ernest Wright, *The Old Testament Against Its Environment* (London: SCM Press, 1950), 22.

[21] Wright, *The Old Testament Against Its Environment*, 28; John N. Oswalt, *The Bible among the Myths: Unique Revelation or Just Ancient Literature?* (Grand Rapids: Zondervan, 2009), 79.

[22] Currid, *Against the Gods*, 40; Oswalt, *The Bible Among the Myths*, 71.

east evolved into monotheism. Fifth, the character of Israel's worship music stood in stark contrast to that of other pagan civilizations, whose worship consisted of orgiastic rites. Calvin Stapert helpfully explains:

> Jewish psalmody was word-oriented, a characteristic that set it apart from the music of the sacrificial rites of the Israelites' pagan neighbors. Pagan sacrificial music typically featured the frenzy-inducing sound of the loud double-reed instruments and the rhythms of orgiastic dancing. Words were superfluous. Temple music was different from pagan music in all these respects: words were primary in it, and they governed the rhythms; instrumental accompaniment was by stringed instruments that supported the monophonic vocal line, perhaps with some heterophonic embellishments,[23] but never covering or distracting attention away from the words; instruments were used independently only for signaling purposes, as when trumpets and cymbals signaled the beginning of the psalm and the places at the end of sections where the worshipers should prostrate themselves.[24]

Sixth, although Israel shares with its neighbors similar worship places and rituals, each of these functions in often radically different ways. For example, unlike pagan sanctuaries, Israel's temple was not a place where the worshipers met the needs of their gods but rather where they responded to his desire to commune with them in the means that he had provided.[25] This leads to what is perhaps the most fundamental difference between Hebrew and pagan worship: pagan worship was initiated by the worshiper who desired to attract the god's attention and earn favor, while Israel's God initiated the worship, and the worshipers simply responded to what God had already done for them.

One of the most picturesque examples of this contrast between true and pagan worship is found in Elijah's confrontation with the prophets of Baal in the northern kingdom during the reign of Ahab. The prophet condemned Ahab for having "abandoned the commandments of the Lord and followed the Baals" (1 Kgs. 18:18). God used him to drive home a poignant lesson: abandoning the commandments of Yahweh and following after false gods brings condemnation. And in order to emphasize this lesson, Elijah proposed a grand contest, a cosmic battle between Baal and Yahweh, between Baal's prophets and the prophet of Yahweh. Ahab agreed and arranged the competition. He sent a proclamation across the whole nation, and all the people

---

[23] In other words, melody was prominent, while there may have been some modest harmony.

[24] Calvin R. Stapert, *A New Song for an Old World: Musical Thought in the Early Church* (Grand Rapids: Wm. B. Eerdmans, 2006), 153.

[25] T. Geraty, "The Jerusalem Temple of the Hebrew Bible in Its Ancient Near Eastern Context," in *The Sanctuary and the Atonement*, ed. Arnold V. Wallenkampf and W. Richard Lesher (Washington, DC: Review and Herald, 1981), 59.

gathered to witness the event on Mt. Carmel. There, Elijah clearly demonstrated central differences between true worship and false worship, differences not merely concerning the object of worship, but the very form of worship. With the worship of Baal, the worshipers initiated the worship. They were the ones who desperately tried to get the attention of their god. Baal had not revealed himself to them nor given them instructions as to how he wanted to be approached; rather, in their theology, Baal was simply the Lord of the land, and so in order to appease him and persuade him to bless them with prosperity, the prophets of Baal had to do things that would please him and meet his needs. This is characteristic of all pagan worship—the worshipers initiate the worship and attempt to call the god down. Their acts of worship were characterized by loud, ecstatic cries, by incessant dancing around the altar, and by self-mutilation. Again, all of this physical activity was an attempt to work up the worshipers into an ecstatic state in order to get the god's attention and persuade him to act on their behalf. And, of course, no one answered. No fire came from heaven, no lightning, not even rain. Elijah took this occasion to mock the futility of this false worship, revealing the essential difference between Baal and Yahweh; in pagan theology, the god is part of nature, limited by time and space, and therefore he has physical needs and grows weary.

But "he who keeps Israel will neither slumber nor sleep" (Ps. 121:4). Yahweh is not part of nature; he transcends nature because he made it. Elijah did not initiate this worship encounter in order to get God's attention, appease him, and meet his needs. On the contrary, the true God is the initiator of worship. God revealed himself in creation, instituting the central worship concepts of sanctuary and priest in the garden and of atonement and sacrifice after Adam and Eve fell into sin. God revealed himself to Abraham, to Isaac, and to Jacob, to Moses, and to David. And God revealed himself to Elijah. Elijah was simply responding to what God had told him to do (1 Kgs. 18:1). And the fact that Elijah's prayer came "at the time of the offering of oblation" (v. 36) is no accident. Elijah was approaching God at the time he had appointed. He did not use the pagan altar, either; rather, Elijah rebuilt the altar of Yahweh that had been torn down. And instead of loud, ecstatic, orgiastic, degrading worship, Elijah simply prayed a modest prayer that itself was not asking for anything that God himself had not already promised, but was rather based in the covenant promises of God: "O Lord, God of Abraham, Isaac, and Israel, let it be known this day that you are God in Israel, and that I am your servant, and that I have done all these things at your word. Answer me, O Lord, answer me, that this people may know that you, O Lord, are God, and that you have turned their hearts back" (1 Kings 18:36-37). Immediately, God answered. It did not take a long, drawn out time of creating the right atmosphere of worship or working up into an emotional frenzy for the fire of God to come down. God had revealed himself to Elijah and told him what to do, and all it took was simple obedience in faith, and God proved himself to be the one true and living God.

The central difference between Hebrew and pagan worship is that Hebrew worship is a response to God's gracious works, while pagan worship is an attempt to appease spiteful gods. Yahweh initiates Hebrew worship. The pagans initiate pagan worship. No Hebrew worship, or Christian worship for that matter, is not merely an attempt to worship the true God using forms familiar from the worship of unbelievers. Hebrew (and Christian) worship is a God-initiated privilege whereby God himself provides a way for communion with him, and his people respond with hearts of confession, thanksgiving, and praise.

Conclusion to Part One

The basis and foundation for Christian religion and worship is found in the Old Testament; every essential element of worship was established by God in the first few chapters of Genesis. God is the initiator of worship, and thus his revelation is central. He revealed himself to Adam, Abraham, Isaac, Jacob, Moses, and David. He prescribed the proper way to approach him in worship, furnishing a divine pattern as the exclusive means ordained by God for worship. The nature of this worship is fellowship and communion with him such that he is glorified and honored. God created Adam as a priest in a sanctuary of his presence whose purpose was to worship and obey. Yet sin prevented the possibility of such communion, and thus God expelled his people from the sanctuary of his presence. God provided, however, a means by which his people could once again draw near to him—atonement. Through the blood sacrifice of a substitute, a worshiper could once again draw near to God in worship, yet not quite as before since the sacrifices themselves were not entirely pure and the worshipers remained sinners themselves. Thus, God made a promise that one day he would provide a perfect sacrifice that would forever crush Satan and sin. Until then, God's people should draw near to him in worship through the means that he prescribed with reverence and dignity, responding to what he has done for them with sincere hearts of praise and thanksgiving. Since mankind has an inherent tendency to corrupt worship, God's people need divine instructions for their worship to be acceptable to him. Specifically, those worship forms that are reflections of pagan worship are prohibited; whenever syncretism occurs, the people inevitably follow after pagan gods. Both following God's commands and proper inward motivation are essential to God-pleasing worship whereby believers commune with God.

This Scripture-based theology formed the worldview of God's people, but it is also important to recognize that many of the general worldview assumptions of even pagan people were, as we discussed at the end of the last chapter, shaped by their nearness in time to the creation of world and God's self-revelation. All people in ancient times, for example, believed in the existence of a spiritual, transcendent reality beyond themselves and interpreted the events of everyday life in relation to that ultimate reality. Quentin Faulkner calls this worldview "world-consciousness" and describes it as being characterized by the following features:

1. It stresses integration into an orderly world or universe (governed and ordered by some higher or transcendent power or powers).

2. It excels at symbolism, myth, ceremony, and ritual—at providing the general, the "big" picture.
3. The primary satisfaction it offers its adherents is security and belonging.[1]

According to Faulkner, "among world-conscious peoples, religion manifests itself in three primary aspects: in myth (content and teachings), in ethos (behavior and morals), and in cultus."[2] Those with this worldview "regard themselves first and foremost as part of a people ... thus they create and perpetuate a tradition."[3]

Yet as we have seen, although believers and unbelievers alike shared some basic assumptions about reality, resulting in some similarities between their approach to cultus and culture, their theology differed considerably. Everything about the Hebrew religion, a combination of a God-entranced worldview with theology derived exclusively from his self-revelation, affected their lives. Nothing was "secular" for faithful Israelites—whether they were rearing children, working in the fields, defeating their enemies, or singing songs of praise, everything was done as unto the Lord and in response to their covenantal relationship with him. Nevertheless, as we have seen, Israel did distinguish between cultus and culture. They did not consider their culture separate from their religion; indeed, their culture flowed from their religious commitments; it was to be holy, set apart from the world. God had created humankind to "worship and obey," and thus God's people were to be a realization of that purpose in everything they did.

But their cultus—the specific rituals and ceremonies of their solemn assemblies of worship—was set apart from the rest of their culture. For example, although every day of the week should be consecrated to the glory of the Lord, the Sabbath was to be kept holy—"set apart"—from the other six days since at the dawn of creation, "God blessed the seventh day and made it holy" (Gen. 2:3). This applied equally to each of the sacred feasts. Likewise, the house of God, the priests, the sacrifices, and the worship music were all to be set apart and consecrated for sacred use.

None of these principles changes in essence in the transition from the Old Testament to the New. Yet with the coming of that promised atoning sacrifice—Jesus Christ—God provides a way for his people to draw near to him in communion as they never could under the Mosaic Law.

---

[1] Quentin Faulkner, *Wiser Than Despair: The Evolution of Ideas in the Relationship of Music and the Christian Church*, 2nd ed. (Simpsonville, SC: Religious Affections Ministries, 2012), 1–2.
[2] Faulkner, *Wiser Than Despair*, 4.
[3] Faulkner, *Wiser Than Despair*, 6.

Conclusion to Part One

Study Guide for Part One
People and Terms

Abraham
acrostic
altar of incense
anaphora
antithetic parallelism
apostrophe
ark of the covenant
atonement
Baal
Babylon
burnt offering
chiasm
communion
creation
David
Day of Atonement
Decalogue
El
Elohim
emblematic parallelism
Ezra
Feast of Firstfruits
Feast of Tabernacles
Feast of Trumpets
Feast of Unleavened Bread
grain offering
guilt offering
high altar
high priest
Holy of Holies
Holy Place
hyperbole
idolatry
Isaiah 6
Jeroboam
khatsotserot
kinnor
lamp stand
laver of bronze
lyre
Melchizedek

memorial
metaphor
Moses
nebel
Passover
peace offering
personification
pivot parallelism
priest
psalm
Sabbath
sacrifice
sanctuary
Shema
shofar
sin offering
Sinai
Sinai liturgy
solemn assembly
Solomon
syncretism
synonymous parallelism
tabernacle
table of showbread
temple
theocracy
tseltselim
"work it and keep it"
world-consciousness
Yahweh

Recommended Resources

Bradshaw, Paul F. *The Search for The Origins of Christian Worship: Sources and Methods for the Study of Early Liturgy.* New York/Oxford: Oxford University Press, 1992.

Currid, John D. *Against the Gods: The Polemical Theology of the Old Testament.* Wheaton, IL: Crossway, 2013.

Edersheim, Alfred. *The Temple, Its Ministry and Services as They Were at the Time of Jesus Christ.* Peabody, MA: Hendrickson Publishers, 1994.

Longman III., Tremper. *How to Read the Psalms.* Downers Grove: IVP Academic, 1988.

Merrill, Eugene H. *Kingdom of Priests: A History of Old Testament Israel.* 2nd edition. Grand Rapids: Baker Academic, 2008.

Conclusion to Part One

Old, Hughes Oliphant. *The Reading and Preaching of the Scriptures in the Worship of the Christian Church: The Biblical Period.* Grand Rapids: Wm. B. Eerdmans, 1998.

Ross, Allen P. *Recalling the Hope of Glory: Biblical Worship from the Garden to the New Creation.* Grand Rapids: Kregel, 2006.

Questions for Discussion and Reflection
1. In what ways does creation and the fall establish the elements and patterns of all worship to follow?
2. Discuss important features of the following Hebrew Worship Periods: Patriarchal Period, Mosaic Period, Period of the Judges, Temple, and Prophets. Note where the primary centers of worship were, how they were instituted, what constituted their primary practices, and what problems occurred.
3. In what ways was Hebrew worship different from the worship of pagan nations?

PART TWO: THE NEW TESTAMENT

For you have not come to what may be touched,
a blazing fire and darkness and gloom and a tempest
and the sound of a trumpet and a voice whose words
made the hearers beg that no further messages be spoken to them.

For they could not endure the order that was given,
"If even a beast touches the mountain, it shall be stoned."
Indeed, so terrifying was the sight that Moses said, "I tremble with fear."

But you have come to Mount Zion
and to the city of the living God, the heavenly Jerusalem,
and to innumerable angels in festal gathering,
and to the assembly of the firstborn who are enrolled in heaven,
and to God, the judge of all,
and to the spirits of the righteous made perfect,
and to Jesus, the mediator of a new covenant,
and to the sprinkled blood
that speaks a better word than the blood of Abel.

Therefore let us be grateful for receiving a kingdom that cannot be shaken,
and thus let us offer to God acceptable worship,
with reverence and awe,
for our God is a consuming fire.

—*Epistle to the Hebrews*, 60 A.D.

Chapter 5
Jesus Christ

After Adam and Eve sinned, God promised that one day a seed of Eve would come whose heel the serpent would bruise; however, that same seed would crush the serpent's head (Gen. 3:15). In the fullness of time, God provided this seed by sending his only begotten Son to be born of a virgin by the Holy Spirit, taking on human flesh, thus enabling him to take the place of sinners with his perfect life and guiltless death.

God with Us
Indeed, the prophet Isaiah had promised that one day Immanuel—"God with us"—would be born of a virgin (Isa. 7:14). At its core, the mission of Jesus Christ was to restore the communion between God and his people that had been broken by sin, forever destroying the barriers preventing people from drawing near to God in worship. Since sinful humans could not come into the presence of a holy God, God himself condescended to draw near to them—"God with us" (Matt. 1:23). The apostle John highlights the relationship between the incarnation of Christ and communion in God's presence when he proclaimed that "the Word became flesh and *tabernacled* among us" (John 1:14 emphasis mine). Just as the tabernacle in the Old Testament was the sanctuary of God's presence to which God's people drew near for communion with God, so Jesus Christ himself was the very presence of God now come to dwell among his people.

Restoring Pure Worship
Jesus clearly emphasized the restoration of true worship as the core of his mission through his identification with the place of God's worship in key points throughout his earthly ministry. The first record of Jesus' life following his birth is his pilgrimage to the temple for Passover when he was twelve years old (Luke 2:41–50). There he gave focused attention to dialogue with the religious teachers such that his parents left the city without him. Confronted by his mother for his failure to accompany them, Jesus replied, "Did you not know I must be in my Father's house" (Luke 2:49)? This was the reason he had come.

Jesus also reveals his mission to restore pure worship by the fact that he cleansed the temple both at the beginning (John 2:13–22) and end (Matt. 21:12–17, Mark 11:15–

19, Luke 19:45–48) of his earthly ministry.[1] What the prophet Malachi had condemned had now become common practice in the worship practices of Israel. The people honored God with their lips and their actions—they followed his instructions to the letter, but they did so with such irreverence that the house of God had become a "den of robbers"—no coincidence, Jesus quoted Jeremiah's condemnation of corrupt worship that led to exile (Jer. 7:11) in his own condemnation of temple worship in his day. Furthermore, the temple cleansings also identified Jesus himself as the sanctuary of God's presence when he indicated to the Jews that he was the temple that would be destroyed and raised up in three days (John 2:19–21).

Frequently during Jesus' public ministry, he condemned the religious leaders of the day for their impure worship. As had become the expectation since the return of the Israelites from exile, the religious leaders in Jesus' day did not worship false gods or engage in syncretistic worship practices. Nevertheless, their central problem also remained consistent with the sins Old Testament prophets condemned; quoting Isaiah this time, Jesus said of the Pharisees and scribes, "This people honors me with their lips, but their heart is far from me" (Matt. 15:8). They obeyed God's instructions regarding how to approach him in worship to a degree, but they did so with insecure, hypocritical hearts. Furthermore, Jesus proclaimed, "in vain do they worship me, teaching as doctrines the commandments of men" (v. 9). While these religious leaders did not break the commands of God for worship by eliminating any of what he had prescribed, they nevertheless added additional worship practices and taught these as necessary for fellowship with God. Supplementing the biblical precepts with practices of their own devising rendered worship vain in God's eyes. Thus, the core problem of the religious leaders of Jesus's day was two-fold, underscoring once again the two-fold essence of God-pleasing worship that was emphasized throughout the Old Testament: (1) insincere hearts and (2) adding to what God had prescribed.

Finally, Jesus stressed the centrality of biblical worship to his mission by formally announcing the beginning of his mission in a synagogue service in Nazareth, which Luke notes "was his custom" (Luke 4:16–30), proclaiming that he was the Messiah promised by the prophet Isaiah. Much of Jesus' ministry involved teaching the Scriptures in services of worship in synagogues throughout the land (Luke 4:31, 38, 44; John 6:59) and in the temple (Matt. 21:14; John 5:14; 7:14, 28; 8:2, 20; 10:23).

---

[1] Debate does exist as to whether John's account of a temple-cleansing near the beginning of his Gospel is indeed a separate occurrence than the one recorded in the Synoptic Gospels or whether John simply moved the account earlier in his report. For a helpful survey of the arguments and defense of a double cleansing, see D. A. Carson, *The Gospel According to John: An Introduction and Commentary* (Grand Rapids: Wm. B. Eerdmans, 1991), 177–178.

Jesus Christ

Culture and Cultus in Jesus' Day
During the 400 years between the close of Malachi's prophecy and the record of the gospels, many significant events occurred in the nation of Israel. The remnant that had returned to Israel from exile had now grown to a vast nation once again. Persian dominance waned, only to be replaced by the Greek Empire in the fourth century BC. Greek influence unified all the Mediterranean world including Israel, with a common Greek language, literature, and philosophy—called "Hellenization." This led Hebrew scholars to translate the Old Testament into Greek. Known in Greek as "The Translation of the Seventy," and later by the Latin title "Septuagint" ("seventy," often abbreviated by the Roman numerals "LXX"), this translation was the Old Testament Scriptures for the Greek-speaking Jews of Jesus' day. Hebrew remained the liturgical language for the Jews, but in addition to Greek, Israelites following the return from exile began to gradually adopt Aramaic, a Semitic language similar to Hebrew that dominated the Middle East during the period, as their primary common tongue.

Rome gradually grew in power in the second century BC, conquering Jerusalem in 63 BC, and becoming an Empire in 2 BC. when Octavian was granted the title *Augustus* by the Roman Senate. Rome established stability in its empire by controlling the governors of various nations under its rule; consequently, it placed a vassal "king" on the throne in Judea, Herod the Great, whose family descended from Esau's line. Roman dominance established a period of unprecedented peace, prosperity, and stability for over two centuries, known as the Pax Romana ("Roman Peace"). In the providence of God, this period provided ideal political and commercial conditions for Christ's coming and the spread of Christianity.

Greco-Roman Religion
As the apostle Paul would later discover in Athens (Acts 17), gods were everywhere in the Greco-Roman world. The multi-national conglomeration that formed the Roman Empire had created a mix of religious traditions by the time Christ came. For some, religious acts had become simply part of mundane life. Others, however, committed themselves to worshiping their deities with fervency, especially those who belonged to one of the various "mystery cults" in devotion to gods like Isis, Cybele, and Dionysus. These cults were characterized by "ecstatic worship, often featuring particularly frenzied processions and festivals."[2] Calvin Stapert aptly summarized the character of Roman worship during this period:

> Ecstatic rituals were not uncommon in Greek and Roman societies, going back centuries before the Christian era. The rituals associated with the worship of

---

[2] Simon B. Jones, *The World of the Early Church: A Social History* (Oxford: Lion Hudson, 2011), 180.

Dionysus or his Roman equivalent, Bacchus, are the classic examples of this type. Drunken revelry, wild music, frenzied dancing, and flagellation and mutilation were their hallmarks.[3]

The Jerusalem Temple

Although the temple rebuilt by Zerubbabel and the returned Hebrew exiles had little of the glory of Solomon's temple, Herod the Great expanded the temple just before the time of Jesus, so much so that it extended even to the area previously occupied by Solomon's palace. Josephus later commented on the fact that visitors to Jerusalem were universally impressed by the grandeur of the temple.[4] The entire temple area spanned more than 1,000 feet long and 1,000 feet wide (about twenty-three acres),[5] consisting of porticos on all four sides, a large courtyard for Gentiles, and the temple, which was surrounded by walls accessible through nine gates. The temple itself contained the Court of Women on the east, and the Priests' Courtyard, where the sacrifices took place before the sanctuary. Within the Priests' Courtyard, the High Altar was at least forty-eight square feet and made entirely of unhewn stone.[6] Herod built the temple proper the same dimensions as Solomon, approximately thirty feet wide, ninety feet long, and sixty feet high.

The Synagogue

Synagogues were also important centers for worship throughout Israel during the life of Christ, yet scholars are uncertain as to their origin. There is no mention of synagogues in the Old Testament; their first appearance is in the Gospels. Their initial formation may have occurred while the people of Israel were in exile, since they had no temple in which to hear the Word of God and pray. Or, synagogues could have been formed after the return of the people from exile, when under Ezra's leadership reading and explanation of Scripture became more important to them. In fact, much of how Nehemiah 8 describes Ezra's reading and explanation of the Law in a solemn assembly carries over into the synagogue practices of Jesus' day. The most traditional view of the matter, held by Jewish historian Josephus, was that Moses himself actually instituted synagogues.

Regardless, synagogues became important, not only as localized places to hear God's Word and pray corporately, but also as the foundation for what would later become corporate worship for the New Testament church. Synagogue services consisted

---

[3] Stapert, *New Song for an Old World*, 135.
[4] Flavius Josephus, *The Jewish War*, 1st cen., Book 5, Chap 5.
[5] Alfred Edersheim, *The Temple, Its Ministry and Services as They Were at the Time of Jesus Christ* (Peabody, MA: Hendrickson Publishers, 1994), 38.
[6] Edersheim, *The Temple, Its Ministry and Services as They Were at the Time of Jesus Christ*, 54.

generally of three parts: Scripture reading, Scripture explanation, and the prayers. A typical service began with a call to worship in the form of a psalm reading, followed by a cycle of formal prayers extolling God as Creator and for his covenant love for Israel:

> Blessed are you Lord
> our God and God of our fathers;
> God of Abraham
> God of Isaac and God of Jacob;
> the great God, powerful and revered;
> exalted God, owner of heaven and earth;
> our shield, and shield of our fathers;
> our refuge in all generations.
> Blessed are you, Lord, shield of Abraham.
> You are powerful, humbling the proud;
> strong, and judging the violent;
> alive forever, raising the dead;
> making wind blow and dew fall;
> sustaining the living, reviving the dead.
> Like the fluttering of an eye,
> make our salvation sprout.
> Blessed are you Lord, reviving the dead.
> You are holy, and revered is your name,
> and there is no god beside you.
> Blessed are you Lord, the holy God.[7]

This was followed by a recitation of the *Shema*, the central Jewish confession of faith, adoration, and obedience (Deut. 6:4–9). A second cycle of prayers commenced, including the recitation of benedictions and prayers on a variety of themes including confession and petition, such as the following:

> Endow us, our Father,
> with understanding from you,
> and discernment and insight from your Torah.
> Blessed are you Lord,
> gracious giver of understanding.
> Cause us to repent, Lord, to you,
> and we will repent.
> Renew our days as at the start.
> Blessed are you Lord,
> who desires repentance.

---

[7] David Instone Brewer, "The Eighteen Benedictions and the Minim before 70 CE," JTS54 (2003): 29–30.

Forgive us our Father,
for we have sinned against you.
Blot out and remove our transgressions
from before your eyes,
for your compassion is great.
Blessed are you Lord, who abundantly forgives.
Look on our affliction and plead our cause,
and redeem us for the sake of your name.
Blessed are you Lord, the redeemer of Israel.
Bless to us, Lord our God,
this year to our benefit,
with all kinds of produce,
and bring near quickly
the final year of our redemption.
Give dew and rain upon the ground,
and satisfy the world
from the storehouses of your goodness,
and give a blessing on the work of our hands.
Blessed are you Lord, who blesses the years.
Hear, Lord our God, the voice of our prayers
and have compassion upon us;
for you are the God of grace and compassion.
Blessed are you Lord, hearer of prayer.[8]

Reading from the Law and Prophets followed, with a response from the Psalms and a sermon explaining the Scripture passage and exhorting the people. This is the point in the service where Jesus was called upon to read the scroll from Isaiah in the Nazareth synagogue as the start of his public ministry. The service concluded with a congregational blessing and Amen, again likely from a psalm. While singing was not considered an element of worship distinct from Scripture reading and prayer, all of the readings and prayers of the service would have been chanted. Nevertheless, since instrumental accompaniment was associated with temple worship, chanting in the synagogue was unaccompanied.

The Baptism of Jesus

Jesus' baptism (Matt. 3:13–17, Mark 1:9–11, Luke 3:21–22) was important both because it identified him as God's chosen Messiah and, in fact, his Son—the Lamb of God who would take away the sin of the world (John 1:29–34), and because it served as a model for later baptismal liturgy. John had established the practice in the Jordan River to encourage the people's repentance, and thus he was hesitant to baptize Jesus.

---

[8] David Instone Brewer, "The Eighteen Benedictions and the Minim before 70 CE," JTS54 (2003): 30–32

Yet Jesus indicated that his baptism was necessary to "fulfill all righteousness" (Matt. 3:15). It was God's will that Jesus be baptized in order to identify himself with the people as the one who would suffer as a substitute for their sins and rise again. God confirmed his pleasure with Jesus' obedience by speaking from heaven—"This is my beloved Son, with whom I am well pleased" (Matt. 3:17), and the Spirit of God descended on him, signifying the special theocratic anointing that God granted to his chosen leaders throughout the Old Testament such as Moses and the elders of Israel (Num. 11:17), Joshua (Deut. 34:9), judges such as Gideon (Judg. 6:34) and Samson (Judg. 13:25), and prophets such as Elijah (1 Kgs. 18:12). He also uniquely came upon Israel's kings, Saul and David (1 Sam. 16:13–14). This act of the Holy Spirit was only given to special leaders of God's people, often resulting in unique wisdom, physical strength, and revelation from God, and Old Testament prophecy also foretold a similar empowerment given by the Spirit to the coming Messiah (Isa. 11:2; 42:1; 48:16; 61:1). Thus, this grand display of all three persons of the triune Godhead left no question as to who Jesus was—the Chosen Prophet, Priest, and King promised long ago.

Jesus's Pattern of Prayer

The gospel accounts frequently record Jesus setting aside dedicated time, usually in the morning or evening, when "he would withdraw to desolate places and pray" (Luke 5:16). For example, just before calling his disciples, Jesus "went out to the mountain to pray, and all night he continued in prayer to God" (Luke 6:12). After feeding the multitude, he "went up on the mountain by himself to pray. When evening came, he was there alone" (Matt. 14:23–24). Peter, James, and John accompanied him on the mountain for prayer, resulting in the Transfiguration (Luke 9:28). And he prayed fervently in the garden of Gethsemane prior to his death (Matt. 26:36–46). He also prayed publicly, at his baptism (Luke 3:21), for little children (Matt. 19:13–15), for his disciples (John 17:6), and for all who would follow him (John 17:20).

Jesus also provided his disciples with a model for prayer, which would come to shape the prayers of his people for centuries to come:

> Our Father in heaven,
> hallowed be your name.
> Your kingdom come,
> your will be done,
> on earth as it is in heaven.
> Give us this day our daily bread,
> and forgive us our debts,
> as we also have forgiven our debtors.
> And lead us not into temptation,
> but deliver us from evil.

For yours is the kingdom, and the power, and the glory forever.
Amen.[9]

Jesus' pattern of prayer becomes important for later development of daily prayer times in the church.

Spirit and Truth
One of the most significant of Jesus' discourses concerning worship is his conversation with the woman at the well in Samaria (John 4:7–26). In this discourse, Jesus helpfully identified both the key continuities and discontinuities between worship in the Old Testament and that in the New. The Samaritans emerged as a people distinct from Israel as a result of intermarriage between Jews that had been left in the land when Assyria invaded and foreigners who immigrated there. They were half-Jews who developed their own unique system of worship on Mt. Gerizim. King Omri of the northern kingdom of Israel had named his capital city Samaria (1 Kgs. 16:24). In essence, the Samaritans were the inevitable fruit of Jeroboam's syncretistic worship in Shechem at the foot of Mt. Gerizim, the general region where Jesus met the woman at the well.

In the course of conversing with Jesus and observing that he was a prophet, the woman asked Jesus about the proper way to worship God. Jesus' reply to the woman helps to expound both the essence of worship and what changed with his coming. The woman focused on the external rituals of worship—the mountain, the temple, the sacrificial system, and the priesthood. Jesus replied that at the time, "salvation is from the Jews" (John 4:22). In other words, the Jewish system of worship is what God prescribed as the proper way to draw near to him; the Samaritans "worship what you do not know."

However, "the hour is coming when neither on this mountain nor in Jerusalem will you worship the Father" (v. 21). Jesus' coming, death, resurrection, and ascension delocalized worship from a physical temple on Mt. Zion. Thus, instead of focusing his answer on the proper physical temple that would soon pass away, Jesus emphasized the essence of what worship had always been: "God is spirit, and those who worship him must worship in spirit and truth" (v. 24). This two-fold description of the essence of worship elucidates the core of what it means to commune with God in worship. To commune with God is to fellowship with him—to converse with him. God speaks to his people (truth), and his people respond back to him with their hearts (spirit). This

---

[9] The final doxology is not found in the oldest Alexandrian manuscripts, but appears in later Byzantine manuscripts, and thus it is found in only English translations that are based on the latter, such as the Authorized Version. Its first use appears to be in the *Didache*, and it resembles a prayer found in 2 Chronicles 29:11: "Yours, O Lord, is the greatness and the power and the glory and the victory and the majesty, for all that is in the heavens and in the earth is yours. Yours is the kingdom, O Lord, and you are exalted as head above all." The doxology is commonly appended to the end of the prayer in Protestant use today.

was the nature of the communion Adam and Eve enjoyed with God in the garden sanctuary before they were expelled from it; it is the essence of what it meant to worship even within the localized Mosaic worship system prescribed by God in the Law, and it continues to be the core of worship after Christ's coming.

The difference is that with his perfect atoning sacrifice, worshipers no longer needed to draw near through the Jewish sacrificial system in the physical temple; they can now worship in spirit and truth through Jesus who is the sacrifice, the priest, and the temple himself. Worship itself does not change with Jesus' coming—worship has always been communion with God in spirit and truth. Jesus' death changed the means to draw near to God, but he did not change the essence of worship.

Institution of the Lord's Supper
The observance of the "Last Supper" by Jesus and his disciples appears in all four gospels, though John does not give details of the meal itself (Matt. 26:26–28; Mark 14:22–24; Luke 22:19, 20). The particular elements of the meal mentioned in the gospel records (and repeated later in 1 Corinthians) each become significant for the development of the observance later by the early church. First, Jesus "blessed" (Matt. 26:26, Mark 14:22) or "gave thanks" (from *eucharisteō*, Luke 22:19) for the bread, which he then "broke" and gave to his disciples, saying, "Take, eat; this is my body." Likewise, "he took a cup, and when he had given thanks he gave it to them, saying, 'Drink of it, all of you, for this is my blood of the covenant which is poured out for many for the forgiveness of sins'" (Matt. 26:27–28; cf. Mark 14:23–24; Luke 22:20). Finally, Jesus and his disciples "sang a hymn" to conclude the meal (Matt. 26:30; Mark 14:26). Both Matthew and Mark use the verb form of the word "hymn" here, but what they sang was likely one of the Hallel psalms (Pss. 113–118), traditionally sung after the concluding prayer of the Passover meal.

There is some debate concerning whether or not the "Last Supper" Jesus shared with his disciples was a Passover meal. Each of the synoptic gospels seem to indicate this, but John's Gospel appears to contradict the timing apparent in the others. In Leviticus 23, God had commanded Moses, "In the first month, on the fourteenth day of the month at twilight, is the Lord's Passover. And on the fifteenth day of the same month is the Feast of Unleavened Bread to the Lord; for seven days you shall eat unleavened bread." Each of the synoptic gospels (Matt. 26:17–20; Mark 14:12–17; Luke 22:7–16) record the day of the Last Supper as "the first day of Unleavened Bread." Already this is a bit confusing and does not appear to correspond to the timing in the Law. However, when we remember that unleavened bread was also eaten during the Passover meal (for that is what was eaten on the eve of the original Passover), it is plausible that Passover itself was also considered part of the seven-day period of eating unleavened bread even though the Feast of Unleavened Bread was technically not until the day following Passover. In fact, Jewish historian Josephus likewise equates the Feast of Unleavened Bread with Passover,[10] so it is likely that this was a common, although technically incorrect, way to refer to the day.

John's Gospel, however, creates an additional problem. While the synoptics each associate the Last Supper with the Passover supper, John records the supper as occurring "*before* the Feast of Passover" (John 13:1). Further, John 18:28 indicates that when the Jewish leaders took Jesus to Caiaphas' headquarters (early Friday morning), they did not go in "so that they would not be defiled, but could eat the Passover." This seems to indicate that the Passover meal had not yet occurred, even after the Last Supper. Finally, John 19:31 clearly indicates that the day on which Jesus died (Friday) was the "day of Preparation" for Passover. So, the synoptics seem to indicate that the Last Supper was the Passover Feast, but John appears as if Jesus died during the time of preparation for Passover. Both cannot be true, can they?

Some suggest that the Last Supper was *not* a Passover feast, since the gospels make no mention of the Passover lamb as part of the supper, the word used for "bread" (*artos*) designated leavened bread, and the traditional four cups of the Passover celebration are not mentioned. Others theorize that Jesus and his disciples ate the meal a day early since Jesus knew he was going to die the next day.

However, one additional alternative exists. Some scholars note that Jews from Galilee measured days differently than Jews from Judea. Galileans measured their day from sunrise to sunrise, while Judeans measured their day from sunset to sunset (similarly to how we do it today). This being the case, Galilean Jews would have slaughtered their Passover animals during the afternoon of Thursday (the day they considered Nisan 14) and eaten their Passover meal later than evening. Judean Jews would have waited another half day, killing their animals Friday afternoon and eating the meal Friday evening. Jesus and his disciples, being Galileans, would have naturally celebrated Passover on Thursday. The Jewish leaders and others in Jerusalem, and indeed any formal celebrations in the temple itself, would have occurred on Friday. Thus, Jesus could have both celebrated the Passover Feast on Thursday in Galilean fashion *and* been killed as the Passover Lamb (1 Cor. 5:7) on Friday.

What is particularly important about this meal is Jesus' statement that the cup "is my blood of the covenant which is poured out for many for the forgiveness of sins," indicating that his death would inaugurate the New Covenant promised to Israel by Old Testament prophets (Isa. 54, 60; Jer. 31–3; Ezek. 36–37). This New Covenant, combined with God's promises to Abraham that in his all the nations would be blessed (Gen. 12:3), will form the New Covenant Church. And like the Passover meal was for

---

[10] Josephus, *The Jewish War*, Book 2, Chap 1.

First Covenant Israel, so the Lord's Supper will become for the church a memorial—a covenant renewal ceremony.

Fulfillment of Old Testament Worship
In the Old Testament economy, God established particular means through which his people were enabled to draw near to him in worship, although since the sacrifices were not completely pure and the worshipers remained sinful, no one could enter God's presence for free and open communion with him. Jesus enabled such communion by himself fulfilling the function of each essential Old Testament worship element. Jesus is the atoning sacrifice, the "lamb of God who takes away the sin of the world" (John 1:29), and the high priest who made "propitiation for the sins of the people" (Heb. 2:17). He is the "bread of life" (John 6:48) on the table of showbread and the "light of the word" (John 8:12), the revelation of God himself (Heb. 1:2–3). He is the altar of incense, interceding on behalf of his people (Heb. 7:25). And ultimately, Jesus is the temple, the embodiment of the presence of God (John 2:21) to which and through which God's people draw near for worship.

Key events in Jesus' life also fulfill the Old Testament feasts. Most notably, as we have already seen, Jesus' atoning death occurred during the Jewish observance of Passover, the feast symbolizing the deliverance of Israel from captivity in Egypt, which is why Paul would later identify Jesus as "our Passover Lamb" (1 Cor. 5:7). Jesus was in the grave during the feast of Unleavened Bread, signifying his sinlessness and the atoning sacrifice for the sins of his people. He rose again from the dead on the day of the feast of Firstfruits, leading Paul to later refer to Jesus as "the firstfruits of those who have fallen asleep" (1 Cor. 15:20). On the feast of Weeks, celebrating God's provision in the beginning of harvest fifty days after Passover (thus, "Pentecost"), God began a great harvest of souls when 3,000 Jews responded to Peter's first public proclamation of the gospel following Jesus' ascension into heaven (Acts 2:41).

The autumn Jewish festivals will likewise be fulfilled by Christ in the future. The announcement of Christ's second coming is frequently associated in the New Testament with the sounding of trumpets (1 Thess. 4:16; 1 Cor. 15:52). That coming will initiate the ultimate Day of Atonement, when the Jewish remnant will "look ... on him whom they have pierced" (Zech. 12:10) and receive him as their Messiah (Rev. 7:4). In that day, Christ will once again tabernacle with his people: "Behold, the dwelling place of God is with man. He will dwell with them, and they will be his people, and God himself will be with them as their God" (Rev. 21:3). In that day, "the mountain of the house of the Lord shall be established as the highest of the mountains, and it shall be lifted up above the hills; and people shall flow to it, and many nations shall come, and say: 'Come, let us go up to the mountain of the Lord, to the house of the God of Jacob, that he may teach us his ways and that we may walk in his paths'" (Mic. 4:1–2). When that happens, the worship of God will be preeminent in the New Jerusalem, where God's people draw near to worship him in his temple, "the Lord God the Almighty and the Lamb" (Rev. 21:22).

The Great Commission
After Jesus died and rose again, he appeared to his disciples and many others, beginning a short period of teaching before he ascended back to heaven. During this time, Jesus prepared his disciples for the mission he was giving to them, telling them, "As the Father has sent me, even so I am sending you" (John 20:21). In other words, just as God the Father sent the Son into the world to accomplish the mission of redeeming his people, so Jesus was now sending his disciples on a mission, and he made that mission explicit just prior to his ascension. Known as the "Great Commission," Jesus commanded his disciples,

> Go therefore and make disciples of all nations, baptizing them in the name of the Father and of the Son and of the Holy Spirit, teaching them to observe all that I have commanded you. And behold, I am with you always, to the end of the age. (Matt. 18:19–20)

The imperative verb in this commission identifies the central purpose for the church, the body of believers the apostles would found: "make disciples." Jesus' mission for his followers was that they would make more followers, and the other participles in this commission as well as descriptions of this commission recorded in Mark and Luke explain how making disciples would take place.

First, making disciples requires proclamation of the gospel. Mark's account of this commission emphasizes this necessity: "Go into all the world and proclaim the gospel to the whole creation" (Mark 16:14). Luke records the content of this gospel message: "Thus it is written, that Christ should suffer and on the third day rise from the dead, and that repentance for the forgiveness of sins should be proclaimed in his name to all nations, beginning from Jerusalem" (Luke 24:46–47). A disciple is a follower of Christ, and the only way to follow him is to repent and believe in him. Second, baptizing new disciples in the name of the Father, Son, and Spirit was to be the visible sign of membership into Christ's body, the church. As we shall see, baptism becomes an important liturgical rite that identified converts with Christ's death, burial, and resurrection. Third, Christ commanded that his followers teach these new disciples to observe all that he had commanded. Here we find explicit instruction regarding the formation of a Christian's religion (his theology and worldview) as well as his behavior (his culture).

Jesus Christ

During what has come to be called Jesus' "High Priestly Prayer" following the Last Supper (John 17), Jesus revealed the central goal of this mission of making disciples. After praying that his disciples would be protected from the world (v. 15) and sanctified in his truth (v. 17), Jesus says that he is sending them into the world (v. 18) with his word (v. 14) so that others would believe in him (v. 20). But then Jesus explains the purpose of this mission:

> That they may all be one, just as you, Father, are in me, and I in you, that they also may be in us, so that the world may believe that you have sent me. The glory that you have given me I have given to them, that they may be one even as we are one, I in them and you in me, that they may become perfectly one, so that the world may know that you sent me and loved them even as you loved me. (vv. 21–23)

Christ's goal for his people is that they would share a profound union with him and with one another. This center of unity is a communion with the glory of God; it is being in God and he in us. It is, as he says later, the love of the Father with which he loved the Son being in us, and Christ in us (v. 26). To put it very simply, the purpose of the mission Christ gave his disciples is communion together with God, the very purpose for which he created them. The immediate context of this prayer, the Last Supper, is no coincidence, for communion with God in his presence is what his people celebrate at the Lord's Table; it is a visible representation of the communion we share with Christ and with each other as his body. And when God's people make their center the worship of God through Christ, set apart from the world by truth, Christ indicates that two things happen: first, as we draw near to fellowship with God, we become one with one another, and second, that very communion we have with God and with one another causes the world to believe in Christ.

In other words, Christ's commission to make disciples is directly connected with his worship—making disciples is making worshipers of God through Christ, and the sincere worship of God's people will help to draw more people in that communion. This important connection between the church's mission and worship is succinctly stated by Devin DeYoung and Greg Gilbert in *What is the Mission of the Church*:

> The mission of the church is to go into the world and make disciples by declaring the gospel of Jesus Christ in the power of the Spirit and gathering these disciples into churches, that they might worship the Lord and obey his commands now and in eternity to the glory of God the Father.[11]

---

[11] Kevin DeYoung and Greg Gilbert, *What Is the Mission of the Church? Making Sense of Social Justice, Shalom, and the Great Commission* (Wheaton: Crossway, 2011), 62.

This was a weighty commission, one that would cost many of his followers their lives, and one that would control the priorities, resources, and energies of his people throughout all church history. Yet Jesus did not leave his people to accomplish this mission alone; rather, he promised that he would be with them always, to the end of the age.

Chapter 6
New Testament Worship

Having accomplished the mission given to him by the Father, Jesus ascended into heaven and left his disciples with their own mission of making more worshipers. But Jesus didn't stop working in the world; rather, Jesus began actively working through his body, the church, to accomplish his purposes in the world. In fact, Luke indicates that his gospel was a record of what Jesus *began* to do and teach (Acts 1:1); his second book records the continuing Acts of Jesus Christ through the church.

The Birth of the Church

Christ's disciples obeyed his command to remain in Jerusalem until he sent them the Holy Spirit and formed his spiritual body. Acts 2 records the amazing event that occurred on the Day of Pentecost—the Holy Spirit descended upon them, attested by visible and audible signs, forming the church and empowering them to accomplish the mission Christ had given them. Jesus had promised his disciples that he would send the Holy Spirit for two purposes: First, he promised that he would baptize them with the Holy Spirit (Acts 1:5). Paul later explained what happens when Christ baptizes believers with the Holy Spirit: "For with one Spirit we were all baptized into one body" (1 Cor. 12:13)—Spirit baptism unifies all Christians into the body of Christ, the church. Second, he promised that the Spirit would give them special ability to witness of him "in Jerusalem and in all Judea and Samaria, and to the end of the earth" (Acts 1:8), and that is exactly what began to happen. On that day, Peter preached a powerful message of judgment and salvation, admonishing the people gathered there to repent and call upon the name of the Lord.

Baptism—Entrance into the Church

Thousands became convicted by Peter's sermon: "So those who received his word were baptized, and there were added that day about three thousand souls" (Acts 2:41). Repentance and faith made these people part of Christ's spiritual body, for which water baptism served as a visible sign. This act identified these new believers as followers of Christ and allowed them to be added to the number of those who were members of the church.

The Infant Church's Continual Commitments

The book of Acts provides the first glimpse of what worship in the newly formed church consisted of. Acts 2:42, immediately following Peter's Pentecost sermon, succinctly describes the core of this gathered assembly of believers. Luke recounts four commitments to which these believers "devoted themselves." The first commitment of this infant church was devotion to apostolic teaching. Jesus had promised his disciples that one benefit of the Holy Spirit's coming was that he would "guide [them] into all the truth" about Christ—he would "take what is [Christ's] and declare it to [them]" (John 16:13–14). In other words, the Holy Spirit led the apostles to understand the truth about Jesus, and they passed it on to others. They instructed these new believers in the teachings of Jesus, how he had fulfilled Old Testament prophesies, and how they should live with each other and be witnesses for Christ. In the course of time, the apostles wrote down this teaching under the inspiration of the Holy Spirit, which became the writings of the New Testament (2 Tim. 3:16; 2 Pet. 1:21).

Next, Luke says that these new believers were devoted to "the fellowship"—literally, "communion" (*koinonia*). These people had a common faith in Jesus Christ and thus a unique fellowship with him and with each other that Jesus had prayed for in his High Priestly Prayer. As the rest of Acts illustrates, this spurred them on to encourage and strengthen one another in that faith, bearing up each other's burdens, and admonishing one another in the things of the Lord. As the author of Hebrews later indicates, this is a key purpose for gathering as the church—"to stir up one another to love and good works, not neglecting to meet together, as is the habit of some, but encouraging one another, and all the more as you see the Day drawing near" (Heb. 10:24–25).

The third commitment of the gathered church was devotion to "the breaking of bread." The definite article, "the," indicates that this is specifically speaking about the Lord's Supper. Jesus, through his apostles, had commanded his people to regularly observe this meal as an expression of their communion with God and with the body of Christ through the shed blood and broken body of Christ (1 Cor. 10:16–17). Gatherings of the early church were so characterized by observing this sacred meal that a worship service was simply described as "gathered together to break bread" (Acts 20:7). Participation in the Lord's Table is, according to Paul, participation with the sacrifice of Christ, and as believers share together and partake of the one bread and the one cup, they demonstrate together their communion with God and each other through Christ. Jesus, through Paul, commanded that believers observe this meal "in remembrance of" him (1 Cor. 11:24, 25), thereby proclaiming his death until he comes again (v. 26). Just as with the Passover memorial, this new ordinance is an active reenactment of the death of Christ on behalf of his people such that they are formed by the act.

The fourth commitment Luke lists of this infant church is devotion to public prayer. Again, there is a definite article, "the," in front of "prayers," which has at least two implications. First, this is describing more than simply individual, private prayer.

New Testament Worship

Private prayer is important, but these believers were devoted to "*the* prayers," meaning public times of prayer together. The other implication is that "the prayers" likely refers to specific prayers that were part of Jewish liturgy. Since every member of this infant church was a Jew, they would have naturally continued using practices from Jewish worship, likely those from their regular synagogue services printed in the previous chapter. In other words, this devotion implies that this early church was devoted to regularly meeting for corporate worship, and these corporate gatherings were so characterized by prayer—by dialogue with God—that they could be called "the prayers."

The rest of the book of Acts demonstrates continued devotion to these commitments. The earliest Jewish Christians continued to worship in the temple (5:42) and in synagogues (15:21). Christians gathered for the express purpose of worship (13:2), and church leaders taught and preached the word of the Lord regularly (15:35), baptizing new converts and adding them to the church. Over time, the first day of the week became a significant day for worship, eventually replacing the Sabbath, since it was the day on which Christ rose from the dead (20:7).

Worship in the Assembly

While the book of Acts gives examples of early churches gathering for worship—Scripture reading, preaching, prayer, and the Lord's Table—the rest of the New Testament further emphasizes this central purpose for church meetings. In particular, several ways in which the New Testament authors describe the church and what it does when it gathers clearly identify the church as a place for worship.

First, the New Testament explicitly defines the gathered church as God's temple. In his letter to the Ephesian church, Paul vividly describes the nature of the church as a building God is constructing, "built on the foundation of the apostles and prophets, Christ Jesus himself being the cornerstone, in whom the whole structure, being joined together, grows into *a holy temple* in the Lord. In him you also are being built together into a *dwelling place for God* by the Spirit" (Eph. 2:20–22 emphasis mine). Likewise, Paul says to the Corinthian church, "Do you not know that you are God's temple and that God's Spirit dwells in you?" (1 Cor. 3:16), and "we are the temple of the living God" (2 Cor. 6:16). These metaphors of the gathered church (the pronouns are plural in each of these texts)[1] being built into a temple for God is not coincidental; the gathered New Testament church is the dwelling place for the Spirit of God in this age in the same way that the temple was God's dwelling place in the Old Testament economy. Communion with God takes place in this temple, built by the Spirit of God and indwelt by him.

---

[1] While these two texts explicitly refer to the gathered church as God's temple, Paul also describes the bodies of individual believers as "a temple of the Holy Spirit within you" (1 Cor. 6:19).

Second, Paul tells Timothy that he wrote his letter so that he "may know how one ought to behave in the *household of God*, which is the church of the living God" (1 Tim. 3:15 emphasis mine). Likewise, he tells Christians that they are "members of the *household of God*," and Hebrews 10:21 describes Jesus as "a great high priest over the *house of God*," specifically in the context of the church meeting together (v. 25 emphasis mine). The phrase "house of God" was a technical term used at the time to describe the sanctuary of God's presence (Matt. 12:4; Mark 2:26; Luke 6:4). In the Old Testament, Jacob had referred to the place where he met with God as "Bethel"—"house of God," and several places refer to the tabernacle as the "house of God" (Judg. 18:30; 1 Chr. 9:25–27) as well as the temple (2 Chronicles 3:3; Ezra 1:4; Neh. 6:10; Ps. 42:4; Ecc. 5:1; Dan. 1:2). Thus, as the temple was the house of God and the place of corporate worship in the Old Testament, so the assembled church is the place of worship today.

Biblical Authority in Worship Practice

One important principle articulated in several places in the New Testament was an emphasis upon the importance of biblical authority for worship practices. Usually, these kinds of discussions came in the context of confronting the legalism of the Jewish religion. Jesus had already condemned the adding of religious practices not prescribed in the Scriptures; the same problems continued with the "Judaizers," Christian converts who taught that it was necessary to adopt Jewish religious practices from the Law of Moses. The church first encountered this when some Jewish Christian converts traveled to Antioch and insisted to the Christians there, "Unless you are circumcised according to the custom of Moses, you cannot be saved" (Acts 15:1). This resulted in the formation of a council of church leadership in Jerusalem, including James, Peter, and Paul, to debate the matter. The council concluded that requiring such religious practices not prescribed for the church was "a yoke on the neck of the disciples" (v. 10).

Paul also explicitly contradicted this teaching in his epistles, insisting that any religious practice not explicitly prescribed by Christ or his apostles for the New Testament church should not be forced upon the corporate body. These rituals were merely "human precepts and teachings" (Col. 2:22); they have "an appearance of wisdom," but they are nevertheless "self-made religion" and "of no value" (v. 23). Paul's discourse in Romans 14 directly addresses issues related to corporate worship such as ceremonially unclean food and sacred days.[2] Some "weaker" Jewish Christians in Rome evidently still honored the Mosaic dietary restrictions and therefore abstained entirely from meat or wine out of concern for their ceremonial purity. They also continued to

---

[2] See Leon Morris, *The Epistle to the Romans* (Grand Rapids: William. B. Eerdmans Publishing, 1988), 12–13.

observe the Jewish Sabbath and holy days. Within the context of "what makes for peace and for mutual upbuilding" (v. 19), Paul insists in verse 5 that "each one should be fully convinced in his own mind" concerning observing sacred days, and in verse 23 he warns that "whoever has doubts is condemned if he eats, because the eating is not from faith. For whatever does not proceed from faith is sin." In other words, one must be careful not to impose upon his own conscience or another person's conscience a religious practice of which he is not fully convinced based on biblical prescription. As individuals, Christians are free to observe religious practices as long as they do not contradict Scripture or consider such practices necessary to salvation; as a corporate body, however, no religious practice may be imposed that has not been prescribed for the church. Paul's goal is that members of the church "live in such harmony with another, in accord with Christ Jesus, that together you may with one voice glorify the God and Father of our Lord Jesus Christ" (Rom. 15:5–6); his goal is a unity of the body in worshiping God that can only be obtained by carefully submitting to what the Bible prescribes for Christian worship.

Elements of New Testament Worship
Therefore, the New Testament explicitly prescribes the elements God desires for the gathered worship of his people.

Scripture Reading
First, Paul commands Timothy, in the context of teaching him how to behave in the house of God, "devote yourself to the public reading of Scripture" (1 Tim. 4:13). In both his letter to the Colossians (4:16) and to the Thessalonians (5:27), Paul also admonishes public Scripture reading. This practice would have continued naturally from synagogue worship and corresponds to the believers' devotion to the apostles' doctrine in Acts 2:42.

Preaching
Likewise corresponding to both synagogue practice and the apostles' doctrine is Paul's command to Timothy to "devote yourself ... to exhortation, to teaching" (1 Tim. 4:13) and "preach the word; be ready in season and out of season; reprove, rebuke, and exhort, with complete patience and teaching" (2 Tim. 4:2). Indeed, the purpose of inspired Scripture is "for teaching, for reproof, for correction, and for training in righteousness, that the man of God may be complete, equipped for every good work" (2 Tim. 3:16–17).

Prayer

A third element corresponding to both the synagogue and Acts 2:42 is Paul's admonition that "supplications, prayers, intercessions, and thanksgivings be made for all people, for kings and all who are in high positions" (1 Tim. 2:1). To the Colossians he also commands, "continue steadfastly in prayer" (4:2), and to the Ephesians he insists, "praying at all times in the Spirit, with all prayer and supplication ... making supplication for all the saints" (6:18). These three elements prescribed for New Testament worship—Scripture reading, preaching, and prayer—would have been natural continuations of Jewish practice in the synagogue liturgy.

Singing

A fourth element of worship prescribed in the New Testament would not have necessarily been considered a separate element, but rather a form of Scripture reading or prayer, and that is singing. In both Ephesians 5:19 and Colossians 3:16, Paul commands gathered believers to sing psalms, hymns, and spiritual songs, thereby "singing and making melody to the Lord with your heart" (Eph. 5:19) and "teaching and admonishing one another in all wisdom" (Col. 3:16).

Scholars disagree as to the exact meaning of the three terms psalms, hymns, and spiritual songs.[3] Traditionally, "psalm" referred to Old Testament Jewish psalms, "hymn" was a common term in the culture denoting poetic expression of praise to deity, and "ode" was a generic term for singing. The term "spiritual" may have been used to modify "songs" so as to designate them as specifically spiritual in contrast to secular songs, or the term could modify all three words. Notably, all three Greek terms are used interchangeably in the titles of psalms in the Greek translation of the Old Testament (LXX). Furthermore, the terms are used interchangeably even within the rest of the New Testament. For example, while Paul typically uses the term "psalm" to refer to Old Testament psalms, in several places he uses the term to refer to Christian hymns (1 Cor. 14:26; Jas. 5:13). Likewise, the reference to a "hymn" in Matthew 26:30 and Mark 14:26 was most likely a psalm, and John calls the "new" songs of Revelation 5 and 15 "odes."

Therefore, since psalms, hymns, and spiritual songs are each used as translations of psalm titles in the LXX and are employed interchangeably in the New Testament, the weight of evidence seems to suggest that Paul did not intend the terms to designate clearly identifiable genre of corporate songs. At very least these passages include a mandate to sing Sprit-inspired Old Testament psalms; no matter how narrowly or broadly one interprets the terms, that Paul commands believers to sing psalms is clear.

---

[3] See Scott Aniol, "Psalms, Hymns, and Spiritual Songs: Assessing the Debate," *Artistic Theologian* 6 (2018): 13–18.

Conversely, no clear argument may be made from these passages alone concerning the warrant for singing songs beyond the Old Testament psalms; because these terms *could* refer only to different types of psalms, one cannot argue with certainty that Paul intended to broaden the church's song beyond inspired psalms in these passages. On the other hand, these passages do not clearly restrict Christian songs to Old Testament psalms either; as with the previous point, the ambiguity of these terms presents enough uncertainty to prevent any dogmatic argument for or against a psalmody-only position. The only certain application to Christian churches from this phrase is that God expects his people to sing a variety of songs, at the very least inspired psalms. Additionally, these passages likely grant warrant for both vocal singing with lyrics and instrumental music, as the term *psallontes*, translated "making melody" in Ephesians 5:19, literally means "to pluck a stringed instrument."[4]

Other New Testament passages, however, may imply the allowance of other songs in addition to psalms in Christian worship (Acts 16:25; 1 Cor. 14:26). It is also relevant to note that several passages in the New Testament epistles are written in a poetic form that may indicate that they were early Christian hymns added to the psalms already in use, such as this Christological poem from 1 Timothy 3:16:

> He was manifested in the flesh,
> vindicated by the Spirit,
> seen by angels,
> proclaimed among the nations,
> believed on in the world,
> taken up in glory.

Other poetic passages in the New Testament include Eph. 1:1–11; Phil. 2:5–11; Col. 1:15–20; Heb. 1:1–3; and 1 Pet. 2:21–25; they quickly became early Christian hymns, especially what are known as the "Lucan Canticles":

> "The Benedictus"[5]—Zechariah's prophetic song (Luke 1:68–79)
>   Blessed be the Lord God of Israel,
>   for he has visited and redeemed his people
>   and has raised up a horn of salvation for us
>   in the house of his servant David,
>   as he spoke by the mouth of his holy prophets from of old,
>   that we should be saved from our enemies
>   and from the hand of all who hate us;
>   to show the mercy promised to our fathers

---

[4] Gerhard Delling, "ψάλλω," *TDNT* 8:490.
[5] The Latin titles for each of the canticles comes from the first phrase of each song.

and to remember his holy covenant,
> the oath that he swore to our father Abraham, to grant us
that we, being delivered from the hand of our enemies,
> might serve him without fear,
> in holiness and righteousness before him all our days.
And you, child, will be called the prophet of the Most High;
> for you will go before the Lord to prepare his ways,
to give knowledge of salvation to his people
> in the forgiveness of their sins,
because of the tender mercy of our God,
> whereby the sunrise shall visit us from on high
to give light to those who sit in darkness and in the shadow of death,
> to guide our feet into the way of peace.

"The Magnificat"—Mary's hymn of praise (Luke 1:46–55)
> My soul magnifies the Lord,
>> and my spirit rejoices in God my Savior,
>> for he has looked on the humble estate of his servant.
> For behold, from now on all generations will call me blessed;
>> for he who is mighty has done great things for me,
>> and holy is his name.
> And his mercy is for those who fear him
>> from generation to generation.
> He has shown strength with his arm;
>> he has scattered the proud in the thoughts of their hearts;
> he has brought down the mighty from their thrones
>> and exalted those of humble estate;
> he has filled the hungry with good things,
>> and the rich he has sent away empty.
> He has helped his servant Israel,
>> in remembrance of his mercy,
> as he spoke to our fathers,
>> to Abraham and to his offspring forever.

"The Gloria"—the angel's song (Luke 2:14)
> Glory to God in the highest,
>> and on earth peace among those with whom he is pleased!

"The Nunc Dimittis"—Simeon's song (Luke 2:29–32)
> Lord, now you are letting your servant depart in peace,
>> according to your word;
> for my eyes have seen your salvation
>> that you have prepared in the presence of all peoples,
> a light for revelation to the Gentiles,
>> and for glory to your people Israel.

New Testament Worship

Giving

A fifth element of worship would have been familiar to Jewish and Gentile converts alike, and that is giving. Paul commanded the Corinthian church, "On the first day of the week, each of you is to put something aside and store it up, as he may prosper, so that there will be no collecting when I come" (1 Cor. 16:2). In its immediate context this refers to giving that was taken to needy believers in Jerusalem (v. 3), an offering he gathered from several of the churches (Rom. 15:27–19; 2 Cor. 8:1–5; Gal. 2:10). However, as Paul indicates that elders should be paid (1 Tim. 5:17–18), it is fitting that such regular, weekly giving be used for that purpose as well, in addition to caring for the particular needs of members of the congregation (Acts 6:1; 1 Tim. 5:3) and other material functions of the church.

Baptism

While the first five elements of worship prescribe for the church naturally continued from Jewish synagogue practice, the final two were unique Christian additions, although they do have some similarity with Jewish practices. The first of these is baptism. In his Great Commission to the disciples, Jesus commanded, "Go therefore and make disciples of all nations, *baptizing them* in the name of the Father and of the Son and of the Holy Spirit" (Matt. 28:19 emphasis mine). Baptism with water is the biblical, prescribed means by which believers in Jesus Christ visibly identify with the church. Since it occurs only once for each church member, this worship element is not necessarily performed each time the church gathers.

The Lord's Supper

The final prescribed worship element is a unique Christian addition, though it finds roots in the Passover meal: The Lord's Supper. The book of Acts describes the meal as "the breaking of bread" (2:42, 46; 20:7–11), and Paul says that he passed on what he calls "the Lord's supper" (1 Cor. 11:20) to the church, having received it from the Lord himself (v. 23). Based on the clear instructions in 1 Corinthians 11 and the accounts of the Last Supper in the synoptic gospels (Matt. 26:17–30; Mark 14:12–26; Luke 22:7–39), the Lord's Supper prescribed in 1 Corinthians 11 contains several elements: prayer of thanks (v. 24), breaking of the bread (v. 24), and eating and drinking of the bread (v. 24) and cup (v. 25). It appears to have originally been celebrated as part of a full meal (vv. 17–34), but eventually—perhaps because of the abuses mentioned in this passage—it was removed from the meal as a separate ritual observance within corporate worship. By the time Jude wrote his epistle, the meal was so closely associated with fellowship that it was called the "love feast" (Jude 1:12).

This meal is to be done "in remembrance" (*anamnēsin*) of Christ's death for the sins of his people, the same kind of "memorial" God commanded of Israel in observing the Passover, an active reenactment of what God has done so that it shapes the worshiper. But it also serves another purpose. Earlier in chapter 10 of 1 Corinthians, Paul explains the significance of the ordinance:

> The cup of blessing that we bless, is it not a participation in the blood of Christ? The bread that we break, is it not a participation in the body of Christ? Because there is one bread, we who are many are one body, for we all partake of the one bread. (vv. 16–17)

The word translated "participation" is the same word translated "fellowship" in Acts 2:42 (*koinōnia*)—a central devotion of the early church. It emphasizes the communion believers in the church have with one another because of their union with Christ himself. Participation in the Lord's Table is fellowship with the sacrifice of Christ, and as believers share together and partake of the one bread and cup, they demonstrate together the unity and communion of the body. This is why the ordinance was given to the church and not just individuals—it is for the whole body to partake together. Members of the body of Christ, who have professed that membership through the sign of baptism (Acts 2:41), and who are living in unity with others in that body (1 Cor. 11:28–34), renew their communion with Christ and with each other through this beautiful drama that Christ himself instituted.

We will see each of these elements of the Lord's Table again as the liturgies of corporate worship develop and expand in the early church and Middle Ages:

- Prayer of thanks (*eucharistéō*)
- Breaking the bread (*fraction*)
- Distribution of the elements ("he gave it to his disciples")
- "This is my body" and "This is my blood"
- Remembrance (*anamnēsis*)
- Communion (*koinōnia*)

Orderly Worship

While the New Testament does not contain any examples or prescriptions of particular liturgies, Paul does address the matter of service order in 1 Corinthians 14:26–33:

> What then, brothers? When you come together, each one has a hymn, a lesson, a revelation, a tongue, or an interpretation. Let all things be done for building up. [27] If any speak in a tongue, let there be only two or at most three, and each in turn, and let someone interpret. [28] But if there is no one to interpret, let each

of them keep silent in church and speak to himself and to God. ²⁹ Let two or three prophets speak, and let the others weigh what is said. ³⁰ If a revelation is made to another sitting there, let the first be silent. ³¹ For you can all prophesy one by one, so that all may learn and all be encouraged, ³² and the spirits of prophets are subject to prophets. ³³ For God is not a God of confusion but of peace.

Apparently, the Corinthian church at the time favored a kind of free, spontaneous worship where any individual could offer a favorite hymn, a lesson, a prophecy, or a message in tongues, resulting in a disorganized and chaotic service (v. 26). Paul corrects this practice by emphasizing that "God is not a God of confusion"—in other words, disorder—"but of peace" (v. 33). On this basis, Paul provides clear principles for order in a worship service.

The purpose of prophecy, Paul contends, is the "upbuilding" of the church (vv. 3–5). "Only two or at most three" people may speak in tongues in any given service, "and each in turn" (v. 27). If there is no one to interpret the tongues, "let each of them keep silent" (v. 28). Only two or three prophets should speak, others should weigh what is said (v. 29), and they should do so one at a time (v. 30) so that "all may learn and all be encouraged" (v. 31). In contrast to what may have been common expectation in pagan worship of the day, worshipers should not expect to be overcome with God's presence such that they lose control in an experience of ecstasy; rather "the spirits of the prophets are subject to prophets" (v. 32).

Although there is debate as to whether tongues and prophecy continue in the church today, the principles in this passage apply to all aspects of a Christian worship service. Paul insists that in a worship service, "all things should be done decently and in order" (v. 40).

The Holy Spirit's Work in Worship

The Holy Spirit of God has worked God's will in the world and particularly in his people since when he "hovered over the face of the waters" to bring order to creation (Gen. 1:2; cf. Job 33:4; Ps. 104:30)—he gave revelation (2 Sam. 23:2), empowered Israel's leaders,[6] gifted Bezalel and Oholiab with skill to build the tabernacle (Exod. 31:1–5; 35:30–35), and dwelt in the midst of Israel (Neh. 9:20; Hag. 2:5; cf. Exod. 29:45). With his coming on the day of Pentecost, however, his work took a new form, which has raised questions for many Christians concerning what to expect as his regular work in worship.

A careful study of the Holy Spirit's activity throughout Scripture, and specifically in the New Testament, reveals what Christians should expect his ordinary work in

---

[6] See Jesus's baptism in the previous chapter.

Christian worship to be. There is no doubt that he sometimes works in extraordinary ways, such as giving revelation (2 Tim. 3:16; 2 Pet. 1:21) and special empowerment of individuals for service (Acts 2:4; 9:17). Yet extraordinary works of the Spirit do not appear to be the ordinary way God works his sovereign will through the course of biblical history. When extraordinary experiences occur, they happen during significant transitional stages in the outworking of God's plan. Sinclair Ferguson helpfully explains:

> In the Scriptures themselves, extraordinary gifts appear to be limited to a few brief periods in biblical history, in which they serve as confirmatory signs of new revelation and its ambassadors, and as a means of establishing and defending the kingdom of God in epochally significant ways. ... Outbreaks of the miraculous sign gifts in the Old Testament were, generally speaking, limited to those periods of redemptive history in which a new stage of covenantal revelation was reached. ... But these sign-deeds were never normative. Nor does the Old Testament suggest they should have continued unabated even throughout the redemptive-historical epoch they inaugurated. ... Consistent with this pattern, the work of Christ and the apostles was confirmed by "signs and wonders."[7]

Rather, the ordinary work of the Holy Spirit throughout Scripture is better characterized as an ordering of the plan and people of God. This describes much, if not all, of what the Holy Spirit does throughout Scripture, including giving revelation, creating life (both physical [Gen. 1:2] and spiritual [Titus 3:5]), and sanctifying individual believers (Rom. 15:16; Gal. 5:22).

This understanding provides a robust picture of what should be the expectation for how the Holy Spirit works in worship. First, his purpose in all he does is to bring order, to both individual Christians and to the Body as a whole. The descriptions in Scripture of the Holy Spirit's activity overwhelmingly attest to this purpose, and this purpose would most naturally extend to his work in corporate worship. He worked to bring peace and blessing to Israel as he dwelt among them in the Old Testament Temple, and he does the same as he dwells within the New Testament Temple. This work begins with his acts of convicting sinners (John 16:8) and regenerating hearts (Titus 3:5), bringing life and order to once dead and disordered lives. This re-ordering continues with his frequently mentioned work of sanctification (Rom. 15:16; 1 Cor. 6:11; 2 Thess. 2:13; 1 Pet. 1:2). He "circumcises the hearts" of believers (Rom. 2:29) and strengthens their inner being (Eph. 3:16), pouring love into their hearts (Rom. 5:5) and leading them to fulfill "the righteous requirement of the law" (Rom. 8:4). Of particular importance for this discussion is a careful focus on what Paul calls "the fruit of the Spirit"

---

[7] Sinclair B. Ferguson, *The Holy Spirit* (Downers Grove, IL: IVP Academic, 1997), 224–225.

in Galatians 5:22–23, the results of such an ordering in the life of the Christian: "love, joy, peace, patience, kindness, goodness, faithfulness, gentleness, self-control." This was his purpose in the foundational gifts he gave to the apostles and others during the formation of the church, and even if those gifts continue today, their purpose remains the same. Paul states that "to each is given the manifestation of the Spirit for the common good" (1 Cor. 12:7). He explicitly connects the Spirit's giving of gifts to bringing order within the church, commanding, "Since you are eager for manifestations of the Spirit, strive to excel in building up the church" (1 Cor. 14:12). The Holy Spirit's gifting of individual Christians with a diversity of ministry abilities serves to build up the unity of the Church—many members of one body (1 Cor. 12:12; Rom. 12:5), with the goal that this body will "attain to the unity of the faith and of the knowledge of the Son of God, to mature manhood, to the measure of the stature of the fullness of Christ" (Eph. 4:13). It is in this context that Paul most clearly defines Spirit baptism—"For in one Spirit we were all baptized into one body" (1 Cor. 12:13)—which, even if the Holy Spirit is the agent, involves an ordering such that the body of Christ is formed and unified. Or, to use another New Testament metaphor for the Church, by the Spirit, believers "are being built together into a dwelling place for God," "a holy temple in the Lord" (Eph. 2:21–22).

Second, one of the most influential and long-lasting works of the Holy Spirit to bring order to his people was the inspiration of his Word; this is why the most frequently described act of the Holy Spirit in Scripture is the giving of revelation, and why, for example, his work of "filling" a believer (Eph. 5:19) is paralleled in Paul's writings with the Word of Christ "richly dwelling" within a Christian (Col. 3:16). The Holy Spirit gave special revelation to disclose the nature and character of God, explain God's requirements, correct sin, and give hope for the future. Likewise, he guided the apostles into the truth (John 16:13) necessary to establish Christian doctrine and set the church in order (1 Tim. 3:15). Ultimately, he inspired a "prophetic word more fully confirmed" (2 Pet. 1:19–21), the canonical Scriptures, given to believers "for teaching, for reproof, for correction, and for training in righteousness, that the man of God may be complete, equipped for every good work" (2 Tim. 3:16–17). The nature of such inspiration is important as well: the Holy Spirit did not inspire the Scriptures by bringing authors into a sort of mystical trance as they were "carried along" (2 Pet. 1:21); rather, inspiration is a divine act wherein each author conscientiously penned the Scriptures (Acts 1:16; 4:25; Heb. 3:7; 1 Cor. 2:12–13) using craftsmanship (e.g., the Psalms), research (e.g., Luke 1:1–4), and available cultural forms and idioms. Spirit-inspired revelation is both for the purpose of order and produced in an orderly fashion. Thus, believers should expect that the Holy Spirit will work today primarily *through* his Word, and he will never act *contrary* to his Word.

The sufficiency of the Spirit-inspired Word of God leads, third, to the conviction that he has given the church in that Word all the revelation necessary concerning the elements he desires to be part of worship as described above: reading the Word, preaching the Word, singing the Word, prayer, giving, baptism, and the Lord's Table. Furthermore, because the Holy Spirit inspired the sufficient revelation concerning the elements for worship, believers should expect that he would naturally work through those elements in the context of worship, what the Reformers would later call the "ordinary means of grace"—these were the primary means Christians should expect the Holy Spirit to ordinarily work his grace into their lives.

This leads to a fourth observation, namely, that believers should expect the Holy Spirit's ordinary work in worship to be that of sanctifying them through the effectual means of grace that he has prescribed in his Word. The regular, disciplined use of these means of grace progressively forms believers into the image of Jesus Christ; these Spirit-ordained elements are the means through which Christians "work out [their] own salvation with fear and trembling, for it is God who works in [them], both to will and to work for his good pleasure (Phil. 2:12–13).

In summary, while the Holy Spirit of God, who with the Father and the Son should be worshiped and glorified, may certainly do whatever he pleases in the world broadly and in corporate worship specifically, he is not a God of disorder, but a God of peace. The testimony of Scripture concerning the ordinary ways he works and a careful study of the New Testament's explicit treatment of his ordinary work in worship should lead Christians to expect disciplined formation when he works. Truly Spirit-led worship is that in which the forms, elements, and content are shaped, guided, and filled with the Spirit-inspired Word for the purpose of the disciplined spiritual formation of his people.

Heavenly Worship

In the book of Revelation, God granted the apostle John a look into the temple of heaven. As with Isaiah during the reign of King Uzziah (Isa. 6), it is no accident that this vision of heavenly worship came at a time when worship on earth was in chaos. In his vision, John observed God himself, sitting on his throne in all of his majestic splendor, surrounded by spectacular heavenly beings. Among other things that occupy their attention, they are singing to God "day and night" (Rev. 4:8). Chapter 4 describes angels surrounding the throne of God, and it relates two songs that those angels are singing to God day and night. The first is "Holy, Holy, Holy, Lord God Almighty" (the *Trisagion*) and the second is "Worthy are you, our Lord and God." But then in Chapter 5 John saw "the Lion of the tribe of Judah, the root of Jesse," a "Lamb standing, as though it had been slain." He saw the Son of God, Jesus Christ, proclaimed as the only

New Testament Worship

one worthy of opening the scroll that would establish his right to rule the Kingdom of God. And in response to this revelation, verse 9 tells us that the angels and the elders sang "a new song," saying:

> Worthy are you to take the scroll and to open its seals, for you were slain, and by your blood you ransomed people for God from every tribe and language and people and nation, and you have made them a kingdom and priests to our God, and they shall reign on the earth.

They sing in the presence of God as expressions attributing worth to God—the essence of worship. Their worship is a response to the nature of God—his holiness, his sovereignty ("Lord God Almighty"), and his eternality ("who was and is and is to come")—and the works of God—creation ("for you created all things") and redemption ("you ransomed people for God"). Their responses of worship are expressions of "honor and glory and thanks" (Rev. 4:9, 11; 5:12, 13).

This picture of the worship of heaven has significance for Christian worship for several reasons. First, since earthly worship, both in the Old Testament and New Testament, is said to be patterned after the worship of heaven, how heavenly worship takes place should inform earthly Christian worship. Second, consequently, Christians since the first century have taken careful notes of the pattern of worship presented in Revelation 4–5. It begins with a Call to Worship: "Come up here" (4:1), followed by a vision of God himself and angels singing the *Trisagion* (4:8) and hymns of praise for creation (4:11). Then follows the presentation of the scroll that reveals the unworthiness of all people to open it (5:1–4) except for the Lamb, he who provided atonement and ransomed a people for God (5:5–12). They respond with a doxology and a choral "Amen" by the four living creatures (5:13–14). Most of the rest of the book foretells God's Word being opened as he enacts his plans for humankind, and the responses of God's people in the form of praise and service (6:1–19:5). The book climaxes with the great Marriage Supper of the Lamb (19:6–21), when a great multitude will sing,

> Hallelujah!
> For the Lord our God
>   the Almighty reigns.
> Let us rejoice and exult
>   and give him the glory,
> for the marriage of the Lamb has come,
>   and his Bride has made herself ready;
> it was granted her to clothe herself
>   with fine linen, bright and pure. (vv. 6–8)

The heavenly temple will descend, and for the first time God's ultimate intention for his people will come to full realization: "Behold, the dwelling place of God is with man. He will dwell with them, and they will be his people, and God himself will be with them as their God" (21:3). The purpose of humankind was communion in the presence of God for his glory, and in that day the purpose will come to pass.

Thus, the structure of worship in Revelation is the same as it has been since the beginning:

> God reveals himself and calls his people to worship
> God's people acknowledge and confess their need for forgiveness
> God provides atonement
> God speaks his Word
> God's people respond with commitment
> God hosts a celebratory feast

From creation to consummation, the corporate worship of God's people is a memorial—a reenactment—of the "theo-logic" of true worship: God's call for his people to commune with him through the sacrifice of atonement that he has provided, listening to his Word, and responding with praise and obedience.

Chapter 7
A Theology of Christian Worship

Synthesizing a theology of worship in the New Testament has been a struggle for Christians since the early church. In particular, how Christ's coming, life, death, and resurrection altered and, in some cases, revolutionized the worship of Old Testament Judaism has been the subject of considerable debate. As we will see in the upcoming chapters, missteps in this matter have led to various—sometimes serious—theological and practical errors. Yet this controversy is not something new. Believers from the earliest years of Christianity—especially those coming out of Judaism—struggled with how to reconcile the transition between Jewish worship and Christian worship. In fact, the confusion escalated to such a point that some apostatized from Christianity in favor of the worship of their Jewish heritage.

The book of Hebrews functions as the New Testament's supreme answer to this challenging dilemma. The author was writing to Jewish Christians who were experiencing intensified persecution and were tempted to reject their Christian beliefs in a return to Judaism. In an attempt to persuade them otherwise, the author explicitly uses Old Testament worship categories—including communion, sanctuary, sacrifices, priesthood, and altar—to help Christians understand the difference between worship in the Old Testament and worship in the New Testament, clearly elucidating the essence of Christian worship. Therefore, a careful study of the message of the book of Hebrews, including its well-developed theology of Christian worship, reveals that while New Testament worship has its roots in Old Testament revelation, worship in and through Jesus Christ is superior to the worship of Judaism.

Draw Near
As we have already seen throughout our study of worship in both the Old and New Testaments, the essence of worship is communion with God in his presence such that he is magnified and glorified. This idea is one of the key themes in the book of Hebrews, communicated throughout the book through the phrase, "draw near" (Greek, *prosérchomai*). This term appears as central in what scholars identify as the three literary climaxes of the book (4:16; 10:22; and 12:22), as well as several other places. Evident from a brief scan of these texts is that this idea of drawing near in the book of Hebrews specifically refers to entering the presence of God for worship. Hebrews 4:16 highlights that the coming of Christians to God in worship is based upon grace, leading to a boldness that the Hebrews at Sinai could not express: "Let us then with confidence *draw near* to the throne of grace." Hebrews 7:25 emphasizes the fact that Christ's

high priestly ministry of intercession makes such an approach possible: "Consequently, he is able to save to the uttermost those who *draw near* to God through him, since he always lives to make intercession for them." In 10:1, the author reveals the insufficiency of animal sacrifices to purify those who come to God in worship: "For since the law has but a shadow of the good things to come instead of the true form of these realities, it can never, by the same sacrifices that are continually offered every year, make perfect those who *draw near*." In contrast, 10:22 proclaims that since believers in Christ have "a great high priest," they may "*draw near* with a true heart in full assurance of faith, with [their] hearts sprinkled clean from an evil conscience and [their] bodies washed with pure water." Hebrews 11:6 further emphasizes the need for faith in coming to God in worship (more below): "And without faith it is impossible to please him, for whoever would *draw near* to God must believe that he exists and that he rewards those who seek him" (all emphasis mine).

A Tale of Two Mountains
In Chapter 12, the author climaxes his argument with a vivid description of drawing near to God for worship in the Old Testament compared with drawing near for Christians. In verses 18–24, he contrasts two mountains—Mt. Sinai, representing Old Testament worship, and Mt. Zion, representing New Testament worship.

> For you have not come to what may be touched, a blazing fire and darkness and gloom and a tempest [19] and the sound of a trumpet and a voice whose words made the hearers beg that no further messages be spoken to them. [20] For they could not endure the order that was given, "If even a beast touches the mountain, it shall be stoned." [21] Indeed, so terrifying was the sight that Moses said, "I tremble with fear."
> [22] But you have come to Mount Zion and to the city of the living God, the heavenly Jerusalem, and to innumerable angels in festal gathering, [23] and to the assembly of the firstborn who are enrolled in heaven, and to God, the judge of all, and to the spirits of the righteous made perfect, [24] and to Jesus, the mediator of a new covenant, and to the sprinkled blood that speaks a better word than the blood of Abel.

Approaching God in the Old Testament is physical—it can be touched; it has visual sensations—burning fire, darkness, gloom, and storm; it has aural sensations—the sound of a trumpet blast and actual words spoken from God himself. In other words, this Old Testament worship was decidedly sensory. This is what naturally comes to mind when considering Old Testament worship; the Jews had a beautiful tabernacle and later a Temple that shone brightly in Jerusalem with elaborate priestly adornments, gold, and fine linens—they could *see* this worship. They had incense and burnt offerings—they could *smell* this worship. Worshipers actually had to lay their hands on the animal as it was being slaughtered, and then they would be given meat from that animal to eat—they could *feel* this worship; they could *taste* this worship. It was all very physical and sensory. It created an experience of the senses that permeated the whole being. The author also describes the response this kind of approach to God created in those who were present. This physical, sensory worship in the Old Testament created very physical reactions—they resisted it; they begged that God stop speaking (12:19)—it was terrifying. Severe judgment was connected to this worship—if they did something wrong, they would be killed. Even an animal that touched Mt. Sinai would be stoned (12:20). Moses himself trembled with fear when God revealed himself in this way (12:21). In other words, the author means to specifically highlight the physical, tangible aspects of this worship.

In contrast, the author uses Mount Zion to represent New Testament worship. Christians are not actually worshiping physically in heaven yet, but in Christ they are worshiping there positionally in a very real sense—they "have come [*prosérchomai*] to Mt. Zion" (12:22). With the New Testament, God no longer has to condescend and enter the fabric of the physical universe to manifest himself to his people; he can now allow his people to ascend into Heaven itself to worship him, which the author argues is superior to the former worship. This is possible because of Jesus' mediation on the behalf of his people (12:24), and thus Christians can now approach God with full confidence in worship.

But here is the important point: this kind of superior worship through Christ is not physical *in its essence*. Living Christians are not physically in heaven yet; when they worship, they are positionally worshiping in heaven with all the angels and saints, but they are doing so *spiritually*. That is the essential difference between these two kinds of worship. Old Testament worship was physical; it was sensory; it happened on earth. New Testament worship, however, is immaterial; it is spiritual; it takes place in heaven.

Discontinuities Between the Mountains
These two mountains and the realities they represent provide the unifying structure for the argument of the book and serve as symbols of worship under the two covenants. Thus, the primary argument of Hebrews is rooted in a theology of worship; the author's method is to contrast the worship they are tempted to leave—spiritual worship in Christ—with the worship they are attracted to—physical worship of the Old Testament. In doing so, the author of Hebrews reveals both discontinuities and continuities between the two ways of approaching God, and he proclaims that worship in Christ is far superior to Old Testament worship.

Revelation of Worship
Throughout the book, the author of Hebrews highlights the essential discontinuity between revelation under the Old Testament and revelation for the Church. Old Testament saints relied heavily upon supernatural, transient means through which to receive revelation from God. The first verse of the book notes what would have been for the Jews the primary source of revelation—prophets. Yet as unique and authoritative as these messengers of God's word were to the Jews, the supreme messenger is now the Word himself (John 1:1). This source of divine revelation "is the radiance of the glory of God and the exact imprint of his nature, and he upholds the universe by the word of his power" (1:3). In other words, he is not simply a messenger of God's revelation—he *is* God and he *is* the revelation. The author focuses on another source of revelation in Chapters 1 and 2—angels. The Jews considered these mysterious beings as special, visible representations of God's word. In contrast to what his readers would have considered the supreme sources of revelation and thus images of the authority of God, the author exalts Jesus Christ as superior, both as the source of revelation and as the very person of God himself.

This verbal revelation is essentially the basis for communion with God. The Word from God delivered through prophets or heavenly messengers was the only means through which Old Testament believers could worship the Lord. Without these supernatural insertions into the earthly realm, people had insufficient knowledge for communion with the Creator. Even then, this knowledge was lacking, for it came sporadically and, at times, impersonally. Yet with the coming of Christ, the revelation that provided a *basis* for communion was also both the *object* and the *means* of that communion.

Location of Worship
Hebrews 12:18–29 is structured around a discontinuity of the location of worship, and the rest of the book reflects this emphasis. In Hebrews 12:18, Sinai stands as a representative for worship under the Law, and thus the location of this worship is first the tabernacle and later the temple. In contrast, worship for a Christian takes place on "Mount Zion and to the city of the living God, the heavenly Jerusalem" (12:22). These synonymous terms refer to the heavenly city, the place where God himself dwells, which is made clear by the groups of participants there: joyful angels, "the assembly of the firstborn," God, and "the spirits of the righteous made perfect" (vv. 22–23). The term "assembly" in verse 22 likely refers to the common sense of New Testament "church" and thus designates post-Pentecost believers, while the latter term describes

A Theology of Christian Worship

Old Testament saints now "made perfect" by the atonement of Christ's blood.[1] So the company of worshipers in this heavenly scene includes angels, New Testament Christians, and Old Testament believers. Here in this heavenly city God actually dwells; the worshipers come to him rather than he coming down to them as in the Sinai experience and his presence in the tabernacle and temple.

The author of Hebrews contrasts these locations in a number of ways throughout the book. He distinguishes between "the true tent that the Lord set up" and the one set up by man (8:1–2). This heavenly tent is "greater and more perfect" since it is "not made with hands, that is, not of this creation" (9:11). He calls the earthly places of worship and all that they entail "copies of the heavenly things" (9:23) and "copies of the true things" (9:24). The Law in general is "a shadow of the good things to come instead of the true form of these realities" (10:1).

The discontinuity between these locations of worship is not, however, a decisive one. Rather, the book of Hebrews develops the understanding that such physical locations of worship in the Old Testament economy were actually prototypes of the actual worship in heaven, where Christians are now seated through Christ. The tent set up by man and the human sacrifices "serve a copy and shadow of the heavenly things" (8:5); Moses had been instructed to construct the earthly tent according to a "pattern" of the heavenly Temple. Thus, a thorough knowledge and understanding of Old Testament worship is critically relevant for the New Testament Church, for it illustrates some of the metaphysical realities of heavenly worship.

Drawing Near to Worship

Drawing near to the presence of God is the fundamental experience of God's people under both covenants, and it is the essence of worship (in both a personal and corporate sense). Descriptions of this approach with relation to the Old Covenant are always negative, however (10:1; 12:18), since those attempting to worship have not been purified; God is essentially unapproachable. In contrast, approach to God in the New Testament is indeed possible because it is mediated by Jesus Christ and is based upon his sacrifice; therefore, Christians can come with boldness and joy. This contrast of response in approaching God is best summarized by the descriptions in 12:18–24: the Hebrews at Sinai "could not endure" the experience, yet Christians worshiping spiritually in the heavenly Temple enter a "festal gathering." Once again, the author distinguishes between the earthly copies and the heavenly realities. On earth, only the High Priest could enter the holy place of the Temple, and that only once a year; in the

---

[1] Homer Kent, *The Epistle to the Hebrews: A Commentary* (Grand Rapids: Baker Book House, 1972), 273. Some see the term ἐκκλησία in verse 22 as being used in its more general sense of "assembly" rather than the technical "church," thus referring to the complete company of God's people. Either way, these are beings in heaven and not on earth.

heavenly temple, every believer may have "confidence to enter the holy places by the blood of Jesus, by the new and living way that he opened for us through the curtain, that is, through his flesh" (10:19–20).

Mediator of Worship
Access to God in worship always involves some kind of mediator, yet the mediators of the Old Testament and New Testament reveal additional discontinuity between the two. Hebrews 12:18–29 lists the mediators of these two covenants—Moses and Jesus—and thus the mediators of worship. Moses' reaction to the Sinai event is revealing: "Indeed, so terrifying was the sight that Moses said, 'I tremble with fear'" (v. 21). Since Moses himself was a sinner, and thus under divine judgment, even as mediator he found the notion of drawing near to God fearsome. In fact, this term is used in Hebrews in the context of judgment from God. The author says of God's promise to judge sin, "It is a fearful thing to fall into the hands of the living God" (10:31). In contrast to Moses, 12:24 points to Jesus as the mediator of New Testament worship. Christ "has been counted worthy of more glory than Moses" (3:3) because he is not simply "faithful in all God's house as a servant"; he is "faithful over God's house as a son" (2:5–6). His mediation is better than Moses' since the covenant he mediates is better (8:6).

Sacrifice of Worship
Likely the most obvious discontinuity between Old Testament and New Testament worship involves the sacrifices of worship. God required Old Testament saints to offer sacrifices with him as means of temporary forgiveness. These sacrifices themselves were imperfect, and they did nothing to change the heart of the one offering the sacrifice. They did not provide full atonement (10:4, 11), but rather a temporary, legal satisfaction of immediate wrath. They could not cleanse sin, but they could "sanctify for the cleansing of the flesh" (9:13). Although these Old Testament sacrifices were limited, they served as "copies" (9:23) of the perfect, complete sacrifice that was to come in the person of Jesus Christ.

In contrast, 12:24 directs the reader's attention to "the sprinkled blood" of Jesus as the basis for New Testament worship. This idea of sprinkling is intricately tied to the ratification of the covenant and harkens back to the sprinkling that ratified the old covenant (9:19-21). Yet the blood is a mere metonymy for the whole of Christ's sacrificial death, which is made clear by its comparison to another violent murder of an innocent victim—that of Abel. According to Hebrews, Abel "is still speaking, although he died" (11:4), and yet the blood of Christ "continues to speak more effectively" (12:24) as a final sacrifice of atonement that makes worship possible. This sacrifice of Christ is an act of grace rather than vengeance as Abel's had been.

A Theology of Christian Worship

Christ is not only the sacrifice, however; he is also the priest who offers the sacrifice. The author highlights this truth as one of the first descriptions of the Son of God in 1:3, noting that after Christ made "purification for sins, he sat down at the right hand of the Majesty on high." The term "purification" is most often used in the New Testament to refer to ritual cleansing, yet in this case it has direct reference to the removal of sin by the sacrifice of Christ. This act of offering one sacrifice and then sitting is in stark contrast to the work of Old Testament priests who had to offer continual sacrifices (10:11–12). The author reiterates this fact in 7:27: "He has no need, like those high priests, to offer sacrifices daily, first for his own sins and then for those of the people, since he did this once for all when he offered up himself." Their sacrifice did not remove sin, but Christ's did. The author of Hebrews speaks of this act of removing sin completely several times throughout the book. He made "propitiation for the sins of the people" (2:17); his sacrifice ensured that God would remember the sins of his people no more" (8:12; 10:17); he was "offered once to bear the sins of many" (9:28); he "offered for all time a single sacrifice for sin" (10:12); he made an "offering for sin" (10:18); he "appeared once for all at the end of the ages to put away sin by the sacrifice of himself" (9:26); his death brought redemption from transgression (9:15). Throughout the book, the author stresses that the Old Covenant could not remove sin, but now Christ has accomplished full atonement (10:2, 4, 6, 11).

Once again, the author portrays Jesus Christ as the bridge between physical and spiritual realities. Christ is able to serve as the high priest of his people because he was both "made like his brothers in every respect" (2:17), and, having "passed through the heavens" (4:14), he "is seated at the right hand of the throne of the Majesty in heaven, a minister in the holy places, in the true tent that the Lord set up, not man" (8:1–2). There he entered, "not by means of the blood of goats and calves but by means of his own blood, thus securing an eternal redemption" (9:12). Physical beings would not be able to worship a spiritual God without a mediator who is both physical and spiritual.

Physicality of Worship

Significant discontinuities exist between these two ways to worship, and it is important to note that each of these cases of discontinuity stems from the author's primary discontinuity, that of the physical vs. the spiritual. Human prophets, a mediator, priests, animal sacrifices, and a temple each represent physical realties that Hebrew worshipers could see, smell, and touch. Yet they all stand in stark contrast to the supreme spiritual reality that replaces them all—Jesus Christ. *He* is the prophet, the mediator, the priest, the sacrifice, and the temple. It is he who stands as the subject, source, and means of true worship. The Old Testament rituals of worship were indeed shadows of the spiritual realities, but they fell short since they could not actually bring someone into the presence of God. With the coming of Christ, however, believers are actually raised up into the very presence of God, not yet physically, but spiritually. This discontinuity reveals the ultimate supremacy of worship in and through Christ over the physical worship of the Old Testament.

Continuities Between the Mountains
Clearly, great discontinuities exist between the worship of Old Testament Israel and the worship of the New Testament Church as expressed throughout the book of Hebrews and summarized in 12:18–29. Yet the book also highlights important continuities that allow the true essence of worship to shine forth clearly.

The God Worshipped
The final phrase in Hebrews 12:18–29, "for our God is a consuming fire," reveals that the object of worship is the same from Old Testament to New Testament worship. Readers would have recognized a clear allusion here to Moses' statement to the Hebrews in Deuteronomy 4:24: "the Lord your God is a consuming fire, a jealous God." The author of Hebrews is emphasizing here, as a final plea to remain faithful to God's covenant, that the God of the New Testament they are being tempted to doubt is the same God of the Old Testament whom they claim to believe.

Worship in Spirit
The metaphor in Hebrews of the church as the temple of God—the location of his presence where they worship him—also highlights a distinct continuity between worship in both testaments. Worship occurred in the Old Testament only where the presence of God's Spirit dwelt; likewise in the New Testament, it is the indwelling of the Holy Spirit of God that makes worship possible. Christians come to enjoy communion with God through the person and work of Jesus Christ, but this happens "in one Spirit" (Eph. 2:18). This also may be part of what Christ meant in John 4 when he said that God is seeking those who will "worship the Father in spirit and truth" (v. 23). Since "God is a spirit" (v. 24) and does not have a body like man, true worship takes place in its essence in the non-corporeal realm of the Spirit, which is why it is essential that the Holy Spirit dwell within the New Testament temple—the church—in the same way he dwelt in the temple of the Old Testament. And while in the Old Testament, worship was specifically localized to that physical, Spirit-indwelt temple, "the hour is now here" (v. 23) that worship takes place wherever two or three Spirit-indwelt believers gather together, for there he is "in the midst of them" (Matt. 18:20).

A Theology of Christian Worship

Consequences of Refusing Worship

The five warning passages in Hebrews (2:1–4; 3:1–4:13; 5:11–6:20; 10:26–29; 12:14–29) stand as an important part of the author's argument and reveal one of the prominent continuities between the Old and New Testament. The author of Hebrews does not relate judgment as present only in the old economy; the consequences of rejecting true worship are the same in both Testaments. Hebrews 12:18–29 itself functions not only as the summary and conclusion of the book but also as the author's final statement of warning—"See that you do not refuse him who is speaking" (v. 25)—and this warning is rooted in a grave continuity between Old Testament and New Testament worship. The author proclaims that the same Judge who descended to earth in order to judge those who rejected him will also Judge from his place in the heavenly city. This is parallel with the first warning of the book: "For since the message declared by angels proved to be reliable, and every transgression or disobedience received a just retribution, how shall we escape if we neglect such a great salvation" (2:2–3). In both of these warning, the author draws on the continuities between the Old Testament and New Testament to demonstrate the reality of certain judgment for those who refuse to worship as God has intended. The other three warning passages are equally as forceful, magnifying the author's concern that his readers not reject Christian worship in favor of that of Judaism. The point is clear: those who refuse to worship Christ will find judgment, but those to do worship him will receive forgiveness and life everlasting.

The Attitude of Approach

The attitude of the worship also remains the same between the Old Testament and New Testament. Hebrews 12:28 admonishes "gratitude," "reverence," and "awe" as appropriate responses of "acceptable worship." True recognition of our place in the heavenly worship causes the believer to express deep gratitude to the Lord. The term "reverence" connotes a kind of reverent piety common to religious speech, but modified by the word "awe," the two terms together express a sense of "fear, terror, or dread" that is lost in many modern translations.[2]

Faith

Faith stands in Hebrews as the supreme continuity between Old Testament and New Testament worship since it functions as an essential link between the physical and spiritual. The author of Hebrews defines faith as "the assurance of things *hoped for*, the conviction of things *not seen*" (11:1 emphasis mine). Two modifiers in the author's definition of faith reveal its connection between physical and spiritual. First, "assurance" has the idea that faith is the basis by which we know spiritual reality for which

---

[2] William Lane, *Hebrews* (Dallas: Word Books, 1991), 487.

we have no present, tangible evidence. "Conviction" has the idea of testing something—in this case "things not seen." The author's point is that faith is what allows physical beings to both know and test spiritual reality. He removes all doubt of his emphasis in 11:3: "By faith we understand that the universe was created by the word of God, so that what *is seen* was not made out of things that are *visible*" (emphasis mine). Faith is the basis for knowing and testing spiritual truth. Without this faith, "it is impossible to please [God], for whoever would draw near to God must believe that he exists and that he rewards those who seek him" (11:6). No physical person can see God or his rewards, but faith allows true believers to know and have confidence in them even though they cannot experience them with their physical senses; thus, faith allows a believer to "draw near" to God in worship spiritually.

The great "faith chapter" of Hebrews (11) highlights, then, Old Testament saints who exhibited true faith, and several cases specifically express how these saints believed in metaphysical realities that they could not perceive with their physical senses. For example, Noah obeyed God's instructions even though what he was warned of was yet "*unseen*" (11:7). Abraham, too, obeyed God, even though he did not "know where he was going" (11:8); instead, "he was looking forward to the city that has foundations, *whose designer and builder is God*" (11:10), that spiritual kingdom described in 12:18–29. Joseph rested in confidence in a future exodus for the Hebrew people, even though he did not experience it himself (11:22). Moses "left Egypt, not being afraid of the anger of the king, for he endured *as seeing him who is invisible*" (11:27). Even Jesus himself is set up as an example of one who "endured the cross" because he was looking forward to the metaphysical "*joy that was set before him*" (12:2 all emphasis mine). In each of these demonstrations of faith, God's true worshipers did not rely on what they could see or touch—in fact, they never experienced the fulfillment of what they had been promised in this life. Instead "these all died in faith, not having received the things promised, but having seen them and greeted them *from afar*" (11:13); they desired "a *better country*"—not a physical one but "a *heavenly* one" (11:16 all emphasis mine). They did not rely on their physical senses but rather on the only sense that can perceive the spiritual—faith.

Thus, what becomes apparent, as exemplified by this central idea of faith, is that all of these continuities between Old Testament and New Testament worship exist *because they are spiritual realities*. Worship's focus, consequences for refusing it, its attitude, and faith are all spiritual in nature both in Old Testament and New Testament worship. This reveals that ultimately, the essence of worship remains unchanged—worship in both testaments is directed to God on the basis of Christ's sacrifice in faith, exhibiting a reverence toward him, and standing forgiven of the judgment that comes to those who refuse. The change of worship between testaments is not in its essence;

the change occurs in the external forms and experience of worship alone. Everything about worship in the Old Testament that was essentially spiritual remains the same, but none of the physical experience is normative for New Testament worship since those physical shadows have been accomplished in Christ.

Draw Near to God through Christ in the Spirit by Faith
The theology of worship from the book of Hebrews is that Christian worship is drawing near to God through Jesus Christ in the Spirit by faith. Worship for the Christian is at its essence spiritual, for as he worships, he participates spiritually through Jesus Christ in the worship of the heavenly Mount. To borrow a phrase from Paul, Christians worship by faith, not by sight (2 Cor. 5:7).

Yet the admonition for corporate worship in Hebrews is rooted in a hope that one day worship as a spiritual reality will become a physical one: "And let us consider how to stir up one another to love and good works, not neglecting to meet together, as is the habit of some, but encouraging one another, and all the more as you see the Day drawing near" (10:24–25). On that Day the spiritual and the physical will be one; when God the Judge shakes the earth (physical) and the heavens (spiritual), only the "things that cannot be shaken [will] remain. Therefore, let us be grateful for receiving a kingdom that cannot be shaken, and thus let us offer to God acceptable worship, with reverence and awe, for our God is a consuming fire" (12:27–29).

Conclusion to Part Two

The Scriptures of the Old and New Testaments lay the necessary foundation for understanding the nature of Christian worship and evaluating everything that happens in subsequent church history. The Bible establishes the nature of worship as communion with God in his presence and on his terms such that he is magnified. The idea of drawing near to God in worship permeates the storyline of Scripture. It is what Adam and Eve enjoyed as they walked with God in the cool the day (Gen. 2:8). It is described in Exodus 19:17 when Moses "brought the people out of the camp to meet God" at the foot of Mt. Sinai. He had told Pharaoh to let the people go so that they might worship their God in the wilderness, and this is exactly what they intended to do at Sinai. It is what Psalm 100 commands of the Hebrews in Temple worship when it says, "Come into his presence with singing and into his courts with praise." It is what Isaiah experienced as he entered the heavenly throne room of God and saw him high and lifted up. It is what Jesus described in John 4 as "spirit and truth." To draw near to God is to enter his very presence in fellowship and obedience.

Ultimately, this is why God created people. God created the world to put on display the excellencies of his own glory, and he created people therein that they might witness that glory and praise him for it. In Isaiah 43:6–7 God proclaims, "Bring my sons from afar and my daughters from the end of the earth, everyone who is called by my name, whom I created for my glory, whom I formed and made." Likewise, Paul commands in 1 Corinthians 10:31, "Whether you eat, or drink, or whatever you do, do all for the glory of God." Worship—magnifying God's worth and glory—is the reason God made humans.

Adam and Eve's fall into sin—their disobedience of God's commandments—was essentially failure to magnify the worthiness of God to be their master and bring him glory, and thus it was a failure to worship him acceptably. This broke the communion they enjoyed with God and propelled them out from the sanctuary of his presence. After they sinned, and they heard God walking in the garden, "the man and his wife hid themselves from the presence of the Lord God" (Gen. 3:8)—they recognized their unworthiness to walk with him. Their sin created a separation between them and their Creator, and they were forced to leave the sanctuary (Gen. 3:23–24), never again able to draw near to the presence of God. All sin is essentially failure to bring God glory (Rom. 3:23)—it is failure to worship him. This failure creates barriers from drawing near to God in worship, and it brings with it severe punishment: eternal separation from the presence of God in hell. Sin prevents people from drawing near to God in worship; it prevents human beings from doing what they were created to do.

However, worship *is* possible through a sacrifice, the vicarious, substitutionary atonement of the Son of God. Sacrifices in the Mosaic system pictured this kind of atonement, but they were unable to "make perfect those who draw near" (Heb. 10:1). But the sacrifice of Christ's sacrifice can perfect those who draw near. Jesus is fully man, and thus he can stand as our substitute, and he is fully God, and thus he can pay an eternal punishment to an eternal, holy God that no normal man could. And because of the perfection and eternality of this sacrifice, it need not be offered day after day after day to atone for sin; it is offered one time and the complete wrath of God is fully appeased.

This is what God pictured when he slew the animal in the garden and covered Adam and Eve's guilt. This is what was pictured when Moses offered a sacrifice at the foot of Mt. Sinai so that the elders of the people could approach God. This is what was pictured each year in Israel on the Day of Atonement when an animal was sacrificed, and the high priest entered the holy place to sprinkle blood on the mercy seat. This is what was pictured when the seraph took a burning coal from the altar and placed it on Isaiah's lips, saying, "your guilt is taken away, and your sin atoned for."

And this is pictured no more beautifully than with what happened at the moment of Christ's death. The gospel accounts of the crucifixion tell us that Jesus cried out with a loud voice and gave up his spirit, and at that exact moment, the veil of the temple on which the angels guarding the sanctuary of God were embroidered was torn in two, as if that veil was the body of the Son of God himself prohibiting entrance into the presence of a holy God, and that access that had been lost by the fall of man is now restored. There is now a new and living way (Heb. 10:20) to draw near to God, and that way is his Son. Thus, those who repent of their sin—their failure to worship—and put their faith and trust in the sacrifice of Jesus Christ on their behalf are saved from separation from God and enabled once again to draw near to him in worship.

What should be apparent is that the essence of worship is itself the language of the gospel—a drawing near to God in relationship with him, made impossible because of sin that demands eternal judgment, yet restored through the substitutionary atonement of the God-man for those who place their faith in him. The gospel of Jesus Christ makes worship possible. The gospel—the good news of Christ's death on our behalf—is a call for people to return to the reason for their existence; it is a plea to accept the simple truths, repent of failure to worship God aright, and call out for forgiveness.

This is what Christians are called to do as we make disciples of all nations. When Christians preach the gospel, they are proclaiming the worthiness of God to be praised, the inability of sinners to draw near to a holy God, and the forgiveness that is possible

Conclusion to Part Two

through faith in Christ's atoning work. Because this faith in Christ requires belief in facts about Christ and his work and trust in him as Savior and Lord, evangelism requires preaching the gospel: "How then will they call on him in whom they have not believed? And how are they to believe in him of whom they have never heard? And how are they to hear without someone preaching" (Rom. 10:14)?

But corporate worship also proclaims the gospel, not that the sermon and hymns will necessarily always be explicitly evangelistic, but in the act of corporate worship itself. Corporate worship is the public acting out of the spiritual realities of worship; it is a dramatic re-creation of drawing near to God through Christ by faith. Christian worship therefore forms worshipers into those who will live out their Christian faith each day of their lives.

Study Guide for Part Two
People and Terms

anamnēsis
baptism
Benedictus
church
communion
"draw near"
eucharistéō
faith
Feast of Firstfruits
Feast of Unleavened Bread
fraction
Gloria
Holy Spirit
hymn
Immanuel
Judaizers
koinonia
Magnificat
Mt. Gerizim
Nunc Dimittis
ode
"Our Father"
Passover
Pentecost
Pharisees
prosérchomai
psallontes
psalm
Samaritans
Septuagint
"spirit and truth"
synagogue
The Great Commission
The Lord's Supper
Trisagion

Conclusion to Part Two

Recommended Resources

Martin, Ralph P. *Worship in the Early Church*. Revised edition. Grand Rapids: Wm. B. Eerdmans, 1975.
Bradshaw, Paul F. *The Search for the Origins of Christian Worship: Sources and Methods for the Study of Early Liturgy*. New York: Oxford University Press, 2002.
Edersheim, Alfred. *The Temple, Its Ministry and Services as They Were at the Time of Jesus Christ*. Peabody, MA: Hendrickson Publishers, 1994.
Ferguson, Sinclair B. *The Holy Spirit*. Downers Grove, IL: IVP Academic, 1997.
Metzger, Marcel. *History of the Liturgy: The Major Stages*. Collegeville, MN: Liturgical Pr, 1997.
Old, Hughes Oliphant. *The Reading and Preaching of the Scriptures in the Worship of the Christian Church: The Biblical Period*. Grand Rapids: Wm. B. Eerdmans, 1998.
Ross, Allen P. *Recalling the Hope of Glory: Biblical Worship from the Garden to the New Creation*. Grand Rapids: Kregel, 2006.

Questions
1. What is the significance of the "Table" in Hebrew and Christian worship practice?
2. Explain important parallels between Hebrew worship, worship in the New Testament church, and heavenly worship.
3. Based on the New Testament's teaching concerning worship, especially in John 4 and the Book of Hebrews, how would you define the essence of Christian worship?

PART THREE: CATHOLIC CHRISTIANITY

Let all mortal flesh keep silence,
and with fear and trembling stand;
ponder nothing earthly minded,
for with blessing in His hand
Christ our God to earth descendeth,
our full homage to demand.

King of kings, yet born of Mary,
as of old on earth He stood,
Lord of lords, in human vesture -
in the body and the blood.
He will give to all the faithful
His own self for heavenly food.

Rank on rank the host of heaven
spreads its vanguard on the way,
as the Light of light descendeth
from the realms of endless day,
that the pow'rs of hell may vanish
as the darkness clears away.

At His feet the six-winged seraph,
cherubim, with sleepless eye,
veil their faces to the Presence,
as with ceaseless voice they cry,
"Alleluia, alleluia!
Alleluia, Lord most high!"

—*Liturgy of St. James*, 4th century

Chapter 8
The Early Church

After the close of the New Testament Scriptures, details concerning how, exactly, Christians worshiped are somewhat difficult to determine. However, several early documents do help to elucidate some of what characterized church gatherings. These include letters from important church leaders like Clement of Rome (35–99 AD), Ignatius in Antioch (c. 35–107), Polycarp (c. 69–155), Clement of Alexandria (c. 150–c. 215), and Justin Martyr's *Apology* (c. 155), an early defense of Christianity. Also, early church orders, documents that gave instructions to new converts and described early baptismal services, help to paint a picture of early Christian worship services. Whether these orders were prescriptive or descriptive is difficult to determine, and they would not have been necessarily indicative of a uniformity in worship during the first three centuries of the church. However, similarity and even direct quotation between various church orders as well as evidence of correspondence between churches during this period establish credibility for these documents as at least instructive concerning how early Christians likely worshiped. The earliest of these is called the *Didache* (Greek for "Teaching"), likely written in the early second century around Antioch.[1] It contained teaching concerning moral living as well as instructions regarding worship practices like baptism, the eucharist, and other aspects of Christian worship. Another Antiochene church order from the third century, the *Didascalia Apostolorum*, was clearly modeled after the *Didache*, expanding its instructions concerning worship. The *Apostolic Tradition* may have come from Rome in the third century as well. Finally, a letter from Pliny the Younger, governor of Pontus and Bithynia, written to Emperor Trajan in 112 AD, provides a helpful description of early Christian practice:

> But they declared that the sum of their guilt or error had amounted only to this, that on an appointed day they had been accustomed to meet before daybreak, and to recite a hymn antiphonally to Christ, as to a god, and to bind themselves by oath, not for the commission of any crime but to abstain from committing theft, robbery, adultery, and breach of faith, and not to deny a deposit when it was claimed. After the conclusion of this ceremony it was their custom to depart and meet again to take food, but it was ordinary and harmless food.[2]

---

[1] See Paul F. Bradshaw, *The Search for the Origins of Christian Worship: Sources and Methods for the Study of Early Liturgy* (New York: Oxford University Press, 2002); Marcel Metzger, *History of the Liturgy: The Major Stages* (Collegeville, MN: Liturgical Press, 1997), 17.

[2] Pliny the Younger, *Letter 10*, c. 112, in Henry Bettenson and Chris Maunder, eds., *Documents of the Christian Church*, 4th ed. (New York: Oxford University Press, 2011), 4.

Though none of these documents can prove with certainty how the services were conducted, and there would not have necessarily been uniformity among the various early churches in worship, we can nevertheless discern a few key elements of early worship.

The Lord's Day

First, an early second-century letter from Ignatius, one of the first pastors of the Church in Antioch, helps to solidify that the first day of the week became for Christians their primary day of worship and that they referred to it as "the Lord's Day." The phrase "Lord's Day" appears only once in the New Testament in Revelation 1:10, where the particular day John is referencing is unclear. However, Ignatius was a disciple of Polycarp, who was a disciple of John himself; thus, since Ignatius explicitly identifies "the Lord's Day" as that day "on which our life as well as theirs shone forth,"[3] John's more ambiguous reference appears more certain to describe the first day of the week as a special, dedicated sacred day. The *Didache* also states, "On every Lord's Day—his special day—come together and break bread and give thanks,"[4] and the early second century *Epistle of Barnabas* states, "Wherefore we also celebrate with gladness the eighth day in which Jesus also rose from the dead."[5] Similarly, Justin Martyr describes Christian gatherings as such: "And on the day called Sunday, all who live in cities or in the country gather together to one place." Justin also presents a full explanation for why this day became significant for Christians:

> We all hold this common gathering on Sunday, since it is the first day, on which God transforming darkness and matter made the universe, and Jesus Christ our Savior rose from the dead on the same day.[6]

At the close of the second century, Tertullian (160–220 AD) observed, "we make Sunday a day of festivity,"[7] a day he specifically calls "the Lord's Day,"[8] and Clement of Alexandria stated that a true Christian, "in fulfilment of the precept, according to the

---

[3] Ignatius, *To the Magnesians*, IX, c. 115, in James F. White, *Documents of Christian Worship: Descriptive and Interpretive Sources* (Louisville, KY: Westminster John Knox Press, 2007), 19.
[4] *The Didache*, XIV, c. 120, in White, *Documents of Christian Worship*, 18.
[5] *The Epistle of Barnabas*, XV, 8–9, c. 100, in White, *Documents of Christian Worship*, 19.
[6] Justin Martyr, *First Apology*, LXVII, c. 155, in White, *Documents of Christian Worship*, 19.
[7] Tertullian, *Ad Nationes*, I:XIII, 197, in Alexander Roberts, James Donaldson, and A. Cleveland Coxe, eds., *Latin Christianity: Its Founder, Tertullian*, vol. 3, The Ante-Nicene Fathers (Buffalo, NY: Christian Literature Company, 1885), 123.
[8] Tertullian, *The Chaplet*, III, in Roberts, Donaldson, and Coxe, *Latin Christianity: Its Founder, Tertullian*, 3:94.

Gospel, keeps the Lord's day, when he abandons an evil disposition, ... glorifying the Lord's resurrection in himself."[9]

Initiation

Entrance into church membership through baptism developed early a preceding time of catechesis for the new believers, which included fasting, instruction on holy living and doctrine, and examination by church leadership. According to Irenaeus (c. 130–c. 202), the central purpose of this time of preparation was "renewing [new believers] from their old habits into the newness of Christ."[10] Church leaders recognized that since new converts were coming from lives accustomed to pagan idolatry and licentious living, they needed to form new practices that would nurture holiness and purity. This formation involved receiving instruction concerning biblical teaching, of course, but it also explains the requirement of fasting and other practices prescribed for the catechumens. This also may account for the beginning of making the sign of the cross, as Tertullian described it: "In all the ordinary occasions of life we furrow our foreheads with the sign of the Cross, in which we glory none the less because it is regarded as our shame by the heathen in presence of whom it is a profession of our faith."[11] Regularly practicing the symbolic gesture would serve to remind Christians of their relationship to Christ and that they have died to sin, helping them to sanctify even the mundane moments of life and to reject their old sinful habits and pursue righteousness. Later, the *Apostolic Tradition* urged catechumens to follow this practice.[12]

As mentioned earlier, church orders may have been compiled for the very purpose of offering instruction to catechumens concerning proper Christian living, and thus they also included instructions for the baptismal service and eucharist to follow. During this period, catechumens were admitted to the first part of worship services in which the Scriptures were read and taught, but they were dismissed prior to celebrating the Lord's Supper since they were not yet in communion with the body. Thus began a distinction between the Service of the Word, sometimes referred to also as the Service of the Catechumenate, and the Service of the Table, sometimes called the Service of the Faithful, separated by a dismissal, from which derives the term "mass."

---

[9] Clement of Alexandria, *Miscellanies*, VII:XII, in Alexander Roberts, James Donaldson, and A. Cleveland Coxe, eds., *Fathers of the Second Century*, vol. 2, The Ante-Nicene Fathers (Buffalo, NT: Christian Literature Company, 1885), 545.

[10] Irenaeus, *Against Heresies*, III:XVII, in Alexander Roberts, James Donaldson, and A. Cleveland Coxe, eds., *The Apostolic Fathers with Justin Martyr and Irenaeus*, vol. 1, The Ante-Nicene Fathers (Buffalo, NY: Christian Literature Company, 1), 444.

[11] Tertullian, *The Chaplet*, 103.

[12] Alexander Roberts, James Donaldson, and A. Cleveland Coxe, eds., *Fathers of the Third Century*, vol. 5, The Ante-Nicene Fathers (Buffalo, NY: Christian Literature Company, 1886), 258.

The period of catechesis spanned anywhere from a few weeks to forty days (corresponding to Christ's forty days of preparation in the wilderness) and climaxed with the baptism, followed by a eucharistic service with the new members. The *Didache* prescribes concerning baptism,

> Baptize in running water, the name of the Father, and of Son, and of the Holy Spirit. If you do not have running water, baptize in some other. If you cannot in cold, then in warm. If you have neither, then pour water on the head three times in the name of the Father, Son, and Holy Spirit. Before the baptism, moreover, the one who baptizes and the one baptized must fast, and any others who can. And you must tell the one being baptized to fast for one or two days beforehand.[13]

Scholarly consensus agrees that baptism in the New Testament and early church would have been full immersion in water,[14] but as is evident in the *Didache*, baptism by pouring appears to have been practiced if no running water was available.

A part of the baptismal ceremony, as described by Tertullian,[15] candidates performed vows denouncing their old life and affirming their new:

> I renounce Satan and his works and his pomps and his worship and his angels and his inventions and all things that are under him. And I associate myself to Christ and believe and am baptized into one unbegotten being.

They also affirmed agreement with core Christian doctrine. What has come to be called the "Apostles' Creed" was likely formulated for this purpose:

> I believe in God, the Father almighty, Creator of heaven and earth,
> and in Jesus Christ, his only Son, our Lord,
> who was conceived by the Holy Spirit, born of the virgin Mary,
> suffered under Pontius Pilate, was crucified, died, and was buried;
> he descended into hell; on the third day he rose again from the dead;
> he ascended into heaven,
> and is seated at the right hand of God the Father almighty;
> from there he will come to judge the living and the dead.
> I believe in the Holy Spirit, the holy catholic church,
> the communion of saints, the forgiveness of sins,
> the resurrection of the body, and life everlasting. Amen.

---

[13] White, *Documents of Christian Worship*, 147.

[14] Angelo Di Berardino, ed., *We Believe in One Holy Catholic and Apostolic Church*, vol. 5, Ancient Christian Doctrine (Downers Grove: Inter-Varsity Press, 2010), 88.

[15] Roberts, Donaldson, and Coxe, *Latin Christianity: Its Founder, Tertullian*, 3:103.

The Early Church

The pastor or deacon would then baptize the candidate, reciting the baptismal formula from Matthew 28:19: "in the name of the Father and of the Son and of the Holy Spirit." A second-century hymn, known later by its Latin title *Gloria Patri*, may have been composed for this purpose:

> Glory be to the Father
> and to the Son and to the Holy Spirit,
> as it was in the beginning,
> is now, and ever shall be,
> world without end. Amen.

Justin Martyr provides the first description of how the church viewed the newly baptized Christian:

> We, however, after thus washing the one who has been convinced and signified his assent, lead him to those who are called brethren, where they are assembled. They then earnestly offer common prayers for themselves and the one who has been illuminated and all others everywhere, that we may be made worthy, having learned the truth, to be found in deed good citizens and keepers of what is commanded, so that we may be saved with eternal salvation. On finishing the prayers we greet each other with a kiss.[16]

Initially, only adults were permitted to progress through catechesis to baptism since children were considered too young to fully understand the significance of what it meant to commit to the Christian faith. However, Christian parents became increasingly concerned for the eternal condition of their children, especially in a time when infant mortality rates were rather high. Thus, some churches began baptizing children as early as the third century, believing that the act would save them from hell if they died, and the practice of baptizing even infants became widely established by the sixth century.[17]

Early Liturgy

Most scholars would agree that the earliest church services began as a natural extension of Jewish synagogue practice with some Christian elements added. Since the earliest Christians were Jews, this would have been only natural. You will recall that synagogue services consisted of three primary elements: reading the Scriptures, instruction from the Scriptures, and the prayers. The earliest church meetings consisted of simple instruction from the Scriptures and prayer, just like the synagogue, but as Acts

---

[16] White, *Documents of Christian Worship*, 148.
[17] Paul B. Newman, *Growing Up in the Middle Ages* (Jefferson, N.C: McFarland, 2007), 22.

2:42 described, Christians added another significant component, "the breaking of bread." Indeed, the Lord himself had commanded them to observe the breaking of bread "in remembrance (*anamnesis*) of him" (1 Cor. 11:24). And so, along with the Service of the Word borrowed from synagogue practice, early Christians added a Service of the Table in which they commemorated Christ's death on their behalf. We know from the New Testament that Christians "broke bread" together in this way, and we even have a description in 1 Corinthians 11 of what they did when they gathered. Paul commanded churches to (1) take bread, (2) give thanks (*eucharisteō*), (3) break it, and (4) consume it, repeating the same steps for the cup (replacing breaking with pouring). The Service of the Word, based on the synagogue, and the Service of the Table, comprised of these four steps from 1 Corinthians, came to characterize early Christian worship.

Several early documents also describe what Christians did when they gathered on the Lord's Day. Pliny states that the Christians "had been accustomed to meet before daybreak, and to recite a hymn antiphonally to Christ, as to a god." They later gathered again "to take food, but it was ordinary and harmless food,"[83] likely referring to the eucharist. The *Didache* and Justin Martyr's *Apology* give much more details. Of the Lord's Supper, the order insists, "You must not let anyone eat or drink of your Eucharist except those baptized in the Lord's name." Before partaking of the meal, believers should come together "confessing your sins so that your sacrifice may be pure." It also prescribes a prayer of thanks for the cup, the "broken bread," and after eating:

> We thank you, our Father, for the holy vine of David, your child, which you have revealed through Jesus, your child. To you be glory forever.
>
> We thank you, our Father, for the life and knowledge which you have revealed through Jesus, your child. To you be glory forever. As this piece of bread was scattered over the hills and then was brought together and made one, so let your Church be brought together from the ends of the earth into your Kingdom. For yours is the glory and the power through Jesus Christ forever.
>
> We thank you, holy Father, for your sacred name which you have lodged in our hearts, and for the knowledge and faith and immortality which you have revealed through Jesus, your child. To you be glory forever. Almighty Master, you have created everything for the sake of your name, and have given men food and drink to enjoy that they may thank you. But to us you have given spiritual food and drink and eternal life through Jesus, your child. Above all, we thank you that you are mighty. To you be glory forever. Remember, Lord, your Church, to save it from all evil and to make it perfect by your love. Make it holy, and gather it together from the four winds into your Kingdom which you have made ready for it. For yours is the power and the glory forever. Let Grace come

and let this world pass away. Hosanna to the God of David! If anyone is holy, let him come. If not, let him repent. Our Lord, come! Amen.[18]

This early Eucharistic prayer is significant since it sets a pattern for the development of others to follow. A modern version of the final section of the prayer is a hymn translation by Bland Tucker (1941):

> Father, we thank Thee who hast planted
> Thy holy Name within our hearts.
> Knowledge and faith and life immortal
> Jesus Thy Son to us imparts.
> Thou, Lord, didst make all for Thy pleasure,
> didst give man food for all his days,
> giving in Christ the Bread eternal;
> Thine is the pow'r, be Thine the praise.
> Watch o'er Thy church, O Lord, in mercy,
> save it from evil, guard it still.
> Perfect it in Thy love, unite it,
> cleansed and conformed unto Thy will.
> As grain, once scattered on the hillsides,
> was in this broken bread made one,
> so from all lands Thy church be gathered
> into Thy kingdom by Thy Son.

Thus, early Christian liturgy as expressed in the *Didache* could be summarized this way:

Service of the Word
Reading of the Scriptures
Sermon
Prayers

Service of the Table
Presentation of the Elements
Prayer of Thanks
Partaking of Communion

Justin Martyr's *Apology* gives a fuller picture of an entire service. When Christians meet on Sunday, Justin describes,

---

[18] White, *Documents of Christian Worship*, 182–183.

the memoirs of the apostles or the writings of the prophets are read as long as time permits. When the reader has finished, the president in a discourse urges and invites [us] to the imitation of these noble things. Then we all stand up together and offer prayers."[19]

This accounts for the three worship practices the early church carried over from the synagogue: Scripture reading, a sermon, and the prayers. Following these prayers, Justin describes the Lord's Supper. First, the believers "greet each another with a kiss," a public expression of their communion together as the body of Christ. The bread and "a cup of water and mixed wine" are then brought forward, and the minister "sends up praise and glory to the Father of the universe through the name of the Son and of the Holy Spirit and offers thanksgiving at some length that we have been deemed worthy to receive these things from him," to which all the people assent with "Amen." The deacons then distribute the bread and wine to the congregation. Finally, "Those who prosper, and who so wish, contribute, each one as much as he chooses to. What is collected is deposited with the president, and he takes care of orphans and widows, and those who are in want on account of sickness or any other cause."[100] Justin explains the significance of this meal for Christians:

> This food we call Eucharist, of which no one is allowed to partake except one who believes that the things we teach are true, and has received the washing for forgiveness of sins and for rebirth, birth, and who lives as Christ handed down to us. For we do not receive these things as common bread or common drink; but as Jesus Christ our Savior being incarnate by God's word took flesh and blood for our salvation, so also we have been taught that the food consecrated by the word of prayer which comes from him, from which our flesh and blood are nourished by transformation, is the flesh and blood of that incarnate Jesus.[20]

Tertullian's *Apology* (c. 197) corroborates the elements of early worship, particularly the Service of the Word. He first notes that Christians gather for prayer: "We meet together as an assembly and congregation, that, offering up prayer to God as with united force, we may wrestle with Him in our supplications." Next, he describes the attention given to Scripture:

> We assemble to read our sacred writings, if any peculiarity of the times makes either forewarning or reminiscence needful. However it be in that respect, with the sacred words we nourish our faith, we animate our hope, we make our confidence more steadfast; and no less by inculcations of God's precepts we confirm

---

[19] White, *Documents of Christian Worship*, 101.
[20] White, *Documents of Christian Worship*, 184–186.

The Early Church

good habits. In the same place also exhortations are made, rebukes and sacred censures are administered.[102]

He further notes that "if he likes, each puts in a small donation; but only if it be his pleasure, and only if he be able," which is disbursed "to support and bury poor people, to supply the wants of boys and girls destitute of means and parents, and of old persons confined now to the house; such, too, as have suffered shipwreck; and if there happen to be any in the mines, or banished to the islands, or shut up in the prisons, for nothing but their fidelity to the cause of God's Church, they become the nurslings of their confession."[21]

The *Apostolic Tradition* (Rome, c. 215) describes an even more expanded liturgy for the celebration of the eucharist. It begins with the "offering," a presentation of the bread and cup to the bishop, followed by the "Salutation":

Bishop: "The Lord be with you."
And all shall say: "And with your spirit."

The "*Sursum Corda*" ("Up hearts") immediately followed:

Bishop: "Lift up your hearts."
All: "We lift them up to the Lord."
Bishop: "Let us give thanks to the Lord our God."
All: "It is fitting and right."

This statement reminded the worshipers that as they drew near to the table, they were actually joining worship in heaven through Christ. Cyprian of Carthage (c. 200–258) is among the earliest to explain the practical significance of this liturgical act:

Moreover, when we stand praying, beloved brethren, we ought to be watchful and earnest with our whole heart, intent on our prayers. Let all carnal and worldly thoughts pass away, nor let the soul at that time think on anything but the object only of its prayer. For this reason also the priest, by way of preface before his prayer, prepares the minds of the brethren by saying, "Lift up your hearts," that so upon the people's response, "We lift them up unto the Lord," he may be reminded that he himself ought to think of nothing but the Lord.[22]

Likewise, Cyril of Jerusalem (313–386 AD) later discussed the theological import of this portion of the liturgy:

---

[21] Roberts, Donaldson, and Coxe, *Latin Christianity: Its Founder, Tertullian*, 3:46.
[22] Cyprian of Carthage, *On the Lord's Prayer*, in Roberts, Donaldson, and Coxe, *Fathers of the Third Century*, 1886, 5:455.

For truly ought we in that most awful hour to have our heart on high with God, and not below, thinking of earth and earthly things. In effect therefore the Priest bids all in that hour to dismiss all cares of this life, or household anxieties, and to have their heart in heaven with the merciful God. ... But let no one come here, who could say with his mouth, "We lift up our hearts unto the Lord," but in his thoughts have his mind concerned with the cares of this life.[23]

This "Preface" initiated the formal eucharistic prayer, which the *Apostolic Tradition* begins with "We render thanks to you, O God ..." The prayer itself expands the elements found in early prayers:

We render thanks to you, O God, through your beloved servant Jesus Christ, whom in the last times you sent to us as a savior and redeemer and angel of your will; who is your inseparable Word, through whom you made all things, and in whom you were well pleased. You sent him from heaven into a virgin's womb; and conceived in the womb, he was made flesh and was manifested as your Son, being born of the Holy Spirit and the Virgin. Fulfilling your will and gaining for you a holy people, he stretched out his hands when he should suffer, that he might release from suffering those who have believed in you.

And when he was betrayed to voluntary suffering that he might destroy death, and break the bonds of the devil, and tread down hell, and shine upon the righteous, and fix a term, and manifest the resurrection, he took bread and gave thanks to you, saying, "Take, eat; this is my body, which shall be broken for you." Likewise also the cup, saying, "This is my blood, which is shed for you; when you do this, you make my remembrance."

Remembering therefore his death and resurrection, we offer to you the bread and the cup, giving you thanks because you have held us worthy to stand before you and minister to you.

And we ask that you would send your Holy Spirit upon the offering of your holy Church; that, gathering her into one, you would grant to all who receive the holy things (to receive) for the fullness of the Holy Spirit for the strengthening of faith in truth; that we may praise and glorify you through your child Jesus Christ; through whom be glory and honor to you, to the Father and the Son, with the Holy Spirit, in your holy Church, both now and to the ages of ages. Amen.[24]

This prayer contains what would later be called *anamnesis*, the "remembrance" of God's works in redemption, the "Words of Institution" from the New Testament, and

---

[23] Cyril of Jerusalem, *Catechetical Lectures*, XXIII, in Philip Schaff and Henry Wace, eds., *S. Cyril of Jerusalem, S. Gregory of Nazianzen*, vol. 7, A Select Library of the Nicene and Post-Nicene Fathers of the Christian Church, Second (New York: Christian Literature Company, 1894), 153–154.

[24] R. C. D. Jasper and G. J. Cuming, *Prayers of the Eucharist: Early and Reformed*, ed. Paul F. Bradshaw and Maxwell E. Johnson, Fourth (Collegeville, MN: Liturgical Press Academic, 2019), 47–48.

epiclesis, "invocation" of the Holy Spirit's blessing. The instructions explicitly state that this prayer is a model and not prescriptive; the bishop may "pray according to his ability."

Thus by the third century, the basic form of the liturgy was consistent with New Testament practice, with the eucharistic prayer receiving the most significant attention and expansion:

Service of the Word
Reading of the Scriptures
Sermon
Prayers

Service of the Table
Presentation of the Elements
Prayer of Thanks
    Salutation
    Sursum Corda
    "We render thanks ..."
    Anamnesis
    Words of Institution
    Epiclesis
    Doxology
Partaking of Communion

Daily Prayer
Emerging from the example of Old Testament Jewish practice (e.g., Ps. 55:17; Dan. 6:10) and continued by Jesus (Mark 1:35; 6:46) and the apostles (Acts 10:3, 9; 16:25) in the New Testament, early Christians began the habit of daily communal prayer, typically both in the morning and evening, and sometimes three times a day. In his treatise *On Prayer*, Tertullian advocated praying "not less than thrice in the day" at the third (sunrise), sixth (noon), and ninth (sunset) hours of the day.[25] Likewise, commenting on the Lord's Prayer, Cyprian observed,

> For both the first hour in its progress to the third shows forth the consummated number of the Trinity, and also the fourth proceeding to the sixth declares another Trinity; and when from the seventh the ninth is completed, the perfect Trinity is numbered every three hours, which spaces of hours the worshippers of God in time past having spiritually decided on, made use of for determined and lawful times for prayer. And subsequently the thing was manifested, that

---

[25] Tertullian, *On Prayer*, XXV, in Roberts, Donaldson, and Coxe, *Latin Christianity: Its Founder, Tertullian*, 3:690.

these things were of old Sacraments, in that anciently righteous men prayed in this manner.[26]

Like with Jewish practice, daily prayers included the reading of Scripture and chanting of psalms and, eventually, other extra-biblical hymn texts. Both the prayers and these newly composed hymns often focused on the subject of light since the morning and evening prayers corresponded to the rising and setting of the sun. An example of an evening prayer comes from the *Apostolic Tradition*:

> We give thanks to you, O God, through your Son Jesus Christ our Lord, because you have enlightened us by revealing the incorruptible light. Therefore, having finished the length of a day, and arriving at the beginning of the night, and having been satisfied with the light of the day which you created for our satisfaction, and since we now do not lack a light for the evening through your grace, we sanctify you and glorify you, through your only Son our Lord Jesus Christ, through whom to you with him be glory and might and honor with the Holy Spirit, now and always, and throughout the ages of the ages. Amen.[27]

An example of an evening hymn is the late second-century Greek *Phos Hilaron*:

> O gladsome Light, O Grace
> of God the Father's face,
> th'eternal splendor wearing;
> celestial, holy, blest,
> our Savior Jesus Christ,
> joyful in Thine appearing.
>
> Now, as day fadeth quite
> we see the evening light,
> our wonted hymn outpouring;
> Father of might unknown,
> Thee, His incarnate Son,
> and Holy Ghost adoring.
>
> To Thee of right belongs
> all praise of holy songs,
> O Son of God, Life-giver;
> Thee, therefore, O Most High,

---

[26] Cyprian of Carthage, *On the Lord's Prayer*, in Roberts, Donaldson, and Coxe, *Fathers of the Third Century*, 1886, 5:456–457.
[27] *The Apostolic Tradition of St. Hippolytus of Rome*, ed. G. Dix (London: S.P.C.K), 51.

the world does glorify
and shall exalt forever.[28]

Singing

Singing in the early church was naturally an extension of Hebrew singing, and thus it had the same general characteristics of singing in Jewish practice. Pliny's letter confirms that early Christians were known to "recite a hymn antiphonally to Christ, as to a god," and Tertullian attested to this as well.[29] Like Jews, early Christians would not necessarily have considered singing as a separate element of worship unto itself, but they rather viewed singing as a way to recite Scripture and offer prayers.

Like synagogue worship, early Christian worship had no instrumental accompaniment, a practice that would have certainly continued as persecution heightened and churches were forced underground. As churches spread, they continued to universally nurture the psalms that had been handed down to them. Furthermore, early Christians composed new hymn texts and cultivated poetic and musical forms consistent with what they inherited. The earliest known hymns were doctrinally rich, often centered on Christological truth, such as an early hymn written by Ignatius of Antioch:

Very flesh, yet Spirit too;
Uncreated, and yet born;
God-and-Man in One agreed
Very-Life-in-Death indeed,
Fruit of God and Mary's seed;
At once impassable and torn
By pain and suffering here below:
Jesus Christ, whom as our Lord we know.[30]

Their musical forms were borrowed from Jewish singing and thus continued in character. In fact, scholars have noted a remarkable similarity between extant melodies from Jewish worship and later Christian chant tunes.[31] Known as plain chant, this early form of Christian singing was modest, church leaders unanimous in their warnings against what Clement of Alexandria described as "extravagant" music in worship. Rather, Clement argued that the church's song should employ "temperate harmonies."[32]

---

[28] Translation, Robert S. Bridges, 1899.
[29] Tertullian, *Apology*, in Roberts, Donaldson, and Coxe, *Latin Christianity: Its Founder, Tertullian*, 3:47.
[30] Ignatius of Antioch, *Epistle to the Ephesians*, trans. Maxwell Staniforth, *Early Christian Writings: The Apostolic Fathers* (New York: Penguin Books, 1986), 63.
[31] Sendrey, *Music in Ancient Israel*, 231–232.
[32] Clement of Alexandria, *Paidagogos* 2, 4 in Johannes Quasten, *Music and Worship in Pagan and Christian Antiquity* (Washington, DC: National Association of Pastoral Musicians, 1983), 68.

This emphasis on modesty in worship music stood in contrast to the pagan worship of the day. Calvin Stapert describes the character of Greek and Roman worship:

> But most of them featured ecstatic, even frenzied and orgiastic, rites. Ecstatic rituals were not uncommon in Greek and Roman societies, going back centuries before the Christian era. The rituals associated with the worship of Dionysus or his Roman equivalent, Bacchus, are the classic examples of this type. Drunken revelry, wild music, frenzied dancing, and flagellation and mutilation were their hallmarks.[33]

Church leaders soundly condemned the pagan musical forms of the culture in which they lived, what James McKinnon characterizes as "vehemence and uniformity."[34] Of this, Stapert observes,

> The uniformity is especially striking considering how different those writers were in other respects. Whether they were Greek-speaking or Latin-speaking, pre- or post-Constantine, conciliatory or antagonistic toward pagan learning, lifelong Christians or converts—whatever their background or personality, they agreed that Christians should distance themselves from some of the music of the surrounding culture.[35]

This rejection of pagan music also led most church leaders to renounce any instrumental accompaniment as well. Clement insisted, "when a man occupies his time with flutes, stringed instruments, choirs, dancing, Egyptian krotala, and other such improper frivolities, he will find that indecency and rudeness are the consequences."[36] They rejected instruments altogether for two reasons: First, they did not want to associate themselves with pagan worship practices. But even more importantly, they believed that the particular instruments used in pagan worship, for the most part, shaped the worshipers in evil ways, such as Clement's comment that the sounds of the instruments led to "indecency and rudeness."[37]

The Liturgical Calendar

The first annual liturgical celebration to emerge among early Christians was understandably that of the death and resurrection of Christ, which early on would have

---

[33] Stapert, *New Song for an Old World*, 135.

[34] James McKinnon, *The Temple, the Church Fathers and Early Western Chant* (Brookfield: Ashgate Publishing, 1998), 69.

[35] Stapert, *New Song for an Old World*, 131.

[36] Clement, *Paidagogos* in Quasten, *Music and Worship in Pagan and Christian Antiquity*, 61.

[37] *Paidagogos* 2, 4 (GCS Clem. I 184 Stählin) in Johannes Quasten, *Music and Worship in Pagan and Christian Antiquity* (Washington, D.C.: National Association of Pastoral Musicians, 1983), 61.

corresponded in time with the Jewish Passover. Often this celebration became the time when new converts were baptized, as Tertullian noted: "The Passover affords a more than usually solemn day for baptism; when, withal, the Lord's passion, in which we are baptized, was completed."[38] Over time, Christian leaders debated whether the resurrection of Christ should always be celebrated on Sunday or if it should correspond to the Jewish Passover, which was determined by the new moon and therefore occurred on different weekdays each year. Eventually, of course, those who argued that it should always fall on Sunday won.

Sacrament

Like ancient Israel, early Christians considered worship on the Lord's Day to be sacred—set apart from the regular, mundane activities of life, and therefore what took place in corporate worship was also sacred. This day was "the Lord's" in a way different from all other days, and the eucharist was a table belonging to the Lord—"the Lord's Table"—in a manner distinct from other tables. The word that emerged to describe the sacred nature of these things was "sacrament." This term comes from the Latin word *sacramentum*, which referred to an oath of allegiance, which itself came from the term *sacrare*, which mean "to consecrate." Notably, this is the very idea Pliny employs to describe what Christians do when they gather, observing that they meet "to bind themselves by an oath." This concept fittingly described both baptism and the Lord's Supper, sacred oaths taken in entrance to and continual communion with the body of Christ. Likely the first to use the term "sacrament" for both baptism and the Lord's Supper was Tertullian.[39] He suggested that in the eucharist, the bread represents (Latin, *repraesentare*) and is the "figuring" (Latin, *figurare*) of Christ's body. Later in his Latin translation of the Greek New Testament, Jerome would use the word *sacramentum* to translate the Greek word *mysterion* ("mystery"),[40] early Christians considering baptism and the Lord's Supper to be mysteries, and Augustine (354–430) would later define a sacrament as "the visible form of an invisible grace."[41]

---

[38] Tertullian, *On Baptism*, in Roberts, Donaldson, and Coxe, *Latin Christianity: Its Founder, Tertullian*, 3:678.
[39] Tertullian, *The Five Books Against Marcion*, in Roberts, Donaldson, and Coxe, *Latin Christianity: Its Founder, Tertullian*, 3:319–474.
[40] Theodore B. Foster, "'Mysterium' and 'Sacramentum' in the Vulgate and Old Latin Versions," *The American Journal of Theology* 19, no. 3 (July 1915).
[41] Augustine, *Questions on the Heptateuch*, III, 84 (c. 410), in White, *Documents of Christian Worship*, 120.

Chapter 9
The Expansion of Worship

The legalization of Christianity by Roman Emperor Constantine I (272–337) in 313 with his Edict of Milan marked the beginning of a period lasting up to the Reformation and Enlightenment that some call "Christendom." Religious toleration in the empire created conditions for the freedom and growth of Christianity to be sure, but when in 391 Emperor Theodosius I made Christianity the Roman Empire's official religion and in the following year outlawed any form of pagan worship, the church began to be the controlling influence in the entirety of the empire.

This shifted what had once been a severely persecuted church to the center of western society, eventually leading to what many believed to be a "Christian civilization." From an evangelical perspective, the dominance of Christian thought during this period had some positive results culturally and even theologically, including for corporate worship. First, persecution against Christians ceased, allowing for freedom of worship, which also provided for the expansion of the liturgy. Additionally, pagan influence over the broader culture was progressively limited, and the church was granted more moral impact in the society at large. Constantine declared Sunday to be an official day of rest, forbidding merchants to trade and closing administrative offices. Since financial support for the church began to be raised through mandatory taxes, this allowed church leadership to shape worship based on what they believed to be best rather than on popular opinion. In fact, the church began to dictate popular opinion; Christianity permeated all of life, including the cultural and artistic endeavors of broader society. Individuals during this period continued to hold a worldview in which they considered reality to be outside themselves—they were part of something larger and transcendent, and the world in which they lived was marked by sin and frailty. Yet the increasing Christian influence provided people a revelation from the Creator of that reality that gave them some hope and direction for life. Thus, they interpreted all of life in its relationship to Scripture and the Church. In other words, to a large extent, Christianity began to be the dominant influence over the worldview and theology of western civilization and thus created the cultural conditions for developing reverent, ceremonial worship and cultivated high art. As Faulkner notes, "The church's liturgy, therefore, was splendid, ceremonial, and ritualistic in part because it was considered to be the divinely revealed earthly counterpart of the worship of God in heaven."[1]

---

[1] Faulkner, *Wiser Than Despair*, 89.

However, these same freedoms and benefits also created conditions for problems to develop. Because Emperor Constantine confessed himself to be a Christian and Theodosius later made Christianity the official religion of the empire, significant numbers of people now began to attend church and identify with Christianity, many of whom had never truly converted. In one sense this was positive—scores of people were now exposed to the Word of God; but it also led to many people believing that citizenship in the empire equated with being a Christian, removing the necessity for sincere personal faith in Christ. It also caused difficulties for church leaders. For one thing, they had to find buildings large enough to accommodate all the people, and thus they procured basilicas originally used as public Roman buildings. What were once simple worship services became elaborate ceremonies in these much larger buildings with bigger congregations. This contributed to a measure of appropriate reverence for the transcendence of God, but often neglected the immanent, personal nature of God communicated in Scripture. Whereas smaller churches exercised a certain measure of flexibility in liturgy, although certain elements between churches would have been the same, now liturgies began to be prescribed. A significant reason for this was the fact that, in order to accommodate the larger congregations, ministers were ordained to serve sometimes without necessary training; thus, theologically educated church leaders prescribed liturgies for the untrained ministers in order to keep them orthodox. Religious freedom, certainly desirable for Christians, also left room for heresy; therefore, eventually church leaders attempted a uniformity of worship practice and creed in order to stem the tide of heresy. Over time, this emerged as a standardized hierarchy of bishops, priests, and deacons and a strict clergy/laity distinction. Further, in an attempt to mimic the worship of heaven, an emphasis on absolute perfection in the liturgy gradually minimized openness by the leadership for "lay" participation. The clergy eventually became mediators between God and the laity, offering acts of worship on behalf of the people.

Liturgy
Much of early Christian worship drew its warrant from explicit New Testament teaching or example and grew organically over time. However, with the new freedoms and growth of worshiping congregations, practices that had begun to develop earlier took new and expanded shape. As Bradshaw notes,

> The so-called Constantinian revolution did not so much inaugurate new liturgical practices and attitudes as create conditions in which some pre-existent

The Expansion of Worship

customs could achieve a greater measure of preeminence than others which were no longer considered appropriate to the changed situation of the church.[2]

Further, very early there appears to be some acceptance of ecclesial tradition as instructive, if not absolutely authoritative, for the practices of Christian worship, especially as the church grew in influence. For example, writing in the mid-fourth century, Basil the Great (c. 329–379) argued the importance of oral tradition in transmitting liturgical practices:

> Concerning the teachings of the Church, whether publicly proclaimed or reserved to members of the household of faith, we have received some from written sources, while others have been given to us secretly, through apostolic tradition. ... For instance (to take the first and most common example), where is the written teaching that we should sign with the sign of the Cross those who, trusting in the Name of Our Lord Jesus Christ, are to be enrolled as catechumens? Which book teaches us to pray facing the East? Have any saints left for us in writing the words to be used in the invocation over the Eucharistic bread and the cup of blessing? As everyone knows, we are not content in the liturgy simply to recite the words recorded by St. Paul and the Gospels, but we add other words both before and after, words of great importance for this mystery. We have received these words from unwritten teaching. We bless the baptismal water and the oil for chrismation as well as the candidate approaching the font. By what written authority do we do this, if not from secret and mystical tradition? ... Are not all these things found in unpublished and unwritten teachings, which our fathers guarded in silence, safe from meddling and petty curiosity? They had learned their lesson well; reverence for the mysteries is best encouraged by silence.[3]

Church leaders continued in this period to produce church orders and other texts in order to provide the necessary direction for leading worship. A fourth-century Syrian order, the *Apostolic Constitutions*, is a work that combines the *Didache*, *Didascalia*, and *Apostolic Tradition* into one composite working, lending credence to the theory that these orders were widely distributed and shared among the churches. The fifth-century *Testamentum Domini* ("Testament of our Lord") is a much-enlarged version of the earlier *Apostolic Tradition*.

Other books contained explicit texts and more detailed instructions for the liturgy. The first was *the sacramentary*, which contained all the texts for use in celebrating the

---

[2] Bradshaw, *The Search for the Origins of Christian Worship: Sources and Methods for the Study of Early Liturgy*, 212.

[3] Basil of Caesarea, *On the Holy Spirit*, trans. David Anderson (Crestwood, NY: St Vladimir's Seminary Press, 1980), 65–66.

Eucharist. *The lectionary* contained Scripture readings for use in each service during the year. Two early examples of lectionaries include the *Armenian Lectionary* and the *Gregorian Lectionary*, both likely from the fifth century. *The antiphonary* or *liber antiphonarius* provided the sung parts of the service for the cantor and choir. Sometime between the end of the tenth century and the thirteenth century, these three books were combined into one book called *the missal*. *Breviaries* contained songs and readings for the divine hours. The *Ordines Romani* developed from the seventh century through the fifteenth and provided directions concerning various acts of the liturgy. Other sermons and letters give additional clarity to the development of worship during the period.

The *Apostolic Constitutions* did not change the Service of the Word much from earlier practice, continuing the pattern of Scripture reading, sermon, and prayer. However, the document does provide a bit more specificity regarding the Scripture readings, indicating that the service should have a reading from the Old Testament, a psalm, an Epistle, and a gospel. However, during this period the eucharistic prayer, originally called the *anaphora* (Greek, "offering") and later in the West the *canon* (Latin, "rule"), expanded considerably. As in the earlier *Apostolic Tradition*, the *Apostolic Constitutions* begins with a Preface consisting of the Salutation and *Sursum Corda*:

> Bishop: "The grace of Almighty God, and the love of our Lord Jesus Christ, and the fellowship of the Holy Ghost, be with you all."
>
> All: "And with your spirit."
>
> Bishop: "Lift up your mind."
>
> All: "We lift it up unto the Lord."
>
> Bishop: "Let us give thanks to the Lord."
>
> All: "It is meet and right to do so."[4]

Then follows the eucharistic prayer itself, including a lengthy *anamnesis* that recounts God's works in creation, Adam and Eve's fall into sin, and Christ's incarnation, holy life, sinless death, resurrection, and ascension. In the middle of the prayer, all the people recite the *Sanctus* (Latin, "Holy"), drawn from the song of angels in Isaiah 6 and Revelation 4:

---

[4] Alexander Roberts, James Donaldson, and A. Cleveland Coxe, eds., *Fathers of the Third and Fourth Centuries*, vol. 7, The Ante-Nicene Fathers (Buffalo, NY: Christian Literature Company, 1886), 486.

The Expansion of Worship

Bishop: "For all these things, glory be to Thee, O Lord Almighty. Thee do the innumerable hosts of angels, archangels, thrones, dominions, principalities, authorities, and powers, Thine everlasting armies, adore. The cherubim and the six-winged seraphim, with twain covering their feet, with train their heads, and with twain flying, say, together with thousand thousands of archangels, and ten thousand times ten thousand of angels, incessantly, and with constant and loud voices,"

All: "Holy, holy, holy, Lord of hosts, heaven and earth are full of his glory: be thou blessed forever. Amen."[5]

The prayer continues with the Words of Institution from 1 Corinthians 11 and the *epiclesis*:

And we beseech Thee that Thou wilt mercifully look down upon these gifts which are here set before Thee, O Thou God, who standest in need of none of our offerings. And do Thou accept them, to the honor of Thy Christ, and send down upon this sacrifice Thine Holy Spirit, the Witness of the Lord Jesus' sufferings, that He may show this bread to be the body of Thy Christ, and the cup to be the blood of Thy Christ, that those who are partakers thereof may be strengthened for piety, may obtain the remission of their sins, may be delivered from the devil and his deceit, may be filled with the Holy Ghost, may be made worthy of Thy Christ, and may obtain eternal, life upon Thy reconciliation to them, O Lord Almighty.[6]

It concluded with prayers of intercession and a Doxology:

Bishop: "For to Thee belongs all glory, and worship, and thanksgiving, honor and adoration, the Father, with the Son, and to the Holy Ghost, both now and always, and for everlasting, and endless ages forever."

All: "Amen."

Bishop: "The peace of God be with you all."

All: "And with thy spirit."

Bidding prayer for the faithful
Bishop: "Holy things for holy persons."

---

[5] Roberts, Donaldson, and Coxe, *Fathers of the Third and Fourth Centuries*, 7:488.
[6] Roberts, Donaldson, and Coxe, *Fathers of the Third and Fourth Centuries*, 7:489.

Changed from Glory into Glory

All: "There is One that is holy; there is one Lord, one Jesus Christ, blessed forever, to the glory of God the Father. Amen. Glory to God in the highest, and on earth peace, good-will among men. Hosanna to the son of David! Blessed be he that cometh in the name of the Lord, being the Lord God who appeared to us, Hosanna in the highest."[7]

Then the elements are distributed, first to the bishop and other church leaders, and then to "all the people in order, with reverence and godly fear, without tumult,"[128] during which Psalm 33 is recited. The service concludes with a prayer of thanks for Communion and a Benediction:

Be gracious to me, and hear me, for Thy name's sake, and bless those that bow down their necks unto Thee, and grant them the petitions of their hearts, which are for their good, and do not reject any one of them from Thy kingdom; but sanctify, guard, cover, and assist them; deliver them from the adversary and every enemy; keep their houses, and guard "their comings in and their goings out."

For to Thee belongs the glory, praise, majesty, worship, and adoration, and to Thy Son Jesus, Thy Christ, our Lord and God and King, and to the Holy Ghost, now and always, for ever and ever. Amen. *And the deacon shall say, Depart in peace.*[8]

This basic shape of the eucharistic liturgy provided the basis for all liturgy to follow:

Service of the Word
Old Testament Reading
Psalm
Epistle
Gospel
Sermon
Prayers

Service of the Table
Presentation of the Elements (Offertory)
Prayer of Thanks
    Salutation
    Sursum Corda
    Anamnesis
    Sanctus
    Words of Institution

---

[7] Roberts, Donaldson, and Coxe, *Fathers of the Third and Fourth Centuries*, 7:490.
[8] Roberts, Donaldson, and Coxe, *Fathers of the Third and Fourth Centuries*, 7:491.

The Expansion of Worship

    Epiclesis
    Doxology
  Partaking of Communion

Liturgy of Hours

During this period of liturgical development, communal daily prayer also expanded. The *Apostolic Constitutions* exhorted, "Offer up your prayers in the morning, at the third hour, the sixth hour, the ninth, the evening, and at cock-crowing."[9] By the end of the fifth century, seven "divine offices" of prayer had emerged, and Benedict of Nursia added an eighth (Prime, which has been eliminated in modern practice) in the sixth century:

Matins (during the night), also called Vigils or Nocturnes
Lauds (at dawn)
Prime (first hour, 6 a.m.)
Terce (third hour, 9 a.m.)
Sext (sixth hour, noon)
None (ninth hour, 3 p.m.)
Vespers (at dusk)
Compline (before retiring)

The Council of Nicaea

In 325, Constantine convened a church council in Nicaea primarily to settle the Arian controversy concerning the deity of the Son of God. The Council produced the Nicene Creed, what would become the most significant liturgical creed of the church. Earlier Christians, especially in Rome, had used what is commonly known as the "Apostles' Creed," likely formulated in the first two centuries. The Nicene Creed expanded to include statements clearly identifying Jesus Christ as "consubstantial" ("of one being") with the Father. Later in 381, the Council of Constantinople expanded the creed even further to contain explicit statements concerning the deity of the Holy Spirit. This "Niceno-Constantinopolitan Creed" is the "Nicene Creed" later officially adopted as the statement of faith in the liturgies of the western church:

We believe in one God, the Father, the Almighty, maker of heaven and earth,
of all that is, seen and unseen.
We believe in one Lord, Jesus Christ, the only Son of God,
eternally begotten of the Father, God from God, Light from Light,
true God from true God, begotten, not made, of one being with the Father.
Through Him all things were made.

---

[9] Roberts, Donaldson, and Coxe, *Fathers of the Third and Fourth Centuries*, 7:496.

For us and for our salvation He came down from heaven:
by the power of the Holy Spirit He became incarnate from the virgin Mary,
and was made man. For our sake He was crucified under Pontius Pilate;
He suffered death and was buried.
On the third day He rose again in accordance with the Scriptures;
He ascended into heaven and is seated at the right hand of the Father.
He will come again in glory to judge the living and the dead,
and His kingdom will have no end.
We believe in the Holy Spirit, the Lord, the Giver of life,
who proceeds from the Father and the Son.
With the Father and the Son He is worshiped and glorified.
He has spoken through the prophets.
We believe in one holy catholic and apostolic church.
We acknowledge one baptism for the forgiveness of sins.
We look for the resurrection of the dead, and the life of the world to come.
Amen.

Second, the Council of Nicaea also addressed the controversy over dating for the celebration of the resurrection of Christ. Though Christ's death and resurrection occurred during the moveable feast of Passover on Nisan 14, according to the gospel accounts, church leaders at Nicaea decided to separate their celebration of Christ's resurrection from the Jewish calendar, which they considered to be disorganized and in error. Consequently, they determined that, contrary to modern Jewish dating of Nisan 14, the celebration of Christ's resurrection should always occur on a Sunday following the vernal equinox (the beginning of spring, when the sun is directly above the equator). Later at the Synod of Whitby in 664, the standard tradition became to observe the holy day on the first Sunday following the full moon after the spring equinox.

Singing

With the legalization of Christianity, the cultural conditions within which the church thrived were such that had not been enjoyed since before the Hebrew exile. This created an environment in which the Judeo-Christian tradition of music in worship thrived and developed. Thus, what Christians sang in worship cultivated what they had been handed from Jewish and early Christian tradition. The fourth-century *Apostolic Constitutions* describes the singing of psalms in response to the reading of Scripture. Medieval Christian leaders continued to promote psalm singing, such as this resounding endorsement by Basil of Caesarea:

> A psalm is the tranquility of souls, the arbitrator of peace, restraining the disorder and turbulence of thoughts, for it softens the passion of the soul and

moderates its unruliness. A psalm forms friendships, unites the divided, mediates between enemies. For who can still consider him an enemy with whom he has sent forth on voice to God? So that the singing of psalms brings love, the greatest of good things, contriving harmony like some bond of union and uniting the people in the symphony of a single choir.

A psalm drives away demons, summons the help of angels, furnishes arms against nightly terrors, and gives respite from daily toil; to little children it is safety, to men in their prime an adornment, to the old a solace, to women their most fitting ornament. It peoples the solitudes, it brings agreement to market places. To novices it is a beginning; to those who are advancing, an increase; to those who are concluding, a confirmation. A psalm is the voice of the Church. It gladdens feast days, it creates grief which is in accord with God's will, for a psalm brings a tear even from a heart of stone.[10]

Plainsong soon developed into more refined chant, the melodies retaining an attention to the natural rise and fall of the doctrinally-rich hymn texts. During the fourth century, hymns were used to combat heresy and promote sound doctrine, as seen in this Christological example by Ambrose of Milan (c. 337–397), the "Father of Christian Hymnody":

O Splendor of God's glory bright,
from Light eternal bringing light,
O Light of light, light's living Spring,
true Day, all days illumining.

Come, very Sun of heaven's love,
in lasting radiance from above,
and pour the Holy Spirit's ray
on all we think or do today.

And now to Thee our pray'r ascend,
O Father, glorious without end;
we plead with sovereign grace for pow'r
to conquer in temptation's hour.

Confirm or will to do the right,
and keep our hearts from envy's blight;
let faith her eager fires renew,
and hate the false, and love the true.

---

[10] Basil of Caesarea, *Homily on the First Psalm*, in William Oliver Strunk, *Source Readings in Music History* (New York: Norton, 1998), 11–12.

> O joyful be the passing day
> with thoughts as pure as morning's ray,
> with faith like noontide shining bright
> our souls unshadowed by the night.
> Dawn's glory gilds the earth and skies,
> let Him, our perfect Morn, arise,
> the Word in God the Father one,
> the Father imaged in the Son.[11]

Church leaders believed singing should express hearts of worship toward God, such as Augustine, who lauded singing for its ability to help Christians express "joy without words."[12] Yet as with Christians before them, they spoke against music that would "arouse passion" or mimic pagan worship.[13]

As early as 422, Pope Celestine I declared that all 150 Psalms be sung through the year by everyone during worship, and thus Psalm chants were added in specific places in the service. In particular, they were sung either as responses to the reading of Scripture (this music came to be called Graduals) or during portions in the service where there would be a lot of moving but no words, such as the entrance of the priests (this was called the Introit), the presentation of the bread and cup (called the Offertory), the blessing of the elements (after the Preface in which the priest refers to joining the angels in worship, and the people respond by singing "Holy, Holy, Holy is the Lord God Almighty"), and the distribution of the elements (during which the words "Lamb of God who takes away the sin of the world" were commonly sung).

During the Middle Ages, service music (as well as readings) developed into two categories identified by the terms "Ordinary" and "Proper." Chants in the service that were "Ordinary" remained consistent each week and have come to be designated by the first words in Latin (or in the first case, Greek). The first chant is *Kyrie, eleison*, derived from the Greek phrase, "Lord, have mercy," in the New Testament (Matt. 15:22; 17:15; 20:30). The second chant is *Gloria in excelsis Deo* from that angels' song in Luke 2:14: "Glory to God in the highest"). As discussed in the previous section, the *Credo* followed, officially becoming part of the Ordinary sometime in the eleventh century. Two Ordinary chants were sung during the Service of the Table, *Sanctus* ("Holy") and *Agnus Dei* ("Lamb of God"), from John the Baptist's identification of Jesus as "the Lamb of God who takes away the sin of the world." Elements within the

---

[11] Translation, composite.

[12] Augustine of Hippo, "Expositions on the Book of Psalms," in Phillip Schaff, ed., *Saint Augustin: Expositions on the Book of Psalms*, vol. 8, A Select Library of the Nicene and Post-Nicene Fathers of the Christian Church, First (New York: Christian Literature Company, 1888), 488.

[13] Isidor, *Epistle I*, in James W. McKinnon, *Music in Early Christian Literature* (Cambridge: Cambridge University Press, 1989), 61.

liturgy that are "Proper" change from week to week as prescribed by a *lectionary*, in order to fit the particular time of the church calendar.

The Liturgical Calendar

Observances of the church calendar developed similarly to the dating of Easter. Letters composed by Athanasius of Alexandria from 329–333 indicate an expansion of celebrating Christ's resurrection to include the six days prior as "the holy days of Pascha," now often called "Holy Week." Later in 334 he enlarged the season even further with a forty-day period of preparation called "The Great Fast" (now called "Lent" from the "lengthening" of hours in spring), forty days corresponding to Christ's period of preparation in the wilderness following his baptism. This practice appears to have solidified by the late-fourth century church order, *Apostolic Constitutions*. As early as the fifth century, Pope Leo I (c. 400–461) decreed that the passion account from Matthew's gospel be read during the Mass for Palm Sunday and on the Wednesday of Holy Week, while John's passion should be read on Friday. Leo is usually credited for developing an emphasis on preaching from texts appropriate for the serving within the church year, a practice that came to be called *lectio selecta*. In early passion chanting, the deacon would chant the text, usually using a different voice for the narrator and various characters, especially Christ (higher for the crowd, lower for Christ). Later by the thirteenth century, different singers chanted the individual characters—a tenor deacon as evangelist, a bass priest as Jesus, and a counter-tenor sub-deacon for the choral parts. A specific celebration of Christ's triumphal entry into Jerusalem at the beginning of Holy Week first appeared in Jerusalem shortly following the Edict of Milan, when Christians there reenacted the event with a procession into the city that included waving palm branches and singing "Hosanna!" However, the earliest mention of regular practice of celebrating Palm Sunday is in the eighth-century Sacramentary of the Abbey of Bobbio in northern Italy, and it soon spread to Rome and became a standard part of the Liturgical Year.

The *Apostolic Constitutions* also mentions the celebration of Christmas, which, from a sermon of John Chrysostom (c. 349–407), appears to have been first celebrated on December 25, 386 in Antioch. The establishment of that particular date arises from an ancient Jewish belief that great prophets of Israel died on the same date as their conception. Early Christians seem to have applied this belief to Jesus; thus, since March 25 was considered to be the original date of Christ's death, they determined that it was also the date of his conception. Then, they simply added nine months to arrive at December 25. The popular notion that the date of Christmas arose from a "Christianization" of the pagan winter solstice festivals lacks any evidence.[14] The

---

[14] Frank C. Senn, *Introduction to Christian Liturgy* (Minneapolis: Fortress Press, 2012), 113–115.

Apostolic Constitutions also prescribes the festival of Epiphany (Greek meaning "to appear") to be celebrated on January 6 in commemoration of the visit of the magi and Jesus' childhood, including his baptism, Ascension Day forty days after Easter, and Pentecost ten days later. It is unclear when Advent first appeared, the period of preparation four weeks prior to Christmas, but monks in France observed the season at least as early as 480. Later, the twelve days between Christmas and Epiphany were celebrated as the extended period of Christmastide.

Thus, by the end of the fifth century, the basic liturgical calendar had been formed:

ADVENT	Four weeks before Christmas	Preparation
CHRISTMAS	December 25–January 5	Christ's Incarnation
EPIPHANY	January 6	The visit of the magi and Christ's baptism
LENT	Forty days prior to Easter	Preparation
HOLY WEEK	Six days before Easter	Christ's suffering and death
EASTER	The first Sunday following the full moon after the spring equinox	Christ's resurrection
ASCENSION	Forty days after Easter	Christ's ascension
PENTECOST	Fifty days after Easter	The coming of the Holy Spirit

Chapter 10
The Unification of Worship

With the basic elements of Christian worship in place by the end of the fifth century, the Middle Ages were a time of further development, expansion, and codification of liturgical practices. As mentioned earlier, worship (and theology) among various churches in the Middle Ages was not necessarily consistent; complete authoritative prescription of liturgical and theological matters did not come until the counter-Reformation Council of Trent in the sixteenth century. However, certain key figures in the Middle Ages did attempt to unify all churches theologically and liturgically, with more or less success.

Unified Worship in the East
While Rome remained central to Christian doctrine and worship in the early years of Christendom, the fact that Constantine centered his government in Byzantium, renamed "Constantinople" in 330, and declared it to be the "New Rome" began to create a division between West and East, first politically, and later ecclesiastically. Due to the shift in political power from West to East, the church in Rome began to consolidate power and influence for itself, increasing the authority of the Bishop of Rome and making Latin the church's official ecclesiastical language, in contrast to the East where Greek remained the dominant language. By the mid-fifth century, two "churches" had formed; although they continued to share common theology for some time (representatives from each participated in the seven ecumenical councils of the church[1]). Two worship traditions—one Byzantine and one Roman— now started developing somewhat independently from each other.

The Byzantine tradition was dominated by Constantinople, but it also included three other major centers of Christianity—Alexandria (Egypt), Antioch (Syria), and Jerusalem—each of which adopted the Byzantine liturgy following the Council of Chalcedon. This liturgy, called the *Byzantine Rite*, developed from "The Divine Liturgy of St. John Chrysostom" in Antioch and became the basis for worship in all Eastern Orthodox Churches today, whether Greek, Slavic, Armenian, Syrian, Romanian, Bulgarian, Serbian, or Russian. While other Orthodox liturgies exist and are still practiced in some churches, the only other liturgies of significance are the much longer and more elaborate liturgy of St. Basil, still commonly used during Lent, Holy

---

[1] Nicaea (325), Constantinople (381), Ephesus (431), Chalcedon (451), Constantinople (553), Constantinople (680–681), Nicaea (787).

Changed from Glory into Glory

Thursday, Easter, Christmas, Epiphany, and Basil's Feast Day (January 1), and the Liturgy of St. James, said to be the liturgy of the first Church of Jerusalem and the oldest liturgy still in common use today, on the feast of St. James (October 23). From the eucharistic prayer of the latter liturgy comes a hymn still in common use today:

> Let all mortal flesh keep silence,
> and with fear and trembling stand;
> ponder nothing earthly minded,
> for with blessing in His hand
> Christ our God to earth descendeth,
> our full homage to demand.
>
> King of kings, yet born of Mary,
> as of old on earth He stood,
> Lord of lords, in human vesture -
> in the body and the blood.
> He will give to all the faithful
> His own self for heavenly food.
>
> Rank on rank the host of heaven
> spreads its vanguard on the way,
> as the Light of light descendeth
> from the realms of endless day,
> that the pow'rs of hell may vanish
> as the darkness clears away.
>
> At His feet the six-winged seraph,
> cherubim, with sleepless eye,
> veil their faces to the Presence,
> as with ceaseless voice they cry,
> "Alleluia, alleluia!
> Alleluia, Lord most high!"[2]

The Divine Liturgy of St. John Chrysostom begins with preparatory rites in which the deacon and priest prepare the Communion elements and say the following:

Priest: "Blessed is the Kingdom of the Father and of the Son and of the Holy Spirit, now and forever and to the ages of ages."

People: "Amen."[3]

---

[2] Translation, Gerard Moultrie, 1864.
[3] *The Divine Liturgy of St. John Chrysostom* (Shawnee, KS: Gideon House Books, 2015).

The Unification of Worship

Then follows what is called the Great Litany, in which the deacon directs the people to pray. He announces various subjects for which to pray:

> For the peace from above and for the salvation of our souls, let us pray to the Lord.
>
> For the peace of the whole world, for the stability of the holy churches of God, and for the unity of all, let us pray to the Lord.
>
> For this holy house and for those who enter it with faith, reverence, and the fear of God, let us pray to the Lord.
>
> For pious and Orthodox Christians, let us pray to the Lord.
>
> For our Archbishop (*Name*), for the honorable presbyterate, for the diaconate in Christ, and for all the clergy and the people, let us pray to the Lord.
> For our country, for the president, and for all in public service, let us pray to the Lord.
>
> For this city, and for every city and land, and for the faithful who live in them, let us pray to the Lord.
>
> For favorable weather, for an abundance of the fruits of the earth, and for peaceful times, let us pray to the Lord.
>
> For those who travel by land, sea, and air, for the sick, the suffering, the captives and for their salvation, let us pray to the Lord.
>
> For our deliverance from all affliction, wrath, danger, and necessity, let us pray to the Lord.
>
> Help us, save us, have mercy on us, and protect us, O God, by Your grace.

The people pray silently as each subject is announced, and they respond with "*Kyrie eleison:* Lord have mercy" following each petition. The third introductory act is the recitation of the Antiphons (prayers or psalms).

The Service of the Word proper begins with what is called the Little Entrance, in which the priest processes, carrying the Gospel Book, blesses the entrance to the sanctuary, and proclaims, "Wisdom. Let us be attentive." Then the people chant the Trisagion Hymn (Greek, "thrice holy"):

Changed from Glory into Glory

> Holy God, Holy Mighty, Holy Immortal, have mercy on us. (*repeated three times*)
>
> Glory to the Father and to the Son and to the Holy Spirit, now and forever and to the ages of ages. Amen.
>
> Holy Immortal, have mercy on us.

The deacon then proclaims, "Let us be attentive," and the priest chants the Epistle reading. The Gospel reading is introduced by a Salutation:

> Priest: "Wisdom. Arise. Let us hear the Holy Gospel. Peace be with all."
>
> People: "And with your spirit."
>
> Priest: "The reading is from the Holy Gospel according to (*Matthew, Mark, Luke, or John*).
>
> People: Glory to you, O Lord, glory to you (*said again after the reading*).

The priest then delivers a sermon based on the gospel reading. The Service of the Word concludes with prayers, first for the catechumens, after which they are dismissed, and then the Prayer of the Faithful, which is essentially a prayer of preparation for the eucharist:

> Again and countless times we fall down before You, and we implore You, O Good One, Who loves mankind: That You, having regarded our prayer, may cleanse our souls and bodies from every defilement of flesh and spirit, and grant to us to stand before Your holy Altar of sacrifice, free of guilt and condemnation. Grant also, O God, to those who pray with us, progress in life, faith, and spiritual understanding. Grant that they always worship You with awe and love, partake of Your Holy Mysteries without guilt or condemnation, and be deemed worthy of Your celestial Kingdom. That, ever guarded by Your might, we may ascribe glory to You, to the Father and to the Son and to the Holy Spirit, now and forever and to the ages of ages.

The Service of the Table begins with the Great Entrance, an elaborate procession of the Communion elements into the sanctuary that is meant to represent Christ's triumphal entry into the heavenly Jerusalem, accompanied by incense and the singing of the Cherubic Hymn:

The Unification of Worship

> Let us, who mystically represent the Cherubim
> and who sing the thrice-holy hymn to the life-creating Trinity,
> now lay aside every worldly care,
> so that we may receive the King of all,
> who is invisibly escorted by the angelical hosts.
> Alleluia. Alleluia. Alleluia.

Then follows another litany in which the deacon leads the congregation to pray for particular matters, and the priest prays the Offertory Prayer. Just before the formal eucharist celebration, the people perform acts that picture the communion they share with one another and with God through Christ. First, they exchange the Kiss of Peace, with which the deacon admonishes, "Let us love one another, that with oneness of mind we may confess," and the people respond, "Father, Son, and Holy Spirit: Trinity, one in essence and undivided." This leads, then, to the affirmation of their common faith in the recitation of the Nicene Creed.

Communion itself includes the Eucharistic Prayer (*Anaphora*), which resembles the western prayer in its basic structure and contents, the singing of "Holy, holy, holy ..." the Words of Institution, the Lord's Prayer, a Communion hymn ("Praise the Lord from the heavens; praise him in the highest. Alleluia."), and partaking of the elements. The service concludes with prayers of thanks, the singing of hymns, and a Benediction:

> May the Holy Trinity protect all of you.
> May the blessing and the mercy of the Lord come upon you.
> By his divine grace and love for mankind,
> now and forever and to the ages of ages.
> Amen.

The Byzantine Church remained fairly consistent throughout the Middle Ages until Constantinople fell to Ottoman Muslims in 1453. This placed the eastern church in an Islamic political situation, which prevented it from inculcating any of the surrounding culture into its worship and preserved the ancient liturgies that are still practiced to this day.

Unified Worship in the West

Theological and ecclesiastic tensions between the eastern and western churches climaxed in 1054 when representatives of Pope Leo IX excommunicated the Patriarch of Constantinople, Michael I Cerularius (c. 1000–1059), who refused to submit to the Pope's authority, and Cerularius responded by excommunicating them. The two churches continued on relatively good terms, but they began to diverge even more in their theology and practice.

While liturgical unity in the East developed rather early, Western liturgical unification took more time. Throughout the Middle Ages, churches in various regions developed separate, although in many ways similar, liturgical practices including the Roman rite (Rome), the Ambrosian rite (Milan), Mozarabic rite (Spain), Gallican rite (France), and Sarum rite (England). Yet two key individuals helped to increase the influence of the Roman rite—a Pope and an Emperor.

Gregory the Great
Pope Gregory I (c. 540–604) is often called the "Father of Christian Worship" because of his influence over liturgical reforms in the late sixth century. Gregory is credited with revising the liturgy, prescribing *Alleluia* to be sung each mass (apparently it had only been sung during Eastertide previously), possibly introducing the Greek *Kyrie* taken from the Eastern Church, inserting the *Pater Noster* ("Our Father") after the canon, and initiating other minor changes.[4] Plainchant that became standardized in the ninth century (see below) was also attributed to Gregory. While it is uncertain how much he did himself or whether he simply initiated and oversaw the reforms, during his tenure the church organized the liturgical and musical materials it had inherited, ordering them according to the liturgical year. Under Gregory, church leadership attempted to establish a uniform repertory of chant throughout the church.

Ordo Romanus Primus
The first *Ordo Romanus*, a rubric for the Mass compiled as early as the seventh century, includes a detailed description of a service around the time Gregory was Pope.[5] The service began with the choir chanting a psalm called the "Introit," during which the Pope and his assistants process to the altar, where he prays silently. The Introit concluded with the *Gloria Patri*, followed by *Kyrie eleison*, after which the Pope began chanting, *Gloria in excelsis Deo*, which was then completed by the choir. Facing east, the Pope began the "Collect," prayers of intercession on behalf of the people. A subdeacon then read the Epistle reading for the day, after which the choir sang a psalm of response, known as a Gradual, and *Alleluia*. A deacon reads the gospel of the day, preceded by attendants diffusing incense. A reading from the Old Testament, found earlier in the *Apostolic Constitutions*, had apparently dropped from most services by the end of the fifth century. The gospel reading finished, the Pope greeted the people with, "The Lord be with you," to which the people replied, "And with your spirit," and the Pope invited them to pray (although no actual prayers follow). Apparently by this time

---

[4] Gregory I, *Epistle XII*, in Philip Schaff and Henry Wace, eds., *Gregory the Great (Part II), Ephraim Syrus, Aphrahat*, vol. 8, A Select Library of the Nicene and Post-Nicene Fathers of the Christian Church, Second (New York: Christian Literature Company, 1898), 8–9.

[5] Edward Godfrey Cuthbert Frederic Atchley, ed., *Ordo Romanus Primus* (London: Alexander Moring, 1905).

the service had no sermon (or was optional), for the *Ordo Romanus* proceeds next directly to the Offering of bread and wine and preparation of the elements for Communion. Some of Gregory's sermons are extant, so he no doubt preached, yet as early as the fifth century an account of services in Rome indicates that "the people are not taught by the bishop, nor by anyone in the Church."[6] The choir sang during the Offering, and when finished, the Pope said the *Sursum Corda*, and the choir began the *Sanctus*. The Pope recited the canon in a low voice, during which attendants performed various acts such as lifting the chalice and bread for him to consecrate, concluding with the Lord's Prayer. After breaking the bread, the choir sang the *Agnus Dei* as the elements were distributed to the clergy. During the communion of the people, the choir sang another psalm. By this time, the people were not permitted to touch the elements directly, having the bread placed in their mouths and receiving wine through a reed. When they were finished, the choir sang the *Gloria Patri*, after which the Pope said the final prayer, and a deacon dismissed the people.

Charles the Great
Although these liturgical reforms developed during the sixth century, it was not until the ninth century that they began to unify and standardize liturgy across the Roman church. This occurred largely due to the political aspirations of Charles I of France, who united much of central and western Europe and was crowned Holy Roman Emperor by Pope Leo III in 800. One of the most significant means Charlemagne used to unify his empire was to standardize liturgy among all the churches. At his request, Leo distributed across the empire the best liturgies and chants, called "Gregorian" because of the popularity of the sixth-century Pope. Charlemagne also encouraged inclusion in the Nicene Creed the phrase "and the Son" to describe the procession of the Holy Spirit, which continues in western liturgy today.

The Pre-Tridentine Roman Rite
Pope Benedict VIII (1012–1024) introduced the Creed into the service at the request of Emperor Henry II (1002–1024), the only element of the Ordinary not yet present in *Ordo Romanus Primus*. Additional ceremonies, incensing, ashes, candles, and prayers were incorporated into the Roman rite after Charlemagne, but the main service structure remained intact. Thus, the basic shape of what is known as the "Pre-Tridentine" (before the Council of Trent) liturgy took the following form (sung elements are marked with an *):

---

[6] Philip Schaff and Henry Wace, eds., *Socrates, Sozomenus: Church Histories*, vol. 2, A Select Library of the Nicene and Post-Nicene Fathers of the Christian Church, Second (New York: Christian Literature Company, 1890), 390.

Service of the Word
*Introit
*Kyrie eleison
*Gloria in excelsis Deo
Collect
Epistle
*Gradual
*Alleluia
Gospel
Sermon (possibly)
*Credo
(Let us pray.)

Service of the Table
*Offertory
Eucharistic Prayer
....Salutation
....Sursum Corda
....Anamnesis
....*Sanctus
....Words of Institution
....Epiclesis
....Pater noster
Communion
....Fraction
....*Agnus Dei
Collect
Ite, misse est

Need for Reformation

Much of the development of worship during the Middle Ages was rooted in biblical prescription, example, and theology. Protestant Christians looking back at this period recognize the errors and heterodoxy that developed within Roman Catholicism during the Middle Ages, yet what must be remembered is that the church did not formally codify or unify around what Protestants consider error until the counter-Reformation Council of Trent in the sixteenth century. And even as erroneous doctrines and practices emerged from the fourth through sixteenth centuries, a core Christianity shaped medieval western civilization. This certainly does not mean that all, or even most, people were genuinely Christian or free from immoral living—quite the opposite. But because of the dominance of Christendom, medieval man affirmed the existence of a God who was both transcendent and personal, believed that this God created and rules the universe, understood that humans were sinful and in need of forgiveness, recognized that Jesus Christ was the Son of God who became incarnate and died to save humanity, and simply came to assume that religion and faith were necessary to human flourishing. These core beliefs produced a social order and culture that was essentially "Christian"—not in the sense of genuine piety, but in the sense of being governed by Christian categories as opposed to pagan or secular.

Nevertheless, heresy did grow, and several aspects of how many Christians worshiped by the end of the fifteenth century made significant reformation necessary. Although the specific dogmas we associate with Roman Catholicism today were not officially canonized until the Council of Trent, which met from 1554–1563, many of the Roman Church's heresy was already developed by the early 1500s. For example, the doctrine of purgatory came in 593, prayer to Mary, saints, and angels in 600, kissing the pope's foot in 709, the canonization of dead saints in 995, the celibacy of the priesthood in 1079, the rosary in 1090, transubstantiation and confessing sins to a priest in 1215, and the seven sacraments in 1439.

Problems specifically with worship can be summarized with the following categories:

Sacrificial Character of the Eucharist
Very early in the development of eucharistic practice, Christians referred to the Lord's Supper as a "sacrifice" or "oblation." While likely that the earliest Christians meant this metaphorically, by the end of the Middle Ages most Christians considering partaking of the bread and cup to be a re-sacrifice of Christ. This particular theological error led to several other abuses.

Transubstantiation
One of the most significant of these abuses was the belief that the bread and wine in the eucharist were literally the body and blood of Christ. Very early on in the development of Christian dogma, participation in the Lord's Table in particular became significant. It is easy to understand why, since this is what made Christians unique from Jews worshiping in the synagogue. For example, Ignatius of Antioch called the Table the "medicine of immortality."[7] It was understandable that they placed such an emphasis on the Table, but they also struggled with a particular statement Christ made during his words of institution. Jesus had said, "This bread *is* my body," and "This cup *is* my blood." Of course, the Protestant Reformers would debate this later, but early on, most Christians leaders took the statement very literally. Ignatius claimed that the

---

[7] Ignatius, *The Epistle of Ignatius to the Ephesians*, in Roberts, Donaldson, and Coxe, *The Apostolic Fathers with Justin Martyr and Irenaeus*, 1:58.

Eucharist "is the flesh of Jesus Christ."[8] Irenaeus, a pastor in the late second century said, "The bread, when it receives the invocation of God, is no longer common bread, but the Eucharist consisting of two realities, the earthly and the heavenly."[9] Likewise, Origin, a third century pastor, claimed, "And this bread becomes by prayer a sacred body, which sanctifies those who sincerely partake of it."[10]

What those earliest Christians meant is a matter of considerable debate. However, a clearer mystical belief concerning the eucharist developed in various places during the Middle Ages, first described as "transubstantiation" in the tenth century. The 1215 Fourth Lateran Council dogmatized this doctrine: "The body and blood of Christ are truly contained in the sacrament of the altar under the forms of bread and wine, the bread being transubstantiated into the body and the wine into the blood by divine power."[11] A short time later, Thomas Aquinas (1225–1274) devised the philosophical rationale for transubstantiation.[12] Aquinas attempted to synthesize Aristotelian philosophy with Christian theology, and this is perhaps no more evident than in his theology of the eucharist. His doctrine sought to explain how the bread and wine could literally be the body and blood of Christ while still looking and tasting like bread and wine. Aquinas used Aristotle's categories of "substance" and "accident" to provide a solution. "Substance" was the very essence of a thing, while "accidents" were a thing's outward, tangible characteristics. Aquinas argued that when the priest uttered the words, "*hoc es corpus meum*" ("this is my body"), the substance of the bread transformed into the body of Christ, while its accidents remained unchanged. The same happened with the wine. From the moment of consecration onward, the wafer and wine, separately or together, are "the Lamb of God" to be adored and received for eternal life. Partaking of the Eucharist results in: (1) forgiveness from venial sins; (2) strengthening against temptation (extinguishing the power of evil desire); and (3) promise of eternal glory and a glorious resurrection. Vatican II (1962–1965) later encouraged frequent or daily participation since it "increases our union with Christ, nourishes the spiritual life more abundantly, strengthens the soul in virtue, and gives the communicant a stronger pledge of eternal happiness."[13]

---

[8] Ignatius, *The Epistle to the Romans*, in Roberts, Donaldson, and Coxe, *The Apostolic Fathers with Justin Martyr and Irenaeus*, 1:77.

[9] Irenaeus, *Against Heresies*, in Roberts, Donaldson, and Coxe, *The Apostolic Fathers with Justin Martyr and Irenaeus*, 1:486.

[10] Origin, *Against Celsus*, in Alexander Roberts, James Donaldson, and A. Cleveland Coxe, eds., *Fathers of the Third Century*, vol. 4, The Ante-Nicene Fathers (Buffalo, NY: Christian Literature Company, 1885), 652.

[11] Philip Schaff, *History of the Christian Church* (New York: Charles Scribner's Sons, 1910), 5:714.

[12] Thomas Aquinas, *Summa Theologica*, Part III (c. 1271), trans. Fathers of the English Dominican Province (New York: Benziger Brothers, 1947), II, 2447–2451.

[13] Robert Joseph Fox, *The Catholic Faith* (Huntington, IN: Our Sunday Visitor, 1983), 212–213.

The Unification of Worship

Sacramentalism

Another abuse was sacramentalism, attributing the efficacy of an act of worship—especially the eucharistic elements—to the outward sign rather than to the inner working of the Holy Spirit. Christians during this period came to believe that just by performing the acts of worship, they received grace from God, whether or not they were spiritually engaged in the act. Along with this belief came the idea of *ex opera operato* ("from the work worked"), the belief that the acts of worship work automatically and independently of the faith of the recipient.

Sacerdotalism

Medieval worship also developed the error of sacerdotalism, the belief in the necessity of a human priest to approach God on the behalf of others. As a result of the drastic increase of church attendance in the fourth century, a strict distinction between clergy and laity had developed wherein the clergy did not trust the illiterate, uneducated masses to worship God appropriately on their own. Thus, the clergy offered "perfected" worship on behalf of the people. The pronouncement by the Council of Laodicea in 363 illustrates this: "No others shall sing in the church, save only the canonical singers, who go up into the ambo and sing from a book."[14] While this was a local council, it illustrates what became common among most churches in the Middle Ages. The quality of worship became measures by the excellence of the music and the aesthetic beauty of the liturgy, and while this facilitated the production of some quite beautiful sacred music during the period, it resulted in "worship" becoming mostly what the priests did in the chancel, which eventually was often distinctly separated from the nave by high rails or even a screen. This clergy/laity separation was only exacerbated by the continued use of Latin as the liturgical language despite the fact that increasing numbers of people did not understand the language. By the end of the fourteenth century, members of the congregation rarely participated in the Lord's Supper, and even when they did, the cup was withheld from them lest some of Christ's blood sprinkle on the unclean. Roman worship had moved from the "work of the people" (*leitourgia*) to the work of the clergy. As even Roman Catholic liturgical scholar Joseph Jungmann notes, "the people were devout and came to worship; but even when they were present at worship, it was still clerical worship. ... The people were not much more than spectators. This resulted largely from the strangeness of the language which was, and remained, Latin. ... The people have become dumb."[15]

---

[14] Philip Schaff and Henry Wace, eds., *The Seven Ecumenical Councils*, vol. 14, A Select Library of the Nicene and Post-Nicene Fathers of the Christian Church, Second (New York: Charles Scribner's Sons, 1900), 132.

[15] Joseph Jungmann, "The State of Liturgical Life on the Eve of the Reformation," in *Pastoral Liturgy* (New York: Herder & Herder, 1962), 67–68.

Preoccupation with Sensory Experience

Medieval Christians likewise became enamored with sensory experience in worship. Church architecture deliberately kept the nave dark and the elevated chancel bright and included ornate, elaborate decorations. Liturgy included rich vestments, processions, and other elaborate ceremonies that included bells and incense in order to create a mystical experience.

Individualization of Piety

All of this resulted in an individualization of piety. The only real benefit of corporate worship was the sacramental experience achieved only by a sacerdotal system and the splendor of the corporate setting. The Service of the Word diminished, and the Service of the Table became a mystical sacrament by which worshipers were infused with grace as they observed the clergy offering a sacrifice on their behalf. Herman Wegman diagnoses the problem:

> The decline in medieval worship must first of all be laid to clericalization and the related individualizing of the piety of the faithful, a piety that grew apart from the liturgy. ... This liturgy was marked by an excess of feasts, by popular customs, and by details and superstitious practices that overlaid the heart of the faith.[16]

Worship that Can Be Touched

Many factors account for the rise of heretical and erroneous theology and practice, including worship, during the Middle Ages. But perhaps one central factor is that in many cases, church leadership derived worship theology and practice primarily or even exclusively from Old Testament Israel—an empire that essentially consisted of a union between the civil and religious found more support and guidelines from the Old Testament than from the New Testament. Therefore, the Old Testament increasingly became the pattern for medieval worship theology and practice, the church becoming the "new Israel." For example, early theologians explicitly explained the ecclesial hierarchy based on its parallels with Old Testament high priest (bishops), priesthood (priests), and Levites (deacons). Theologians used the Old Testament as the basis for priestly vestments, mandatory tithing, infant baptism, altars, sacrifice, richly adorned sanctuary, incense, processions, and ceremonies. As early as the third century, for example, Tertullian described standing "at God's altar ... [for the] participation of the sacrifice" and proclaimed, "we ought to escort with the pomp of good works, amid

---

[16] Herman A. Wegman, *Christian Worship in East and West: A Study Guide to Liturgical History* (New York: Pueblo Publishing Co., 1985), 217.

The Unification of Worship

psalms and hymns, unto God's altar, to obtain for us all good things from God."[17] Whether he meant this in the New Testament metaphorical sense is debatable, but this kind of language unquestionably became more literal in later worship practice. Priority given to the Old Testament for worship theology also accounts for the sacramentalism, sacerdotalism, and preoccupation with sensory experience that came to characterize worship by the end of the fifteenth century. Christians desired a "worship that can be touched" led by human mediators.

However, a second factor contributing to errant theology and practice of worship was that some theologians, rightly understanding that Christian worship is participation with the worship of heaven (Heb. 12:22–24), nevertheless failed to recognize that this is currently something to be accepted in faith as a spiritual reality rather than expected as a physical experience. Medieval Christians wanted to experience the worship of heaven tangibly here on earth, either expecting that heaven came down to them while they worshiped or that they were led into the heavenly temple through the sacramental ceremonies. Therefore, if not bringing into worship altars and incense and adornments by appealing to Old Testament Israel, some drew from pictures of heavenly worship, especially those from the book of Revelation. Even the church architecture pictured this theology, with the nave where the people sat symbolizing earth, the "sanctuary" where the mass took place a picture of heaven. In this way, they desired a heavenly worship "that can be touched."

Worship—along with many other aspects of Christian theology—was in desperate need of Reformation.

---

[17] Tertullian, *On Prayer*, in Roberts, Donaldson, and Coxe, *Latin Christianity: Its Founder, Tertullian*, 3:687, 690.

Conclusion to Part Three

Medieval worldview in general did not shift from that of ancient times: people believed in the reality of the immaterial, and they believed that this immaterial reality was what was truly real. The spiritual and material functioned as a unified whole, meaning in this life finding its source in the ultimate reality of the spiritual world.

What changed was the dominant theology, both for good and for ill. Positively, as Christianity spread to become the dominant force in the West, the unstated assumption that a spiritual world existed became defined in explicit terms of Christian Theism. Medievals believed that all things "live and move and have their being" (Acts 17:28) in the Creator who "is before all things, and in him all things hold together" (Col. 1:17). Again, this did not mean everyone was truly Christian—there was plenty of immorality, unbelief, and corruption, even within (or, perhaps, especially within) the church. Yet the dominant Christian imagination of the Middle Ages was to consider everything as part of a unified harmony governed by God, regulated by his law, and intended for his glory. This religious perspective of the Middle Ages significantly affected both culture and cultus. Culturally, a transcendent Theistic worldview became the crucible in which rich artistic endeavors flourished. The church itself became a sort of conservatory of the arts, many of the greatest artists of the period being churchmen who created art as a means to picture the divine and nourish the soul. Even the folk art of the period flourished in this environment that Faulkner called "World-consciousness." In a sense, culture and cultus interacted in ways very similar to the golden age of ancient Israel. As we have seen, public worship became more and more concerned with the transcendent, often to the neglect of the immanent, with highly ornate architecture, iconography, music, ceremonies, and other accoutrements. The dominant worldview led people to recognize the necessity of corporate worship for their spiritual and physical welfare.

Negatively, however, late Medievals began to understand the relationship between the material and immaterial world sacramentally, that is, they believed that experiencing God came as a result of physical things—sacred places, rituals, relics, and ceremonies. This was a considerable shift from the spirituality of early Christians who believed the reverse, that knowledge and meaning in the physical world came as a result of knowing God. In other words, earlier Christians began with transcendent reality rooted in God and moved from that basis toward an understanding of particulars in the material world. Late medieval scholastic theologians, most significantly Thomas Aquinas, began with the particulars and worked toward the universals, a philosophy now called moderate (or "Thomistic") realism. This subtle shift from the Christian realism of early Christianity turned seismic with other theologians, such as William of Ockham (1285–1347). While Aquinas still taught that meaning in the material world finds its source in the *nature* of God himself (as early Christians had as well), Ockham argued that meaning in the world existed based on the *will* of God; thus, truth, morality, and beauty are not intrinsic. This way of thinking will eventually lead to the nominalism of the eighteenth century and have considerable impact on culture and the church.

Conclusion to Part Three

Study Guide for Part Three
People and Terms

Advent
Agnus Dei
Ambrose of Milan
anamnesis
anaphora
antiphonary
Apostles' Creed
Apostolic Constitutions
Apostolic Tradition
Ascension
Augustine of Hippo
baptism
Byzantine Rite
Byzantium
canon
Charlemagne
Christendom
Christmas
Collect
Compline
Constantine
Constantinople
Council of Constantinople
Council of Nicaea
Credo
Didache
Didascalia Apostolorum
doxology
Easter
Eastertide
Edict of Milan
epiclesis
Epiphany
eucharist
eucharistic prayer
ex opera operato
Gloria in excelsis
Gloria Patri
Good Friday
Gradual
Gregory I

Holy Week
Introit
Ite, misse est
Justin Martyr's *Apology*
Kyrie eleison
Lauds
lectionary
Lent
Lord's Day
Mass
Matins
Nicene Creed
None
Offertory
Ordinary
Ordo Romanus Primus
Palm Sunday
Pascha
Pater Noster
Pentecost
plainchant
Pliny the Younger
Preface
Pre-Tridenine Roman Rite
Prime
Proper
sacerdotalism
sacrament
sacramentalism
sacramentary
Salutation
Sanctus
Service of the Table
Service of the Word
Sext
Sursum Corda
Terce
transubstantiation
Vespers
Words of Institution

Recommended Resources
Bettenson, Henry, and Chris Maunder, eds. *Documents of the Christian Church*. 4th ed. New York: Oxford University Press, 2011.

Bradshaw, Paul F. *Early Christian Worship: A Basic Introduction to Ideas and Practice*. Collegeville, MN: Liturgical Press, 2010.

Bradshaw, Paul F. *Reconstructing Early Christian Worship*. Reprint edition. Collegeville, MN: Liturgical Press, 2011.

Bradshaw, Paul F. *The Search for the Origins of Christian Worship: Sources and Methods for the Study of Early Liturgy*. New York: Oxford University Press, 2002.

Cook, William R. and Ronald B. Herzman. *The Medieval Worldview: An Introduction*, 3rd ed.

Dix, Gregory. *The Shape of the Liturgy*. Second. London: T&T Clark, 2015.

Jasper, R. C. D., and G. J. Cuming. *Prayers of the Eucharist: Early and Reformed*. Edited by Paul F. Bradshaw and Maxwell E. Johnson. Fourth. Collegeville, MN: Liturgical Press Academic, 2019.

Metzger, Marcel. *History of the Liturgy: The Major Stages*. Collegeville, MN: Liturgical Pr, 1997.

Needham, Nick. *2,000 Years of Christ's Power*. United Kingdom: Christian Focus Publications, 2016, vols. 1, 2.

Senn, Frank C. *Introduction to Christian Liturgy*. Minneapolis: Fortress Press, 2012.

Thompson, Bard. *Liturgies of the Western Church*. St. Louis: Fortress Press, 1980.

White, James F. *Documents of Christian Worship: Descriptive and Interpretive Sources*. Louisville, KY: Westminster John Knox Press, 2007.

Questions for Discussion and Reflection
1. Describe the development of Christian liturgy from the New Testament to 500, naming key extant documents, important figures, and major liturgical issues.
2. What was the relationship between the Christian cultus and pagan cultus and culture prior to the legalization of Christianity in 313?
3. Explain both positive and negative effects upon worship from the development of Christendom after the Edict of Milan.
4. Discuss the errors that developed in Christian worship by the end of the middle ages, and explain how these errors evolved.

PART FOUR: REFORMATION

O Lord Jesus Christ, which art the true Sun of the world,
evermore arising, and never going down,
which by thy most wholesome appearing and sight,
dost bring forth, preserve, nourish, and refresh all things,
as well that are in heaven, as also that are on earth:

we beseech thee mercifully and favorably to shine into our hearts,
that the night and darkness of sins,
and the mists of errors on every side driven away,
thou brightly shining within our hearts,
we may all our life space go without any stumbling or offence,
and may decently and seemly walk, as in the day time,
being pure and clean from the works of darkness,
and abounding in all good works which God hath prepared for us to walk in:
which with the Father and with the Holy Ghost
livest and reignest for ever and ever.
Amen.

—Thomas Cranmer, 1567

Chapter 11
The German Reformation

It would be a mistake to assume that worship (or theology, for that matter) evolved in a single, unified, unbroken stream from the close of the New Testament canon to the sixteenth century; indeed, although there was largely one "Church" in the West during the medieval period, beliefs and practices varied to a certain extent depending on region and even particular pastors and theologians. Nevertheless, as we have already observed, the church as a whole was in much need of reform by the end of the fifteenth century, both theologically and liturgically.

The immediate causes for Reformation in various regions, as well as what caused divisions among various Reformation figures, are diverse. However, much of what lay at the core of what both unified Reformers in their reaction against the Roman Catholic Church and what ended up dividing them in the end, involved theology and practice of worship. This was certainly true for Martin Luther (1483–1546), the German theologian who sparked the Reformation and laid important groundwork for reforms in worship.

Martin Luther was born to a poor German family, and from a very early age he developed a love for music. Luther's father wanted him to be a lawyer, but through a series of unusual events, Luther eventually entered a friary and began to study theology. In 1507, he was ordained to the priesthood, and in 1508 he began teaching theology at the University of Wittenberg. Between 1513 and 1517, Luther slowly began to rediscover the doctrine of justification by faith alone in Christ alone. He soon realized that the "righteousness of God" he read in Romans was not just the righteousness that God demanded of sinful people, but also the righteousness that he credited to those who believe in him. This began Luther's reformational thinking. On October 31, 1517, Luther wrote to Albrecht, Archbishop of Mainz and Magdeburg, protesting the sale of indulgences. He enclosed in his letter a copy of his "Disputation of Martin Luther on the Power and Efficacy of Indulgences," which came to be known as "The 95 Theses." Whether or not he actually posted them on the door of the church at Wittenberg is disputed.

Liturgical Reform
Much of what Luther and other Reformers sought to reform was, of course, theological; yet as we have seen throughout this book, *lex orandi, lex credendi*—religion and liturgy impact each other and cannot be treated as if they are completely separate. Luther recognized this reality, and thus much of his efforts involved liturgical reform.

Luther knew that some of what had developed in the liturgy of the mass both reflected the errant theology of salvation and sanctification that concerned him and had profound formative effects upon the lay people who regularly participated.

Eucharist

In one of Martin Luther's most significant early works, *A Prelude Concerning the Babylonian Captivity of the Church* (1520), he argued against what he considered three "captivities" concerning the Lord's Supper: withholding the cup from the laity, the doctrine of transubstantiation, and understanding the mass as a sacrifice. As to the first "captivity," Luther argued for the universality of the cup by noting Christ's statement in the words of institution, "Drink of it, all of you" (Matt. 26:27). Medieval theologians had interpreted the "all" as referring to the cup, but Luther demonstrated that grammatically, "all" referred to "you" in Christ's command, and thus insisted that all believers should partake. He argued, "But they are the sinners, who forbid the giving of both [bread and cup] to those who wish to exercise this choice. The fault lies not with the laity, but with the priests. The sacrament does not belong to the priests but to all men."[1]

As to the second, Luther argued against the philosophical explanation of the presence of Christ in the eucharist from Aristotle through the writings of Aquinas. He complained, "What shall we say when Aristotle and the doctrines of men are made to be the arbiters of such lofty and divine matters?"[2] He insisted that Christ is really present in the bread and wine itself, but the substance of the elements does not change. Instead, he presented what he called "sacramental union"—the idea that Christ is present spiritually:

> Therefore, it is entirely correct to say, if one points to the bread, "This is Christ's body," and whoever sees the bread sees Christ's body, as John says that he saw the Holy Spirit when he saw the dove, as we have heard. Thus also it is correct to say, "He who takes hold of this bread, takes hold of Christ's body; and he who eats this bread, eats Christ's body; he who crushes this bread with teeth or tongue, crushes with teeth or tongue the body of Christ." And yet it remains absolutely true that no one sees or grasps or eats or chews Christ's body in the way he visibly sees and chews any other flesh. What one does to the bread is rightly and properly attributed to the body of Christ by virtue of the sacramental union.[3]

---

[1] Martin Luther, *The Babylonian Captivity of the Church*, 1520, in *Luther's Works* (Philadelphia: Fortress Press, 1999), 36:27.

[2] Pelikan, Oswald, and Lehmann, *Luther's Works*, 36:33.

[3] Martin Luther, *Confession Concerning Christ's Supper*, 1528, in Pelikan, Oswald, and Lehmann, *Luther's Works*, 37:300.

Yet, he insisted, "even though philosophy cannot grasp this, faith grasps it nonetheless. And the authority of God's Word is greater than the capacity of our intellect to grasp it."[4]

As to the third "captivity," which Luther believed to be "far the most wicked abuse of all,"[156] he argued that there is no Scriptural basis for understanding the Mass as a sacrifice, and he stressed the need for personal faith in those who wished to participate. The mass is not, Luther insisted, "a work which may be communicated to others, but the object of faith, ... for the strengthening and nourishing of each one's own faith."[5] He argued,

> Now, the more closely our mass resembles that first mass of all, which Christ performed at the Last Supper, the more Christian it will be. But Christ's mass was most simple, without any display of vestments, gestures, chants, or other ceremonies, so that if it had been necessary to offer the mass as a sacrifice, then Christ's institution of it was not complete.[6]

Luther built on his arguments from *Babylonian Captivity* in his 1521 work, *The Misuse of the Mass*. In this work Luther argued that the false teachings concerning the Mass were based on errant conception of the priesthood: "Every true Christian really ought to know that in the New Testament there is no outward, visible priest, except those whom the devil has exalted and set up through human lies. We have only one single priest, Christ, who has sacrificed himself for us and all of us with him."[7] He then argued that no Scripture supports the idea that the Mass is a continual sacrifice, proclaiming, "Therefore I conclude on unshakeable grounds and with a good conscience that to offer mass as a sacrifice, and to have anointed and tonsured priests as is now the custom, is nothing else than to slander and deny Christ and to abrogate and remove his priesthood and all his law."[8] In his characteristically poignant manner, Luther laid the blame for these heresies in the papacy itself, pleading,

> I implore you, Christian friend, for God's sake, do not let yourself be moved one whit by the golden crowns and pearl mitres, red hats and cloaks, gold, silver, precious stones, mules, horses and retinue, with all the glory, ornament and splendor of the popes, cardinals and bishops, those lost sheep; but believe Paul in the Holy Spirit: these are not bishops, but idols, puppets, camouflages and wonders of the wrath of God.[9]

---

[4] Luther, *Babylonian Captivity*, Pelikan, Oswald, and Lehmann, *Luther's Works*, 36:35.
[5] Pelikan, Oswald, and Lehmann, *Luther's Works*, 36:51.
[6] Pelikan, Oswald, and Lehmann, *Luther's Works*, 36:52.
[7] Martin Luther, *The Misuse of the Mass*, 1521, in Pelikan, Oswald, and Lehmann, *Luther's Works*, 36:138.
[8] Pelikan, Oswald, and Lehmann, *Luther's Works*, 36:142.
[9] Pelikan, Oswald, and Lehmann, *Luther's Works*, 36:156.

The German Mass

These fierce attacks against the Roman Mass did not, however, imply that Luther believed every part of the sacred service to be heretical. On the contrary, Luther argued, "It would be good to keep the whole liturgy with its music, omitting only the canon."[10] He truly believed that "the service now in common use everywhere goes back to genuine Christian beginnings."[11] Luther did not object to the forms of the liturgy *per se*, but only those particular parts (most especially the eucharistic prayer and all that it symbolized) that conflicted with biblical teaching. He explained, "It is not now nor ever has been our intention to abolish the liturgical service of God completely, but rather to purify the one that is now in use from the wretched accretions which corrupt it and to point out an evangelical use."[12]

Luther's first attempt to correct these errors while maintaining what he could was in the formation of the *Formulae Missae* (1523), in which he retained the basic outline of the Roman mass and even retained the Latin, while removing what he considered the heretical elements of the canon. Although this satisfied him in terms of removing what was heresy, since the common people did not understand Latin, Luther set out to develop a distinctly German Mass (*Deutsche Messe*) in 1526, which, while in the vernacular, nevertheless maintained most of the general liturgical outline.[13] For the Kyrie he kept the Greek but supplied a simplified melody. He wrote his own German paraphrase of the Creed, "Wir glauben alle an einen Gott" ("We All Believe in One True God"), supplied a new hymn for the Sanctus, "Jesaja dem Propheten das geschah" (a paraphrase of Isaiah 6), and suggested singing "the German Agnus Dei" in place of the Latin. Later, the German hymn "Kyrie, Gott Vater in Ewigkeit" ("Kyrie, God Father in Heaven Above") replaced the Greek Kyrie, and Decius' "Allein Gott in der Höh sei Her" ("All Glory Be to God on High") replaced the Gloria of the Roman mass. He explicitly encouraged congregational participation, including ample indications, "then the whole congregational sings." Eventually, Lutherans replaced each part of the mass Ordinary with German hymns:

Kyrie: *Kyrie, Gott Vater in ewigkeit*
Gloria: *Allein Gott in der Höh sei Her*
Credo: *Wir glauben all an einen Gott*

---

[10] Martin Luther, "Table Talk No. 4676: The Introduction of Reforms in Leipzig, Continuation of the Preceding Entry," June 25, 1539, in Pelikan, Oswald, and Lehmann, *Luther's Works*, 54:361.

[11] Martin Luther, *Concerning the Order of Public Worship*, 1523, in Pelikan, Oswald, and Lehmann, *Luther's Works*, 53:11.

[12] Pelikan, Oswald, and Lehmann, *Luther's Works*, 53:20.

[13] Martin Luther, *The German Mass and Order of Service*, 1526, in Pelikan, Oswald, and Lehmann, *Luther's Works*, 53:51-90.

Sanctus: *Jesaha dem Propheten das gesachah*
Agnus Dei: *Christe, du Lamm Gottes*, or *O Lamm Gottes, unshuldig*[14]

He also placed a high emphasis upon preaching, stating in the preface to his *Duetsche Messe*, "The preaching and teaching of God's Word is the most important part of the divine service."[15] Luther did not advocate abolishing the Latin Mass entirely; indeed, it still continued especially in university cities.

Thus, Luther's German service emphasized the Service of the Word, while revising the theology and practice of the eucharist. He never intended for his service to become "a rigid law to bind or entangle anyone's conscience,"[16] but based on what he wrote in both liturgies, a basic shape for Lutheran worship took form:

Service of the Word
Introit (Hymn or Psalm)
German Kyrie
German Gloria
Prayer
Epistle
Hymn
Gospel
German Creed
Sermon

Service of the Table
Offertory
Eucharistic Prayer
    Salutation
    Sursum Corda
    The Lord's Prayer paraphrased
    Prayer of Thanks
Communion
    Words of Institution
    German Sanctus
    German Agnus Dei
Prayer of Thanks
Benediction

---

[14] See Robin A. Leaver, *Luther's Liturgical Music: Principles and Implications* (Minneapolis: Fortress Press, 2017), 301.
[15] *Luther's Works*, 53:68.
[16] Pelikan, Oswald, and Lehmann, *Luther's Works*, 53:61.

The Liturgical Calendar

Luther's reforms continued the observance of the four major festivals of the church year—Christmas (including Advent), Easter (including Lent), Pentecost (including Ascension) and Trinity Sunday (including other subsequent festival Sundays). However, he eliminated Corpus Christi, saints' days, and Marian festivals. He argued in the preface to his *Fomula Missae*, "We think that all the feasts of the saints should be abrogated, or if anything in them deserves it, it should be brought into the Sunday sermon."[17] Lutherans practiced the forty days of Lent and Holy Week but did not prohibit meat or observe other restrictions as did the Romanists:

> Lent, Palm Sunday, and Holy Week shall be retained, not to force anyone to fast, but to preserve the Passion history and the Gospels appointed for that season. This, however, does not include the Lenten veil, throwing of palms, veiling of pictures, and whatever else there is of such tomfoolery—nor chanting the four Passions, nor preaching on the Passion for eight hours on Good Friday. Holy Week shall be like any other week save that the Passion history be explained every day for an hour throughout the week or on as many days as may be desirable, and that the sacrament be given to everyone who desires it. For among Christians the whole service should center in the Word and sacrament.[18]

Music

Luther famously observed, "Indeed I plainly judge, and do not hesitate to affirm, that except for theology there is no art that could be put on the same level with music."[19] Luther's most notable reform with regard to the music of worship was to put the singing back into the mouths of the people. The process by which he accomplished this goal follows similarly the path by which he reformed the Mass. First, Luther removed any heretical texts from the current hymns. Commenting on the songs of the Roman Church, Luther observed,

> And indeed, they also possess a lot of splendid, beautiful songs and music, especially in the cathedral and parish churches. But these are used to adorn all sorts of impure and idolatrous texts. Therefore, we have unclothed these idolatrous, lifeless, and foolish texts, and divested them of their beautiful music. We have put this music on the living and holy Word of God in order to sing, praise, and honor it. We want the beautiful art of music to be properly used to serve her dear Creator and his Christians. He is thereby praised and honored and we are

---

[17] Martin Luther, *Formula Missae et Communionis pro Ecclesia Vuittembergensi*, 1523, in Pelikan, Oswald, and Lehmann, *Luther's Works*, 53:23.

[18] Luther, *German Mass*, *Luther's Works*, 53:90.

[19] Martin Luther, "Letter to Louis Senfl," 1530, in Pelikan, Oswald, and Lehmann, *Luther's Works*, 49:428.

made better and stronger in faith when his holy Word is impressed on our hearts by sweet music.[20]

Yet this was not enough for Luther. Very soon he insisted that the people sing in their own vernacular language, an argument he rooted in the Bible itself:

> Thus it was not without reason that the fathers and prophets wanted nothing else to be associated as closely with the Word of God as music. Therefore, we have so many hymns and Psalms where message and music join to move the listener's soul, while in other living beings and [sounding] bodies music remains a language without words. After all, the gift of language combined with the gift of song was only given to man to let him know that he should praise God with both word and music, namely, by proclaiming [the Word of God] through music and by providing sweet melodies with words.[21]

He stated in the Preface to his Latin Mass:

> I also wish that we had as many songs as possible in the vernacular which the people could sing during mass, immediately after the gradual and also after the Sanctus and Agnus Dei. For who doubts that originally all the people sang these which now only the choir sings or responds to while the bishop is consecrating? ... But poets are wanting among us, or not yet known, who could compose evangelical and spiritual songs, as Paul calls them (Col. 3:16), worthy to be used in the church of God. ... I mention this to encourage any German poets to compose evangelical hymns for us.[22]

The first natural step in that direction was to begin translating the available Latin hymns into German. Examples include "Allein Gott in der Höh sei Ehr" ("All Glory Be to God on High," Nicolaus Decius, 1523) from the Latin "Gloria in excelsis," "Komm, Heiliger Geist" ("Come, Holy Ghost," Martin Luther, 1523) from "Veni, Sancte Spiritus" (Pope Innocent III, thirteenth c.), and "Christum wir sollen loben schon" ("Now Praise We Christ," Martin Luther, 1524) from "A solis ortus cardine" (Caelius Sedulius, fifth c.). Furthermore, Luther borrowed tunes from Gregorian chant and other Roman Catholic office hymns for his early German hymns. Examples include ALL EHR' UND LOB SOLL GOTTES SEIN (*Kirchengesangbuch*, Strassburg, 1541) from the tenth-century *Gloria tempore paschali* and KYRIE, GOTT VATER IN EWIGKEIT (c. 1541) from the tenth-century *Kyrie fons bonitatis*. However,

---

[20] Martin Luther, "Preface to the *Burial Hymns*," 1542, in Pelikan, Oswald, and Lehmann, *Luther's Works*, 53:327–328.
[21] Martin Luther, "Preface to Georg Rhau's *Symphoniae Iucundae*, 1538, in Pelikan, Oswald, and Lehmann, *Luther's Works*, 53:323–324.
[22] Luther, *Formula Missae*, Pelikan, Oswald, and Lehmann, *Luther's Works*, 53:36–37.

translating from a syllable-timed language (Latin) to a stress-timed language (German) produced a somewhat awkward hymn that didn't "feel" right with the original Latin tunes. Regardless, Luther recognized that this is where the process must begin. He could not expect an indigenous hymnody to develop overnight, and he was convinced that the indigenous Christians in his culture must not ignore the vast wealth of Christian hymnody that had developed in the tradition of the church. Thus, Luther recognized the value in at least beginning with translations of what was already available in Latin, even if the translations did not feel natural quite yet.

Nevertheless, Luther did desire to cultivate a truly German hymnody, so his next step was to begin writing new German texts of the same quality and character of the Latin texts but with poetry that was stress-timed. He still sometimes used tunes that were available to him from the Latin tradition, which continued to be awkwardly matched with the new German lyrics. Yet, he bemoaned,

> But I would very much like to have a true German character. For to translate the Latin text and retain the Latin tone or notes has my sanction, though it doesn't sound polished or well done. Both the text and notes, accent, melody, and manner of rendering ought to grow out of the true mother tongue and its inflection.[23]

Luther then began to collect the best of German folk tunes to use with the new German texts. Sometimes this was successful, but other times the strong association of a tune with its secular lyrics caused distractions. Luther also did have available to him German sacred folk hymns that he could readily bring into the church. These were Christian songs that had been written by Germans in years past, not for corporate worship (which had been in Latin) but for daily devotion. Many of these were usable in the now German language services.

Finally, Luther encouraged Germans to write new tunes that flowed naturally from German syllabic stress, often employing the traditional bar form (AAB) of German folk tunes. Even then, he and other musicians modeled their new tunes after the noble character of the Latin chant melodies, Albert Schweitzer noting that Luther's EIN FESTE BERG was "woven out of Gregorian reminiscences,"[24] but they wrote the tunes so that the cadence matched the stress-timed nature of the German language.

Luther's genius was that he combined the most accessible of high art with the best of folk art to create the Lutheran chorale, and his efforts produced scores of influential German hymnals. In 1524 the earliest known collections of hymns were published, beginning with *Achtliederbuch*, which contained eight hymns, four of which were

---

[23] Luther, *German Mass*, Pelikan, Oswald, and Lehmann, *Luther's Works*, 53:54.
[24] Albert Schweitzer, *J. S. Bach*, trans. Ernest Newman (Neptune City, NJ: Paganiniana, 1980), 1:16.

written by Luther. Two other important hymnals were published in 1524, Enchiridion, oder *Handbuchlein* ("Little Handbook"), and *Geystliche Gesangk Buchleyn* ("Little Book of Sacred Songs"). The first of these contained twenty-five hymns, eighteen penned by Luther, and the second contained thirty-eight hymns, twenty-four by Luther. Luther personally supervised the publication of both the second and third collections, as well as several others between 1526 and 1545. His best-known hymn, *Einfeste Burg ist unser Gott* ("A Mighty Fortress is Our God"), first appeared in the 1529 collection, and the 1545 publication included all but two of his thirty-seven hymns.

> A mighty fortress is our God, a bulwark never failing;
> Our helper He, amid the flood of mortal ills prevailing:
> For still our ancient foe doth seek to work us woe;
> His craft and power are great, and, armed with cruel hate,
> On earth is not his equal.[25]

Hymnody flourished in later orthodox Lutheranism. The primary poet and hymn writer of orthodox Lutheranism was Paul Gerhardt (1607–1676), who wrote more than a hundred German hymns that accurately expressed the Lutheran conception of piety. His musician, Johann Crüger (1598–1662), provided the tunes for most of Gerhardt's hymns, and thus his musical output well expresses that piety as well.

Orthodox Lutherans placed discussions of music squarely in the category of *adiaphora* (see below).[26] They saw music as indifferent, but quite beneficial for Christian purposes within the liturgy. Meiser notes, "What about the fact that music serves to increase devotion, to restrain the evil spirit, to recall the human heart from sadness and sorrow, and also to impress the things heard more firmly upon the memory?"[27] They considered singing as the overflow of a heart of praise to God and as a preview of what Christians would enjoy in heaven. Theophil Grossgebauer said in 1667 of singing in corporate worship, "No more beautiful harmony can be found than this; it is nothing less than a type and foretaste of the eternal gathering in heaven."[28]

Yet because they saw it as both spiritually indifferent but also beneficial, they were very careful as to what kind of music they would allow in the public worship. For example, Dannhauer required that music be "sacred, glowing with love, humble, dignified, the praise of God sung by the voice of men and instruments with becoming grace

---

[25] Translation, Frederick H. Hedge, 1852.
[26] Johann Gerhard, *Loci Theologici*, 1610, V, 249; translated in Friedrich Kalb, *Theology of Worship in 17th Century Lutheranism*, trans. Henry P.A. Hamann (St. Louis: Concordia Publishing House, 1964), 139.
[27] Balthasar Meisner, *Collegium Adiaphoristicum*, 1663, 220; translated in Kalb, *Theology of Worship*, 141.
[28] Theophil Grossgebauer, *Wächterstimme Aus Dem Verwüsteten Zion (Drei Geistreiche Schriften)*, 1667, 194; translated in Kalb, *Theology of Worship*, 79.

and majesty," contrasted with "profane music, which is unspiritual, frivolous, proud, irreverent."[29] Likewise, Meiser insisted,

> Let all levity, and sensualism be absent [in music]. On the contrary, let gravity and a pious intent of the mind prevail, which does not contemplate and pursue bare harmony but devoutly fits and joins to it the inmost desires and emotions. For unless a ready spirit is joined to the turns of the voice and a vigilant and fervent heart to the varied words, we weary God and ourselves in vain with that melody. For not our voice but our prayer, not musical chords but the heart, and a heart not clamoring but loving, sings in the ear of God.[30]

They also rejected for liturgical use even serious music that was not directly connected to the Word of God. Brochmand insisted in 1664,

> Although we also disapprove of wanton songs, even the sweetest, and think that they should not be permitted either publicly or privately; and although we judge that even serious tunes, if not set to religious words, are not fit for the house of God; nevertheless, we cannot disapprove in the house of God, the singing of hymns whose contents are taken from Holy Writ; for God's Spirit approves such hymns both in the Old Testament (Ps. 150:4) and in the New Testament (Eph. 5:19).[31]

As important as music was, however, it always served theology and was subservient to the sermon. Music in worship had always to be "sung according to the nature of the gospel."[32] This is why Luther insisted that the music be sung in the vernacular of the people.

Baptism

The third significant worship reform was in the matter of baptism. Rome taught that a baptized infant was forgiven for both original and actual sin. According to a Papal Bull of 1439,

> The effect of this sacrament is the remission of all sin, original and actual; likewise of all punishment which is due for sin. As a consequence, no satisfaction for past sins is enjoined upon those who are baptized; and if they die before they

---

[29] Johann Konrad Dannhauer, *Hodsophia Christiana Seu Theologia Positiva*, 1666, 511; translated in Kalb, *Theology of Worship*, 142.
[30] Meisner, *Collegium Adiaphoristicum*, 220; translated in Kalb, *Theology of Worship*, 142.
[31] Jesper Rasmussen Brochmand, *Universae Theologiae Systema*, 1664, I, 50f.; translated in Kalb, *Theology of Worship*, 142–143.
[32] Charles Sanford Terry, *J. S. Bach's Cantata Texts, Sacred and Secular, with a Reconstruction of the Leipzig Liturgy of His Period* (London, 1926), 36.

commit any sin, they attain immediately to the kingdom of heaven and the vision of God.[33]

Luther believed that faith was a prerequisite for baptism but insisted that infants could exercise faith. He claimed,

> [The infant] comes to Christ in baptism, as John came to him, and as the children were brought to him, that his word and work might be effective in them, move them, and make them holy, because his Word and work cannot be without fruit. Yet it has this effect alone in the child. Were it to fail here it would fail everywhere and be in vain, which is impossible.[34]

Scripture as Normative

In reforming the Church's worship, Luther followed an overarching principle that can really be broken into three:

1. All liturgical elements that were contrary to the teachings of the Scripture were removed.
2. All those elements that were commanded by God were retained.
3. Those things that were neither commanded nor forbidden were considered *adiaphora* (Greek, "things indifferent").

This principle that set the Scripture as normative for Christian worship significantly changed the perspective from that of Rome. Yet since Luther did not insist that worship be absolutely *regulated* by the Word of God, but only that it follow the Scriptures as a *normative* rule, he retained in Lutheran worship many of the Roman innovations that he considered *adiaphora*—not forbidden, and therefore acceptable.

Luther himself struggled with how to treat *adiaphora*. He said of worship in *The Babylonians Captivity of the Church*, "We must be particularly careful to put aside whatever has been added to its original simple institution by the zeal and devotion of men: such things as vestments, ornaments, chants, prayer, organs, candles, and the whole pageantry of outward things."[35] Yet later, in *Brief Confession Concerning the Holy Sacrament* (1544), he alters his early judgment:

---

[33] Pope Eugene IV, in the Bull "Exultate Deo" (1439). See Charles George Herbermann, ed., *The Catholic Encyclopedia: An International Work of Reference on the Constitution, Doctrine, Discipline, and History of the Catholic Church*, vol. 2 (New York: Appleton, 1907), 259.

[34] Martin Luther, *Concerning Rebaptism*, 1528, in *Luther's Works*, 40:244.

[35] Luther, *Babylonian Captivity*, *Luther's Works*, 36:36.

For whatever is free, that is, neither commanded nor prohibited, by which one can neither sin nor obtain merit, this should be in our control as something subject to our reason so that we might employ it or not employ it, uphold it or drop it, according to our pleasure and need, without sinning and endangering our conscience.[36]

The Book of Concord

After the death of Martin Luther in 1546 and his collaborator Philip Melanchthon (b. 1497) in 1560, Lutheranism experienced a period of struggle. Internal debates over certain theological matters as well as external pressure from both Calvinists and Romanists alike motivated Lutheran leaders to unify themselves around their unique theology and practice. They achieved this unity through drafting the *Book of Concord*. This doctrinal standard consists of ten creedal documents that framed Lutheran orthodoxy, including a Preface, the three ecumenical creeds (the Apostles' Creed, Nicene Creed, and Athanasian Creed), the *Augsburg Confession*, the *Apology of the Augsburg Confession* (by Melanchthon), the *Small* and *Large Catechisms* of Luther, Luther's *Smalcald Articles*, Melanchthon's *Treatise on the Power and Primacy of the Power*, and the *Formula of Concord*, a confession written specifically to articulate key doctrinal issues and creating order in ecclesiastical and liturgical matters for the unification of Lutheranism. The final document of the Book was written by Jakob Andreae (1528–1590) and Martin Chemnitz (1522–1586) in order to unify all Lutherans around a single confession of faith and to settle disputes over *adiaphora* and other doctrinal and practical matters.

In particular, the *Formula of Concord* served to finalize debates concerning *adiaphora* in worship that had continued following Luther's death. In 1548, Holy Roman Emperor Charles V tried to unite Protestants and Catholics in his realm with the Augsburg Interim: Charles had entered an agreement with the Pope and invaded all of the Lutheran strongholds in the land. He ordered Protestants to adopt seven sacraments while allowing for priests to marry and for laity to receive both the bread and the cup. John Calvin wrote against it, but Philip Melanchthon was willing to compromise for the sake of the people (he was even willing to call the seven sacraments *adiaphora*). However, a significant number of other Luther theologians, led by Matthias Flacius (1520–1575), refused and thus were stripped of their offices, some banished, and some executed. In order to reach compromise, Melanchthon drew up the Leipzig Interim, an attempt to affirm Lutheran doctrinal beliefs while compromising on *adiaphora* such as church rituals. Calvin wrote a letter of rebuke to Melanchthon concerning the Leipzig Interim, claiming that Melanchthon "overextended the category of

---

[36] Luther, *Brief Confession Concerning the Holy Sacrament*, 1544, in *Luther's Works*, 38:316.

adiaphora." However, in the 1577 *Formula of Concord*, the position of Melanchthon prevailed. Article X, "Church Rites, Commonly Called *Adiaphora*" states:

> We believe, teach, and confess that the community of God in every place and at every time has the right, authority, and power to change, to reduce, or to increase ceremonies according to its circumstances, as long as it does so without frivolity and offense but in an orderly and appropriate way, as at any time may seem to be most profitable, beneficial, and salutary for good order, Christian discipline, evangelical decorum, and the edification of the church.[37]

Yet although the official position was that such *adiaphora* could be eliminated at will by individual congregations, by the seventeenth century some ceremonies, while considered not necessary to the essence of worship, were nevertheless deemed necessary for a proper worship service to take place. Thus, Friedrich Baldiun could write in 1628, "Divine worship cannot be without ceremonies; and though the ceremonies are not part of worship, they are yet its supports and ornaments."[38] In fact, Balthasar Meisner took an additional step when he noted, commenting on 1 Corinthians 14:26,

> The apostle has noted certain matters derived from their useful purpose on account of which rites and ceremonies can and should be introduced into the church; and if they are confined within those limits, even an uncommon use of ceremonies in the matter of religion and in the interest of piety is advantageous.[39]

This became the prevailing accepted position for orthodox Lutheranism.

---

[37] Theodore G Tappert, ed., *The Book of Concord the Confessions of the Evangelical Lutheran Church*. (Philadelphia: Mühlenberg Press, 1959), 612.

[38] Friedrich Balduin, *Tractatus Luculentus ... de ... Casibus ... Conscientiae* (Wittenberg: 1628, n.d.), 1135; translated in Kalb, *Theology of Worship*, 106.

[39] Meisner, *Collegium Adiaphoristicum*, 13; translated in Kalb, *Theology of Worship*, 109.

Chapter 12
Worship Regulated by Scripture

Many of Martin Luther's concerns and priorities were shared by other key leaders at the time. The five so-called "*Solas*"—*Sola Scriptura* ("Scripture alone"), *Sola Gratia* ("grace alone"), *Sola Fide* ("faith alone"), *Solus Christus* ("Christ alone"), and *Soli Deo Gloria* ("glory of God alone")—became consistent battle cries among emerging Protestant theologians. Even in worship, Reformers agreed in their renunciation of the sacrificial character of the mass and transubstantiation, as well as in their insistence in use of vernacular languages. Other matters—especially with regard to worship—divided them. In particular, reformations in Zurich, Strasbourg, and Geneva combined to form what is now known as the "Reformed" tradition.

Ulrich Zwingli

Ulrich Zwingli (1484–1531) began a Reformation in the Swiss Confederation just a few years after Luther, his first public controversy occurring in 1522 when he preached against fasting during Lent, encouraging his congregation to go ahead and eat sausage (known later as the "Affair of the Sausages"). His reforms continued in 1523 with his publication of *An Attack on the Canon of the Mass*, where he composed new prayers to replace the canon. Zwingli was pastor of the Great Minster in Zürich, where he sought to enforce his reforms through the city council and through public preaching.

Scripture as Regulative
In many respects, Zwingli's concerns with Roman Catholic theology and worship were nearly identical to Luther's, yet a few matters prevented them from unifying. Zwingli was committed to church practice being regulated by Scripture alone, leading him to advocate much more radical reforms than even Luther did. He disagreed with Luther's governing principle of worship, insisting that worship practices must have explicit biblical warrant, causing him to denounce images, other ceremonial adornments, and even music from public worship since he could find no warrant for them in the New Testament.[1] His new vernacular liturgy, *Act or Custom of the Lord's Supper* (1525), was far simpler than Luther's, consisting of Scripture reading, preaching, and prayer. Zwingli adamantly opposed the use of images in worship, a conviction that came to be

---

[1] Charles Garside, *Zwingli and the Arts* (New Haven: Yale University Press, 1966), 38, 44.

known as *iconoclasm*. He was convinced that worship was at its core spiritual, and thus "it is clear and indisputable that no external element or action can purify the soul."[2]

Memorial

While he held the Eucharist to be important, he believed that it had been grossly perverted, particularly with the doctrine of transubstantiation. Yet, while Luther and Zwingli agreed in their repudiation of transubstantiation, they could not come to a consensus on the meaning of "this is my body," the only one of fifteen articles in the Marburg Articles (an attempt at Lutheran and Zwinglian unification) the Zwinglians could not sign.[3] Luther argued that Christ could be literally present in sacramental union with the elements, while Zwingli insisted that Christ was present only at the Father's right hand and that the elements of the Lord's Supper were a memorial only; Christ's words were not to be taken literally:

> For it is clear that if they insist upon a literal interpretation of the word "is" in the saying of Christ: "This is my body," they must inevitably maintain that Christ is literally there, and therefore they must also maintain that he is broken, and pressed with the teeth. Even if all the senses dispute it, that is what they must inevitably maintain if the word "is" is taken literally, as we have already shown. Hence, they themselves recognize that the word "is" is not to be taken literally.[4]

Because he was concerned about the abuses, Zwingli's Communion services took place sitting around tables and occurred only once a quarter—on Christmas, Easter, Pentecost, and the patronal festival of Zurich (September 11)—rather than weekly. He stressed that the nature of the meal was thanksgiving: "This memorial is a thanksgiving and a rejoicing before Almighty God for the benefit which he has manifested to us through his Son."[5] During the celebration of the Lord's Table, the congregation recited the Gloria, the Apostles' Creed, and Psalm 113.

Zwingli also introduced *lectio continuo* preaching, that is, preaching successively through books of the Bible rather than the Roman tradition of *lectio selecta* (continued by Luther) of following a prescribed lectionary. "The people must be educated in the Word of God," Zwingli wrote, "so that neither vestments nor song have a part in the Mass."[6] He eliminated music altogether, finding no warrant for singing in the New Testament. As to the New Testament admonition to sing, Zwingli wrote, "Here Paul

---

[2] Ulrich Zwingli, *Of Baptism*, 1525, in G. W. Bromiley, ed., *Zwingli and Bullinger*, Library of Christian Classics (Philadelphia: Westminster Press, 1953), 156.

[3] Details of the Marburg Colloquy between Luther and Zwingli are described in *Luther's Works*, 38:15-39.

[4] Ulrich Zwingli, *On the Lord's Supper*, 1526, in Bromiley, *Zwingli and Bullinger*, 195.

[5] Ulrich Zwingli, "The Lord's Supper as administered in Zurich, 13 Apr. 1525," in Beresford James Kidd, *Documents Illustrative of the Continental Reformation* (Charleston, SC: BiblioBazaar, 2009), 444.

[6] Quoted in Garside, *Zwingli and the Arts*, 54.

does not teach mumbling and murmuring in the churches, but shows us the true song that is pleasing to God, that we sing the praise and glory of God not with our voices, like the Jewish singers, but with our hearts."[7]

Other Swiss Reformers

Another important Reformer in the Swiss Confederation, especially for liturgical reform, was Johannes Oecolampadius (1482–1531). Oecolampadius ministered in Basel, stimulating theological and liturgical reforms at least as early as Zwingli. In particular, his emphasis upon personal examination and church discipline in his 1526 *Form and Manner of the Lord's Supper* later influenced both Martin Bucer and John Calvin. Oecolampadius began his liturgy,

> All those who desire to receive the Sacraments, I admonish by the love of Christ to examine themselves beforehand, whether they know and have the mystery of the Sacrament, so that the pearls are not case before the swine, and they become guilty of the body and blood of Christ.[8]

Zwingli died in 1531 in a battle defending Zürich from five Catholic states that had aligned themselves in opposition to Zwingli's reforms and attacked the city. His reforms continued in Zürich, however, and spread throughout the Swiss Confederation, largely through the influence of his successor, Heinrich Bullinger (1504–1575). Bullinger organized and refined Zwingli's reforms, penning the Second Helvetic Confession in 1561, which was eventually adopted by Reformed churches through Switzerland, Scotland, Hungary, and France, and has come to be one of the most influential Reformed confessions. He also published *Christian Order and Custom* in 1535 as a slight revision of Zwingli's liturgy.

Service of the Word
Scripture Greeting
Prayers
    Illumination
    Intercession
    The Lord's Prayer
Scripture Reading
Sermon

---

[7] Garside, *Zwingli and the Arts*, 45.

[8] Johannes Oecolampadius, *Form and Manner of the Lord's Supper*, 1526, in Jonathan Gibson and Mark Earngey, eds., *Reformation Worship: Liturgies from the Past for the Present* (Greensboro, NC: New Growth Press, 2018), 153.

Service of the Table
Exposition of the Gospel and the Lord's Supper
Confession
1 Corinthians 11:20-29
Gloria
Salutation
John 6:47–63
The Apostles' Creed
Exhortation
    The Lord's Prayer
    Sursum Corda
    Prayer of Consecration
    Words of Institution
    Communion
        John 13–17
    Prayer of Thanks (or Psalm 113)
Words of Exhortation and Comfort
Benediction

Anabaptists

The term "Anabaptist" ("again baptizer") has been applied to various groups that arose during the sixteenth century who came to the conviction that according to New Testament example and prescription, only believers should be baptized. Unlike other Reformation groups—even later Baptists—Anabaptists do not constitute one, unified tradition; rather, groups that came to credobaptist ("believers baptism") convictions, in contrast to paedobaptist ("infant baptism"), varied in other theological and practical matters. Yet, exploration of the roots of these Anabaptist groups reveals some common characteristics, including with how they worshiped.

Among the earliest Anabaptists, those known as the Swiss Brethren, started as followers of Zwingli in Zurich. Some of them, such as Conrad Grebel (c. 1498–1526), Felix Manz, Balthasar Hubmaier (c. 1485–1528), and George Blaurock (1492–1529), and Michael Sattler (c. 1500–1527) affirmed Zwingli's reforms but thought he did not go far enough, especially in the matter of baptism. They argued, beginning in 1525, that a consistent application of Zwingli's emphasis on strict biblical authority necessarily led to credobaptist convictions since they could find infant baptism nowhere in the New Testament. Zwingli considered infant baptism "true and valid,"[9] and the Zürich council forbad what they considered "rebaptisms," resulting in execution by drowning of Manz and others.

---

[9] Zwingli, *Of Baptism, Zwingli and Bullinger*, 123.

Worship Regulated by Scripture

These "Radical Reformers" spread the doctrine of believer's baptism among dispirit groups like the Swiss Brethren, Hutterites, and Mennonites, followers of Menno Simons (1496–1561). Figures in these movements consistently demanded that all doctrine and practice should be based exclusively on clear biblical prescription and that there should be no compromise made with man-made innovations or traditions. Furthermore, rather than having a centralized ecclesial body formulate official statements of faith to which all must ascribe, which even Zwingli advocated, these groups insisted that each local congregation was free to establish its own faith and practice based upon the Word of God alone. Michael Sattler led a meeting of Swiss Anabaptists in 1527 to produce the Schleitheim Confession, which represents many of these core values.

> Baptism shall be given to all those who have been taught repentance and the amendment of life and [who] believe truly that their sins are taken away through Christ and to all those who desire to walk in the resurrection of Jesus Christ and be buried with him in death, so that they might rise with him; to all those who with such an understanding themselves desire and request it from us; hereby is excluded all infant baptism, the greatest and first abomination of the Pope. For this you have the reasons and the testimony of the writings and the practice of the apostles. We wish simply yet resolutely and with assurance to hold to the same.[10]

These convictions, of course, affected how Anabaptist groups worshiped. For the most part, Anabaptists rejected liturgical books, insisting that each congregation had the right to worship as they believed most consistent with New Testament example and precept. This central principle renders generalization concerning Anabaptist worship impossible, yet since these groups attempted to derive their worship practice from Scripture, several common characteristics appear. They all, of course, reserved baptism for those who expressly professed faith, and also insisted that only believers who had been baptized could participate in Communion. They also stressed the necessity of purity for those taking Communion, emphasizing church discipline, what they referred to as "the ban" (Matt. 18:15–18)—prohibiting those living in unrepentant sin from joining in the Lord's Table.

Likely the most influential Anabaptist in terms of liturgical reforms was Balthasar Hubmaier. His 1527 "A Form for Christ's Supper" outlines a service with detail unusual for most Anabaptists.[11] His service began with confession, instructing the congregation to recite,

---

[10] *The Schleitheim Confession*, 1527, trans. Walter Klaassen, *Anabaptism in Outline* (Scottdale, PA: Herald Press, 1981), 168.

[11] Balthasar Hubmaier, "A Form for Christ's Supper," 1527, in Robert Webber, ed., *Twenty Centuries of Christian Worship*, The Complete Library of Christian Worship (Nashville: Star Song Pub. Group, 1994), 2:216–225.

"Father we have sinned against heaven and against thee" (Luke 15:21). We are not worthy to be called thy children. But speak a word of consolation and our souls will be made whole. God be gracious to us sinners (Luke 19:1ff). May the almighty, eternal and gracious God have mercy on all our sins and forgive us graciously, and when he has forgiven us, lead us into eternal life without blemish or impurity, through Jesus Christ our Lord and Savior. Amen.[202]

The service moved immediately then to the priest "explaining the Scriptures concerning Christ," followed by questions from the congregation, which constituted the Service of the Word. Then followed preparation for the Lord's Table, which included an exposition of 1 Corinthians 11 and silent prayer. Hubmaier instructs that "the priest shall point out clearly and expressly that the bread is bread and the wine, wine and not flesh and blood, as has long been believed." The priest continued by leading the congregation through a series of vows in which they pledge their commitment to love God, serve him, and care for their neighbors and each other. A short eucharistic prayer followed:

We praise and thank thee, Lord God, Creator of the Heavens and earth, for all thy goodness toward us. Especially hast thou so sincerely loved us that thou didst give thy most-beloved Son for us unto death so that each one who believes in him may not be lost but have eternal life (John 3:16; 1 John 4:9; Rom. 8:32). Be thou honored, praised, and magnified now, forever, always and eternally. Amen.[202]

The Words of Institution were interspersed with distribution and consumption of the elements, and the service concluded with a charge to the congregation and benediction: "Arise and go forth in the peace of Christ Jesus. The grace of God be with us all. Amen."[202]

Hubmaier's service seems to have omitted music altogether; however, both Felix Manz and George Blaurock composed hymns, and hymnody flourished among other Anabaptist groups. Anabaptist hymns were both theologically sturdy and devotionally warm, such as this from Manz:

I will delight in singing,
in God o'er-joys my heart;
for grace He is me bringing,
that I from death depart,
which lasting ever, hath no end;

Worship Regulated by Scripture

I praise Thee Christ from heaven,
who dost my grief attend.[12]

A group of Anabaptists in Bavaria published a collection of hymns called the *Ausbund* in 1564, still in use today by the Amish (a second set of descendants from Menno Simons). The Mennonites later cultivated a four-part, a cappella hymn-singing tradition.

Martin Bucer

Martin Bucer (1491–1551) is an often-overlooked Reformer, but one who interacted with each of the other key Reformers and had significant influence particularly on worship reforms. Bucer ministered in Strasbourg, Germany and was heavily impacted by Martin Luther, but since Strasbourg was closely allied with the Swiss, he followed more in the Reformed tradition of Zwingli and Calvin than Luther. Bucer acted as a sort of mediator between Luther and Zwingli, urging them to unite, welcomed Calvin in Strasbourg for a period (more below), worked with Melanchthon on the Wittenberg Concord, a foundational document for Lutheranism, and in the final years of his life influenced Thomas Cranmer in England.

When Bucer arrived in Strasbourg in 1523, one of his first goals was to enact worship reforms and create a new liturgy. The Reformation there had already begun in earnest, but the liturgy in common use was simply a German translation of the Latin mass. His most significant work on the subject, *Grund und Ursach* ("Ground and Reason"),[13] completed the following year, condemned the idea of the mass as sacrifice, calling it "superstition,"[14] and stressed the idea of Communion in the service instead. Bucer insisted that worship that is "proper and pleasing to God"[15] must always be based upon "the sole, clear Word of God."[16] He produced three service books beginning in 1525 and published in 1526 the *Strasbourg Psalter*, culminating with the 1539 *The Psalter with Complete Church Practice*. Bucer replaced the sanctuary altar with a table in order to return the symbolism to a meal rather than a sacrifice, arguing, "we have only one altar, one sacrifice, and one priest—all of these are Christ."[17] He intentionally used the term "Lord's Supper" instead of "mass"[18] and sought to bring the reading and preaching of the Word (*lectio continuo*) back to a place of significance

---

[12] Trans., John J. Overholt, 1989.
[13] Martin Bucer, *Ground and Reason*, 1524, in Ottomar Frederick Cypris, *Martin Bucer's Ground and Reason: English Translation and Commentary* (Yulee, Florida: Good Samaritan Books, 2017).
[14] Cypris, *Martin Bucer's Ground and Reason*, 110.
[15] Cypris, *Martin Bucer's Ground and Reason*, 103.
[16] Cypris, *Martin Bucer's Ground and Reason*, 90.
[17] Cypris, *Martin Bucer's Ground and Reason*, 133.
[18] Cypris, *Martin Bucer's Ground and Reason*, 87.

alongside the Table. He rejected what he considered ceremonies of human origin, including vestments, insisting that church leaders had no right to invent new forms or to "enrich" existing forms with such innovations which either hid or replaced the basically biblical signs in worship. He noted,

> The Lord instituted nothing physical in his supper except the eating and drinking alone, and that for the sake of the spiritual, namely as in memory of him. ... [Yet] we have observed that many cared neither to consider seriously the physical reception nor the spiritual memorial, but instead, just as before, were satisfied with seeing and material adoration.[19]

Like his eucharistic theology, Bucer's service stood midway between those of Luther and Zwingli, reflecting the simplicity of biblically-regulated worship, yet retaining the basic order of the pre-Tridentine mass, including many of its elements, and advocating singing psalms and hymns:

Service of the Word
Confession
Pardon
Psalm or Hymns
Kyrie Eleison
Gloria in Excelsis
Prayer for Illumination
Psalm
Gospel
Sermon
Apostles' Creed (or Psalm or Hymn)

Service of the Table
Offertory
Eucharistic Prayer
    Salutation
    Prayer of Thanks
Communion
    Exhortation
    Words of Institution
    Hymn or Psalm
Prayers
Benediction

---

[19] Cypris, *Martin Bucer's Ground and Reason*, 117–118.

Ever desiring unity, Bucer attempted to unify Protestants and Catholics in Germany, separate from Rome. However, after the governing council of Strasbourg accepted the Augsburg Interim at the behest of Charles V in 1548, which re-imposed Catholic worship practices, Bucer was exiled to England, where he lived and interacted with Thomas Cranmer for the final years of his life.

John Calvin

Reformation among French-speaking people flourished under the leadership of John Calvin (1509–1564). Calvin had been educated in law rather than the priesthood, but after his conversion around 1530, he fled persecution to join the Reformation in Geneva in 1536 along with William Farel (1489–1531), where he began to preach *lectio continuo* through the Pauline epistles. The governing council of the city held considerable control over ecclesiastical matters in Geneva, at first resisting Calvin's reforms. They expelled Calvin from the city, who accepted the invitation of Martin Bucer to pastor French refugees in the city of Strasbourg. While there, Calvin began work on what would be his influential psalter and began to make liturgical revisions based on those implemented in German by Bucer. In 1541 the Genevan council invited Calvin back, and he ministered there until his death in 1564.

Scripture as Regulative

Similar to Zwingli and Bucer, Calvin's central goal was to return to the simple worship practices of the early church, strictly following biblical prescription. He argued that "a part of the reverence that is paid to [God] consists simply in worshiping him as he commands, mingling no inventions of our own."[20] He interpreted the Second Commandment as God defining "lawful worship, that is, a spiritual worship established by himself"[21] and insisted upon "the rejection of any mode of worship that is not sanctioned by the command of God."[22] Calvin also agreed with Zwingli and Bucer concerning iconoclasm. He argued,

> We think it unlawful to give a visible shape to God, because God himself has forbidden it, and because it cannot be done without, in some degree, tarnishing his glory. And lest any should think that we are singular in this opinion, those acquainted with the productions of sound divines will find that they have always disapproved of it. If it be unlawful to make any corporeal representation of God, still more unlawful must it be to worship such a representation instead of God,

---

[20] John Calvin, *Institutes of the Christian Religion* (Philadelphia: Westminster John Knox Press, 1960), 4.10.23.

[21] Calvin, *Institutes*, 2.8.17.

[22] John Calvin, *The Necessity of Reforming the Church*, trans. H. Beveridge (Philadelphia: Presbyterian Board of Publication, 1844), 23.

or to worship God in it. The only things, therefore, which ought to be painted or sculptured, are things which can be presented to the eye; the majesty of God, which is far beyond the reach of any eye, must not be dishonored by unbecoming representations.[23]

Calvin employed a particular argument of emphasizing the critical discontinuity between Old Testament worship and New Testament worship in much of his worship reforms. For example, in commenting on Roman Catholic worship, Calvin exclaimed, "What shall I say of ceremonies, the effect of which has been, that we have almost buried Christ, and returned to Jewish figures?"[24] He complained, "A new Judaism, as a substitute for that which God had distinctly abrogated, has again been reared up by means of numerous puerile extravagances, collected from different quarters."[25] He criticized the priesthood, noting, "Then, as if he were some successor of Aaron, he pretends that he offers a sacrifice to expiate the sins of the people."[26]

Music

Although Calvin agreed with Zwingli concerning biblical authority over worship practice, like Bucer he did not agree entirely with Zwingli on music in worship. While his goal was still biblical simplicity, he did allow unaccompanied, unison psalm singing, since he found support for such practices in Scripture. He argued that the practice was "very ancient" and done "among the apostles,"[27] and insisted that songs "incite us to prayer and to praise God, to meditate on his works, in order to love, fear, honor, and glorify him."[28] Calvin considered singing to be a form of prayer, noting that one kind of prayer consists of "words alone," while the other consists of "singing." He insisted, however, that Christians sing only inspired Scripture: "Now what St. Augustine says is true, that no one can sing things worthy of God, except what he may have received from him; when we shall have moved all around to search here and there, we shall find no better nor more proper songs to do this than the Psalms of David."[29] Over the course of the next twenty years, Calvin helped encourage the publication of several editions of the *Genevan Psalter*, an influential collection of metrical psalms with texts by Clement Marot (1497–1544) and Theodore Beza (1519–1605) and tunes by Louis Bourgeois (c. 1510–1560) and Claude Goudimel (c. 1510–1572). Its final editions in 1562 contained all 150 psalms with 125 tunes. He insisted that the character of music

---

[23] Calvin, *Institutes*, 1.11.12.
[24] Calvin, *Institutes*, 4.10.14.
[25] Calvin, *The Necessity of Reforming the Church*, 21.
[26] Calvin, *The Necessity of Reforming the Church*, 30.
[27] Calvin, *Institutes*, 3.20.32.
[28] John Calvin, "Preface to the *Genevan Psalter*, 1542, in *Hymnology: A Collection of Source Readings* (Lanham, MD: Scarecrow Press, 1996), 67.
[29] Music, *Hymnology*, 67.

in worship fit its solemn purpose, however, having "weight" and "majesty" rather than being "light" or "frivolous."[30] While he found warrant for singing in Scripture, Calvin did not approve instruments as Luther did. He argued that, while God allowed the people of Israel to use instruments in their worship, this practice terminated with the gospel.

Form of Church Prayers

In 1542 Calvin published a service book called *The Form of Church Prayers and Hymns*, which presented the liturgy he used in Geneva. He suggested in the Preface to his *Genevan Psalter* published in the same year, "Now there are briefly three things which our Lord commanded us to observe in our spiritual assemblies: namely, the preaching of his Word, prayers public and solemn, and the administration of the sacraments."[31] The service book's subtitle emphasizes Calvin's central concern: "According to the Custom of the Ancient Church." The liturgy he formulated for Geneva emphasized this biblical simplicity while not altogether ignoring what had developed in the previous centuries.[32] Calvin maintained his own unique understanding of the presence of Christ in the Supper, asserting that Christ was not actually present in the elements but that "all that Christ himself is and has is conveyed" to believers through the Spirit of Christ at the Supper.[33]

Calvin's service began with Psalm 124:8: "Our help is in the name of the Lord, who made heaven and earth." The first major element of the service, then, was corporate confession. He noted,

> Seeing that in every sacred assembly we stand in the view of God and angels, in what way should our service begin but in acknowledging our own unworthiness? ... In short, by this key a door of prayer is opened privately for each, and publicly for all.[34]

Calvin regularly began his services with a reading of the Ten Commandments, and after each commandment, the congregation would sing, *Kyrie eleison*, "Lord have mercy." He believed that in repenting each week through reading the Ten Commandments and singing a prayer of repentance, the people in his congregation would be formed into people who lived lives of repentance. Then followed a psalm, the reading of Scripture, and the sermon. Like Zwingli, Calvin abandoned lectionaries in favor of

---

[30] *Hymnology*, 67–68.
[31] Calvin, "Preface," Music, *Hymnology*, 63.
[32] See Hughes Oliphant Old, *The Patristic Roots of Reformed Worship New American Edition* (Black Mountain, NC: Worship Press, 2004).
[33] Calvin, *Institutes*, 4.14.12.
[34] Calvin, *Institutes*, 3.4.11.

lectio continuo preaching. Intercessory prayers and a paraphrase of the Lord's Prayer followed the sermon.

Calvin desired that Communion be observed "at least once a week,"[35] but the ruling council of Geneva would not allow it, instead following Zwingli's example of quarterly celebration. When observing the Table, his service transitioned between the Service of the Word and Communion with the traditional practice of affirming the Apostles' Creed, although for Calvin this consisted of a sung version. The service contained a prayer of thanks, including an invocation and the Lord's Prayer. Interestingly, here Calvin preserved the traditional *Sursum Corda*, yet as a prose monologue:

> Let us raise our hearts and minds on high, where Jesus Christ is, in the glory of his Father, and from whence we look for him at our redemption.[36]

In Calvin's eucharistic theology, he recovered the New Testament idea that in Christ and by the Holy Spirit, worshipers are raised to join in with the worship of heaven, represented at this climactic moment in the service:

> Let us not be bemused by these earthly and corruptible elements which we see with the eye, and touch with the hand, in order to seek him there, as if he were enclosed in the bread or wine. Our souls will only then be disposed to be nourished and vivified by his substance, when they are thus raised above all earthly things, and carried as high as heaven, to enter the kingdom of God where he dwells. Let us therefore be content to have the bread and the wine as signs and evidences, spiritually seeking the reality where the word of God promises that we shall find it.[37]

After reading the Words of Institution from 1 Corinthians 11, which unlike Luther and Bucer preceded the eucharistic prayer, the people partook of Communion, during which they sang a psalm of thanksgiving (Psalm 138). When all had finished, another prayer of thanksgiving was offered, and the service concluded with a final psalm of praise. Here is an outline of Calvin's service:

Service of the Word
Psalm 124:8
Ten Commandments
French Kyrie
Pardon
Psalm

---

[35] Calvin, *Institutes*, 4.17.43.
[36] ohn Calvin, *The Form of Church Prayers*, 1542, in *Prayers of the Eucharist*, 287.
[37] *Prayers of the Eucharist*, 287.

Prayer for Illumination
Gospel
Sermon
Intercessory Prayers
Paraphrase of the Lord's Prayer
Apostles' Creed

Service of the Table
Offertory
Words of Institution
Exhortation
Eucharistic Prayer
    Sursum Corda
    Prayer of Thanks
Communion
    Psalm
Prayer of Thanks
Psalm or Canticle
Benediction

Calvin's worship reforms in Geneva became the influential standard and model for several other traditions and have come to characterize quintessential Reformed worship. Calvin achieved unity with Zwingli's successor, Heinrich Bullinger (1504–1575), and subsequently the rest of the Swiss Reformed, in the *Consensus Tigurinus* of 1549, further defining the Reformed tradition.

One particular comment Calvin made in the context of his liturgical reforms supports the central focus of this book. When challenged by opponents that his concerns about worship were unnecessary, Calvin replied, "It is not true, as has been alleged, that we dispute about a worthless shadow. The whole substance of the Christian religion is brought into question."[38] Calvin recognized the formative relationship between liturgy and the Christian religion.

---

[38] Calvin, *The Necessity of Reforming the Church*, 103.

Chapter 13
The English Reformation

The Protestant Reformation stands as a prime example of the interplay between religion and liturgy—worldview, theology, cultus, and culture, and as is often the case, it is impossible to neatly determine cause and effect. Political power struggles, corruption in church leadership, scientific discoveries, advancements in technology, and genuine spiritual concerns all worked together to produce the theological and liturgical reforms of the sixteenth and seventeenth centuries. Yet in England, political issues had perhaps an even greater influence over reformations than in other regions.

The Church of England
While the reformations on the European continent found impetus in sincere desire for theological correction, the beginning of reformation in England had a less noble motivation. Because King Henry VIII (1491–1547) was forbidden by the Pope to annul his marriage with Catherine of Aragon simply because she could not provide him a male heir, the king demanded that Parliament declare independence from Rome. In 1534, Parliament passed the Acts of Supremacy, making Henry "supreme head in earth of the Church of England."

The Book of Common Prayer
However, Thomas Cranmer (1489–1556), the newly appointed Archbishop of Canterbury, shared many of the theological concerns that Luther and the other continental reformers had, and thus was able to promote similar reforms in the Church of England, particularly after Henry died in 1547 and Edward VI (1537–1553; son of Henry's third wife, Jane Seymour), came to the throne, whom Cranmer had tutored as a boy and who took interest in religious reform. During Edward's reign, Cranmer oversaw the compilation of two editions of the *Book of Common Prayer*, the governing liturgical guide for the Church of England. The first edition (1549) emphasized congregational participation, translated the Roman rite into English, drastically revised the eucharistic prayer, and removed transubstantiation language. However, having been forced to leave Strasbourg after it was retaken by the Holy Roman Empire, Martin Bucer took refuge in England and encouraged Cranmer to make more drastic reforms. Bucer's influence resulted in a second edition of the *Book of Common Prayer* in 1552, which removed the word "mass" from the liturgy, replaced the "altar" with a Communion table, forbad vestments for clergy, moved the Gloria to the end of the service, and

removed the Agnus Dei and Benedictus. Thus with this second edition, worship in England began to resemble more the reforms of Calvin and Bucer than Luther. Cranmer's prayers are noted particularly for the beauty of language, such as this prayer of confession from the Morning Prayer service, which first appeared in the 1552 edition, still used in many traditions today:

> Almighty and most merciful Father, we have erred, and strayed from thy ways like lost sheep. We have followed too much the devices and desires of our own hearts. We have offended against thy holy laws. We have left undone those things which we ought to have done, and we have done those things which we ought not to have done, and there is no health in us. But thou, O Lord, have mercy upon us, miserable offenders. Spare thou those, O God, who confess their faults. Restore thou those who are penitent, according to thy promises declared unto mankind in Christ Jesus our Lord. And grant, O most merciful Father, for his sake, that we may hereafter live a godly, righteous, and sober life, to the glory of thy holy Name. Amen.

Persecution under Bloody Mary

The 1552 book was only used for one year, however. In the following year Edward died, and Mary I (1516–1558; daughter of Henry's first wife, Catherine of Aragon), re-established Roman Catholicism in England and severely persecuted English Protestants, including the execution of Thomas Cranmer. Some Protestants fled England during Mary's reign. One such exile was Scottish Reformer John Knox. Knox had been living in London since 1549, after his release from Scottish prison due to his Protestant faith. He left England in 1554 and spent most of his exile in Geneva, where he was heavily influenced by John Calvin's theology and worship reforms. Knox reflected Calvin's conviction concerning biblical authority over worship practice when he argued, "All worshiping, honoring, or service invented by the brain of man in the religion of God, without his own express commandment is idolatry."[1] In 1556, Knox produced *The Forme of Prayers* based on Calvin's service book.

Anglo-Catholicism under Elizabeth

After Mary died in 1558 and Elizabeth I (1533–1603; daughter of Henry's second wife, Anne Boleyn) took the throne in England, Knox returned to Scotland and helped to spark a Reformation there with many of the same reforms as those in Geneva. While Elizabeth's personal religious convictions are uncertain, she desired peace and unity in England between the Catholics, Protestants, and a growing number of so-called

---

[1] John Knox, "A Notable Sermon or Confession Made by John Knox, April 4, 1550: Wherein Is Evidently Proved That the Mass Is, and Always Has Been, Abominable Before God, and to Be Idolatry," in *Writings of the Rev. John Knox* (Philadelphia: Presbyterian Board of Publication, 1842), 166.

"Puritans" who were advocating for even more radical reforms. These Puritans did not believe that the Reformation in England had progressed far enough, particularly as regulated by Scripture. Parliament passed a second Act of Supremacy in 1559, re-establishing the Church of England once again, along with an Act of Uniformity, which made church attendance compulsory and revised the *Book of Common Prayer* to restore some features of the 1549 edition such as vestments and a less strict definition of real presence in the eucharist.

The Church of England also attempted to maintain peace with church music. While service music and choral anthems began to appear for the trained musicians, Puritan influence led the congregations to sing metrical psalms. In 1562, the same year that the complete edition of the *Genevan Psalter* was published, John Day published *The Whole Booke of Psalmes, collected into Engish metre by T. Sternhold, I Hopkins, & Others*. This "Old Version" of the psalms dominated English singing until a "New Version" by Nahum Tate and Nicholas Brady was published in 1696. During the same period, exiles who had spent time in Geneva published several volumes of the *Anglo-Genevan Psalter*.

The 1662 *Prayer Book*, revised and published after the English Civil War (see below), established the liturgy for the Anglican Church through the twentieth century and is still the official Prayer Book of the Church of England. In most respects it was essentially Cranmer's 1549 Prayer Book with some additions from the 1552 book and other minor changes. The service begins with an Introit psalm or hymn, during which the priest proceeds to the altar. While the people kneel, the priest says the Lord's Prayer and the Collect for Purity:

> ALMIGHTY God, unto whom all hearts be open, all desires known, and from whom no secrets are hid; Cleanse the thoughts of our hearts by the inspiration of thy Holy Spirit, that we may perfectly love thee, and worthily magnify thy holy Name, through Christ our Lord. Amen.

Then turning toward the congregation, the priest reads the Ten Commandments; after each commandment, the people reply with *Kyrie eleison*: "Lord, have mercy upon us, and incline our hearts to keep this law." Following the final commandment, they say, "Lord, have mercy upon us, and write all these thy laws in our hearts, we beseech thee." The priest then prays the collect of the day. An Epistle reading, with a hymn of response, and Gospel reading follow, after which the people recite the Nicene Creed, and the priest delivers the sermon. Following the sermon, the priest prepares the Communion elements, during which a hymn may be sung, and the priest then leads intercessory prayers for the Church. He then invites the faithful to partake of Communion, exhorting them to confess their sins to the Lord, using the following prayer:

Almighty God, Father of our Lord Jesus Christ, Maker of all things, Judge of all men; we acknowledge and bewail our manifold sins and wickedness, which we from time to time most grievously have committed, by thought, word, and deed, against thy divine Majesty, provoking most justly thy wrath and indignation against us. We do earnestly repent, and are heartily sorry for these our misdoings, the remembrance of them is grievous unto us; the burthen of them is intolerable. Have mercy upon us, have mercy upon us, most merciful Father; for thy Son our Lord Jesus Christ's sake, forgive us all that is past, and grant that we may ever hereafter serve and please thee in newness of life, to the honor and glory of thy Name, through Jesus Christ our Lord. Amen.

The priest then pronounces the Absolution and Words of Comfort from Scripture:

Almighty God our heavenly Father, who of his great mercy hath promised forgiveness of sins to all them that with hearty repentance and true faith turn unto him; have mercy upon you, pardon and deliver you from all your sins, confirm and strengthen you in all goodness, and bring you to everlasting life, through Jesus Christ our Lord. Amen.

Hear what comfortable words our savior Christ saith unto all that truly turn to him.

Come unto me all that travail and are heavy laden, and I will refresh you (Matt. 11:28).

So God loved the world, that he gave his only begotten Son, to the end that all that believe in him should not perish, but have everlasting life. (John 3:16)

This is a true saying, and worthy of all men to be received, that Jesus Christ came into the world to save sinners (1 Tim. 1:15).

If any man sin, we have an Advocate with the Father, Jesus Christ the righteous, and he is the propitiation for our sins (1 John 2:1).

The eucharistic prayer follows, beginning with the *Sursum Corda* and proceeding with the prayer of thanks and the Sanctus in English. Then the prayer continues with expression of humility, consecration, including the Words of Institution. He then receives Communion himself, distributes to any other clergy, and invites the people to partake. The congregation joins together with the Lord's Prayer once all have communed, and the priest prays a Prayer of Oblation or Thanksgiving. The Service concludes with the Gloria in English and a Benediction. Here is a basic outline of the service:

Service of the Word
Introit Psalm or Hymn
The Lord's Prayer (short version)
Collect for Purity

Ten Commandments
English Kyrie
Collect
Epistle
Gradual Hymn
Gospel
Nicene Creed
Sermon (optional)

Service of the Table
Offertory (with optional hymn)
Intercessory Prayer
Exhortation
Confession and Absolution
Eucharistic Prayer
    Sursum Corda
    Preface
    English Sanctus
    Words of Institution
Communion (with optional English Agnus Dei)
The Lord's Prayer (long version)
Prayer
English Gloria
Benediction

Puritan Worship

Conflict between the growing Puritan faction and the bishops during the reign of James I (from 1603 to 1625) and especially Charles I (from 1625 to 1649) eventually led Parliament to appoint in 1643 an Assembly of theologians, including Anglican bishops and Puritans (many from Scotland) to meet in Westminster Abbey and discuss restructuring the Church of England. The Assembly produced four key documents that reflected significant Calvinist Puritan influence in both theology and worship practice: A Confession of Faith, a Larger and Shorter Catechism, and a *Directory for the Public Worship of God*. The *Directory*, more of a guide for public worship than a prescriptive prayer book, centered worship around the reading of Scripture and insisted only what Scripture mandates for worship may be included in public worship. Like Calvin and Knox before them, the Westminster divines rooted their regulative principle in their doctrine of Scripture:

> The whole counsel of God, concerning all things necessary for his own glory, man's salvation, faith, and life, is either expressly set down in Scripture, or by good and necessary consequence may be deduced from Scripture: unto which

nothing at any time is to be added, whether by new revelations of the Spirit, or traditions of men. (Westminster Confession of Faith [WCF] 1:6)

Their bibliology would not allow for any additions to worship beyond what God had prescribed in his Word:

But the acceptable way of worshipping the true God is instituted by himself, and so limited by his own revealed will, that he may not be worshipped according to the imaginations and devices of men, or the suggestions of Satan, under any visible representation or any other way not prescribed in the holy Scripture. (WCF 22:1)

The regulative principle of Calvin, Knox, and the Puritans found its rationale not only in logical extension of the doctrine of *sola Scriptura*, but also in the conviction that church authority was limited by clear scriptural precepts and had no right to constrain the free consciences of individual Christians. As the Westminster Confession explained,

God alone is Lord of the conscience, and hath left it free from the doctrines and commandments of men which are in any thing contrary to his Word, or beside it in matters of faith or worship. So that to believe such doctrines, or to obey such commandments out of conscience, is to betray true liberty of conscience; and the requiring an implicit faith, and an absolute and blind obedience, is to destroy liberty of conscience, and reason also. (WCF 20:2)

The *Directory* does, however, present a basic liturgical structure for use in corporate worship. The service begins with an opening prayer that acknowledges the greatness of God and the unworthiness of man, requesting that God would bless and accept the people's worship. Then followed a reading from Scripture, "ordinarily one chapter of each Testament," *lectio continuo* from week to week through the whole Bible. The congregation would then sing a psalm, and the minister offers a prayer before the sermon, first focused on confession of sin and forgiveness in Christ, followed by general petitions and a prayer for the ministry of the Word. The sermon commenced, accompanied afterwards by a prayer of petitions based on the sermon and sometimes the Lord's Prayer. An optional psalm transitions between the Word and Table, which was "frequently to be celebrated."[2] Communion consisted of a brief exhortation and warning concerning the proper use of the sacrament, a blessing of the elements "by the Word of Institution and Prayer,"[3] the Eucharistic Prayer, distribution of the elements, a post-

---

[2] *The Directory for the Public Worship of God* (Philadelphia: William S. Young, 1851), 491.
[3] *Directory for the Public Worship of God*, 492.

Communion prayer, and collection of alms for the poor. The following is the basic order of worship as recommended in the Westminster *Directory*:

Service of the Word
Call to Worship
Prayer
   Confession
   Pardon
   Illumination
Old Testament Reading
     New Testament Reading
Psalm
Prayer
   Confession
   Pardon
   Intercession
Scripture Reading
Sermon
Prayer of Thanks
Psalm

Service of the Table
Exhortation and Invitation
Words of Institution
Eucharistic Prayer
Communion
Exhortation
Psalm or Canticle
Benediction

These documents were only employed by the Church of England, however, during the Commonwealth (1653–1659) after Civil War. Upon the restoration of the monarchy in 1661, the *Book of Common Prayer* was republished with little revision, though the Westminster Standards remain important for denominations that trace their lineage back to English Puritans. Anglican worship in the late-seventeenth and eighteenth centuries gradually devolved, with a progressive neglect of the eucharist and diminishing of true piety, leading to the rise of many dissenting and non-conformist groups from within the Church.

Baptists
In addition to the Puritans, who sought more radical reforms within the Anglican Church that would bring it closer to what they considered biblical fidelity, others also

objected to the union of church and state in England and therefore left the Church entirely. These so-called "Separatists" splintered into several different dissenting factions, but one such group fled England for Amsterdam in the early seventeenth century under the leadership of John Smyth (c. 1544–1612) and Thomas Helwys (c. 1575–1616), and influenced by Mennonites there, came to the conviction that only believers should be baptized. This group became known as Baptists.

Like the Puritans, the governing principle of these early Baptists was commitment to explicit, New Testament commands for doctrine and practice. Thus, failing to recognize any direct commands in Scripture, they aggressively opposed any kind of formalism in worship. "The Spirit is quenched," Smyth argued, "by set forms of worship, for therein the spirit is not at liberty to utter itself, but is bounded in."[4] They were opposed to congregational singing or even the reading of Scripture in a public service; everything had to be spontaneous:

> We hold that the worship of the New Testament properly so called is spiritual proceeding originally from the heart, and that the reading out of a book (though a lawful ecclesiastical action) is no part of spiritual worship.[5]

A 1609 letter from a member of Smyth's congregation presents a helpful picture of a typical early Baptist service:

> We begin with a prayer, after read some one or two chapters of the Bible; give the sense thereof and confer upon the same; that done, we lay aside our books and after a solemn prayer made by the first speaker he propoundeth some text out of the Scripture and prophesieth out of the same by the space of one hour to three quarters of an hour. After him standeth up a second speaker and prophesieth out of the said text the like time and space, sometimes more, sometimes less. After him, the third, the fourth, the fifth &c, as the time will give leave. Then the first speaker concludeth with prayer as he began with prayer, with an exhortation to contribution to the poor, which collection being made is also concluded with prayer.[6]

Thomas Helwys returned with the congregation to London in 1612 and established a church there, beginning what is called the General Baptist movement, due to the theology of general atonement held by these congregations. These General Baptists were characterized by free, spontaneous worship and aversion to doctrinal creeds.

---

[4] John Smyth, *The Differences of the Churches*, 1608 in W. T. Whitley, ed., *The Works of John Smyth* (Cambridge: Cambridge University Press, 1915), I:277.
[5] *The Works of John Smyth*, I:273.
[6] Barrington Raymond White, *The English Separatist Tradition: From the Marian Martyrs to the Pilgrim Fathers* (Oxford: Oxford University Press, 1971), 126–127.

The English Reformation

Other English Separatists with more Calvinistic theology came to Baptist convictions later in the seventeenth century, being called Particular Baptists due to their doctrine of particular redemption. While these Particular Baptists affirmed believer's baptism and strict scriptural regulation of worship, they were more open to forming confessions of faith and simple formality in worship. In 1644 a group of Particular Baptists created the London Confession of Faith, revised in 1689 as the Second London Baptist Confession, a document still influential among Reformed Baptists today. The wording of the 1689 Second London Baptist Confession is almost identical to the 1646 Westminster Confession of Faith, except for on key doctrines such as baptism and church government.

Particular Baptist leaders wrote in 1645 the following in response to Edmond Calamy's defense of infant baptism: "But your infant baptism is a religious worship, for which there is no command, nor any example, written in the Scripture of truth."[7] Likewise, Hercules Collins (1646–1702) noted about infant baptism, "We have neither precept nor example for that practice in all the Book of God."[8] In their 1688 *Confession*, London Baptists argued against infant baptism on the basis that it was not prescribed in Scripture.[9] Furthermore, these Baptists' commitment to the mode of immersion sprang from their conviction that this is exactly what the New Testament prescribed. John Norcott (1621–1676), for example, rejected the mode of sprinkling, because "God is a jealous God, and stands upon small things in matters of Worship."[10] Thus, the 1644 London Confession articulated the "way and manner" of baptism and defined it as "dipping or plunging under water," and the 1689 Confession insisted that "immersion, or dipping of the person in water, is necessary to the due administration of this ordinance."[11]

The 1689 Baptist Confession also differed with the Westminster Confession on the matter of church polity. The LBC (London Baptist Confession) contains several more articles in its chapter on the church than does the WCF, including this statement on the organization of a church:

> A particular church, gathered and completely organized according to the mind of Christ, consists of officers and members; and the officers appointed by Christ to be chosen and set apart by the church (so called and gathered), for the peculiar

---

[7] Benjamin Cox, Hanserd Knollys, and William Kiffin, *A Declaration Concerning The Publike Dispute Which Should Have Been in the Publike Meetinghouse of Alderman-Bury* (London: n.p., 1645), 10, 11.

[8] Hercules Collins, *An Orthodox Catechism: Being the Sum of Christian Religion Contained in the Law and Gospel* (London: n.p., 1680), 26–27.

[9] *Confession of Faith, Put Forth by the Elders and Brethren of Many Congregations of Christians, (Baptized Upon Profession of Their Faith) in London and the Country, A* (London: n.p., 1688), 114–115.

[10] John Norcott, *Baptism Discovered Plainly & Faithfully, According to the Word of God* (American Baptist Publication Society, 1878), 31.

[11] William Latane Lumpkin, *Baptist Confessions of Faith* (Judson Press, 2011), 6, 291.

administration of ordinances, and execution of power or duty, which he entrusts them with, or calls them to, to be continued to the end of the world, are bishops or elders, and deacons. (LBC 26:8)

The WCF contains no such statement on how a church should be organized. The LBC furthermore eliminated the chapter "Of Synods and Councils" (WCF 31) since Baptists did not find New Testament warrant for such. Church autonomy, congregational government, and the limiting of church offices to elders and deacons each illustrates these Baptists' concern that their polity be governed by explicit New Testament prescription.

On the subject of worship, however, language in the London Baptist Confession is very similar to the earlier Westminster Confession. Early English Baptists clearly insisted, like their Presbyterian counterparts, "The acceptable way of worshipping the true God is instituted by himself" (LBC 22:1 parallel to WCF 21:1). Furthermore, many of the early English Baptist leaders explicitly articulated a clearly defined regulative principle. For example, John Spilsbury (1593–1668) declared, "The holy Scripture is the only place where any ordinance of God in the case aforesaid is to be found, they being the fountain-head, containing all the instituted Rules of both of Church and ordinances."[12] John Gill (1697–1771) later proclaimed, "Now for an act of religious worship there must be a command of God. God is a jealous God, and will not suffer anything to be admitted into the worship of him, but what is according to his word and will."[13] These Baptists were not simply articulating the doctrine of *Sola Scriptura* or emphasizing the authority of Scripture upon church practice, as any good Protestant would. Rather, they were insisting that the practices of the church be limited to what Scripture—specifically, the New Testament—commanded, and as William Kiffin (1616–1701) noted, "that where a rule and express law is prescribed to men, that very prescription, is an express prohibition of the contrary."[14] This concern among Baptists continued well into the early nineteenth century, as seen by John Fawcett's (1740–1817) very direct assertion,

> No acts of worship can properly be called holy, but such as the Almighty has enjoined. No man, nor any body of men have any authority to invent rites and ceremonies of worship; to change the ordinances which he has established; or to invent new ones ... The divine Word is the only safe directory in what relates to his own immediate service. The question is not what we may think becoming,

---

[12] John Spilsbury, *A Treatise Concerning the Lawfull Subject of Baptisme* (London: n.p., 1643), 89.

[13] John Gill, *A Body of Practical Divinity: Or a System of Practical Truths, Deduced from the Sacred Scriptures* (The Baptist Standard Bearer, Inc., 2001), 899.

[14] William Kiffin, *A Sober Discourse of Right to Church Communion* (Baptist Standard Bearer, Incorporated, 2006), 28–29.

The English Reformation

decent or proper, but what our gracious Master has authorized as such. In matters of religion, nothing bears the stamp of holiness but what God has ordained.[15]

Notably, these Baptists believed that their application of the regulative principle was more consistent than that of other groups, a matter that will be explored below. Matthew Ward summarizes well the Baptist position, in contrast to both the normative principle of the Anglicans and what Baptists considered the inconsistent regulative principle of the Presbyterians:

> The same Anglicans who had rejected the popish practices of crucifixes, beads, praying to the Saints, icons, and pilgrimages had retained bowing at the name of Jesus, signing the cross in baptism, wearing the surplice in preaching, and kneeling at the Lord's Supper. The same Presbyterians who had rejected those latter practices had retained the church hierarchy, a directory of worship, infant baptism, and compulsory church attendance and tithes. The Baptists saw inconsistency therein and wanted to practice a consistent application of Scripture in their worship because they desired true reverence for God and true humility before him.[16]

One of the clearest examples of the difference between the Reformed regulative principle and that of the Baptists is in a difference in wording concerning biblical authority over worship between their two confessions. As was shown earlier, the 1689 London Baptist Confession is almost identical to the Westminster Confession in its articulation of the regulative principle. Yet in one very important change, the LBC reveals a stricter application of the principle than that of the WCF. Baptists changed the statement "or by good and necessary consequence may be deduced from Scripture" in WCF 1.6 to "or necessarily contained in the Holy Scripture" in LBC 1.6. Puritans demanded that the elements of worship have clear biblical warrant but were willing to be flexible as to the forms those elements took as long as those forms "by good and necessary consequence may be deduced from Scripture" (WCF 1:6). Baptists, on the other hand, insisted that all aspects of church practice be "expressly set down or necessarily contained in the Holy Scripture."

Particular Baptists also accepted congregational singing relatively early, first successfully argued by Benjamin Keach in his 1691 *The Breach Repaired in God's Worship*. He believed singing in worship to be "so clear an Ordinance in God's Word" and

---

[15] John Fawcett, *The Holiness Which Becometh the House of the Lord* (Halifax: Holden and Dawson, 1808), 25.

[16] Matthew Ward, *Pure Worship: The Early English Baptist Distinctive* (Eugene, OR: Pickwick Publications, 2014), 141.

declared, "The holy Ghost doth injoin [sic] the Gospel-Churches to sing *Psalms*, as well as *Hymns*, and *spiritual Songs*. Will you take upon you to countermand God's holy Precept?"[17] In particular, he first introduced the singing of hymns to his congregation at the end of their Lord's Supper observance because of the biblical example of Christ and his disciples at the end of the Last Supper (Matt. 26:30; Mark 14:26). He inquired,

> Did not Christ sing an Hymn after the Supper? Would he have left that as a Pattern to us, and annexed it to such a pure Gospel-Ordinance, had it been a Ceremony, and only belonging to the Jewish Worship?[18]

Other Dissenting Congregations

Other Separatist and Puritan groups came and went during the seventeenth and eighteenth centuries, all determined to follow Scriptural prescription as literally as possible, leading them to resist interference by the state Church. This very core conviction, however, caused many sectarian debates and irreconcilable disagreements such that, in some cases, a given church would separate itself off from every other. Because of this lack of unity combined with their reticence to use formal liturgical texts, generalizations concerning their worship are difficult to make. However, several groups and individuals, which eventually formed into Congregationalists, Presbyterians, and Baptists, deserve mention.

The Pilgrims

Anglican minister John Robinson (1575–1625), due to his concern for what he called "free prayer," that is, "prayers conceived first in our hearts before they be brought forth in our lips,"[19] led his congregation to separate from the Church of England. Insistent that the prescribed liturgies of a prayer book were "unnatural, bastardly, and profane,"[248] he moved his congregation to Plymouth, Massachusetts in 1620. These "Pilgrims" maintained the simple, Scripture-regulated services they advocated in England and sang from a metrical psalter compiled in 1612 by Henry Ainsworth, which they considered to be more literal than Sternhold and Hopkins.

New England Puritans

The new world provided a safe haven also for Puritans who had given up hope of reforming the Church in England. Settling first in Salem and Boston, Massachusetts in 1629 and 1630, these Puritans considered themselves still Anglicans, but those who

---

[17] Benjamin Keach, *The Breach Repaired in God's Worship* (London: Hancock, 1691), 99, 129.
[18] Keach, *The Breach Repaired*, 73.
[19] Quoted from Bryan D. Spinks, *From the Lord and "The Best Reformed Churches": A Study of the Eucharistic Liturgy in the English Puritan and Separatist Traditions, 1550-1633* (Eugene, OR: Wipf & Stock, 2004), 32.

worshiped in pure, biblical fashion. Boston pastor John Cotton (1584–1652) provided in his 1645 *The Way of the Churches of Christ in New England* a helpful picture of worship among these Puritans.[20] They began the service with "prayers and intercessions and thanksgiving for ourselves and for all men, not in any prescribed form of prayer, or studied liturgies, but in such manner as the Spirit of grace and or prayer (who teacheth all the people of God, what and how to pray, Rom. 8:26, 27) helpeth our infirmities."[248] This was followed by the singing of a psalm and the reading and preaching of Scripture. The congregation sang more psalms "many times after" the sermon. They celebrated the Lord's Supper "once a month at least,"[21] not according to "any set forms prescribed to us, but conceived by the Minister." The Minister simply blessed the bread, broke it, and gave it to all to eat, followed by the same with the cup.

Like the Separatist Pilgrims, New England Puritans also considered the Old Version not literal enough, producing a new psalter in 1640, the *Bay Psalm Book*, the first book published in the new world. Later, largely as a result of the First Great Awakening and particularly the influence of George Whitefield, churches in the colonies began to also include the hymns of Isaac Watts, whose hymns dominated worship in America thereafter. Other congregations eventually made their way to the American colonies, such as Congregationalists, Dutch Reformed, German Reformed, Lutheran, Scottish Presbyterians, and Baptists, each bringing with them the worship practices typical of their English traditions.

Dissenting Worship in England

While some Separatists and Puritans found freedom to worship in the new world, others remained in England and formed independent congregations there, attempting to establish pure worship. A few accounts of services in such churches help to provide a picture of what worship was like.

Isaac Watts (1674–1748), an independent pastor in London, stood in this tradition of simple, Bible-regulated worship. Watts is likely best known as the Father of English hymnody, authoring some of the most well-known English hymns such as "O God, Our Help in Ages Past," "When I Survey the Wondrous Cross," and "Jesus Shall Reign." Not satisfied with the poor condition of metrical psalm singing in English churches, Watts set out to produce hymns that were both theologically rich and singable for a musically untrained congregation. He produced four separate hymn collections, including his "Christianizations" of psalms in *The Psalms of David Imitated in*

---

[20] John Cotton, *The Way of the Churches of Christ in New-England* (London: Printed by Matthew Simmons, 1645), 66–69.

[21] John Cotton, Letter to Edward Winslow, 1646, quoted from Doug Adams, *Meeting House to Camp Meeting: Toward a History of American Free Church Worship* (Saratoga, CA: Modern Liturgy-Resource Publications, 1981), 31.

the Language of the New Testament (1719). Watts also authored an influential *Guide to Prayer* (1715), and an early account of worship of his church, Bury Street Church of London, presents a helpful picture of what constituted worship in independent (as well as Particular Baptist) churches in England at the time:

Psalm
Short prayer
Exposition of Scripture
Optional psalm or hymn
Prayer
Sermon
Psalm or hymn
Short prayer
Benediction[22]

Communion was celebrated during an afternoon service on the first Sunday of the month, following a shorter Service of the Word, and consisting of the Words of Institution, "that it may every be kept in mind to regulate every part of the practice," and "a short prayer of eight or ten minutes" to bless the elements.[23]

This service structure seems to characterize the other accounts of Dissenting worship in the time, including that of Presbyterian Richard Baxter (1615–1691) in 1690[24] and Rothwell Independent Meeting in Northampton around 1700.[25]

---

[22] From the Bury Street Church records, originally printed by John Rippon in *The Baptist Annual Register* of 1800–1801 and reprinted in T. G. Crippon, "From the Bury Street Church Records," *Transactions of the Congregational Historical Society*, 6, 1913, 334–342.

[23] Crippon, "From the Bury Street Church Records," *Transactions of the Congregational Historical Society*, 6, 1913, 334, 336.

[24] Journal of Rober Kirk, 1690, quoted in Donald Maclean, *London at Worship: 1689–1690* (Manchester: Presbyterian Historical Society, 1928).

[25] *Account of the Doctrine and Discipline of Mr. Richard Davis of Rothwell in the County of Northampton, and Those of His Separation* (London: n.p., 1700), 20–21.

Conclusion to Part Four

For both religion and liturgy, the sixteenth and seventeenth centuries saw the beginnings of fragmentation. What for hundreds of years had been cultural and liturgical unity flowing from the dominance of Christian religion began to splinter, paving the way for a fundamental shift in worldview.

Theologically, of course, this period was a time of significant reform. The Protestant Reformers, and even counter-Reformation Roman Catholics, consciously emphasized a return to ancient beliefs and practices. The dominant worldview of the sixteenth and seventeenth centuries remained fairly consistent with what had come before, but fractures began to appear. As in the past, subtle changes in underlying worldview were both for good and ill. For both theological and cultural reasons, this period saw a gradual shift from a dominant emphasis on community to a focus on the individual. Positively, this created a deep appreciation for the value of human dignity and forced people to consider whether they had a personal relationship with God through Christ or if they were simply trusting the Church for their salvation. Negatively, this eventually led to an overly optimistic view of what humanity could do on its own, elevating the individual above all else, including community and even God.

Culturally, the sixteenth and seventeenth centuries can be characterized by a renewed interest in ancient documents and traditions—"Ad fontes!" ("to the sources") was the cry of the day, finding expression both in the study of the humanities and classical Greek and Roman literature as well as the translation of Scripture from its original Hebrew and Greek into modern vernacular. But this was also a period in which a culture that had for a long time been cultivated within a united Christian environment now began to give way to splintering culture influenced by competing value systems. The situation did not change overnight, of course—philosophical shifts always precede change in the culture.

While disagreements concerning worship theology and practice created irreconcilable division between various theologians and their adherents, largely the cause of denominationalism following the Protestant Reformation, much about the essence of worship among these dispirit groups remained consistent and unified. Each group maintained a focus on worship in their primary gatherings, a worship that was characterized by reverence and intentional faithfulness to Scripture, though what this faithfulness required sometimes differed. This common understanding of the nature of worship, despite many disagreements concerning particular practices, allowed these groups to unify in several different respects.

Changed from Glory into Glory

Musically, traditions springing from the Reformation were both divided and unified. On the one hand, music does present an example of an issue that historically divided the Reformers. For example, Luther promoted the liberal use of psalms and hymns in worship, Zwingli prohibited music altogether, and Calvin limited singing to psalms without instrumental accompaniment. However, this division can be interpreted primarily as a result of the more significant matter of the regulative principle vs. the normative principle, as discussed above. All three Reformers agreed concerning good music's spiritual benefits and cautioned against the degenerating influence of some music.[1] What separated them is whether they believed they had biblical warrant for particular musical practices (or, in Luther's case, whether biblical warrant was even necessary).

Furthermore, even though differences over the governing principle of worship did lead to distinctions in practice with worship music, groups springing from these early Reformers shared their songs across denominational lines. For example, many of the earliest Lutheran hymns were translations of Latin texts from the Roman Church. Lutheran chorale texts, in turn, were brought to the Anglican tradition, first through Myles Coverdale's *Goostly Psalmes and Spirituall Songes drawen out of the Holy Scripture* (c. 1535–1536). According to Reynolds and Music, "Of its 41 hymns, 36 were translations from German sources, one of which was the first English version of *En'feste Burg*."[2] Other Lutheran hymn texts were delivered to other denominations through the translations of those like Methodist John Wesley—an example is "Jesus, Thy Blood and Righteousness" (1740) from "Christi Blut und Gerechtigkeit" by Nikolaus von Zinzendorf (1739)—and Anglican Catherine Winkworth, whose translations include "All Glory be to God on High" (1863) from "Allein Gott in der Höh sei Her," "Come, Holy Spirit, God and Lord" (1855) from "Komm, Heiliger Geist," "Now Thank We All Our God" (1858) from "Nun Danket Alle Gott" (Martin Rinkart, 1636), and "Praise to the Lord, the Almighty" (1863) from "Lobe den Herren" (Joachim Neander, 1680). Additionally, the Genevan Psalter arose out of the psalmody-only Calvinist tradition, but "within little more than a decade it was translated into several other European languages."[3]

The other factor that influenced the transdenominational nature of traditional psalmody and hymnody is the fact that tunes were exchanged liberally between psalm/hymn texts and thus across denominational lines as well. For example, Luther borrowed tunes from Gregorian chant and other Roman Catholic office hymns for his

---

[1] See Robert Loman Harrell, "A Comparison of Secular Elements in the Chorales of Martin Luther with Rock Elements in Church Music of the 1960's and 1970's" (M.A. thesis, Bob Jones University, 1975).

[2] William J Reynolds and David W. Music, *A Survey of Christian Hymnody*, Fifth Edition (Carol Stream, IL: Hope Publishing Company, 2010), 63.

[3] Reynolds and Music, *A Survey of Christian Hymnody*, 50.

Conclusion to Part Four

early German hymns. Further, many tunes originally composed for Lutherans were transplanted when their corresponding texts were translated and brought into other denominations. Likewise, tunes from the Genevan Psalter made their way into the Anglican Sternhold and Hopkins Psalter, primarily through the Anglo-Genevan Psalter. This Psalter, which contained English versifications for all the Genevan tunes, was created while English Protestants lived in exile in Geneva during the reign of Queen Mary (reigned 1553–1558). The lasting influence of Genevan psalm singing upon Anglican practice can be seen in the use of several common tunes such as OLD 100TH by Louis Bourgeois (originally Psalm 134 in the Genevan Psalter).

Finally, while each of the Reformers reshaped their liturgies to greater or lesser degrees in response to Roman Catholic abuses, most post-Reformation denominational groups traditionally preserved a similar shape to their worship services. As we have seen, in his 1523 *Formula Missae*, Luther retained most of the pre-Tridentine Roman liturgy, the only substantial change being in the language of the canon. Even in his 1526 *Deutsche Messe*, Luther preserved much of the shape of the liturgy, simply replacing Latin elements with vernacular hymns and readings. Likewise John Calvin, despite his strict adherence to the regulative principle, nevertheless also reflected the shape of the pre-Tridentine liturgy, though much simplified, in his Genevan liturgy.

Study Guide for Part Four
People and Terms

Acts of Supremacy
adiaphora
Anabaptist
Anglican Church
Ausbund
Babylonian Captivity
Baptist
bar form
Bay Psalm Book
Book of Common Prayer
Bucer, Martin
Bullinger, Heinrich
Calvin, John
chorale
Church of England
Cranmer, Thomas
Deutsche Messe
Elizabeth I
Form of Church Prayers
Formula of Concord
Formulae Missae
Genevan Psalter
Grund und Ursach
Helwys, Thomas
Henry VIII
Hubmaier, Balthasar
Keach, Benjamin
Knox, John
lectio continuo
lectio selecta
London Baptist Confession
Luther, Martin
Manz, Felix
Mary I
Mennonite
normative principle
Pilgrims
Puritan
Radical Reformers
regulative principle
sacramental union

Conclusion to Part Four

Schleitheim Confession
Separatist
Smyth, John
Solas
Sternhold and Hopkins
Strasbourg
Watts, Isaac
Westminster Assembly
Westminster *Directory*
Zürich
Zwingli, Ulrich

Recommended Resources
Bettenson, Henry, and Chris Maunder, eds. *Documents of the Christian Church*. 4th ed. New York: Oxford University Press, 2011.
Gibson, Jonathan, and Mark Earngey, eds. *Reformation Woship: Liturgies from the Past for the Present*. Greensboro, NC: New Growth Press, 2018.
Jasper, R. C. D., and G. J. Cuming. *Prayers of the Eucharist: Early and Reformed*. Edited by Paul F. Bradshaw and Maxwell E. Johnson. Fourth. Colegeville, MN: Liturgical Press Academic, 2019.
Lindberg, Carter. *The European Reformations*. 2nd Edition. Malden, MA: Wiley-Blackwell, 2009.
Thompson, Bard. *Liturgies of the Western Church*. St. Louis: Fortress Press, 1980.
White, James F. *Documents of Christian Worship: Descriptive and Interpretive Sources*. Louisville, KY: Westminster John Knox Press, 2007.
White, James F. *Protestant Worship: Traditions in Transition*. Louisville, KY: Westminster John Knox Press, 1989.

Questions for Discussion and Reflection
1. Explain the particular aspects of late medieval theology and practice of worship with which the Reformers disagreed and which aspects of worship they retained.
2. Describe the differences in worship theology and practice between each major Reformer, and explain what aspects of worship remained consistent among them.
3. Compare and contrast the normative principle of worship with the regulative principle of worship.

PART FIVE: SHIFTING SANDS

Behold the glories of the Lamb
amidst His Father's throne!
Prepare new honors for His name,
and songs before unknown.

Let elders worship at His feet,
the church adore around,
with vials full of odors sweet,
and harps of sweeter sound.

Now to the Lamb that once was slain
be endless blessings paid;
salvation, glory, joy, remain
forever on Thy head.

Thou hast redeemed our souls with blood,
hast set the pris'ners free,
hast made us kings and priests to God,
and we shall reign with Thee.

—Isaac Watts, 1707

Chapter 14
A New Worldview Emerges

Many factors gradually led to the end of the close church/state union of Christendom in the West. Several of these, ironically, came as a result of the dominance of Christianity. The fifteenth-century Renaissance, which emphasized classical learning rooted in original sources, flourished among Christian theologians, but also began to dismantle unilateral control of the Church. The quick impact of the Reformation, also, could have only happened because Christianity was such a central part of society; most people already believed in the reality of God and the Bible as his divine revelation, and once the Scriptures were translated into the language of the people, these underlying assumptions provided the fertile ground for Protestant theologians to argue their reforms. Likewise, even advancements in science in the sixteenth and seventeenth centuries, beginning with the Copernican Revolution in 1543 and culminating with Isaac Newton's discoveries, arose out of Christian curiosity to truly know God and what he had made. Each of these movements—the Renaissance, Reformation, and Scientific Revolution—were, for the most part, thoroughly Christian at their core, yet they each also contributed to the weakening of Christianity's influence.

For example, the seventeenth-century Scientific Revolution inevitably led to skepticism toward anything that could not be proven through human reason, including anything supernatural. Philosophers such as René Descartes (1596–1650), John Locke (1632–1704), and Voltaire (1694–1778) provided a philosophical framework for the natural sciences rooted in independent human reason, effectually divorcing reason from faith. Descartes' most famous maxim, *Cogito, ergo sum*, "I think, therefore I am," centered the foundation for knowledge in self rather than in divine revelation, beginning a shift in what constitutes the final authority for understanding the world from faith in God's divine revelation to human reason. Whereas Augustine had said, *Credo, ut intelligas*, "Believe, so that you may understand," Descartes made understanding primary. Locke, on the other hand, valued empirical perception through the senses as necessary for human understanding, and thus all truth must be established on the basis of something like the scientific method of observation and testing. Reason alone would become the basis for truth and morality.

This elevation of reason and science over faith—known as "The Enlightenment" or "The Age of Reason"—was, in the words of Abraham Kuyper, "the expulsion of God from practical and theoretical life,"[1] what Rod Dreher describes as "the decisive break

---

[1] Abraham Kuyper, *Lectures on Calvinism* (Grand Rapids: Wm. B. Eerdmans, 1931), 23–24.

with the Christian legacy of the West."[2] The position that the church had enjoyed as the dominant influence over all of culture in the West was over. Kuyper poignantly described the ultimate goal of this period:

> Voltaire's mad cry, "Down with the scoundrel," was aimed at Christ himself, but this cry was merely the expression of the most hidden thought from which the French Revolution sprang. The fanatic outcry of another philosopher, "We no more need a God," and the odious shibboleth, "No God, no Master," of the Convention;—these were the sacrilegious watchwords which at the time heralded the liberation of man as an emancipation from all Divine Authority.[3]

Reason was now in control, and a purely secular culture began to emerge for the first time in western civilization, leading to German philosopher Friedrich Nietzsche to proclaim in 1882, "God is dead."[4] As David Wells astutely observes,

> The Enlightenment world liberated us to dream dreams of the world's renovation and of ourselves at its center, standing erect and proud, recasting the whole sorry scheme of things bare-handed, as it were, leaning only on our own reason and goodness. It also liberated us to perceive illusion as reality. The illusion was that the forces at work within human life were benign, that life was bound and moved by the hidden purposes of an impersonal Good that would, in the end, serve only the high purposes the Enlightenment had imagined.[5]

Secular Worldview

As we explore how philosophical changes in the West impacted worldview, theology, and ultimately the broader culture as well as the church and worship, it is important to spend some time considering the relationship between reason and faith for Christians before the Enlightenment and after. What happened as a result of the Enlightenment was a complete redefinition of both reason and faith based on changes in fundamental worldview assumptions, significantly impacting Christian theology and worship.

---

[2] Rod Dreher, *The Benedict Option: A Strategy for Christians in a Post-Christian Nation* (New York: Sentinel, 2017), 35.

[3] Kuyper, *Lectures on Calvinism*, 10.

[4] Friedrich Nietzsche, *Also Sprach Zarathustra: Ein Buch für Alle und Keinen*, 1883, trans. Thomas Wayne (New York: Algora Publishing, 2003), 67.

[5] David F. Wells, *No Place for Truth: Or Whatever Happened to Evangelical Theology?* (Grand Rapids: Wm. B. Eerdmans Publishing, 1994), 57–58.

A New World Emerges

Reason and Faith

The elevation of reason over faith in the eighteenth century took two general forms. First, pure naturalists relied upon reason as the ultimate authority by which all notions must be judged; in other words, naturalists will not consider rational any notion that allows for the supernatural or otherwise contradicts the foundational assumptions of naturalism. Similarly, empiricists insisted that a notion must have some sort of empirical evidence in order to be considered reasonable. In each of these cases, naturalists or empiricists defined reason on the basis of their foundational assumptions, which assumes reason as its own self-evident authority.

Previously, Christian theologians defined reason differently, not considering it to be the ultimate and independent authority. For Christians, God's revelation is the supreme authority by which all notions must be judged. This does not mean Christians rejected reason prior to the Enlightenment; rather, Christians acknowledged reason as a God-given tool that allows people, by employing various laws of logic, to judge whether or not a notion corresponds to reality, that is, whether or not it is true.

The definition of faith also hinges upon whether one presupposes naturalist/empiricist principles or the truth and authority of God's revelation. For example, naturalists might define faith as "believing in spite of evidence to the contrary." Their definition of reason is constrained by their underlying assumption that immaterial reality is an impossibility. In contrast, faith defined biblically is confident belief in what is "not seen" (Heb. 11:1), that is, belief in that for which there is no empirical proof. For example, Abraham believed and obeyed God even though "he did not know where he was going" (Heb. 11:8). He believed without empirical proof, but it was perfectly reasonable for him to believe God if reason is defined as a faculty of human cognition that allows a person to judge whether something is true or dependable.

Defining reason and faith in these ways should make determining their relationship simple for Christians. Just as naturalists/empiricists root their understanding of those terms in naturalist/empiricist presuppositions, so Christians understand their relationship based on revelation concerning the reality of God and his creation. Christians understand (reason) by faith (Heb. 11:3). God created the universe and everything in it (Gen. 1:1–2:1), and this includes both what is material and immaterial (Col. 1:16). He rules all things in his universe (Eph. 4:6), and "in him all things hold together" (Col. 1:17). All things exist and function on the basis of God's creation and rule of all things (Rom. 11:36). These truths alone implicitly ensure the absolute reasonableness of the Christian faith. If reason is that faculty by which a person determines whether a notion corresponds with reality, and if God is the creator and ruler of reality, then all that God has said is self-attestingly reasonable. There may be no apparent empirical evidence for every Christian belief, and a Christian may not understand the reasonableness of every biblical claim, but he can be assured that his faith is indeed reasonable because of the impossibility of the contrary.

In fact, unbelief—whether naturalist or empiricist—is inherently irrational. Because God created all things, and because all people are made in his image, God has already revealed himself to all people; all people know God (Rom. 1:19–20). The reasons for God are "plain," and all people "clearly perceive" this evidence of the existence of God. Reason leads to belief in these things, for the very laws of logic themselves depend for their existence upon the reality of the Christian God. Yet, all people suffer from the noetic effects of sin (Rom. 1:21), and thus they suppress this plain knowledge of true reality; all people are born doubting what is self-evident and rational.

Therefore, Christians can assume the reasonableness of their faith as self-evident. For Christians, reason is not the foundation or source of faith, but rather an instrument of faith. This is an important distinction that can give Christians confidence that what they believe is true, but that also ensures that they "honor the Lord as holy" (1 Pet. 3:13) in affirming the supreme authority of God's revelation in their worldview and, consequently, in their entire lives.

Self-Conscious Worldview

However, naturalist and empiricist philosophy began quickly to spread, first among the elite intelligencia, and eventually to the public largely through culture. The ultimate result of these philosophical shifts was a fundamental change in *worldview* from metaphysical realism to nominalism, which denies transcendent reality and intrinsic meaning—ultimately reality exists in what can be experienced with the physical senses. Faulkner describes the worldview that dominates post-Enlightenment as "self-conscious"—indeed, he calls the Enlightenment "The Self-Conscious Revolution"[6]—and characterizes it as follows:

1. It excels in detail, in providing reasonable answers to various specific elements of the complex mysteries of the universe.
2. To do this, it insists on organization and efficiency.
3. The primary satisfactions it offers to its adherents are a sense of freedom, initiative, and adventure.[7]

As Faulkner notes, each of these emphases have always been somewhat inherent in the world-conscious worldview of Christianity, but in healthy measure. However,

---

[6] Faulkner, *Wiser Than Despair*, 161.
[7] Faulkner, *Wiser Than Despair*, 2.

the appreciation of human individuality grew steadily stronger in the wake of Renaissance humanism. Among its many effects were a rise in the estimation of private, individual worship as over against cultic worship (which is always communal in spirit) and a corresponding slackening of the indispensable requirement for full participation in cultic events.[8]

He further explains, "The cult places God at the absolute, unrivaled center of consciousness. When the consciousness of God as the center is dislodged by a focus on the human self as the center of interest and concern, then the cult is inevitably transformed."[9]

Secular Theology

This fundamental shift of worldview put Christians in an awkward position because many of their beliefs were not able to be proven through empirical evidence, leading many toward a rejection of God altogether. People in the eighteenth century did not throw away any conception of God immediately, of course. Changes in philosophy and culture, as quickly as they did occur during this period, do not happen overnight.

Deism

Yet a new theology emerged as a result of change in worldview. This theology first affirmed the existence of a Creator God, but one who had not revealed himself to humanity nor has any contact with them now. Combination of a nominalist worldview with this new theology created the religion of Deism, a drastically secularized portrait of the relationship between God and man. Most of the Founding Fathers of America were Deists.

This also changed their view of Scripture. Working from the basis of naturalist assumptions, German higher critics attempted to "demythologize" Scripture by extracting the biblical "narrative" (*Geschichte*) from the historical "event" (*Historie*). They began to argue that a group of Hebrew editors composed the Pentateuch after the return from exile out of a desire to unify the struggling nation around a common religious heritage, most of which is fabricated from myths and legends. Thus, they claimed that the Old Testament's historical genre was rooted in the erroneous supernaturalist worldview of its time and concluded that biblical events were recorded on the basis of cultural conventions rather than revealed truth.

---

[8] Faulkner, *Wiser Than Despair*, 11.
[9] Faulkner, *Wiser Than Despair*, 165–166.

Changed from Glory into Glory

Darwinism

While early Enlightenment philosophers were Deists, affirming the existence but impersonality of God, by the nineteenth century the dominant worldview shifted to pure materialism. The rational basis for explaining the world in purely natural terms without the need to acknowledge a Creator was Charles Darwin's (1809–1882) 1859 *The Origin of Species by Means of Natural Selection or the Preservation of Favored Races in the Struggle for Life*. Man was now understood to be a machine, his actions the product of chemical reactions, with no inherent morality or value at all. This naturalist evolutionary explanation also spread to other philosophical disciplines, such as anthropology and its insistence upon the value-free nature of culture. For example, the father of British anthropology, Edward Tylor, applied Darwin's evolutionary theories to the way people behave in different societies, formulating a conception of the idea of culture that continues to this day. Even religion, in this theory, is merely one aspect of culture that has simply evolved in human societies.[10]

Pluralism

What these developments have created is essentially a new religion—a secular religion dominated by the central doctrine of pluralism, which D. A. Carson describes:

> Any notion that a particular ideological or religious claim is intrinsically superior to another is *necessarily* wrong. The only absolute creed is the creed of pluralism. No religion has the right to pronounce itself right or true, and the others false, or even (in the majority view) relatively inferior.[11]

Pragmatism

A final essential component of the secular religion is pragmatism, the first distinctly American school of philosophy, formulated by John Dewey, William James, and John Sanders Peirce. Peirce succinctly articulated the core of pragmatism: "Consider the practical effects of the objects of your conception. Then, your conception of those effects is the whole of your conception of the object."[12] These philosophers wanted to bring the successes of scientific problem solving to other realms of life, and therefore what answers practical needs becomes the most important. James defined truth on the basis of what has "cash value in experiential terms." He argued, "true ideas are those that we can assimilate, validate, corroborate, and verify. False ideas are those that we

---

[10] Tylor, *Primitive Culture*.

[11] D. A. Carson, *The Gagging of God: Christianity Confronts Pluralism* (Grand Rapids: Zondervan, 1996), 19. Emphasis original.

[12] Charles Peirce, "How to Make Our Ideas Clear," 1878, in *The Essential Peirce, Volume 1: Selected Philosophical Writings (1867–1893)* (Bloomington, IN: Indiana University Press, 1992), 124–141.

cannot."[13] Dewey, whose influence in America spans from education to politics and art, believed that practical answers to real problems was more important than theoretical contemplation. Experience is ultimate, for only through testing what works can we come to know what is true.[14] Since only the natural world exists, and therefore there are no transcendent universal moral principles, the ends justify the means in the secular religion.

Secular Culture

The Industrial Revolution, often said to have begun with the development of steam power in the early 1800s, also had significant impact on culture and, consequently, the church and worship. As technological advancements made communication and travel easier, local folk cultures began to lose their distinctiveness, and a new mass culture emerged. This newly formed "pop" culture had as its core mass appeal and commercial interests. "New" or "contemporary" became axiomatic values since with technology, new is usually better. C. S. Lewis helpfully explains how as a result of the rise of machines, "what other ages would have called 'permanence'" now became simply "old" and "outdated":

> It is the image of old machines being superseded by new and better ones. For in the world of machines the new most often really is better and the primitive really is the clumsy. And this image, potent in all our minds, reigns almost without rival in the minds of the uneducated. For to them, after their marriage and the births of their children, the very milestones of life are technical advances. From the old push-bike and thence to the little car; from gramophone to radio and from radio to television; from the range to the stove; these are the very stages of their pilgrimage.[15]

This belief that new is always better is often an unconscious assumption; in other words, a significant change in culture has created a shift of worldview.

Emotion

One important philosophical shift that occurred as a result of the Enlightenment and had significant impact on broader culture was the emergence of the naturalistic category of "emotion." When theologians and philosophers prior to the Age of Reason spoke about human sensibilities, they used nuanced categories of "affections of the soul," such as love, joy, and peace, and "appetites (or passions) of the body," like

---

[13] Williams James, *The Meaning of Truth* (New York: Longmans Green, and Co., 1909), v–vi.

[14] John Dewey, *Logic: The Theory of Inquiry* (New York: Henry Holt and Company, 1938), 154.

[15] C. S. Lewis, "De Descriptione Temporum," in *They Asked for a Paper: Papers and Addresses* (London: Geoffrey Bles, 1962), 21.

hunger, sexual desire, and anger. This conception of human faculties appears all the way back in Greek philosophers, who used the metaphors of the *splanchna* (chest) to designate the noble affections and the *koilia* (belly) for the base appetites. In the New Testament, the apostle Paul employed such categories as well, urging Christians to put on the "affections" (*splanchna*) of compassion, kindness, humility, meekness, and patience (Col. 3:12) and describing enemies of Christ as those whose "god is their belly (*koilia*)" (Phil. 3:19).

This way of understanding human sensibility dominated Christian thought and philosophy from the Patristic period through the Reformation.[16] The affections were the core of spirituality and were to be nurtured, developed, and encouraged; the appetites, while not evil (in contrast to Gnosticism), must be kept under control lest they overpower the intellect. Theologians believed that the Bible taught a holistic dualism where material and immaterial combined to compose man; thus, while the body and spirit are both good and constantly interact and influence one another, and physical expression is part of the way God created his people, biblical worship should aim at cultivating both the intellect and affections as well as calming the passions. With music in worship, for example, second-century theologian Clement of Alexandria argued, "We must abominate extravagant music, which enervates men's souls, and leads to changefulness—now mournful, and then licentious and voluptuous, and then frenzied and frantic."[17] Rather, the church's hymnody should employ "temperate harmonies." Likewise, Augustine later insisted that while the affections were at the core of Christian religion, the passions must be controlled by reason,[18] Thomas Aquinas likewise maintained a distinction between the soul's affections and the body's passions,[19] and sixteenth-century Reformers such as Calvin agreed, considering worship to consist centrally of pious affections,[20] while yielding entirely to "fleshly desires" was sin.[21]

In contrast to this premodern way of thinking, the purely naturalistic environment of the Enlightenment created a new psychological category philosophers called "emotion"—non-cognitive, purely physical, involuntary feelings.

---

[16] See Thomas Dixon, *From Passions to Emotions: The Creation of a Secular Psychological Category* (Cambridge: Cambridge University Press, 2006).

[17] Clement of Alexandria, *Stromateis*, trans. in Robert A. Skeris, Χρομα Θεου, I:78, quoted in Faulkner, *Wiser Than Despair*, 69.

[18] See Ryan J. Martin, *Understanding Affections in the Theology of Jonathan Edwards: "The High Exercises of Divine Love"* (London: T&T Clark, 2018), 37–46.

[19] Martin, *Understanding Affections in the Theology of Jonathan Edwards*, 49–56.

[20] Calvin, *Institutes*, 3.7.5.

[21] John Calvin, *Commentaries on the First Twenty Chapters of the Book of the Prophet Ezekiel*, trans. Thomas Myers (Grand Rapids: Baker Book House, 1979), 115.

A New World Emerges

Romanticism

This new psychological philosophy of emotion, combined with increasing secularism, affected the culture broadly and the church specifically, including their view of art and music. Premodern thought, understanding music to be directly connected to the heart, and understanding a distinction between the affections and passions, consequently understood a distinction between kinds of music. Some music inherently targets the spirit—the mind, the affections, and the will, while other music is designed simply to artificially create a physical experience of the senses. Augustine and the Reformers used the biblical terms "spiritual" and "carnal" to describe this distinction, while non-Christians have used the terms "classical" and "romantic."

After the Enlightenment had taken hold, Friedrich Nietzsche used the labels "Apollonian" and "Dionysian." Both Dionysus and Apollo were mythological Greek gods associated with music. Apollo was the god of reason and logic and was considered the god of music since the Greeks thought of good music as a great expression of order and pattern (*a la* Pythagorus and Plato). Dionysus, on the other hand, was the god of wine and revelry and was worshiped with loud, raucous music accompanied by pipes and drums. Nietzsche used these names, then, to describe the distinction that had been made in the past between kinds of music. In an article applying this to sacred music, Daniel Reuning explains this distinction in kinds of music:

> Music that communicates emotions with a Dionysian force is that kind which excites us to enjoy our emotions by being thoroughly involved or engrossed in them with our entire person. Our enjoyment of the emotion then becomes ego-directed, driven by the desire for self-gratification. This direction often shows itself in keen physical involvement; people become emotionally involved through stomping of the feet, swaying of the body, clapping of the hands, and waving of the arms. Music that solicits from us this kind of emotional response allows us to enjoy our emotions from the inside and very experientially. This kind of music is clearly anthropocentric in nature, because it turns man to himself, rather than away from himself, with the result that he becomes the appreciating center of his own emotions and experiences. Herein lies the goal of all entertainment and popular music, which must please or gratify the self if it is going to sell.[22]

The difference between Apollonian and Dionysian music is basically what it targets in man. Apollonian music targets the spirit of man—the mind, the affections, and the will. Once the spirit is moved by such music, it may often result in some kind of physical sensation, but that is not the target; it is a result. Dionysian music targets the

---

[22] Daniel Reuning, "Luther and Music," *Concordia Theological Journal* 48, no. 1 (January 1984): 18.

passions of man—the physical feelings themselves for their own sake. It artificially stimulates such feelings.

In the wake of the Enlightenment, Dionysian music rose to dominance—the goal of music in the broader culture became to excite human passions rather than calm them, and this gradually impacted music in worship as well. Faulkner helpfully summarizes how the Enlightenment affects the music of western culture:[23]

- The goal of music is to excite human passions rather than to calm them.
- Music provides entertainment and diversion rather than the shaping of content.
- The best kind of music is characterized by constant variety rather than order and modesty.
- Individuality and originality are virtues in musical composition and performance rather than cultivating a noble tradition.
- The gauge of music's excellence is popular acclaim rather than its ability to shape content in an appropriate manner.
- The best kind of music is "natural" and unlearned rather than skilled and ordered.
- Music is purely scientific without any ethical dimension.
- Music is unimportant rather than that which orders men's souls.

This is not to say that theologians prior to the Enlightenment saw no connection between worship, music, and the heart; indeed they certainly did. However, losing the older distinctions between "affections" and "appetites," lumping both together in a nebulous category of "emotion" or "feeling," led to a reality in which "music's historic anchors to the church and its worship—carrying praise, prayer, the story, and proclaiming the Word—were obscured or removed."[24] Faulkner concludes,

> Music (for that matter, all the arts) had become a theological orphan. In fact, no important theological movement, either in the nineteenth or twentieth century, has concerned itself in any profound way with the significance of harmony, order, or beauty in Christian life or cult.[25]

Pop Culture

Savvy entrepreneurs, of course, noticed the shift in worldview and, taking advantage of newly invented means of mass communication, sought an opportunity to cash in. In order to appeal to the largest number of consumers, pop culture began to produce

---

[23] See Faulkner, *Wiser Than Despair*, 172–179.
[24] Paul Westermeyer, *Te Deum: The Church and Music* (Minneapolis: Fortress Press, 1998), 230.
[25] Faulkner, *Wiser Than Despair*, 190.

art that created immediate results, valuing novelty above all else. Instead of arising from the "bottom up" from the people, as the traditional folk culture had, pop culture was created "top down" by businessmen for the purpose of profit. Furthermore, instead of having as its goal the ennoblement of humanity, as had traditional high culture, pop culture aimed for immediate gratification. Kenneth Myers helpfully compares and contrasts this new pop culture with traditional folk and high culture.[26]

Myers's Comparison of Popular Culture with Traditional/High Culture

Popular Culture	Traditional and High Culture
Focuses on the new	Focuses on the timeless
Discourages reflection	Encourages reflections
Pursued casually to "kill time"	Pursued with deliberation
Gives us what we want, tells us what we already know	Offers us what we could not have imagined
Relies on instant accessibility; encourages impatience	Requires training; encourages patience
Emphasizes information and trivia	Emphasizes knowledge and wisdom
Encourages quantitative concerns	Encourages qualitative concerns
Celebrates fame	Celebrates ability
Appeals to sentimentality	Appeals to appropriate, proportioned emotions
Context and form governed by requirements of the market	Content and form governed by requirements of created order
Formulas are the substance	Formulas are the tools
Relies on spectacle, tending to violence and prurience	Relies on formal dynamics and the power of symbols (including language)
Aesthetic power in reminding of something else	Aesthetic power in intrinsic attributes
Individualistic	Communal
Leaves us where it found us	Transforms sensibilities
Incapable of deep or sustained attention	Capable of repeated, careful attention

---

[26] Kenneth Myers, *All God's Children and Blue Suede Shoes: Christians and Popular Culture* (Wheaton: Crossway Books, 1989), 120.

Lacks ambiguity	Allusive, suggests the transcendent
No discontinuity between life and art	Relies on "Secondary World" conventions
Reflects the desires of the self	Encourages understanding of others
Tends toward relativism	Tends toward submission to standards
Used	Received

Both Myers and Faulkner demonstrate how traditional high culture, with its "ability to provide some transcendent perspective," corresponds to and cultivated the premodern realist worldview, while pop culture, with its "tendency to encourage a self-centered perspective," corresponds to and cultivates the post-Enlightenment nominalist worldview.[27]

Cultivated, Commercial, and Communal Culture
This change that occurred culturally in the early nineteenth century, particularly in America, formed a new distinction between "classical" art and "popular" culture. Whereas in Europe, and even in early America, what was popular culturally came out of the cultivated tradition of high culture, the individualism, freedom, and commercialism inherent in American democracy created an environment at the turn of the century in which what was popular as that which was simple, immediate, "rugged," and personal. This created three distinct cultural streams, what could be described as "cultivated," "commercial," and "communal." Cultivated culture is the high art built on classical models, commercial culture is the popular culture of the marketplace, and communal culture is the simple vernacular culture. Yet regardless of what terms one uses, such cultural divides became increasingly evident during this time. The eighteenth century became known for music characteristic of rugged, rural, American indigenous tradition, yet the nineteenth century was in many respects a reaction against this in favor of what some would consider a more refined "European" tradition. Added to this distinction was the growing industry of music entrepreneurs who published what they thought would sell, not necessarily what was either representative of American indigenous culture of European art. Thus a growing distinction between folk, popular, and high culture became more and more apparent. This became true, not only of secular culture in general, but also of the inner culture of the church.

---

[27] Myers, *All God's Children*, 122. This is, essentially, the entire argument of Faulkner's book.

Secularized Worship

An initial response to the rise of secularism by Christians was to accept a separation of reason and faith and attempt to affirm both. However, adopting the rationalist redefinition of reason also ended up redefining faith as something ultimately "emotional" rather than rational. Instead of refuting these new philosophical developments by proving that they are self-refuting, many professing Christians actually accepted the premise that this new way of thinking was "intellectual" and sought refuge by denying the need for the intellect.

As a result of these philosophical changes and the growth of secular society, "emotion" entered the void left by a growing absence of religion, and in many cases the liturgies and music of worship devolved into a mere aestheticism—worship of beauty and tradition for the feelings they create, feelings assumed to be the very core of religiosity. Friedrich Schleiermacher (1768-1834), considered the "Father of Modern Liberal Theology," described religious piety as "essentially a state of feeling."[28] Religion eventually became defined as individual and private expression of emotion divorced from doctrine, leading to worship that shunned the intellect and attempted to speak simply and directly to the worshipers' emotions.

A Dilemma

By the mid-nineteenth century, western society had been forever changed. As the secular culture moved further and further away from the traditional beliefs and practices of Christendom, Protestant churches were faced with a dilemma—continue to cultivate their historic worship traditions, and risk becoming increasingly alien compared with the rest of culture or reject the church's traditions and adapt to the culture in order to remain influential. Christianity's cultural influence was increasingly diminished, and as the surrounding culture plunged into popularized secularism, the church's traditional forms became foreign.

Churches responded in one of two ways: First, the traditionally liturgical churches attempted to revive Christianity through "a renewal of their historic liturgies," but heavily influenced by what Faulkner calls "aestheticism," which valued beauty for its own sake, and "historicism," which valued tradition simply out of a belief that old is better.[29] The response characterizes what are sometimes called "Mainline Denominations," as well as groups with more loyalty to historical traditions and liturgies, such as various Lutheran and Anglican (or Episcopal) synods. Active cultivation of worship culture slowed considerably but was preserved. Second, the new evangelical churches

---

[28] Friedrich Schleiermacher, *The Christian Faith*, ed. H. R. Mackintosh and J. S. Stewart (London: T&T Clark, 1999), 11.

[29] Faulkner, *Wiser Than Despair*, 188.

reacted against rationalism, initiating "vigorous attempts at revival"[30] through methods that would eventually lead them to break from the worship traditions they inherited in the name of effectiveness and relevance.

As we shall see, what all of this meant for worship forms is that active cultivation virtually stopped. The church still had the hymns and liturgies that had been nurtured for thousands of years, but now talented poets and musicians stopped writing for the church and began writing for money. For a while, they continued writing in the noble artistic forms that had been handed down to them, but with high culture broken off from any moral direction, it eventually all but died away. Whatever high culture now existed was devoid of any significant Christian values. In the church, ritual and ceremony became suspicious or even embarrassing to the reasonable, modern mind, and worship gradually became seen as merely emotional expression.

---

[30] Faulkner, *Wiser Than Despair*, 189.

Chapter 15
The Rise of Evangelical Worship

The dethroning of Christianity by reason left churches in an awkward position. Should churches continue cultivating the Judeo-Christian worship tradition and become progressively alienated from their surrounding culture, or should they "contextualize" and abandon their tradition for a new one that follows the lead of pop culture? Evangelical churches ultimately chose the latter path.

German Pietism

Pietism was a reform movement within orthodox Lutheranism that had significant impact in the late seventeenth century to mid-eighteenth century. The Pietist movement began in Germany in 1675 with Philipp Jakob Spener's (1635–1705) *Pia Desideria*, in which he spoke against polemical theology and high liturgy in favor of practical Christianity and simple devotion. The Pietists believed that the Reformation had been only half successful and that Lutheranism needed further reforms. They considered orthodox Lutheranism to be "dead" and instead emphasized a personal relationship with Christ. They were particularly against the strictness of the church year and of what they considered "elaborate" church music, "as if God were to be worshiped with noise and not in spirit and in truth."[1] Pietist Johann Samuel Stryk (1668–1715) described church music in the early eighteenth century as

> (1) contrary to the genius of the New Testament church, and not agreeing with the example of the primitive church; (2) superfluous; (3) useless, as not promoting but impending divine worship; (4) superstitious, while men imagine that the glory of God can be promoted in this wise.[2]

He especially dismissed the chanting of prayers and Scripture readings: "The gospels and epistles of the apostles are not hymns; why then are they sung like hymns?"[3] In contrast, Pietists produced more devotional hymns focused on the heart. Key to this development was Nicholas Ludwig, Count von Zinzendorf (1700–1760), a wealthy noble who provided asylum for Moravians, descendants of John Hus, fleeing Bohemia. Zinzendorf wrote hymns himself, edited Moravian hymnals, and considered himself

---

[1] Johann Samuel Stryk, *De Iure Sabbathi*, 1702, 121; translated in Kalb, *Theology of Worship*, 149.
[2] Stryk, *De Iure Sabbathi*, 121ff.; translated in Kalb, *Theology of Worship*, 149.
[3] Stryk, *De Iure Sabbathi*, 125; translated in Kalb, *Theology of Worship*, 149.

to be "Minister and Cantor, known to the congregation."[4] Orthodox Lutherans such as Erdmann Neumeister (1671–1756) strongly rejected many of the Pietist themes. In fact, Neumeister called Zinzendorf "the apostle of Satan."[5]

American Revival

Similar to the formation of Christendom in the fourth century, American democracy had both positive and negative effects for Christianity and its worship. On the positive side, the new world provided freedom for the new colonists to worship according to their convictions rather than state mandate, which is why many groups that affirmed the regulative principle made their way to the American colonies.

Worship in Colonial America

As Chapter 13 described, worship in the colonies, dominated by Puritans and Separatists that had fled England, was characterized by simple, Scripture-regulated worship that included Scripture reading, prayer, a sermon, and psalm singing. Negatively, true piety began quickly to wane, especially by the eighteenth century. Several factors account for this: First, growing influence of Enlightenment rationalism led to an institutionalized religion in America not much different from what had occurred in Europe. This also led, second, to theological liberalism in both institutions of higher learning (such as Harvard after 1701) and among churches. Third, churches in New England began to accept into membership anyone who could affirm an orthodox creed and basic life morality, without necessitating a testimony of personal conversion (known as the "Half-Way Covenant"), filling the churches with unregenerate members. Fourth, freedom and individualism in America, combined with the increased unregenerate condition of many of its citizens, gave rise to growing worldliness and, eventually, lack of church attendance altogether.

Jonathan Edwards and the First Great Awakening

Likely the greatest theologian America has ever produced, Jonathan Edwards (1703–1758) lived and ministered just as the significant philosophical and theological shifts of the Enlightenment were beginning to impact culture, the church, and Christian worship. Pastoring a Congregationalist church in Northampton, Massachusetts, Edwards recognized the sad condition of true Christian piety in New England:

---

[4] Walter Blankenburg, "The Music of the Behemian Brethren," in Friedrich Blume, ed., *Protestant Church Music: A History* (New York: Gollancz, 1975), 601.

[5] Erdmann Neumeister, *Räuch-Opfer*, trans. in Jaroslav Jan Pelikan, *Bach Among the Theologians* (Phila: Fortress Press, 1986), 56.

The Rise of Evangelical Worship

> Licentiousness for some years prevailed among the youth of the town; they were many of them very much addicted to night walking, and frequenting the tavern, and lewd practices, wherein some, by their example, exceedingly corrupted others. It was their manner very frequently to get together in conventions of both sexes for mirth and jollity, which were called frolics; and they would often spend the greater part of the night in them, without regard to any order in the families they belonged to; and indeed family government did too much fail in the town. ... There had also long prevailed ... a spirit of contention between two parties, into which they had for many years been divided; by which they maintained a jealousy one of the other, and were prepared to oppose one another in all public affairs.[6]

In response, he ended unregenerate church membership in his congregation and began to faithfully preach the gospel. His goal was to lead the people

> to a conviction of their absolute dependence on [God's] sovereign power and grace, and an universal necessity of a mediator. This has been effected by leading them more and more to a sense of their exceeding wickedness and guiltiness in his sight; their pollution, and the insufficiency of their own righteousness; that they can in no wise help themselves, and that God would be wholly just and righteous in rejecting them and all that they do, and in casing them off forever.[7]

His vivid preaching produced beginning in 1734 what he would later call a "surprising work of God": "The Spirit of God began extraordinarily to set in and wonderfully to work among us; and there were very suddenly, one after another, five or six persons, who were, to all appearances, savingly converted, and some of them wrought upon in a very remarkable manner."[8] This same kind of work of the Spirit began to spread to other towns in Massachusetts and Connecticut over the next months and years.

After Edwards published in 1737 his first account of the revival, "A Faithful Narrative of the Surprising Work of God," George Whitefield (1714–1770) came from England in 1740 to begin a tour of preaching in the colonies. Whitefield was known for dramatic, emotional preaching. Newspapers all through New England began to promote Whitefield's meetings, and vast crowds gathered in churches and outdoor meetings to hear him, many of them affected visibly by his preaching. He eventually made his way to Northampton, where he spent time with Edwards, who, while very complimentary of Whitefield, counseled him to be careful with sensationalism and

---

[6] Jonathan Edwards, "A Faithful Narrative of the Surprising Work of God," (1737), in *The Works of Jonathan Edwards*, vol. 1 (Carlisle, PA: Banner of Truth Trust, 1984), 347.
[7] Edwards, "A Faithful Narrative of the Surprising Work of God," 1:351.
[8] Edwards, "A Faithful Narrative of the Surprising Work of God (1737)," 1:348.

enthusiasms. Sarah Edwards wrote of Whitefield, "He makes less of doctrines than our American preachers generally do and aims at affecting the heart."[9]

The vast number of conversions taking place in churches in the American colonies between 1730 and 1740, sometimes accompanied by intense physical responses, led to two extremes. On the one hand, some Christian leaders considered the physical responses as the defining characteristic of the awakening and thus sought to recreate such experiences through means to stir up emotion. A prime example of this was New York Presbyterian minister, James Davenport (1716–1757), whose services became characterized by irregularity and disorder, "his hands extended, his head thrown back, and his eyes staring up to heaven, attended with so much disorder, that they looked more like a company of Bacchanalians [worshipers of Bacchus, Roman god of drunken revelry] after a bad frolic, than sober Christians who had been worshiping God" (*Boston Evening-Post*, July 5, 1742).[10]

Other leaders rejected the validity of the awakening altogether because they saw what was happening as merely excesses of emotionalism, such as Charles Chauncy in his 1743 *Seasonable Thoughts on the State of Religion in New England*. Chauncy was an Enlightenment rationalist through and through who considered theology to be the "handmaid to reason," valued natural theology over revealed theology, and argued that the revival was a work of over-zealous fanatics, an assertion he substantiated by appealing to the emotional excesses and disorder. But even theologically conservative "Old Light" Calvinists opposed what they considered the "extremism" of the revival.

Both of these responses came as a result of the newly growing secular understanding of "emotion," and Edwards rejected both. His reply was to emphasize the distinction between religious affections and physical responses, defining religion as consisting in the affections, which may or may not manifest themselves in external feelings or expression. Edwards argued,

> The affections and passions are frequently spoken of as the same, and yet in the more common use of speech, there is in some respect a difference. Affection is a word that in the ordinary signification, seems to be something more extensive than passion, being used for all vigorous lively actings of the will or inclination, but passion for those that are more sudden, and whose effects on the animal spirits are more violent, and the mind more over powered, and less in its own command.[11]

---

[9] Quoted in Harry S. Stout, *The Divine Dramatist: George Whitefield and the Rise of Modern Evangelicalism*, 50465th edition (Grand Rapids: Wm. B. Eerdmans, 1991), 126–127.

[10] Quoted in Edwin Gaustad, *The Great Awakening in New England* (Chicago: Quadrangle Books, 1957), 39.

[11] Jonathan Edwards, *The Religious Affections* (1746), in *The Works of Jonathan Edwards*, 2:98.

He insisted that, while physical expression, excitement, and intensity may result from the Holy Spirit's convicting work, they are in actuality "signs of nothing"—they neither define nor disprove true revival. Rather, the only way to measure true conversion or any other spiritual experience is over time, examining whether a person perseveres and grows in the Christian faith.

Some time after the awakening, Edwards noted that the more genuine conversions were those, not necessarily accompanied by intense physical externals, but those characterized by "greater solemnity and greater humility and self-distrust, and greater engagedness after holy living and perseverance."[12] In fact, Edwards admitted that he should have been more careful during the time, many of the conversions that were actually resting on the emotional experience later proven to be false. This period of revival America would soon prove to be a tipping point for what evangelical Christians came to expect as characteristic of spiritual experience, including in worship.

The Wesleys and Methodism
Reaction to the increasing lack of sincere devotion in the Church of England took two primary forms, one in the eighteenth century, and the other in the nineteenth (see Oxford Movement below). The first was what might be called an "evangelical" response, which sought to revive the church through an emphasis on personal holiness and piety. This movement is perhaps best represented by the leadership of John and Charles Wesley.

John (1703–1791) and Charles (1707–1788) Wesley were Anglican ministers who became concerned with revisions of the *Book of Common Prayer* and lack of piety within the Church, consequently stimulating a reform movement later called Methodism, after the stringent routines they advocated toward personal holiness. The brothers had been significantly impacted by the Pietism of Moravian Brethren with whom they shared a boat traveling to the New World; the Moravians were immigrating to the colonies to start a new life, and the Wesleys were traveling as Anglican missionaries. Both brothers were not actually converted until 1738, after Charles came under conviction in a German Lutheran church, John soon converting as well.

The Wesleys advocated weekly Communion, fasting, celebration of holy days, and other "methodical" observances of Christian practices. In 1784 John produced his revision of the prayer book, *The Sunday Service*, shortening the service to allow more room for preaching, hymn singing, and weekly observance of the Lord's Supper. John did not at all reject the *Book of Common Prayer*, affirming in 1784, "I believe there is no liturgy in the world, either in ancient or modern language, which breathes more of

---

[12] Edwards, *The Works of Jonathan Edwards*, 16:125.

a solid, scriptural, rational piety, than the *Common Prayer* of the Church of England."[13] He tried to establish a mediating position between those advocating for and against fixed forms by providing a formal eucharistic rite, but then adding, "Then the elder, if he see it expedient, may put up an extempore prayer."[14]

In addition to Methodism, the Wesleys are known best for their hymns, which also help to illustrate their liturgical theology. They knew that singing formed people perhaps better than anything else, and they used the power of poetry set to music for just this purpose. Charles composed over six thousand hymns on various doctrinal themes, always infused with the deep piety that lay at the core of their theology. Some of his more well-known hymns include "And Can It Be" (1738), "O, for a Thousand Tongues to Sing" (1739), "Christ the Lord Is Risen Today" (1739), "Hark! The Herald Angels Sing" (1739), and "Love Divine, All Love's Excelling" (1747). In contrast to Isaac Watts' more straightforward, objective texts, Charles employed more complex, intricate poetic devices and meter. Also, in contrast to Watts' more Calvinistic theology, Charles' hymns reflect the brothers' Arminianism. Finally, John taught a doctrine he called "entire sanctification," whereby believers in this life could reach a state of "perfect love" in which they would be freed from the desire to sin. This doctrine, too, found expression in Charles' hymns, such as "Love Divine, All Love's Excelling" (1747):

> Breathe, O breathe Thy loving Spirit
> into every troubled breast!
> Let us all in Thee inherit;
> let us find that second rest.
> Take away our bent to sinning;
> Alpha and Omega be;
> end of faith, as its beginning,
> set our hearts at liberty.

In addition to Charles' new hymn compositions, John translated many hymns from German to English, recognizing the rich Lutheran heritage of hymnody already available. He gave special attention to hymns of German Pietism, translating hymns like "Jesus, Thy Blood and Righteousness" in 1740 from Nikolaus von Zinzendorf's "Christi Blut und Gerechtigkeit."

> Jesus, Thy blood and righteousness
> my beauty are, my glorious dress;

---

[13] Letter of John Wesley to Coke, Asbury, and "our brethren in North America," September 10, 1784, printed with *The Sunday Service* in Bard Thompson, *Liturgies of the Western Church* (St. Louis: Fortress Press, 1980), 416.

[14] John Wesley, *John Wesley's Sunday Service for the Methodists in North America*, Bicentennial Edition (Nashville: United Methodist Publishing House, 1984), 138.

'midst flaming worlds, in these arrayed,
with joy shall I lift up my head.

John was also particularly concerned with the quality of singing and that appropriate tunes be used. In 1761, he appended "Instructions for singing" to *Select Hymns* as well as prescriptions for specific hymns tunes for each text, something rare in hymnals of the day. His instructions to the singers were direct:

1. Learn these tunes before you learn any others; afterwards learn as many as you please.
2. Sing them exactly as they are printed here, without altering or mending them at all; and if you have learned to sing them otherwise, unlearn it as soon as you can.
3. Sing all. See that you join with the congregation as frequently as you can. Let not a slight degree of weakness or weariness hinder you. If it is a cross to you, take it up, and you will find it a blessing.
4. Sing lustily and with a good courage. Beware of singing as if you were half dead, or half asleep; but lift up your voice with strength. Be no more afraid of your voice now, nor more ashamed of its being heard, than when you sung the songs of Satan.
5. Sing modestly. Do not bawl, so as to be heard above or distinct from the rest of the congregation, that you may not destroy the harmony; but strive to unite your voices together, so as to make one clear melodious sound.
6. Sing in time. Whatever time is sung be sure to keep with it. Do not run before nor stay behind it; but attend close to the leading voices, and move therewith as exactly as you can; and take care not to sing too slow. This drawling way naturally steals on all who are lazy; and it is high time to drive it out from us, and sing all our tunes just as quick as we did at first.
7. Above all sing spiritually. Have an eye to God in every word you sing. Aim at pleasing him more than yourself, or any other creature. In order to do this attend strictly to the sense of what you sing, and see that your heart is not carried away with the sound, but offered to God continually; so shall your singing be such as the Lord will approve here, and reward you when he cometh in the clouds of heaven.[15]

John drew from a variety of sources for his prescribed tunes, including psalters, German chorale tunes, earlier hymn tune collections, and tunes newly composed for Charles' texts by local musician, John F. Lampe (1703-1751).[16] He resisted the

---

[15] John Wesley, "Instructions for Singing," in *Select Hymns*, 1761, reprinted in Franz Hildebrandt, Oliver A. Beckerlegge, and James Dale, eds., *The Works of John Wesley*, vol. 7 (Oxford: Clarendon Press, 1983), 765.
[16] Oliver A. Beckerlegge and Franz Hildebrandt, "Wesley's Tunes for the *Collection*, 1786," in *The Works of John Wesley*, vol. 7, 770.

polyphony of "modern music," avoiding anything that would obscure the words, yet he also made some strikingly revolutionary comments in "Thoughts on the Power of Music" that Westermeyer considers "a pivotal move toward Romanticism and music's role in arousing emotions."[17] In the treatise, John appears to object to counterpoint and even harmony on the basis that it does not "move the passions" as ancient, monophonic music once did. In modern music, only "when the music has been extremely simple and inartificial, the composer having attended to melody, not harmony," John argued, "the natural power of music to move the passions has appeared."[18] This emphasis demonstrates a characteristic early evangelical mix of interest in personal piety in worship and an increasing Romanticism, especially with regard to music in the church.[19] As Eric Routley notes,

> There is in him a creative conflict ... between the residue of Puritanism and the proleptic Romanticism. ... No seventeenth-century Puritan would have dreamed of saying that it was music's purpose, in or out of church, to arouse emotions; if it did, they did not approve it. But to John, music's primary purpose was just this.[20]

American Revivalism

The nineteenth century in America was a critical time in its cultural, political, and religious development. The nation was still reeling from its Revolution near the end of the previous century, the new government was expanding the political system, and the citizens were enjoying their first tastes of democratic freedom.

American Democracy

Democratic liberty especially significantly shaped both the religious dynamic and—very much related—the cultural tides of the United States. In the southern colonies in particular, the Great Awakening had "forged new and aggressive religious forces in the Baptists and the Methodists and started them on their amazing development, which was to make them the most numerous religious bodies in the new nation. In other words, it marks the real beginning of the democratizing of religion in America."[21] Both

---

[17] Westermeyer, *Te Deum*, 214.
[18] John Wesley, "Thoughts on the Power of Music," 1779, in *The Works of John Wesley*, 7:777.
[19] See Carlton R. Young, *Music of the Heart: John and Charles Wesley on Church Music and Musicians* (Carol Stream: Hope Publishing Company, 1995), 84–105.
[20] Erik Routley, *The Musical Wesleys* (Oxford: Oxford University Press, 1968), 22–23.
[21] William Warren Sweet, *Religion in Colonial America* (New York: Charles Scribner's Sons, 1942), 292.

The Rise of Evangelical Worship

Nathan O. Hatch[22] and Mark A. Noll[23] have shown how America's democracy altered Christianity considerably, and this is perhaps no more evident than in its worship. Americans became known for a kind of "rugged individualism" and distrust of systems of authority or anything that resembled class distinctions. Individuals expected to have a say in how they lived and what they believed, and these sentiments contributed to the development of American culture as well, especially in the church.

Religion in America experienced changes concurrent with, and likely influenced by, the emerging democratic ideas. Religious life became more personal and individualistic, free to all and less dependent upon any sovereign act of God. This shift is evident in the stark contrast between the First Great Awakening of the eighteenth century—led by strong Calvinists such as Jonathan Edwards and George Whitefield—and the Second Great Awakening of the early nineteenth century, whose primary figure was Charles G. Finney, an outspoken Arminian who believed that conversion was not a supernatural work of a sovereign God, but an individual decision by anyone who decided to choose God (more below).

The growing Baptist and Methodist congregations in America began to lose their English theological and liturgical roots. Baptists in America were originally Particular Baptists who brought with them the theology and worship practices of their English forbears. Eventually, however, as Baptists were influenced by "New Lights" and began to move west, both their theology and worship began to take a freer form. Methodists in America, led first by Bishop Francis Asbury (1745–1816) replaced John Wesley's prayer book in 1792 with a much shorter book of guidelines for worship, believing that "they could pray better, and with more devotion while their eyes were shut, than they could with their eyes open."[24] Methodists moving to the frontier ignored forms altogether and encouraged simple, exciting songs such as Edward Payson Hammond's "Come to Jesus, come to Jesus, / Come to Jesus just now."

Rural Camp Meetings

Changes in liturgical practice can be seen perhaps most clearly in the rural camp meetings that began to emerge in the early nineteenth century. These were interdenominational gatherings, often including the Lord's Supper,[25] characterized by extreme

---

[22] Nathan O. Hatch, *The Democratization of American Christianity* (New Haven: Yale University Press, 1989).

[23] Mark A. Noll, *America's God: From Jonathan Edwards to Abraham Lincoln* (New York: Oxford University Press, 2002).

[24] Jesse Lee, *A Short History of the Methodists*, facsimile of 1810 ed. (Rutland, VT: Academic Books, 1974), 107.

[25] See William Warren Sweet, *The Story of Religion in America* (New York: Joanna Cotler Books, 1950), 223–242.

Changed from Glory into Glory

emotional expression[26] and congregational singing of choruses. The quintessential model for all subsequent camp meeting revivals was the Cane Ridge (Kentucky) meeting of 1801. Attended by crowds between 10,000 and 25,000 people, the meeting became characterized by shouting, prostrations, singing, laughing, emotional fits, and even barking.[27] Camp meetings spread from Cane Ridge throughout the rural frontier.

James White suggests that a new liturgical structure—a "tripartite ... service of the Word"—emerged from these camp meetings that has come to characterize American evangelical worship ever since: it begins with "a service of song and praise which places great emphasis on music," moves to a "highly evangelistic [sermon], calling souls to conversion," and climaxes with "a call to those who have been converted to acknowledge this change in their lives by coming forward, being baptized, or making some other indication of their new being."[28] This public "invitation," sometimes referred to as an "altar call," became the focal point of a camp meeting service. Baptist elder Lemuel Burkitt described one of the first of these in North Carolina in 1850:

> Numbers, apparently under strong conviction, would come and fall down before the Lord at the feet of the ministers, and crave an interest in their prayers. ... It had a powerful effect on the spectators to see their wives, their husbands, children, neighbors, etc. so solicitous for the salvation of their souls; and was sometimes a means of their conversion. ... The act of coming to be prayed for in this manner had a good effect on the persons who came, in that they knew the eyes of the congregation were on them, and if they did fall off afterwards it would be a disgrace to them, and cause others to deride them; this, therefore, was a spur to push them forward.[29]

The nature of these meetings necessitated a simple, emotionally-charged kind of song that would keep the attention of the masses of people while inciting them to spiritual change. Camp meeting leaders, therefore, took those hymns that had been staples of congregational singing and altered them to meet their needs, most often appending a chorus to the end of an existing hymn text, such as this example of adding a chorus to Robert Robinson's 1757 "Come, Thou Fount of Every Blessing":

Robinson's text:
Come, Thou Fount of ev'ry blessing,

---

[26] Jerald C. Brauer, *Protestantism in America: A Narrative History* (Louisville, KY: Westminster Press, 1953), 108–109.

[27] Charles Albert Johnson, *The Frontier Camp Meeting: Religion's Harvest Time* (Dallas: Southern Methodist Univ Press, 1955), chap. 4.

[28] James F. White, *Introduction to Christian Worship*, Third (Nashville: Abingdon Press, 2010), 164.

[29] Lemuel Burkitt and Jesse Read, *A Concise History of the Kehukee Baptist Association, from Its Original Rise down to 1803* (Philadelphia: Lippincott, Grambo, & Company, 1850), 150–151.

tune my heart to sing Thy grace;
streams of mercy, never ceasing,
call for songs of loudest praise.

Added camp meeting refrain:
I am bound for the kingdom,
will you go to glory with me?
Hallelujah, praise the Lord.

This was the beginning of what would later be called "gospel songs," and eventually, these choruses were separated to stand on their own. Newly formed "Sunday schools" found these choruses, and other new songs modeled after them, as perfect for use with children, and eventually these songs made their way into urban revival meetings and church services.

One significant group that emerged from this frontier tradition was what came to be known as the Christian Church (Disciples of Christ) and the Churches of Christ, founded by Barton Stone (1772–1844), Thomas Campbell (1763–1854), and Alexander Campbell (1788–1866). This movement strongly emphasized biblical authority in all matters of worship, arguing, "Nothing ought to be received into the faith or worship of the church, or to be made a term of communion among Christians, that is not as old as the New Testament."[30] Based on this principle, they insisted that churches celebrate the Lord's Table every Sunday and that no instrumental accompaniment be used in corporate worship.

Charles G. Finney
The first influential Christian leader to strategically integrate Enlightenment psychology and pop culture with Christian practice was nineteenth-century Revivalist Charles G. Finney (1792–1875). Influenced by theologian Nathaniel Taylor's "New Haven Theology," Finney denied the imputation of Adam's sin to all humankind, and thus, "We deny that the human condition is morally depraved;"[31] sin comes only from choice, not from nature. Therefore, "the sinner has all the faculties and natural abilities requisite to render perfect obedience to God;"[32] most people are simply morally weak and lack the will to do so. "All [the sinner] needs," Finney argued, "is to be induced to use these powers and attributes as he ought."[33] As for Christian sanctification, Finney was influenced by Wesleyan Perfectionism, insisting that given the right conditions,

---

[30] Thomas Campbell, "Declaration and Address," in *American Christianity*, ed. H. Shelton Smith, Robert T. Handy, and Lefferts A. Loetscher, vol. 1 (New York: Charles Scribner's Sons, 1960), 584.
[31] Charles Grandison Finney, *Lectures on Systematic Theology* (London: William Tegg and Co., 1851), 391.
[32] Finney, *Lectures on Systematic Theology*, 408.
[33] Finney, *Lectures on Systematic Theology*, 408.

Christians could experience "entire sanctification."[34] Because Finney believed that conversion and sanctification could be produced by human means, he sought to create experiences in his services that would "induce" sinners to accept the claims of Christianity or be motivated to complete sanctification. In his *Revival Lectures*, Finney insisted that "there is nothing in religion beyond the ordinary powers of nature," and revival is therefore "a result of the use of the appropriate means."[322] In order to create revival, then, "God has found it necessary to take advantage of the excitability there is in mankind, to produce powerful excitements among them, before he can lead them to obey."[35] He argued, "there must be excitement sufficient to wake up the dormant moral powers."[36]

Finney argued that in order to create the necessary excitement, churches must employ "new measures" since "The Tradition of the Elders" (the title of one of his sermons) that were familiar to the congregation would never produce the desired results. Many of the measures for which he advocated had first appeared in early nineteenth-century rural camp meetings, such as altar calls and the use of choruses, but Finney brought them into the urban mainstream. Finney found the newly emerging pop culture as the perfect tool for creating exciting experiences because it was immediate, and it stimulated excitement. Finney urged those writing and leading music in his meetings to look to the advertisers of the day for inspiration. This new way of thinking affected not only the content and style of worship and music, but it transformed the view of the church and its worship. Music for church services was chosen based on whatever would create an exciting atmosphere for unbelievers or believers. Liturgy within corporate worship eventually began to mimic that of an evangelistic meeting, with an altar call replacing the Lord's Table as the climax of the service. Finney's revivalist measures marked a decided break with the Judeo-Christian worship tradition.

Finney's philosophy began a trend to create emotional experiences in the church that was kept alive in the revivalist tradition in the years to come. D. L. Moody (1837–1899) and his famous song leader, Ira Sankey (1840–1908), were widely known for their emotional, experience-oriented preaching and music, helping to further ingrain these kinds of methods into the church's worship so that every service became an evangelistic revival meeting. Sankey popularized "evangelistic song leading" and soloists in services, composing songs reminiscent of older camp meeting choruses. Sankey published a collection of his songs in 1873 and then teamed with Sunday School song author Philip Bliss (1838–1876) to compile *Gospel Hymns and Sacred Songs* in 1875, which included songs by the most prolific author of gospel songs, Fanny Crosby

---

[34] Finney, *Lectures on Systematic Theology*, 405–407.
[35] Charles G. Finney, *Revivals of Religion* (Boston: John P. Jewett & Company, 1858), 9.
[36] Finney, *Revivals of Religion*, 11.

(1820–1915). *Gospel Hymns* was printed in six total editions through 1894, when a final edition included 739 gospel songs. Later, Homer Rodeheaver (1880–1955), song leader to revivalist Billy Sunday (1862–1935), taught that "Creating the proper atmosphere for the character of the meeting to be held is an important office of the director." He taught song leaders how using certain songs and directing methods could create the right "emotional conditioning."[37] Liturgically, a new service structure developed that consisted of a "song service," the sermon, and a climactic altar call.

A New Worship Tradition

Liturgical historian James White argues that the rural camp meetings and urban revivalism created a new worship tradition, which he suggests was adopted by "most of the traditions of Protestant worship" and "provided a 'black hole' that tended to swallow up many of the distinctive characteristics of previous traditions."[38] This new tradition minimized the Lord's supper and baptism, a "concert-stage arrangement with the choir elevated and facing the congregation" developed, services celebrating distinctly American holidays replaced the Christian year, and extemporaneous prayer became the established norm. Church music, in particular, took on an entirely different function within services. Its purpose now became preliminary preparation for the sermon, used to unite the congregation and create a "sense of expectancy." The music had no identifiable liturgical function; rather, "it was used to embellish, and the actual sequence during the first minutes did not seem of great importance."[39]

The Oxford Movement

In England, as similar evangelical revivalism spread, a strong Anglo-Catholic contingent within the Anglican Church opposed what they considered to be the extreme emotionalism of the evangelical revivals but also sought to correct what they considered stagnation in the Church of England. Come to be known as the "Oxford Movement," due to its beginnings at Oxford University, theologians such as John Keble (1792–1866), John Henry Newman (1801–1890), John Mason Neale (1818–1866), and Frederich Faber (1814–1863) sought to forge a middle way between Anglicanism and Roman Catholicism. The movement had such a significant effect upon Anglicanism that many late medieval Roman Catholic practices were reintroduced into worship, including emphasis on weekly celebration of the eucharist, vestments, observation of the church year, and other liturgical rituals. Sacramental theology likewise shifted to

---

[37] Homer Rodeheaver, *Song Leadership: A Practical Manual for All Who Want to Help Folks Sing Together* (Winona Lake, IN: Rodeheaver, 1941), 8, 30.
[38] James F. White, *Protestant Worship: Traditions in Transition* (Louisville, KY: Westminster John Knox Press, 1989), 178–179.
[39] White, *Protestant Worship*, 185.

stress Christ's real presence in the eucharist and the necessity of confession to a priest. The movement also impacted the Episcopal Church in the United States.

Musically, the Oxford Movement produced three primary contributions. First, they encouraged translations of Latin, Greek, and German hymns into English. Neale produced several important translations of Latin hymns, such as "O Come, O Come, Emmanuel," "Let All Mortal Flesh Keep Silence," and "Of the Father's Love Begotten." Second, they composed original hymns such as "Sun of My Soul" (John Keble), "Crown Him with Many Crowns" (Matthew Bridges), and "Faith of our Fathers" (Frederick Faber). Finally, in 1860–1861 they published *Hymns Ancient and Modern*, one of the most significant and influential hymnals of the century, and organ and choral music flourished as well.

Two Worship Philosophies

In the wake of eighteenth-century Enlightenment and nineteenth-century revivalism, evangelical Christianity evidenced two distinct philosophies of worship. The first was the conservative philosophy that generally characterized each of the post-Reformation groups despite their idiosyncratic differences. This conservative philosophy desired to preserve the theology and practices of biblical worship, mediated through the tradition of the church to various degrees. Both those who followed a more normative principle of worship and those who affirmed a regulative principle nevertheless desired that their worship take the shape of whatever preserves biblical tradition. Following revivalist movements, this philosophy continued to characterize what are sometimes called "Reformed" traditions, referring to these groups' continued adherence to post-Reformation confessions, liturgies, and hymnody.

The second philosophy, newly formed by revivalist theology and becoming the more significant to characterize evangelical churches, was a more progressive philosophy. Instead of employing a regulative principle, restricting its worship to explicit biblical prescription, or even a normative principle, where church traditions not necessarily prescribed in Scripture carry more weight, this progressive philosophy employs an "effective principle of worship," where worship takes the shape of whatever accomplishes the church's objectives. The driving impulse of such a philosophy is the means of accomplishing the objective of evangelism or the spiritual grown of Christians, and often both in combination. While churches following such a philosophy certainly desire to be biblical in their doctrine and practice, they consider contextualization of methods into newer, more relevant forms to be the necessary means by which both unbelievers are brought to faith and Christians are spiritually stimulated. This legacy of evangelical revivalism has come to characterize what are sometimes called "Free church" traditions.

Chapter 16
Contemporary Worship

When surveying the various changes in worship theology and practices throughout history, as we have been doing in this book, what is notable is the pendulum that has swung between unity and diversity among different traditions. Early Christian and medieval worship formed a theology and practice that, while not absolutely unified, was nevertheless fairly consistent. Reformation worship splintered practice into several different traditions, while maintaining a generally unified core theology of worship. Nineteenth-century revivalism began to bring once diverse denominations back into unity around its newly devised evangelical theology and practice of worship. The final step in worship's evolution is an almost complete unification simply referred to as "Contemporary Worship."

In their insightful *Concise History of Contemporary Worship, Lovin' on Jesus*, Swee Hong Lim and Lester Ruth convincingly demonstrate five key sources of contemporary worship:

1. Youth ministry
2. Pentecostalism
3. The baby boomer generation
4. Jesus people
5. Church growth missiology[1]

While youth ministry, baby boomers, and Jesus people have, indeed, significantly affected the evolution of worship theology and practice, the most significant contributors to contemporary worship are Pentecostalism and the Church Growth movement, both of which deserve attention here.

Pentecostalism
Pentecostalism emerged in the early twentieth century, combining the Methodist holiness movement and revivalism with a conviction that the miraculous signs of the apostolic era continue today. Its beginning is traditionally dated as December 31, 1900, when in Topeka, Kansas Agnes Ozmen reportedly began to speak in tongues after Charles Parham (1873–1929) laid his hands on her, which Parham interpreted to be evidence of the Spirit baptism. This led others to report the same experience,

---
[1] Swee Hong Lim and Lester Ruth, *Lovin' on Jesus: A Concise History of Contemporary Worship* (Nashville: Abingdon Press, 2017), 16–23.

culminating with a three-year-long Azusa Street revival (1906–1909), which attracted much attention and sparked the spread of the Pentecostal movement. As the title of one important history of this event indicates, participants at the revival believed they were experiencing "Heaven Below."[2] Leaders within this movement stressed the need for a crisis moment and work of the Holy Spirit to engender conversion and spiritual growth. This theology led them to consider baptism of the Holy Spirit to be something separate and subsequent to salvation, an event evidenced by speaking in tongues and other miraculous gifts. Their theology was rooted in, among other theological influences, Wesleyan Perfectionism and Charles Finney's theology of entire sanctification.

Whereas Pentecostalism initially produced its own denominations, the so-called Second Wave Charismatic Movement (including the Jesus People mentioned by Lim and Ruth above) began to spread Pentecostal theology to already established denominations. A Third Wave (sometimes called "Neo-Charismaticism") shifted rationale for the continuation of the miraculous gifts from baptism of the Spirit to an inaugurated eschatology,[3] well-expressed in Jack Hayford's chorus, "Majesty, kingdom authority, flows from his throne, unto his own; his anthem raise." Despite their (sometimes considerable) differences, what each of these groups share is the belief that the Holy Spirit manifests himself in physical and often miraculous ways in worship.

Praise & Worship

In many respects, Pentecostalism can be credited for recovering a focus on worship within the revivalist evangelical traditions that had shifted the focus of the Sunday morning service from worship to evangelism and revival. However, continuationist theology and expectations concerning how the Holy Spirit works led to a redefinition of worship from that of Reformed traditions to what they considered more consistent with New Testament teaching. Charismatic theologians argue that the Holy Spirit's primary work in worship is that of making God's presence known in observable, tangible ways such that worshipers can truly encounter God. This theology places a high emphasis and expectation in worship upon physical expressiveness and intensity, resulting in what is sometimes called a "Praise and Worship" theology of worship. The goal, in this theology, is to experience the presence of God in worship, but praise is considered the means through which Christians do so.

Praise and worship theology seeks to provide a "blueprint for a worship service" that ensures worshipers will truly "enter the presence of God."[4] Fundamental to this theology is the idea that in Scripture, praise is inherently connected to God's

---

[2] Grant Wacker, *Heaven Below: Early Pentecostals and American Culture* (Cambridge, MA: Harvard University Press, 2003).

[3] Peter C. Wagner, *The Third Wave of the Holy Spirit* (Ann Arbor, MI: Servant Books, 1988).

[4] Terry Law, *How to Enter the Presence of God* (Tulsa: Victory House, 1994), 69.

presence—in fact, praise is the very means of entering the presence of God. A central text underlying this idea is Psalm 22:3: "Yet you are holy, enthroned on the praises of Israel." Early Pentecostal authors, such as Reg Layzell and Bob Sorge,[5] taught that this text and others reveal that, in the words of Judson Cornwall, "the path into the presence of God [is] praise."[6] This leads to the understanding that praise and worship are distinct; as Cornwall suggests, "Praise is the vehicle of expression that brings us into God's presence. But worship is what we do once we gain an entrance to that presence."[7] Thurlow Spurr explains more thoroughly the distinction between the two:

> Praise and worship are not the same. Praise is thanking God for the blessings, the benefits, the good things. It is an expression of love, gratitude, and appreciation. Worship involves a more intense level of personal communication with God, centering on his person. In concentrated worship, there is a sort of detachment from everything external as one enters God's presence.[8]

Contemporary worship leader Darlene Zschech represents well Praise & Worship theology:

> The word says that God *inhabits* the praises of His people (Psalm 22:3). It's amazing to think that God, in all His fullness, inhabits and dwells in *our* praises of Him. ... Our praise is irresistible to God. As soon as He hears us call His name, He is ready to answer us. That is the God we serve. Every time the praise and worship team with our musicians, singers, production teams, dancers, and actors begin to praise God, His presence comes in like a flood. Even though we live in His presence, His love is *lavished* on us in a miraculous way when we praise Him.[9]

Flow

This theology affected liturgical practice. Breaking from a confessional liturgical structure, Praise and Worship instead aims to bring the worshiper through a series of emotional stages from rousing "praise" to intimate "worship." Judson Cornwall explains the process:

---

[5] Reg Layzell, *Unto Perfection: The Truth about the Present Restoration Revival* (Mount-lake Terrace: The King's Temple, 1979), 120–121; Bob Sorge, *Exploring Worship: A Practical Guide to Praise & Worship* (Canandaigua, NY: Oasis House, 1987).

[6] Judson Cornwall, *Let Us Praise* (Plainfield, N.J: Logos Associates, 1973), 26.

[7] Judson Cornwall, *Let Us Worship* (Plainfield, NJ: Bridge Pub., 1983), 49.

[8] Thurlow Spurr, "Praise: More Than a 'Festival.' It's a Way of Life," *Charisma* 11, no. 6 (August 1977): 13.

[9] Darlene Zschech, *Extravagant Worship: Holy, Holy, Holy Is the Lord God Almighty Who Was and Is, and Is to Come* (Minneapolis: Bethany House, 2002), 54–55 Emphasis original.

> Praise begins by applauding God's power, but it often brings us close enough to God that worship can respond to God's presence. While the energy of praise is toward what God does, the energy of worship is toward who God is. The first is concerning with God's performance, while the second is occupied with God's personage. The thrust of worship, therefore, is higher than the thrust of praise.[10]

Praise and Worship liturgy is centered around the emotional "flow" of the music; worship leaders are encouraged to begin with enthusiastic songs of thanksgiving, leading the worshipers to an emotional "soulish worship," and then bringing the mood to an intimate expression where "a gentle sustained chord on the organ and a song of the Spirit on the lips of the leaders should be more than sufficient to carry a worship response of the entire congregation for a protracted period of time."[11] Zac Hicks suggests, "Part of leading a worship service's flow ... involves keeping the awareness of God's real, abiding presence before his worshipers. As all of the elements of worship pass by, the one constant—the True Flow—is the presence of the Holy Spirit himself." This kind of flow, according to Hicks, "lies in understanding and guiding your worship service's emotional journey."[12] "Grouping songs in such a way that they flow together," worship leader Carl Tuttle explains, "is essential to a good worship experience."[13] Lim and Ruth describe the earliest guides written to help worship leaders achieve flow, David Blomgren's 1978 *The Song of the Lord*:

> The flow should move continuously with no interruptions; the flow should move naturally (using connections from the songs' content, keys, and tempos); and the flow should move toward a goal of a climactic experience of true worship of God. Blomgren spelled out technical aspects for achieving proper flow: the content of the songs in sequence makes sense, having scriptural and thematic relatedness; the key signatures are conductive to easy, unjarring, and smooth transitions between songs; the tempos of the songs (usually faster to slower overall with songs having similar tempos grouped) contributing to a growing sense of closer encounter with God.[14]

The Tabernacle Model of Worship

Praise and Worship theology produced a liturgical shape that uses the typology of the Hebrew tabernacle or temple as the foundation for its worship design to describe this emotional progression through which worshipers are led to experience "the manifest

---

[10] Cornwall, *Let Us Worship*, 146.
[11] Cornwall, *Let Us Worship*, 158.
[12] Zac M. Hicks, *The Worship Pastor: A Call to Ministry for Worship Leaders and Teams* (Grand Rapids: Zondervan, 2016), 184.
[13] Carl Tuttle, "Song Selection & New Song Introduction," in In *Worship Leaders Training Manual* (Anaheim, CA: Worship Resource Center/Vineyard Ministries International, 1987), 141.
[14] Lim and Ruth, *Lovin' on Jesus*, 33.

presence of God."³⁴³ Advocates often appeal to Psalm 95 or Psalm 100 as concise examples of their model, noting that Psalm 95 progresses from songs of rejoicing, to thanksgiving, to praise, and then to reverence, which they define as the prescribed flow of worship. Psalm 100 is an even more clear picture of the model, what Eddie Espinosa calls a "journey into the holy of holies of the temple or tabernacle":

> Make a joyful noise to the Lord, all the earth!
> Serve the Lord with gladness!
> Come into his presence with singing!
> Know that the Lord, he is God!
> It is he who made us, and we are his;
> we are his people, and the sheep of his pasture.
> Enter his gates with thanksgiving,
> and his courts with praise!
> Give thanks to him; bless his name!
> For the Lord is good;
> his steadfast love endures forever,
> and his faithfulness to all generations.

Tabernacle worship, they reason, began with "fun songs" outside the tabernacle, followed by songs of thanksgiving, leading to worship songs as they entered the holy place and intimate songs in God's presence within the holy of holies.[15] This formed what is sometimes referred to as the "Tabernacle Model," the "Vineyard Model," or the "Five Phase Pattern" of worship:

Invitation	Songs of Personal Testimony in the Camp
Engagement	Through the Gates with Thanksgiving
Exaltation	Into His Courts with Praise
Adoration	Solemn Worship inside the Holy Place
Intimacy	In the Holy of Holies

Musical Sacramentality

In addition to appealing to Old Testament worship as a foundation for their theology and practice of worship, Pentecostals also often appeal to the worship of heaven, suggesting that since Christians now worship through Christ in the heavenly temple (Heb. 12:22–24), we should expect to tangibly experience God's manifest presence, whether through a visible display of his glory, miraculous gifts, or emotional rapture. The goal of music and the "worship leader" is to "usher worshipers" into the presence of God

---

[15] Eddie Espinosa, "Worship Leading," in *Worship Leaders Training Manual* (Anaheim, CA: Worship Resource Center/Vineyard Ministries International, 1987), 81–82.

in heaven, to "bring the congregational worshipers into a corporate awareness of God's manifest presence."[16] As Michael Farley observes,

> Sacrifices were tangible means of grace that God used to draw people near to him experientially and relationally, and thus they were a kind of sacrament. If worship music falls within the category of sacrifice, then it accomplishes the same broadly sacramental function, namely, to be a tangible means through which God reveals himself and enables us to experience his special presence with us.[17]

This change in theology of worship led to a new understanding of worship music perhaps best described by Ruth Ann Ashton's 1993 *God's Presence through Music*,[18] raising the matter of musical style to a level of significance that Lim and Ruth describe as "musical sacramentality," where music is now considered a primary means through which "God's presence could be encountered in worship."[19] Further, this perspective has developed an *ex opera operato* expectation similar to that of medieval worship. As Lim and Ruth note,

> As the idea of the sacramentality of praise developed, it usually picked up another quality that has characterized [Medieval] understanding of the Eucharist: a confidence in its instrumental effectiveness. In other words, the sacrament achieves what it symbolizes. ... When God's people praise, God will be present. The teachers of praise and worship are confident in this instrumental effectiveness for praise.[20]

Lim and Ruth observe that while more recently explicit language of sacramentality has lessened among more recent Pentecostal authors, "what have not waned are the root sentiments behind this theology of sacramental praise: a desire to encounter the divine through music and a sense that when God is present God is present in active power."[21]

Transdenominational Impact

The Pentecostal Praise & Worship theology and practice have since spread to other non-charismatic churches and denominations through the popularity of music produced from these movements, adaption of the theology by Church Growth advocates

---

[16] Barry Griffing, "Releasing Charismatic Worship," in *Restoring Praise & Worship to the Church* (Shippensburg, PA: Revival Press, 1989), 92.
[17] Michael Farley, email correspondence in Hicks, *The Worship Pastor*, 35.
[18] Runn Ann Ashton, *God's Presence through Music* (South Bend, IN: Lesea Publishing Co., 1993).
[19] Lim and Ruth, *Lovin' on Jesus*, 18.
[20] Lim and Ruth, *Lovin' on Jesus*, 134.
[21] Lim and Ruth, *Lovin' on Jesus*, 131.

(more below), and even from within more modern "liturgical renewal" movements. An example of the latter is Robert Webber, who combined traditional liturgical theology with contemporary Pentecostal foundation in his promotion of "Ancient-Future Worship."[22] Webber observed, "What I see in the future is a convergence of worship traditions, a convergence of the liturgical, traditional nonliturgical (like many Baptists), and the Praise and Worship tradition."[23] Zac Hicks is a more recent example, who recounts his journey from what he describes as "a kind of 'default charismatic,' thinking and believing that God's presence was located solely in the surprising, unexpected, unplanned, goose-bump moments of worship" to what he describes as falling "in love with all things liturgical and historical, locating God's presence primarily in the sacraments."[24] He says that "the sacramental traditions remind us that we can feel his presence in a powerful and multisensory way as we touch, taste, see, and smell Jesus, through the Spirit, in baptism and Communion."[25] "But later," he notes, "God lifted my head and opened my ears to listen to his Spirit's work in the broader church, among *all* the traditions."[26] No matter how we worship, he argues, "We should build the language of presence and encounter into worship."[27]

Arguably, the default expectation of contemporary evangelical worshipers is that the Holy Spirit works in worship in such a way so as to create an extraordinary experience, well expressed in the popular worship song by Bryan and Katie Torwalt:

Holy spirit, You are welcome here
Come flood this place and fill the atmosphere
Your glory, God, is what our hearts long for
To be overcome by Your presence, Lord[28]

Many theologians and authors who have helped to shape contemporary evangelical worship embody a theology of the Holy Spirit's primary work as that of making God's presence known. For example, Wayne Gruden argues, "The work of the Holy Spirit is to manifest the active presence of God in the world, and especially the church. ... It seems that one of his primary purposes in the new covenant age," Grudem continues, "is to manifest the presence of God, to give indications that make the presence of God

---

[22] Robert E. Webber and John Wilvliet, *Ancient-Future Worship: Proclaiming and Enacting God's Narrative* (Grand Rapids: Baker Books, 2008).
[23] Robert Webber, "Enter His Courts with Praise: A New Style of Worship Is Sweeping the Church," *Reformed Worship* 20 (June 1991).
[24] Hicks, *The Worship Pastor*, 34.
[25] Hicks, *The Worship Pastor*, 37.
[26] Hicks, *The Worship Pastor*, 34.
[27] Hicks, *The Worship Pastor*, 38.
[28] Bryan Torwalt and Katie Torwalt, "Holy Spirit," 2011, https://songselect.ccli.com/Songs/6087919/holy-spirit. This is a CCLI Top 10 song.

known. ... To be in the Holy Spirit is really to be in an atmosphere of God's manifested presence."[29] Zac Hicks agrees: "The Holy Spirit has an agenda in manifesting his presence to us."[30]

Lim and Ruth suggest that with its "revisioning of a New Testament emphasis upon the active presence and ministry of the Holy Spirit,"[31] "Pentecostalism's shaping of contemporary worship has been both through its own internal development and through an influencing of other Protestants in worship piety and practice," including the following ways its theology has shaped contemporary worship:

1. mainstreaming the desire to be physical and expressive in worship
2. highlighting intensity as a liturgical virtue
3. a certain expectation of experience to the forms of contemporary worship
4. a musical sacramentality [that] raises the importance of the worship set as well as the musicians leading this set.[32]

They explain, "Pentecostalism contributed contemporary worship's sacramentality, that is, both the expectation that God's presence could be encountered in worship and the normal means by which this encounter would happen," creating an "expectation for encountering God, active and present through the Holy Spirit."[33] Daniel Albrecht agrees:

> The presence of the Holy Spirit then is fundamental to a Pentecostal perspective of worship. The conviction that the Spirit is present in worship is one of the deepest beliefs in a Pentecostal liturgical vision. The expectancy of the Spirit's presence is often palpable in the liturgy. ... Their liturgical rites and sensibilities encourage becoming consciously present to God—even as God's presence is expected to become very real in worship.[34]

Monique M. Ingalls agrees with this assessment after her ten-year study (2007 to 2017) of contemporary worship in several different settings.[35] She notes the connection between centrality of contemporary worship music and the desire of worshipers to experience "a personal encounter with God during congregational singing."[36] This

---

[29] Wayne Grudem, *Systematic Theology* (Grand Rapids: Zondervan, 1995), 634, 641, 648.
[30] Hicks, *The Worship Pastor*, 33.
[31] Lim and Ruth, *Lovin' on Jesus*, 17–18.
[32] Lim and Ruth, *Lovin' on Jesus*, 18.
[33] Lim and Ruth, *Lovin' on Jesus*, 18.
[34] Daniel E. Albrecht, "Worshiping and the Spirit: Transmuting Liturgy Pentecostally," in *The Spirit in Worship—Worship in the Spirit*, ed. Teresa Berger and Bryan D. Spinks (Collegeville, MN: Liturgical Press, 2009), 239.
[35] Monique M. Ingalls, *Singing the Congregation: How Contemporary Worship Music Forms Evangelical Community* (New York: Oxford University Press, 2018).
[36] Ingalls, *Singing the Congregation*, 85.

Contemporary Worship

expectation in worship can even reach the point, she says, of describing the longing for such an experience with phrases like "worship fix" or "worship junkie." She observes, "The language of addiction ... evidences the overwhelming success of the major worship brands in not just responding to felt needs, but also actively producing desire."[37] Often this expectation has been created by professionalized worship music, including "worship concerts," that have set the standard for what to expect in church: "Understanding their worship concert activities as worship shapes what evangelicals expect of a 'worship experience' in other settings," she suggests.[38]

Thus, worship in which the Holy Spirit is directly active is often necessarily connected with engaging music, spontaneity, and "freedom" of form. Worship that is formal, structured, and regulated is the opposite of "Spirit-led" worship in this view. As Lim and Ruth note, most contemporary worship, impacted as it is by this understanding of the Holy Spirit's work in worship, considers "extemporaneity as a mark of worship that is true and of the Holy Spirit, that is, worship in Spirit and truth (John 4:24). This view of extemporaneity" they observe, "has been held widely within Free Church ways of worship."[39] According to a 2010 study by Faith Communities Today, the percentage of Protestant churches characterized by contemporary Praise and Worship rose from 29% in 2000 to 43% in 2010. The percentage change was even higher when they factored out mainline denominations and focused exclusively on Evangelical Protestants (from 35% to 51%).[40] Today, the worship in a majority of evangelical churches is more characterized by Praise and Worship philosophy and contemporary music than by traditional practices rooted in the Reformation or earlier. What Albrecht observes of Pentecostal worship has become the standard expectation for most of evangelicalism:

> In the midst of radical receptivity, an encounter with the Holy Spirit may occur. Pentecostals envision such encounters as integral to the worship experience. While an overwhelming or overpowering experience of/in the Spirit is neither rare nor routine for a particular Pentecostal worshiper, the experiential dimension of worship is fundamental. The liturgical vision sees God as present in the service; consequently, Pentecostals reason that a direct experience of God is a normal expectation.[41]

---

[37] Ingalls, *Singing the Congregation*, 204.
[38] Ingalls, *Singing the Congregation*, 42.
[39] Lim and Ruth, *Lovin' on Jesus*, 38.
[40] Marjorie H. Royle, "Facts on Worship: 2010" (Faith Communities Today, 2010), 12.
[41] Albrecht, "Worshiping and the Spirit: Transmuting Liturgy Pentecostally," 240.

Church Growth

Arising from application of missiological principles to North American church ministry philosophy in the 1960s and 1970s, the church growth movement sought to explain in sociological terms why some churches grew and others did not and to advocate strategies and techniques for accomplishing the desired growth. Donald McGavran is often credited as the first significant author to promote church growth strategies,[42] which very quickly developed into the application of business marketing techniques in order to grow a church, such as this striking statement from George Barna: "My contention, based on careful study of data and the activities of American church, is that the major problem plaguing the church is its failure to embrace a marketing orientation in what has become a marketing-driven environment."[43] Church growth experts advocate proactively changing methodology—including reformatting church services—in order to grow the church. For example, Peter Wagner urged "consecrated pragmatism" when evaluating a church's traditional practices:

> The Church Growth Movement has always stressed pragmatism, and still does even though many have criticized it. It is not the kind of pragmatism that comprises doctrine or ethics or the kind that dehumanizes people by using them as means toward an end. It is, however, the kind of consecrated pragmatism which ruthlessly examines traditional methodologies and programs asking the tough questions. If some sort of ministry in the church is not reaching intended goals, consecrated pragmatism says there is something wrong which needs to be corrected.[44]

Megachurches such as Willow Creek Community Church in South Barington, IL, pastored by Bill Hybels,[45] and Saddleback Valley Community Church in Lake Forest, CA, pastored by Rick Warren,[46] came to lead the charge in revising traditional church services in favor of "seeker-sensitive" services that would draw the unchurched.

Church growth advocates quickly found that one of the most successful tactics for attracting new people to services was to adopt Praise and Worship methodology, particularly its music and concept of flow, without necessarily affirming its theology. For example, church growth leaders such as Ed Dobson taught that "a style of music that would get [unchurched people] moving in a physical way (nodding heads and tapping

---

[42] First in *The Bridges of God: A Study in the Strategy of Missions* (New York: Friendship Press, 1955).
[43] George Barna, *Marketing the Church* (Colorado Springs: Navpress, 1988), 23.
[44] C. Peter Wagner, *Leading Your Church to Growth* (Ventura, CA: Regal Books, 1984), 201.
[45] Lynne and Bill Hybels, *Rediscovering Church: The Story and Vision of Willow Creek Community* (Grand Rapids: Zondervan, 1995).
[46] Rick Warren, *The Purpose Driven Church: Growth without Compromising Your Message and Mission* (Grand Rapids: Zondervan, 2007).

feet) would help break down their defenses."[47] Likewise, Rick Warren argued that "the style of music you choose to use in your services will be ... *the* most influential factor in determining who your church reaches for Christ and whether or not your church grows. You must match your music to the kind of people God wants your church to reach."[48] Saddleback's music leader, Rick Muchow, deliberately applied the "flow" theology of Pentecostal worship to the church's seeker services, creating what they called the IMPACT model in which songs would "Inspire Movement to Praise to Adoration to Commitment to a song to Tie it together."[375] Resemblance between this model and the tabernacle model of Pentecostal worship is unmistakable:

> The songs should move from a "hand clapper" (an up-beat song about God) to a "hand holder") a community song where the worshiping assembly engages as one in dialogue with God), to a "hand raiser" (a more intimate song where the worshiper sings in the first person to God), and then, at the end of the service, another "hand holder."[49]

This philosophy affected preaching as well, such as Leith Anderson's insistence that

> words like "ought," "should," and "must" punctuated the older style in which the preacher told the audience what to do. The new style explains the issues, presents the alternatives, and then seeks to persuade—but clearly leaves the decision up to the listener. Modern Americans don't want their politicians, doctors, or pastors telling them what to do. They want to be well informed and decide for themselves.[50]

In reality, church growth philosophy and resultant methodologies were not new—they were the natural development of principles first successfully promoted in the revivalism efforts of Charles Finney. What church growth advocates did was to update these principles with modern marketing strategies and combine them with the perceived creativity and innovation of Pentecostal worship, creating what Peter Wagner called "the new apostolic churches."[51]

---

[47] Edward G. Dobson, *Starting a Seeker Sensitive Service: How Traditional Churches Can Reach the Unchurched* (Grand Rapids: Zondervan, 1993), 42–43.
[48] Warren, *The Purpose Driven Church*, 280. Emphasis original.
[49] Interview with Rich Muchow, in Lim and Ruth, *Lovin' on Jesus*, 34–35.
[50] Leith Anderson, *A Church for the 21st Century: Bringing Change to Your Church to Meet the Challenges of a Changing Society* (Grand Rapids: Bethany House, 1992), 209.
[51] Peter C. Wagner, *The New Apostolic Churches* (Ventura, CA: Regal Books, 1998).

Worship Defined as Music

Both the Praise and Worship and Church Growth movements emphasize musical style as a predominant feature of a church above traditional doctrinal and ecclesiastical distinctives such that an increasing number of evangelical Christians today choose their church based on worship style over traditional confessional reasons. As David Holeton observes, "When people move from one region of the country to another or even to another part of the city, denomination is less and less their first criterion in finding a new parish." Instead, people choose their church more based on the style of worship and programs the church has to offer.[52] In a 2009 study of megachurches, researchers found that worship style was the number one factor that attracted attenders to megachurches, with denominational affiliation eighth on the list under the church reputation, music/arts, and adult programs.[53] Likewise, a 2016 Pew Research study demonstrated that 74% of Americans searching for a church based their decision on worship style,[54] and a 2017 Gallup poll showed music to be a major factor in choosing a church, more important than any doctrinal or denominational concerns.[55]

Since the Reformation, worship theology and practice has always been central to denominational distinctiveness. Yet as we have seen, psalmody, hymnody, and liturgy have traditionally provided a means for appropriate unity across denominational lines without diminishing the importance of theological matters. Contemporary worship trends, however, have raised musical style to a place of prominence that tends to make style more important for a church's identity than doctrinal issues.

What distinguishes traditional songs and liturgy from contemporary Praise and Worship songs and liturgy in this comparison is not the transdenominational character of their lyrics or tunes; as we have observed, this is a characteristic feature of most successful congregational songs as well as historic liturgies throughout history. What distinguishes them is the importance placed upon the contemporaneity of musical style in each category. On the one hand, traditional psalms, hymns, and liturgy were both transdenominational and transcultural. Contemporary worship songs and structure, however, reflect current culture rather than transcend it. Thus "relevant" stylistic matters and appealing to particular cultural demographics have become central to a

---

[52] David R. Holeton, "'Religion Without Denomination? The Significance of Denominations for Church and Society': Some Reactions," *Communio Viatorum* 44 (January 1, 2002): 40.

[53] Scott Thumma and Warren Bird, "Not Who You Think They Are: The Real Story of People Who Attend America's Megachurches" (Hartford, CT: Hartford Institute for Religious Research, 2009), 15.

[54] Pew Research Center, "Choosing a New Church or House of Worship," *Pew Research Center's Religion & Public Life Project*, August 23, 206, http://assets.pewresearch.org/wp-content/uploads/sites/11/2016/08/Choosing-Congregations-08-19-FULL-PDF-for-web-2.pdf.

[55] Lydia Saad, "Sermon Content Is What Appeals Most to Churchgoers," Gallup News Service, April 14, 2017, http://www.gallup.com/poll/208529/sermon-content-appeals-churchgoers.aspx.

church's identity rather than important confessional matters that have historically defined denominations in the wake of the Reformation.

Emergent Worship

Postmodernism was a late-twentieth-century philosophical reaction against the extreme optimism in human progress characteristic of post-Enlightenment Modernism. Worldwide poverty, illness, and two world wars led to an increasing distrust in mankind's reason and what it could produce, resulting in a growing skepticism for anything absolute or objective. Postmodernism generally asserts that reality cannot be known in any objective way. Truth, morality, and beauty are merely a matter of perspective, and thus truth, morality, and beauty are relative to one's community. There is no metanarrative by which all things may be assessed.

This philosophical movement impacted broader in culture in many ways clearly negative to biblical Christianity and its worship. Its denial of absolutes, pluralism, rejection of authority, consumer appetite, individual subjectivity, and insistence upon cultural neutrality served to further increase the chasm between Christianity and culture that had begun with Modernism. However, postmodernism's reaction against secular modernism creates some positive results for Christianity as well. Postmoderns tend to distrust reason alone, becoming open to the mystical or miraculous; they recognize that not all truth can be easily proven through the scientific method and that presuppositions influence the understanding of truth. They tend to desire community and authenticity, eschewing artificially packaged entertainment for its own sake, and are interested in arts and ancient traditions.

These philosophical and culture developments laid the groundwork for another shift in Christian theology and worship practice, first beginning with the Emergent Church.[56] Emergent church leaders argued that churches must contextualize theology and practice in order to be relevant to postmodern unbelievers and believers alike. Everything must be set in a postmodern context, including practice and even theology. These leaders began to question whether Scripture had an overarching meta-narrative, suggesting instead that each culture's presuppositions would affect how it came to the text of Scripture and developed its theology and practice.

Worship in churches impacted by emergent theology tended to emphasize authenticity instead of performance, mystery and multisensory experiences, relationship and community, and symbols and stories. Emergent worship was quite eclectic, drawing its liturgical practices and artistic expressions both from ancient tradition and contemporary culture, leading Robert Webber to describe it as "Ancient/Future

---

[56] See D. A. Carson, *Becoming Conversant with the Emerging Church: Understanding a Movement and Its Implications* (Grand Rapids: Zondervan, 2005).

Worship." It rejected what it considered the "attractional worship" philosophy of the church growth movement in favor of services designed to foster true worship among postmodern Christians.

Missional Worship

Some conservative evangelical theologians objected to emergent leader's denial of Scripture's metanarrative and over-contextualization of doctrine, but they agreed that practice must be contextualized to a postmodern context.[57] Because of the liberal tendencies of emergent theology, these theologians eventually adopted the term "missional" to describe their philosophy and argued that everything explicitly addressed in Scripture is absolute and must not be changed, while anything not in Scripture is relative.[58] This resulted in a firm defense of traditional Protestant theology combined with sometimes radical departures from traditional practices, including worship. They consider worship to be primarily for believers instead of unchurched "seekers," but since even believers are postmodern, worship practice should be contextualized to this postmodern context. Furthermore, unbelievers are still welcome in corporate worship, and so even though worship is not designed specifically for them, it should be "intelligible" for unbelievers.[59]

Ecumenical Worship and Liturgical Renewal

Although this book focuses primarily on the roots and streams of evangelical worship, liturgical developments within Roman Catholicism and other mainline Protestant denominations have contributed to relatively small but growing "liturgical renewal" movements.

Vatican II

One significant development in Roman Catholic worship in the twentieth century affected the worship of other traditions as well. Between 1962 and 1965, Popes John XXIII and later Paul VI presided over the Second Ecumenical Council of the Vatican, commonly known as Vatican II. The council's primary concern was to address the relationship between the RCC and the rest of the modern world, and this resulted in considerable liturgical reforms. The council produced in 1963 the *Constitution on the Sacred Liturgy*, which ended the centuries-long insistence that all worship practices

---

[57] Mark Driscoll, *Confessions of a Reformission Rev.: Hard Lessons from an Emerging Missional Church (The Leadership Network Innovation)*, Revised (Grand Rapids: Zondervan, 2006).

[58] Darrell Guder, *Missional Church: A Vision for the Sending of the Church in North America* (Grand Rapids: Wm. B. Eerdmans, 1998).

[59] For a full history and assessment of missional worship, see Scott Aniol, *By the Waters of Babylon: Worship in a Post-Christian Culture* (Grand Rapids: Kregel Ministry, 2015).

across the Church remain uniform in structure and language, instead allowing churches within different nations and cultures to develop their worship in ways closer aligned to their own local identities. The *Constitution* called for "full, conscious, and active participation" (Part 14) in worship, and thus the liturgy was translated into various vernacular languages. Preaching also became more important to the Sunday mass, and congregational song became emphasized, with much more freedom to contextualize musical forms to popular idioms. Many other liturgical rites and liturgies were updated, even providing four canons for mass (heavily influenced by the *Apostolic Tradition*) from which clergy may choose.

One result of this modernization of worship within Roman Catholicism has been a more openness by some Protestants toward Catholic liturgical practices. Since the liturgies themselves, translated into the vernacular, have become more accessible to those who do not understand Latin, various Protestants have begun to be impacted by these liturgies.

Anglicanism
The Oxford Movement in England had already begun to create a dialogue between Anglicanism and Roman Catholicism in the nineteenth century, and by the twentieth century, the Church of England had incorporated many liturgical revisions that brought it closer to Roman Catholic worship, including the adoption of medieval vestments, lighting candles, burning incense, and physical rituals by priests within the liturgy. In 1912, the Church published a new English Missal, which was strongly influenced by the Eucharistic rite of the 1662 *Book of Common Prayer* and the Latin Roman Missal. Even more significant changes were made in the late twentieth century with the *Alternative Service Book* (1980) and *Common Worship* (2000), considered an updated alternative to the 1662 *Book of Common Prayer* (which is still also in common use). Much of the wording, especially in the text of the Eucharist, is identical to the Roman Missal, leading many to observe that Anglican worship based in these texts has returned in many ways to pre-Cranmer practices.

Lutheran
Some Lutheran churches, too, have been impacted by the ecumenical renewal movements. The Evangelical Lutheran Church in America (ELCA) has adopted many liturgical practices drawn from Roman Catholic and Anglican traditions, such as pre-Reformation vestments, feast days, and the sign of the cross, and much of the wording of commonly used liturgies are the same as the Roman Missal. The more conservative Lutheran Church–Missouri Synod (LCMS) has recovered Lutheran liturgical practices that had been for some time overlooked.

Methodist

In the latter nineteenth and twentieth centuries, many Methodists began to recover more formal worship. Even as early as 1859, Thomas O. Summers (1812–1882) reprinted Wesley's *Sunday Service* and helped to establish a standard liturgy. Yet as Methodists became more educated and affluent in the twentieth century, the free emotionalism of frontier Methodism was replaced by the aestheticism of more liturgical worship as well as social activism, climaxing with the publication of a new *Book of Worship* in 1945 that included formal services and emphasized confession and the creeds. In 1970, a Commission on Worship began to integrate the Roman Catholic rites from Vatican II into Methodist liturgy, producing *The Sacrament of the Lord's Supper* in 1972.

Conclusion to Part Five

What is critical to recognize is that the difference between pre-Enlightenment and post-Enlightenment worldview, theology, culture, and cultus is not simply change of degree but fundamental change in *kind*. What has occurred since the eighteenth century is the creation of what David Bentley Hart calls an "imaginative chasm between the premodern and modern worlds. Human beings now in a sense inhabited a universe different from that inhabited by their ancestors."[1]

Further, because of the fragmentation created in the wake of both the Reformation and Enlightenment, it is no longer sufficient to describe "*the* theology" of this period. Rather, many theolog*ies*—both traditionally Christian and "secular"—have emerged. Christian theology can be somewhat simplistically divided into two broad categories, evangelical and liberal. Evangelical theology has continued to affirm the inspiration and veracity of Scripture and thus traditional doctrines such as the deity and atonement of Christ, and it proclaims the necessity of repentance and faith in Christ for the forgiveness of sins. Liberal Christianity of various forms questions certain aspects of traditional theology such as the virgin birth of Christ and tends to center its religious life in social activism over against insisting upon "born again" conversion.

The cultural changes resulting from the Enlightenment are perhaps best epitomized in the American and French Revolutions, where democratic ideals overthrew aristocratic and monarchical dominance. As with most of the changes we've surveyed in this book, these revolutions were both positive and negative. New freedom of religion allowed Christians to worship according to their conscience instead of state mandate. This led some groups toward more purity of religion and less nominal Christianity. Yet extreme individualism, especially in America, continued the growth of privatized, individualistic religion.

The dominant theology of "secular" religion is hedonism—worship of self. What is prized most greatly in modern society is self-expression and pleasure, fueled by the growth of commercialism as the driving force of economic life, the cultural result of the Industrial Revolution. The growing dominance of the secular religion has produced an increasingly hedonistic society, perhaps reaching its tipping point in the Sexual Revolution of the 1960s, notable results including the national legalization by the Supreme Court of abortion in 1973 and of same-sex marriage in 2015 as well as the

---

[1] David Bentley Hart, *The Experience of God: Being, Consciousness, Bliss* (New Haven, CT: Yale University Press, 2013), 62.

normalization of transgenderism in recent years. Charles Taylor describes the present culture well:

> Everyone has a right to develop their own form of life, grounded on their own sense of what is really important or of value. People are called upon to be true to themselves and to seek their own self-fulfillment. What this consists of, each must, in the last instance, determine for him- or herself. No one else can or should try to dictate its content.[2]

---

[2] Charles Taylor, *The Ethics of Authenticity* (Cambridge, MA: Harvard University Press, 1992), 14.

Conclusion to Part Five

Study Guide for Part Five
People and Terms

"manifest presence"
affections
Age of Reason
altar call
appetites
camp meetings
charismaticism
church growth movement
commercial culture
communal culture
conservative philosophy
contemporary worship
Cornwall, Judson
cultivated culture
Darwin, Charles
Deism
democracy
Descartes, René
Edwards, Jonathan
effective principle
emergent
emotion
empiricism
Enlightenment
Espinosa, Eddie
faith
Finney, Charles G.
Five Phase Pattern
flow
folk culture
gospel song
Great Awakening
high culture
humanism
Hybels, Bill
Industrial Revolution
mass culture
Methodism
missional
Modernism
Moravians

naturalism
new measures
normative principle
Oxford Movement
passions
Pentecostalism
Pietism
pluralism
pop culture
Postmodernism
pragmatism
Praise & Worship
progressive philosophy
reason
regulative principle
revival
revivalism
Romanticism
sacramentality
Scientific Revolution
secularism
self-consciousness
Tabernacle Model
Vatican II
Wagner, Peter
Warren, Rick
Wesley, Charles
Wesley, John
Whitefield, George
Wimber, John
Zinzendorf, Nicholas

Recommended Resources
Faulkner, Quentin. *Wiser Than Despair: The Evolution of Ideas in the Relationship of Music and the Christian Church*. 2nd ed. Simpsonville, SC: Religious Affections Ministries, 2012.
Lim, Swee Hong, and Lester Ruth. *Lovin' on Jesus: A Concise History of Contemporary Worship*. Nashville: Abingdon Press, 2017.
Murray, Iain H. *Revival and Revivalism*. Carlisle, PA: Banner of Truth, 1994.
Needham, Nick. *2,000 Years of Christ's Power Vol 4: The Age of Religious Conflict*. United Kingdom: Christian Focus Publications, 2016.
Noll, Mark A. *A History of Christianity in the United States and Canada*. Grand Rapids: W.B. Eerdmans, 1992.

Wells, David F. *No Place for Truth: Or Whatever Happened to Evangelical Theology?* Grand Rapids: Wm. B. Eerdmans Publishing, 1994.

White, James F. *Protestant Worship: Traditions in Transition.* Louisville, KY: Westminster John Knox Press, 1989.

Questions for Discussion and Reflection
1. Discuss the factors leading up to the Enlightenment and the philosophical and practical results in Christian theology and worship.
2. Explain Jonathan Edwards's philosophy of affections and passions and discuss its impact upon an understanding of conversion, spirituality, and worship.
3. Discuss Charles Finney's theology and methods, including their impact on evangelical worship.
4. Explain the historical theological influences that created contemporary worship.

PART SIX: LOOKING FORWARD

Love divine, all loves excelling,
joy of heav'n, to earth come down,
fix in us Thy humble dwelling;
all Thy faithful mercies crown.
Jesus, Thou art all compassion;
pure, unbounded love Thou art;
visit us with Thy salvation;
enter ev'ry trembling heart.

Come, Almighty, to deliver;
let us all Thy life receive;
suddenly return and never,
nevermore Thy temples leave.
Thee we would be always blessing,
serve Thee as Thy hosts above,
pray and praise Thee without ceasing,
glory in Thy perfect love.

Finish then Thy new creation;
pure and spotless let us be.
Let us see Thy great salvation
perfectly restored in Thee.
Changed from glory into glory,
till in heav'n we take our place,
till we cast our crowns before Thee,
lost in wonder, love, and praise.

—Charles Wesley, 1747

Chapter 17
By the Waters of Babylon:
Worship in a Post-Christian Culture

When faithful Hebrews gathered by a river in Babylon to worship, they could not help but recognize the clear antithesis between true worship and false worship. They were God's people in a strange land; they had no homes, no place for worship; they were a unique people with a unique identity, but they were aliens and strangers. When they were in their land, Israel's cultus and culture fit together perfectly under the Law of God—at least that's how it was supposed to be. Now, however, the Hebrews found themselves in a cultural situation that was hostile to their religion and pure worship.

And so they sat down and wept; they hung up their lyres, the predominate instrument of accompaniment for temple worship. Their captors mocked them: "Sing for us one of your worship songs!" (v.3) But the captive Hebrews could not. "How shall we sing the Lord's song in a foreign land?" (v. 4) Yet the author of Psalm 137 wishes not to forget God in the midst of exile, as so many of the other people did. He does not want to forget Jerusalem, the place of God's worship. He says that if he forgets the true worship of God, then may it be that he loses his skill to play the lyre or to sing, for he does not want to use these skills except in the praise of Yahweh.

The Church in Exile
What is particularly instructive for us in the church today is that New Testament authors often use language to describe our situation that refers back to Israel's experience in exile by way of analogy. Consider, for example, the idea of Babylon. In the New Testament, particularly in the book of Revelation, the title Babylon is given to the enemies of God (Rev. 14:8, 16:19, 17:5, 18:2), representative of everything that is contrary and hostile to God, his worship, and his people. And isn't that exactly how Scripture describes this present age? Galatians 1:4 calls this "the present *evil* age"(emphasis mine), and 2 Corinthians 4:4 identifies the "god of this world" as one who has "blinded the minds of the unbelievers, to keep them from seeing the light of the gospel of the glory of Christ," this one who Ephesians 2:2 calls "the prince of the power of the air, the spirit that is now at work in the sons of disobedience." Jesus said that this world hates him, because he "testifies about it that its works are evil" (John 7:7). In other words, there appear to be striking similarities between the Babylon in which the Jewish exiles found themselves and how the New Testament describes the age in which we Christians find ourselves.

Or consider the idea of Zion and Jerusalem. In Psalm 137, these refer to a literal city, but even in the Psalm these titles represent more than merely a physical location—they represent the place where God's presence dwelt, the place of true worship. In the New Testament, the terms "Zion" and "Jerusalem" are likewise often used metaphorically in reference to the place of God's presence and true worship. Probably the most vivid example is the one we looked at in Chapter 7 from Hebrews 12:22: "But you have come to Mount Zion and to the city of the living God, the heavenly Jerusalem." As we saw, God's presence is in the temple of heaven, and when we Christians worship, we are actually joining with the worship of heaven, uniting our voices with innumerable angels in festal gathering and saints who have gone before us. Ephesians 2:6 tells us that we Christians have been raised up with Christ and have been seated with him in the heavenly places. In fact, in verse 19 of the same chapter, Paul calls us "fellow citizens with the saints and members of the household of God," and Philippians 3:20 states that our citizenship is not here on earth; our citizenship is in heaven itself.

You see, when we consider how the New Testament describes this present age, it sounds a whole lot like Babylon, and when we consider how the New Testament describes our citizenship in the place of God's presence and worship, it sounds a whole lot like a distant city where we have our citizenship but where we do not currently dwell. And to make this comparison even more apparent, consider how Peter refers to the church today. First Peter 1:17 calls our current situation as Christians "the time of your exile," and 2:11 specifically calls us "sojourners and exiles." In other words, we who are members of Christ's church in this present age are, like Israel, God's people in exile. Like Israel, our citizenship is in Zion, a city far away where God's presence dwells in his temple and where pure worship takes place. Like Israel, we find ourselves by the waters of Babylon, amidst a people whose ruler hates God, his worship, and his people.

Dual Citizens
Yet many Christians today have lost sight of this antithesis between true worship and the false worship of those around us. One reason for this is that the fundamental worldview assumptions that dominated for so long prior to the Enlightenment, especially during Christendom, still linger in some respects in western society. Their effects are still evident for two reasons: First, as we have seen throughout this study, nothing changes quickly. Assumptions about reality have gradually shifted since the eighteenth century, sometimes drastically, but mostly slowly. Nevertheless, because religion produces culture, and culture evolves slowly over time, many elements of current culture—even pop culture—retain elements of a worldview compatible with biblical truth. This is especially true in the West, where for hundreds of years culture was

rooted in basic, universal principles sometimes called "Jude-Christian." That political system has been gradually moving away from those principles, perhaps more so recently than in previous generations, but because our system prevents quick change, biblical values do still exist.

The second reason worldview assumptions compatible with Christianity still exist is this: since God created the world and everything in it to flourish under conditions consistent with his nature and will, operating on the assumptions of a biblical worldview just works better. Unbelieving people often "borrow" from the biblical worldview because they instinctively recognize that living in a contrary way leads to destruction. For example, in *Mere Christianity*, C. S. Lewis noted remarkable similarity among the moral codes of diverse civilizations as evidence for universal principles embedded by God in the very fabric of the world.[1] Most successful civilizations recognize the wisdom in outlawing certain acts like murder and theft, even if they have no explicitly creedal basis for such laws.

This makes our situation somewhat more challenging to navigate. On the one hand, Christians are citizens of another kingdom in exile among a pagan people. But on the other hand, even unbelieving societies can sometimes reflect universal, transcendent values consistent with what the Bible teaches. This creates a dilemma: how much must Christians—especially our worship—be distinct from pagan religions if those pagans sometimes stumble onto truth?

Yet this challenge is not unique after all—Israel in exile actually had a similar situation. Consider what the prophet Jeremiah commanded the people as they were being taken off into exile in Babylon:

> Thus says the Lord of hosts, the God of Israel, to all the exiles whom I have sent into exile from Jerusalem to Babylon: ⁵ Build houses and live in them; plant gardens and eat their produce. ⁶ Take wives and have sons and daughters; take wives for your sons, and give your daughters in marriage, that they may bear sons and daughters; multiply there, and do not decrease. ⁷ But seek the welfare of the city where I have sent you into exile, and pray to the Lord on its behalf, for in its welfare you will find your welfare. (Jer. 29:4–7)

You see, God did not expect his people to remain completely and utterly distinct from their captors in every respect. In fact, they were supposed to build houses, plant gardens, get married, and have children, and they were even supposed to seek the welfare of Babylon. We see this kind of thing exemplified with one of the accounts of captivity covered in Chapter 4: Daniel refused to stop praying to Yahweh, and he would not

---

[1] C. S. Lewis, *Mere Christianity* (San Francisco: HarperSanFrancisco, 2002), 6; c.f. C. S Lewis, *The Abolition of Man* (New York: HarperOne, 2001), 83–101.

pray to the king or eat meat that was associated with pagan worship, and yet he willingly allowed himself to be educated in the literature and language of Babylon and even served in political leadership, as did others of the people of Israel. Because even pagans retain the image of God and often borrow basic assumptions about reality that are actually true, they can sometimes do good things—they can build structurally-sound houses, they can plant fruitful gardens—the Hanging Gardens of Babylon are one of the Seven Wonders of the Ancient World, they can devise successful political systems, they can produce worthy art, and they can teach things that are true. So in these cases—when what pagans do in culture actually reflects values consistent with biblical Christianity, God's people can stand alongside unbelieving people, participating in and contributing to society. In fact, God commands his people to actually seek the welfare of the city and pray on its behalf, because since they are living as exiles in this land, its welfare is their welfare.

The same is true for the New Testament church. Jesus was clear: render to Caesar that which is Caesar's, because the welfare of the city is also our welfare. A healthy government that protects the innocent and punishes injustice is a good thing, even if that government is pagan. In the context of teaching Christians how to live as sojourners and exiles, Peter specifically says that we should submit to earthly authorities and even honor them (1 Pet. 2:13–18), because the welfare of the city is also our welfare. Government was instituted by God himself, and inasmuch as governing officials rule with equity and justice, they are doing exactly what God intends for them to do. Like Jeremiah, Paul commands that "supplications, prayers, intercessions, and thanksgivings be made for all people, for kings and all who are in high positions, that we may lead a peaceful and quiet life, godly and dignified in every way" (1 Tim. 2:1–2).

Therefore, there is a very real sense in which we as Christians, very similar to Israel in Babylonian exile, are dual citizens. We are first and foremost citizens of a future city, the heavenly Jerusalem, where the presence of God dwells and where he is worshiped in truth and purity. But we are also citizens of the present earthly city, in which we contribute to society, submit to and pray for governmental authorities, and participate in various aspects of cultural endeavors.

Secular Religion, Cultus, and Culture
Nevertheless, while we may legitimately build houses, plant gardens, and participate in the political process, enjoying the literature and education of the foreign land in which we are exiles, we may only do so if those aspects of the culture indeed embody values and assumptions consistent with biblical Christianity. This was the case in certain respects in Babylon, and it is sometimes the case in western society, especially due to the long influence of Christianity on western culture. However, when pagan *religion*

manifests itself in the cultus and culture of a society, God's people must be utterly distinct. As we have seen several times throughout this study, there is a strict antithesis between the belief systems and worship practices of God's people and pagan people. And this is increasingly so in the West as well. Since at least the rise of secular humanism, basic assumptions about the nature of reality have been changing. I described several of them in Chapter 14: naturalism, empiricism, Darwinism, and later a complete rejection of absolutes, combined with the hedonism that naturally rises in a depraved heart, have drastically altered dominant assumptions in Western society concerning meaning and purpose in life. The central religion of a secularized west is that of pluralism and pragmatism—no particular ideology is better than another, and the ends justify the means. Thus, as western culture continues to reflect secularist values, Christians will find themselves increasingly separated from that culture.

Furthermore, while there may be commonality between Christians and pagans with regard to the everyday aspects of life in some cases, *worship* must remain distinct. We, like Israel, must recognize ourselves in a situation in which true worship will always be at odds with the prevailing beliefs and values of the world, will always be mocked and maligned by unbelieving people, and will always be countercultural to pagan worship.

Bowing to Secular Idols
And yet, as western culture increasingly embodies the values of secular religion, the effect of these changes upon Christianity has not been negligible. Lack of overt paganism during the period of Christendom in a way desensitized Christians to the need for vigilant separation from the world. Furthermore, the secularization of the West following the Age of Reason has made it somewhat more difficult to discern the antithesis between Christianity and the world's religion. Because of the lingering effects of Christendom, false religion today is often packed in wrappings that make it seem less overtly pagan. Unlike Israel in Babylon, for example, we don't have pagan kings commanding us to bow down and worship huge statues of themselves. We don't see altars and human sacrifices going on around us, because the "sophisticated modern mind" doesn't believe in the supernatural. But our Babylon is no less pagan—secularism is just a different kind of paganism that manifests itself in the culture it influences. Secular paganism doesn't worship idols of gold or bow down to false kings as gods; rather, today's paganism worships financial prosperity, hedonism, entertainment, immorality, and self.

The problem is that Christians haven't always recognized these emerging values and assumptions, unknowingly adopting them as they embrace what they consider to be neutral aspects of secular culture. In short, many Christians don't recognize secularism to be the religion (worldview + theology) that it is. As Rod Dreher notes, instead of recognizing and resisting the increasing secularization of the West, many Christians succumbed to it, having placed "unwarranted confidence in the health of our religious institutions."[2] Dreher offers his proposal, not just because the culture is so bad, but because Western Christianity is so bad. He continues, "The changes that have overtaken the West in modern times have revolutionized everything, even the church, which no longer forms souls but caters to selves."[3] He observes that most professing Christians in America have identified their Christianity with being American and have adopted what was more accurately described by Christian Smith and Melinda Lundquist Denton in 2005 as Moralistic Therapeutic Deism.[4] The core theology of many evangelicals today can be summarized by the following beliefs:

1. A God exists who created and orders the world and watches over human life on earth.
2. God wants people to be good, nice, and fair to each other, as taught in the Bible and by most world religions.
3. The central goal of life is to be happy and to feel good about oneself.
4. God does not need to be particularly involved in one's life except when he is needed to resolve a problem.
5. Good people go to heaven when they die.

Others have also described the effects of the secular religion upon Christianity. David Wells has assessed the effects of modernity and postmodernity on Christianity in a thorough manner like few others. He argues that, as a result of the increasing secularization of the west, theology in the church "has become dismembered" such that confessional beliefs (theology) have been divorced from the cultivation of virtue manifested in holy living (culture). Wells argues, "theology is disappearing ... in the sense that while its articles of belief are still professed, they are no longer defining what it means to be an evangelical or how evangelicalism should be practiced. At its center there is now a vacuum into which modernity is pouring, and the result is a faith that, unlike historic orthodoxy, is no longer defining itself theologically."[5] In a later book, Wells described the result of the disappearance of theology as "the weightlessness of

---

[2] Rod Dreher, *The Benedict Option: A Strategy for Christians in a Post-Christian Nation* (New York: Sentinel, 2017), 9.

[3] Dreher, *The Benedict Option*, 9.

[4] Christian Smith and Melinda Lundquist Denton, *Soul Searching: The Religious and Spiritual Lives of American Teenagers* (New York: Oxford University Press, 2005). Smith followed up his research in 2011 with a study of 18-to-23-year-olds and found MTD to be largely the presumed theology.

[5] Wells, *No Place for Truth*, 109.

God."[6] Building from Wells' critique, Michael Lawrence well describes the state of many churches today:

> The church has become enamored with business practice and psychological method. Her leaders are expected to be CEO's, not pastor-theologians. The church's public gatherings are designed to be events that appeal to the outsider, rather than assemblies that give corporate expression to our identity as the people of God. And our habits of thought tend to be shaped more by polling data, the blogosphere, and the image-driven nature of television than they do the Bible. The thoughts of God and his glory, our nobility and depravity, and this world's value and transience—thoughts that shaped and characterized the minds of previous generations of Christians—rest lightly, if at all, on the church today.[7]

D. A. Carson also assessed the impact of secular pluralism on evangelical Christianity. He suggests that "it is difficult to avoid the conclusion that profound *selfism*—self-centeredness elevated to an unrecognized principle of interpretation—governs not only much of Western culture, but, of more interest to us at the moment, much of the Western church."[8] He observes that this increasing "selfism" manifests itself primarily in churches that are "too pragmatic, hedonistic, relativistic, given to emotion rather than thought, and in short, self-centered."[9] This has climaxed in a fundamental consumerism within the church:

> In a former age, insatiable desire was understood to be a principal source of frustration, something to be opposed. Now it is to be cultivated as the engine that drives economic development. The endemic consumerism of the age feeds our greed, and even defines our humanity: we are not primarily worshipers, or thinkers, or God's image-bearers, or lovers, but *consumers*.[10]

Thomas Bergler described the influence of secular culture on Christianity as "the juvenilization of American Christianity," which he argues has "undermined Christian maturity:

> First, the faith has become overly identified with emotional comfort. And it is only a short step from a personalized, emotionally comforting faith to a self-

---

[6] David F. Wells, *God in the Wasteland: The Reality of Truth in a World of Fading Dreams* (Grand Rapids: Wm. B. Eerdmans, 1994), 88.
[7] Michael Lawrence, *Biblical Theology in the Life of the Church: A Guide for Ministry* (Wheaton: Crossway, 2010), 110.
[8] Carson, *Gagging of God*, 462. Emphasis original.
[9] Carson, *Gagging of God*, 463.
[10] Carson, *Gagging of God*, 463. Emphasis original.

centered one. Second, far too many Christians are inarticulate, indifferent, or confused about their theological beliefs. They view theology as an optional extra to faith, and assume that religious beliefs are a matter of personal preference. Many would be uncomfortable with the idea of believing something just because the Bible, the church, or some other religious authority teaches it. And they are particularly resistant to church teachings that impose behavioral restrictions. If we believe that a mature faith involves more than good feelings, vague beliefs, and living however we want, we must conclude that juvenilization has revitalized American Christianity at the cost of leaving many individuals mired in spiritual immaturity.[11]

Ultimately, what has happened to much of evangelical Christianity can be assessed as nothing short of worldliness, which is how John MacArthur described the church's embrace of pragmatism. He argues, "Modernists gained ground early and easily among evangelicals by decrying the importance of doctrine (which was deemed divisive and unnecessarily pedantic) while championing the importance of charity and good works."[12] The result?

> Today more than ever, evangelical church leaders are held captive to the notion that their main duty toward the world is to study the trends of popular culture and try desperately to get on every passing bandwagon as quickly as possible. Some pastors literally devote most of their energies to learning whatever happens to be the latest worldly craze, and then they desperately seek a way to blend themes and references from those fads into their sermons and Sunday-school programs. The goal, still, is to woo people into the kingdom by making Christianity seem cool and contemporary. As a result, people in evangelical pews have become utterly obsessed with superficial trends and silly fashions. In fact, evangelical Christians may be more addicted to quickly passing fads than any other single demographic or subculture, including preteen girls.[13]

Cultus

All of these various changes in worldview, theology, and culture among Christians have without doubt affected worship to one degree or another. Here too, however, two realities are present when we consider the formative relationship between religion and liturgy. First, worship philosophy and practice has not changed quickly or necessarily all at once. Especially for more confessional churches that deliberately tie themselves to a particular church tradition, elements of historic worship still exist. In "free

---

[11] Thomas E Bergler, *The Juvenilization of American Christianity* (Grand Rapids: William B. Eerdmans, 2012), 225.

[12] John F. MacArthur, *Ashamed of the Gospel: When the Church Becomes Like the World*, 3rd ed. (Wheaton: Crossway Books, 2010), 206.

[13] MacArthur, *Ashamed of the Gospel*, 32.

churches," changes may be more evident, but even there, certain aspects of historic and biblical worship linger. Second, it is not always simple to assess what changes in worship practice are simply changes that reflect the same underlying theology, or which changes actually result from the kinds of secularization the authors above describe. Some clearly are, but others are less easy to discern.

This is why, as we evaluate the *lex orandi, lex credendi* relationship we have been tracing through the book, it is important that we carefully compare and contrast modern worship philosophies and practices, parsing them for their meaning, and evaluating what kinds of religious commitments they embody. In recent years, several interesting taxonomies of worship philosophies have been published in an attempt to do just this, classifying various views in a similar way one might classify positions concerning the return of Christ, whether or not regeneration precedes faith, or the proper mode of baptism. For example, Zondervan published a counterpoint book in 2004, *Exploring the Worship Spectrum: Six Views*, classifying worship philosophies as

Formal-Liturgical Worship (Paul F. M. Zahl)
Traditional Hymn-Based Worship (Harold M. Best)
Contemporary Music-Driven Worship (Joe Horness)
Charismatic Worship (Don Williams)
Blended Worship (Robert Webber)
Emerging Worship (Sally Morgenthaler).[14]

Broadman and Holman's attempt in 2009, titled *Perspectives on Christian Worship: Five Views*, classified these perspectives as

Liturgical Worship (Timothy C. J. Quill)
Traditional Evangelical Worship (J. Ligon Duncan)
Contemporary Worship (Dan Wilt)
Blended Worship (Mark Dever)
Emerging Worship (Dan Kimball).[15]

While the information in books like these may be interesting and helpful to a certain degree, if the study of worship history in this book has revealed anything, it is that attempting to classify worship philosophy and practice in a simplistic way is virtually impossible. The biggest difficulty with each of these taxonomies is a common one: the various philosophies of worship throughout history or currently held today cannot really be put on a simple sliding scale. For example "Contemporary Worship" today

---

[14] Paul Basden, ed., *Exploring the Worship Spectrum: Six Views* (Grand Rapids: Zondervan, 2004).
[15] J. Matthew Pinson, ed., *Perspectives on Christian Worship: Five Views* (Nashville: B&H Publishing Group, 2009).

could describe anything from Hillsong to Keith Getty, and although Judson Cornwall and Bob Kauflin might both be considered "charismatic" and share certain aspects of their worship theology in common, in practice they are far different.

What would be more helpful is to recognize that worship philosophy actually encompasses several categories of classification that should be taken into account when assessing the philosophy of a particular theologian, author, speaker, or church.

Governing Principle

The first question to ask regarding a person's or church's worship is what governing principle primarily drives their decisions concerning what to include in worship. Although even these principles contain some variation within them, those that have already been discussed in our historical survey are helpful. The *regulative principle* determines that whatever elements of worship are not prescribed in Scripture are therefore forbidden. Those who follow this principle will tend to have more simple, unadorned worship, giving less weight to extra-biblical worship traditions that have developed in the church and will be less likely to concern themselves with shaping the worship service according to what is contextual in present society. The *normative principle* is more willing to retain certain practices in worship that have grown up within Christian tradition over time but do not necessarily have explicit biblical prescription. Churches that follow this principle might include more ornate liturgical acts, for example. Those who adopt an *effective principle* will be primarily concerned with shaping worship according to what will most successfully accomplish their purpose and will be more likely to give priority to contextualizing worship in the current culture in order to be more relevant to it.

Purpose

The second classification involves what a person or church considers the main purpose of the primary church service(s). First, a church might have as its primary goal the *attraction* of unchurched and/or unsaved people, such that such individuals might be evangelized and brought into the church. Second, a church might see as its main purpose the *revival* of Christian people. Sometimes churches might also see their purpose as a combination of the two. Third, a church may consider the aim of its service to be an *experience of worship*. This focus here is on believers worshiping the Lord, but worship specifically defined such that the church makes certain that its service order, music, and preaching all move the worshiper in such a way that he is able to experience the presence of God. A fourth kind of church might also desire that its services primarily enable Christians to worship God, but *worship defined as reenactment*. A church of this sort is less concerned with what people *feel* in the service and more concerned with simply enacting a liturgy that responds to and renews the covenantal relationship between God and his people.

Content
A third classification directs attention to the content of a typical service, assessing whether that content is more *doctrinally weighty* or *doctrinally simple*. Here is certainly a sliding scale; usually churches either deliberately include lots of lengthy Scripture readings, songs with weighty lyrics, and more intellectually-driven preaching on the one hand, or more simplicity and accessibility in content on the other.

Relationship to Culture
What an individual or church believes concerning the relationship between the artistic forms in public worship and the dominant culture of the surrounding society is a fifth category for assessing worship philosophy. Here I have chosen to use terms commonly associated with worship philosophy, which, while certainly not perfect, nevertheless commonly connote certain perspectives. The first category under this heading could be called a *progressive* philosophy of culture. This position values cultural contextualization, considers cultural forms like music as primarily neutral containers for delivering content, and therefore seeks to make the artistic expressions of its services sound similar to the expressions of the surrounding culture. On the other end of the spectrum is a more *conservative* philosophy of cultural expression in worship. While those who adopt this posture are not opposed to anything new, they give greater weight to preserving the artistic forms and liturgies of the past, believing them to be better vehicles for worship than forms that resemble the dominant culture since they consider artistic expression to have moral impact. In between these two poles is a position that considers the conservatives too extreme while also being wary of the newest cultural expressions. This view could be called *traditional*, characterizing those who oppose modern pop styles of music, for example, while also considering older hymns too "stuffy."

Liturgy
Finally, examining a church's typical service order helps to classify its worship. First, some employ what might be called a *gospel-shaped* liturgy. This would describe several of the historic confessional liturgies surveyed in this book including those of pre-Tridentine Rome, Martin Luther, John Calvin, the Westminster divines, and the *Book of Common Prayer*.

	MEDIEVAL	LUTHER	CALVIN	WESTMINSTER	ANGLICAN
REVELATION & ADORATION	Introit	Introit Hymn / Psalm	Psalm 124:8	Call to Worship	Introit Psalm / Hymn
CONFESSION	*Kyrie*	*Kyrie*	10 Commandments *Kyrie*	Prayer Confession	Collect for Purity 10 Commandments *Kyrie*
PROPITIATION	*Gloria* Collect	*Gloria* Prayer	Assurance of Pardon	Prayer of Pardon	Collect
INSTRUCTION	Readings Psalms Sermon	Readings Psalm, Hymn Creed Sermon	Psalm Prayer Gospel Sermon	Readings Psalm Sermon	Readings Psalm, Hymn Creed Sermon
DEDICATION	*Credo* Prayer Offertory	Offertory	Prayer Apostle's Creed Offertory	Prayer of Thanks Psalm	Offertory
COMMUNION	The Lord's Table *Sanctus* *Agnus Dei*	The Lord's Table *Sanctus* *Agnus Dei*	The Lord's Table Psalm	The Lord's Table	Intercessory Prayer The Lord's Table *Agnus Dei* The Lord's Prayer
COMMISSION	Collect Dismissal	Benediction	Psalm, Canticle Benediction	Psalm, Canticle Benediction	Prayer *Gloria* Benediction

More modern expressions of this liturgy include what is sometimes called the "Isaiah Six model," deriving its liturgy from Isaiah's vision of heavenly worship:

Revelation
Adoration
Confession
Pardon
Instruction
Dedication
Communion (Supplication and/or the Lord's Table)
Commission

This basic liturgical shape has also been advocated recently by Constance Cherry, Bryan Chapell, James K. A. Smith, Robbie Castleman, and Mike Cosper, among others.[16]

A second liturgical shape could be described as *revivalist*. In such a service, the purpose of music is to set the mood for the service, preparing the people's hearts to receive the message from God's Word, which is considered central to the service. The climax of the service is the invitation, where sinners come forward to receive Christ and/or Christians come forward to rededicate themselves to serving the Lord. Often with this kind of service order, all of the music is chosen around a theme that corresponds to the sermon of the day.

Music Service
Sermon
Invitation

A third service order concerns itself primarily with *flow*. This service structure typically derives from an understanding of the purpose of the service as experiencing the presence of God and considers the emotional progression of the worshipers through the service as key to accomplishing this purpose. It describes the "Five Phase Model" of John Wimber and Eddie Espinosa as well as the Praise and Worship "Tabernacle Model" of Judson Cornwall.

Praise and Worship
    Invitation   Songs of Personal Testimony in the Camp
    Engagement   Through the Gates with Thanksgiving
    Exaltation   Into His Courts with Praise
    Adoration   Solemn Worship inside the Holy Place
    Intimacy   In the Holy of Holies
Sermon and other elements follow

---

[16] Bryan Chapell, *Christ-Centered Worship: Letting the Gospel Shape Our Practice* (Grand Rapids: Baker Academic, 2009); Constance M Cherry, *The Worship Architect: A Blueprint for Designing Culturally Relevant and Biblically Faithful Services* (Grand Rapids: Baker Academic, 2010); Robbie F. Castleman, *Story-Shaped Worship: Following Patterns from the Bible and History* (Downers Grove, IL: InterVarsity Press, 2013); Mike Cosper, *Rhythms of Grace: How the Church's Worship Tells the Story of the Gospel* (Wheaton: Crossway Books, 2013); James K. A. Smith, *Imagining the Kingdom: How Worship Works* (Grand Rapids: Baker Academic, 2013). For a review of these works, see Scott Aniol, "Gospel-Shaped Worship: A Review of Recent Literature," *Artistic Theologian* 2 (2013): 106–113.

Taxonomy of Worship Philosophies.

Descriptive terms under each of these categories can help to classify different worship philosophies, and since these philosophies don't fit well on a sliding scale, these terms can be mixed. For example, a Presbyterian church might be a combination of regulative principle, worship as reenactment, doctrinally weighty, conservative culturally, with a historic gospel-shaped liturgy, while a Lutheran church might differ only in its governing principle. These two churches differ in only one area, but their services would likely look completely different, and thus it would be simplistic to classify them both under one label. Likewise, one charismatic church might adopt an effective principle, worship as experience, doctrinally simply content, progressive culture, and a flow liturgy, while another might share all of those characteristics but with doctrinally weighty songs and expositional preaching. It would be misleading to lump both of those churches together under the umbrella of "Charismatic Worship Philosophy."

Instead, in assessing and evaluating worship philosophies and practices, it would be more helpful to use these five categories to form a more robust taxonomy.

GOVERNING PRINCIPLE	PURPOSE	CONTENT
Regulative Principle	Attraction	Doctrinally Weighty
Normative Principle	Revivalism	Doctrinally Simple
Effective Principle	Worship as Experience	
	Worship as Reenactment	

RELATIONSHIP TO CULTURE	LITURGY	
Progressive	Historic/Gospel	
Traditional	Revivalist	
Conservative	Praise & Worship (Flow)	

Chapter 18
Practice Makes Perfect:
How Corporate Worship Makes Disciples

The purpose of this book has been to explore the formative relationship between religion (worldview + theology) and liturgy (cultus + culture). But to what end? If we recognize that how we worship both reveals and forms our religion—our explicit beliefs and our implicit assumptions about reality, then simply recognizing how we *have been formed* is not enough; we need to have a fundamental purpose for how we *should be formed* and make liturgical decisions accordingly. In this Chapter, I would like to make my central argument more explicit, using the liturgical history as the foundation. We need to start with our purpose, and for that, we turn to the fundamental mission Christ gave to his body, the Great Commission.

Worship and the Great Commission
Christ's great commissions to churches was to "make disciples" (Matt. 28:19-20). Churches accomplish this mission through proclaiming the gospel, through "baptizing them in the name of the Father and of the Son and of the Holy Spirit," and through "teaching them to observe all that I have commanded."[1] Christian disciples are a new people of God whose behavior should emerge from and reflect their biblical beliefs and values. This is why Scripture gives such attention to the behavior of Christians; it should be holy as God is holy (1 Peter 1:16). Yet although Christians are new creatures (2 Cor. 5:17) with new hearts of obedience to Christ (Rom. 6:17-18), holy behavior is not something that comes automatically. Observing Christ's commands, as the Great Commission explicitly states, is something that must be taught—it is a learned moral behavior.

Yet in a day in which Christianity has become very personal and individualistic, and corporate worship in particular has become merely an experience or a time of individual "authentic" expression, the relationship between corporate worship and the church's mission of making disciples is often missed. On the one hand, some pastors believe that corporate worship is something entirely separate from discipleship; on the other hand, some pastors, recognizing their need to obey Christ's mandate in the Great Commission, turn corporate worship into either an evangelistic crusade or a lecture

---

[1] For a thorough argument for this understanding of the church's mission, see Kevin DeYoung and Greg Gilbert, *What Is the Mission of the Church? Making Sense of Social Justice, Shalom, and the Great Commission* (Wheaton: Crossway, 2011); David M. Doran, *For the Sake of His Name: Challenging a New Generation for World Missions* (Allen Park, MI: Student Global Impact, 2002).

hall. Neither of these rightly understands the role corporate worship plays in making disciples.

How Is a Disciple Made?
An important question every pastor must ask is how he can lead his church to accomplish the mission of making disciples. Since making disciples is the primary command of the Great Commission, this task involves not only the proclamation of the gospel but also teaching and nurturing new converts. Sharing the gospel is the first step toward making disciples, but it is not enough. In other words, true conversion is not simply assent to certain facts; it is a life-changing entrance into communion with God. It is "turn[ing] to God from idols to serve a living and true God" (1 Thess. 1:9–10).

Understanding that discipleship begins with evangelism but involves more, the question remains as to how churches accomplish their mission of forming disciples. Certainly, much of what is involved with such disciple-making is the formation of theology through teaching and preaching. Without a proper set of beliefs, one will not behave in a manner worthy of Christ. However, data transmission is not all there is to discipleship for at least three reasons. First, Christian behavior is more than simply a collection of right beliefs. Jesus did not just say, "teaching them all that I have commanded"; he said, "teaching them *to observe* all that I have commanded" (Matt. 28:19, emphasis mine). Christian behavior is a collection of skills, and development of a skillset requires more than a certain amount of knowledge. Reading a book about golf may be helpful in learning to play the sport, but it is going to take more than that. The same is true with learning to play an instrument or fly an airplane. A certain amount of book knowledge is necessary, but these skills require something more. And so "teaching" in Matthew 28 involves more than just instructing the mind, it also concerns imparting a skillset.

Second, making disciples is more than data transmission because the reality is that most actions are not the result of deliberate, rational reflection upon beliefs. Some are, but most of how people act on a daily basis is due to ingrained habits. A pastor may proclaim the gospel to someone and then diligently teach him biblical doctrines, but that will not necessarily make a disciple who is characterized by Christian moral living, especially if a new convert has many habitual behaviors that conflict with biblical living. A drug addict will still have to deal with his addiction, a petty thief may find himself unintentionally slipping things off the shelf into his pocket, and a lazy husband will have difficulty finding the energy necessary to help with the kids. Old habits die hard, even for Christians.

Third, whether or not people are acting on the basis of a deliberate decision or a habitual response, people ultimately will act not primarily based on the knowledge in their minds, but rather on the inclinations of their hearts—the Christian religion is more than just theology; it also includes worldview, a fundamental orientation of the heart, and ultimately a person's heart is what motivates them to behave to certain ways. A child who is terrified of dogs will not pet one no matter how many statistics you give her about the docile nature of domesticated canines. A man whose heart is captivated by pornography will sin continually no matter how much he knows it is wrong. Another way of saying this is that people act more based on their desires than on their knowledge. The way many pastors try to combat this reality is to urge people to live according to their beliefs rather than their hearts, but it is not quite that simple. The problem is not that people have replaced what drives their actions with their hearts, instead of their minds. They cannot help but be driven by the inclinations of their hearts, and philosophers from Plato to Augustine to Edwards to Lewis all recognized this.[2] If the intellect and the heart conflict, people will most often do what they want to do rather than what they know they should do; this is the nature of humanity.

In other words, our proper concern about Christian behavior must take into consideration the nature of religion I presented in Chapter 1 and have illustrated throughout this book—religion is more than theology; it also includes worldview, a fundamental orientation of the heart. Thus, in order to cultivate holy living—in order to accomplish the mission of the church and make disciples—churches must concern themselves with nurturing moral virtue, a biblical heart orientation.

Inclination

This leads to the question of how moral virtue is formed and cultivated. First, as I noted in Chapter 14, it is important to remember that there is a difference between higher and lower inclinations. The lower inclinations—or passions—are those impulses that respond primarily to physical appetites. Paul describes those who live according to these lower appetites: "their god is their belly" (Phil. 3:19). When set in conflict with the mind, these lower appetites will always dominate since people act primarily on the basis of inclination. A second aspect to human inclinations are the higher inclinations—or affections—of the soul. As we have already seen, Christian theologians including Paul, Augustine, Aquinas, Calvin, and Edwards all taught this distinction.

Virtue, a biblical heart orientation, is produced by the cultivation of the affections toward what is right and good, leading us to act accordingly. We still nevertheless act according to our inclinations, but as C. S. Lewis so famously stated, "The head rules

---

[2] See, for example, Plato, *The Republic*, 9:571–580; Augustine, *City of God*, 14:6; Lewis, *The Abolition of Man*, 24; Edwards, *The Works of Jonathan Edwards*, 2:96.

the belly through the chest."[3] Our theology carries into our practice only when we have deliberately shaped our worldview to match our theology. Therefore, if church leaders want to produce disciples characterized by holy behavior, then they must give attention to cultivating noble inclinations for what is true and good. Yet the question remains, how do churches teach people's affections? How do we shape worldview?

Habits
The earlier analogy of skill development is helpful here. Developing a good golf swing or learning to play the piano requires knowing the right information, but it also requires rehearsing those skills learned in a book over and over again. Skill development requires doing, not just data transmission. It requires the cultivation of habits that become second nature. The same is true for cultivating noble affections that will produce holy behavior; it takes training. Holiness, according to Hebrews 12:14, is something a Christian must "strive for." Paul told Timothy to discipline himself for the purpose of godliness (1 Tim. 4:7). Holy behavior takes practice. Once again, Lewis is helpful. He describes the "chest"—the higher inclinations—as "emotions organized by trained habits into stable sentiments."[4] Mark Noll describes Edwards' view of the affections as "habitual inclinations at the core of a person's being."[5] The disciplined formation of habits is essential for the formation of holy living because habit is what trains the affections. Thus, cultivating holy behavior involves shaping the affections through habitual practices.

Community
Such habitual behaviors are cultivated most significantly in the context of community. As I noted in Chapter 1, and as we have witnessed through the story of God's people, worldview, theology, and behaviors never develop on an individual basis; rather, they always evolve within the environment of a community of people. And this is exactly how God intended it to be. "It is not good that the man should be alone," God said of Adam (Gen. 2:18), and this extends to discipleship. God never intended for us to develop our worldview and theology on our own; he gave us the church for that. Christ baptized us with the Spirit into his body, the church, gifting each member with a diversity of ministry functions (1 Cor. 12) so that we all might be built up "to mature manhood, to the measure of the stature of the fullness of Christ" (Eph. 4:13). It is in the church, in the community of God's people, where formation of worldview and theology best take place.

---

[3] Lewis, *The Abolition of Man*, 24.
[4] Lewis, *The Abolition of Man*, 24–25.
[5] Mark A Noll, *America's God: From Jonathan Edwards to Abraham Lincoln* (Oxford: Oxford University, 2005), 23.

Corporate Worship Makes Disciples

Worked In—Work Out

Furthermore, this kind of formation can only happen by the power of the Spirit of God. Sanctification is a synergistic process whereby the Holy Spirit of God works in the life of a believer to "work out his salvation with fear and trembling" (Phil. 2:12–13). It is God who works in believers to will and to do of his good pleasure. The Holy Spirit is the agent that differentiates a person who is enslaved by legalistic habits and one who intentionally nurtures habits that will shape his soul. An individual without the Holy Spirit can develop all the right habits, but this will not transform his life without the Holy Spirit's activity in his heart. Paul made this necessity explicit: "And we all, with unveiled face, beholding the glory of the Lord, are being transformed into the same image from one degree of glory to another. For this comes from the Lord who is the Sprit" (2 Cor. 3:18). The Holy Spirit works this kind of transformation through the Revelation he inspired (2 Tim. 3:16; 2 Pet. 1:21) in such a way that he changes the entirety of who we are—not just our intellectual beliefs, although those certainly change, but also the fundamental orientation of our hearts—our worldview. This is what Paul referred to when he commanded, "be transformed by the renewal of your *mind*" (Rom. 12:2). The word "mind" here, similar to "heart," encompasses a person's "total inner or moral attitude"[6]—his worldview. Through his Word, God transforms minds that were once debased (Rom. 1:28), futile (Eph. 4:17), defiled (Titus 1:15), depraved (1 Tim. 6:50), and corrupted (2 Tim. 3:8) into the mind of Christ (1 Cor. 2:16).

Liturgy's Role in Forming Disciples

What I have argued here, and demonstrated through the liturgical story in this book, is that moral virtue is shaped by the cultivation of inclinations through habitual behavior in community. Discipleship is thus concerned with the behavior (*ergon*) of a people (*laos*). Considering discipleship in this way reveals the significance of corporate worship for cultivating such behavior, for *laos* combined with *ergon* equates to *leitourgia*. The behavior of a people is shaped by its liturgies.

As we have seen throughout the history, liturgies have several characteristics. The first two are embedded in the root words themselves. First, liturgies are behaviors; they are *works*. They are informed by beliefs, and they are reflections of values, but at their essence, liturgies are what people do. This is why liturgy is so essentially connected to moral behavior. Yet not all actions are liturgies. The second characteristic of liturgies is that they are the *people's* work—they are communal behaviors. But not all communal behavior is liturgy. The third characteristic of liturgies is that they are a kind of ritual. In other words, they are habitual practices; liturgies do the same thing over and over again. This point is likely the biggest reason many evangelicals squirm at the

---

[6] Johannes Behm and Ernst Würthwein, "νοῦς," *TDNT*, 4:952.

mention of liturgy. For a number of reasons, some Christians have been conditioned to see habitual, repetitious ritual as inauthentic, hypocritical, and ultimately "vain repetition." Yet it is this very quality that makes liturgies so powerful in cultivating behavior. Consider again the problem with viewing discipleship as only data transmission. Holy living is a skillset that Christians must develop, and such skillsets require practice. What is practice if not ritual? It is doing the same action over and over again, not as an end in itself, but toward the end of developing skill. Repetition is not a deficiency of liturgy; it is actually liturgy's greatest strength and why, for example, Donald Whitney categorizes public worship as a "spiritual discipline."[7]

Many times the aversion to liturgy is that it is just going through the motions; but there is virtue to going through the motions. Going through the motions is not a mark of hypocrisy; going through the motions is a mark of maturity. It is, indeed, certainly possible to perform a ritual in a way that renders it vain repetition. But rituals in themselves are not inherently vain; rather they are necessary for the formation of virtue. Anyone can tell the difference between a piano student who is running through her scales just because she has to and one who is performing the repetitious exercise with intentionality because she knows that it is through such a ritual that she will become a better pianist. This is exactly where the Holy Spirit's work is essential; without the Holy Spirit, liturgy becomes dry, mundane, and enslaving. But with the Holy Spirit's active participation, liturgy becomes God's tool for spiritual formation.

The goal is that after practicing the scale or the swing over and over again, you will be able to perform it without even thinking, and this solves the second problem with viewing discipleship as only the transmission of doctrine: most of our daily actions result not from deliberate choice but from the habits we have formed through ritual. The issue is not whether people will be formed by liturgy, but which liturgies will form them. Much of how people act has developed through rituals. Most people have a particular morning routine. That routine may or may not be informed originally by deliberate choices, but regardless, people eventually perform the same morning rituals without really thinking about it. From driving to work to typing on a computer to making the coffee, most of human behavior has been shaped by habitual practices.

The Form of the Liturgy
Behavior is shaped by liturgies because, as Lewis stated, human inclinations are organized through trained habits, and habits are formed through rituals. And it is the shape of those rituals that cultivates the habits, because the form of the liturgy embodies certain values, just like this book's opening illustration of the path through the forest. As

---

[7] Donald S. Whitney, *Spiritual Disciplines for the Christian Life* (Colorado Springs: NavPress, 1997), 101–117.

we have seen, liturgies are developed over long periods of time, at first with very deliberate values in view, and those values are worn into the liturgies through regular use. And when people practice such liturgies, they are shaped by the values that have formed them, whether they recognize it or not.

Worldly Liturgies
Our aim here has been to discover how Christians can cultivate higher inclinations toward what is true and good, but we must recognize that the reverse also happens—deformation of our inclinations. Again, our actions are not always the outcome of rational choices, and this is true of sinful behavior as well. Sometimes we sin deliberately and willfully; but often sinful action is the result of ingrained habits, and those habits have been formed through worldly liturgies.

The rhythms of worldly routines are shaping our inclinations and the inclinations of people in our churches maybe more than we would like to admit. These are routines and habits that are part of the cultural environment all around us—remember, like cultus, culture is liturgical. And the problem is that it is because they are liturgies that people have a very difficult time both recognizing how they are being shaped and even considering living without them. If we wish to make disciples—if we wish to teach the people in our churches to observe all that Christ has commanded them—then we must do something to counteract the effects of the worldly liturgies that are affecting them each and every day. Part of what will counteract their effects is doctrinal preaching, but because our religion and behavior involve more than just correct theology, shaping Christian behavior toward Christ-likeness requires more than data transmission.

Corporate Worship
This is where it will be useful to narrow the definition of *leitourgia* to how it has been used at least since the LXX as the work of the people in corporate worship. Many Christians today consider corporate worship as simply a Christian's expression of authentic devotion toward God. Yet liturgy—considered now in terms of corporate worship—is not just an expression of "authentic" devotion; liturgy is formative. It is not just expressive, and this is why repetition is necessary, for repetition is necessary for formation. An understanding of the formative nature of liturgy uncovers the fact that *how* Christians worship also significantly affects their behavior.

This is how corporate worship fits into the Great Commission: the liturgy of a church shapes the liturgy of life. How a church worships week in and week out forms the people—it molds their behavior by shaping their inclinations through habitual practices, because the shape of the liturgy transmits its values. Like that path through the forest, when people travel along the liturgy that we have provided for them, they will inevitably be shaped by the values and beliefs worn into it. It is in Christian liturgy that a Christian's heart, as Lewis said, is "organized by trained habits into stable sentiments," where a Christian's inclinations are discipled and trained, and where the negative effects of worldly liturgies may be counteracted.

Reenactment
Because the Holy Spirit works transformation of this sort in our lives only through the Word he inspired, it is critical that our worship be shaped and guided by who God is, what God does, and what God says. Therefore, both the content and form of our worship services must be derived from the Scriptures. As we witnessed in Part One, Scripture is filled with liturgies, and these liturgies help explain both the purpose of liturgy and how one should be formed in order to nurture virtue. In particular, the liturgies of Scripture illustrate that biblical liturgies shape the people of God through reenactment of what God has done. In this way biblical liturgy is not human work toward God; rather, it is God's work upon his people.

As we have seen, God prescribed for Israel a liturgical year that shaped their relationship with him by reenacting the covenant that he had established with them and the ways in which he had redeemed them. This is a stark difference between biblical liturgies and pagan liturgies. Pagan liturgies involve rituals designed to attract a god's attention and manipulate him to do something for the worshiper; biblical liturgies rehearse what God has already done in order that the worshiper's affections and life might be formed and shaped.

A few reminders from Israel's liturgical year will illustrate this. The Sabbath itself was a regular reenactment of God's rest on the seventh day of creation, and as Jesus later indicated, "the Sabbath was made for man" (Mark 2:27) in order to shape him into a certain kind of person through a weekly routine. The most holy of days for Israel was the Day of Atonement (Lev. 16), a Feast Day containing a very carefully prescribed liturgy that pictured spiritual realities through reenactment. The cleansings, the sacrifices, the sprinkling of blood, and the scapegoat all formed the people through their participation into those who recognized the holiness of God, the horrors of sin, and the necessity of atonement. The Passover and Feast of the Unleavened Bread had a carefully prescribed liturgy that shaped the people by their participation in it. It was a reenactment of the historical event of the first Passover, and this is exactly why liturgies are so powerful; by reenacting these events, a person is formed as if he had been there himself. In Exodus 12:14, God called the feast a "memorial," a ritual reenactment by which a person enters into the past event and is thus shaped by it. Fifteen hundred years later, while celebrating the Passover memorial himself, Jesus Christ established a new ordinance, complete with a carefully prescribed liturgy, and commanded his disciples, "Do this in remembrance of me." This *anamnesis*—this "remembrance"—is an active reenactment of the death of Christ on behalf of his people in such a way that Christians are shaped by the act. Each of these examples serve to illustrate the point that biblical liturgies should reenact God's work for his people and thereby form his people into those whose lives are driven by a recognition of what he has done for them.

Formed by the Gospel
Liturgies form disciples because they both embody and shape beliefs and values. It follows, then, that how people worship both *reveals* their beliefs and values and *forms* their beliefs and values. *Lex orandi, lex credendi*—"the law of prayer is the law of belief." This is why it is essential that we carefully consider how the liturgies of our churches shape the inclinations, and therefore the lives, of our church members. These are things that occur every single week—they are habits that are shaping the inclinations, and therefore behavior, of people in churches.

The structure of a biblical liturgy follows the logic of the gospel and is thus a reenactment of the gospel. The logic of the gospel is this: God reveals himself and calls us to worship him, and individuals respond with adoration and confession of their sins as they recognize their unworthiness to be in his presence. God responds by forgiving sins through Christ and welcoming believers into his presence, where they hear him speak, they commit to obedience, they bring their petitions to him, and they enjoy open and free communion.

This is the same logic that informs historic Christian liturgy: Worshipers begin with God's call for them to worship him, followed by adoration and praise. They then confess their sins to him and receive assurance of pardon in Christ. They thank him for their salvation, they hear his Word preached, and they respond with dedication. And the climax of all historic Christian worship has always been expression of communion with God, either through drawing near to him in prayer, or more often in historic liturgies, through celebrating the Lord's Table. To eat at Christ's Table is the most powerful expression that Christians are accepted by him. All of the Scripture readings, prayers, and songs in this liturgy are carefully chosen for their appropriateness in a particular function within the gospel-shaped structure.

  Revelation
  Adoration
  Confession
  Pardon
  Instruction
  Dedication
  Communion
  Commission

Aesthetics

What is important about a corporate worship service is not just what is said from the pulpit or the doctrine of the hymns, for there are aspects of Christian piety that are inarticulable; much of Christian piety is learned only through doing, and that is what art is—the purpose of art is to incarnate values, and we experience those values as we participate in the art. As Mark Twain once quipped, "A man who carries a cat by the tail learns something he can learn in no other way." This is the power of aesthetics, and so this extends beyond the shape of the liturgy itself to the other aesthetic forms employed in corporate worship. Poetry, music, architecture, and rhetoric each embody inarticulable aspects of Christian virtue that through their use express those virtues. A story is told that once when Robert Schumann played a new composition and someone asked him what it meant, "he simply replied, "It means this" and played it again.[8] The liturgies and art forms of Christian worship embody and form certain aspects of Christian discipleship in a way that nothing else can. Art like poems and songs allow the artist to express aspects of experience that are deeper than words such that a person can experience for himself the realities the artist creates in a way that would not be possible if the artist simply described the experience. Thus through participation in such aesthetic and liturgical acts, the embedded meaning of those acts are worn into the participant.

This is why the Bible itself is not simply a collection of propositional statements of doctrine. Rather, the Bible is a work of literature employing aesthetic devices such as metaphor, simile, tautology, anadiplosis, chiasmus, climax, antithesis, paradox, allegory, metonymy, synecdoche, hyperbole, personification, and a whole host of others to communicate what could not be otherwise. The shape of Scripture, not only its truth claims, shapes Christian living, and thus the shape of Scripture must inform the shape of liturgies today.

Tradition

The implication of this is that all of the various cultural institutions, forms, artistic expressions, media, languages, and systems of thought are what they are today based on hundreds, and in some cases thousands, of years of nurture and development. This is what we call "tradition." As we have studied the development of worship theology and practice through the history of the church, we noted the various worship traditions that have emerged from biblical Christianity. It would be very tempting to insist that instead of relying on inherited tradition, we should instead simply study what the Bible says and apply it to today. This is a noble goal, but it is actually impossible to attain.

---

[8] Donald Whittle, *Christianity and the Arts* (London: A. R. Mowbray, 1966), 52.

Corporate Worship Makes Disciples

We always inherit a tradition; we cannot help it. No one wakes up one morning and decides to do something of which he has had no personal knowledge or experience. No one decides to build a house who has not first inherited some idea of what a house should look like and how it should function. He may choose to deviate from what he has received, but his deviation is, nevertheless, influenced by and building upon what has come before him. Likewise, those who wish to lead biblical worship will always be impacted by what they have inherited. The question is not *whether* current worship practice will build upon tradition but rather *which* tradition(s) today's church leaders choose to build upon.

This understanding and appreciation for tradition is both biblical and unavoidable. For example, Paul appeals to the "customs" of the churches as an actual basis of argument in his discussion of head coverings in 1 Corinthians 11:16. As Paul commands others to imitate him (Phil. 3:17), so we are to imitate the traditions and practices of those who have come before us. Even the observance of the Lord's Supper is based not only upon direct revelation given to Paul, but also apostolic tradition (1 Cor. 11:2–34). The biblical command to honor parents and elders is more than simply an attitude, but a direction and disposition. This principle is even implied in Matthew 18:15–20. Jesus clearly states that two or three believers gathered in an official capacity to make a decision for the full assembly possess a certain amount of derivative authority because God is "among them." Certainly, this authority applies most directly to discipline situations contextually, yet the principle applies more broadly. This authority is not infallible and equal with Scripture, as the Romanist view of Church tradition argues, but it is real authority, nonetheless. These biblical principles should make us very cautious about quickly rejecting the customs, practices, and traditions of those within the Christian heritage. Finally, the importance of tradition is expressed in passages like 2 Timothy 2:2: "And what you have heard from me in the presence of many witnesses entrust to faithful men who will be able to teach others also." Passing values and practices from one generation to another is exactly how Christianity is perpetuated. This is true especially for worship.

It is also unavoidable. There are many core doctrines of the Christian faith, for example, whose articulations we hold firmly even though the particular ways in which those doctrines are stated are not directly from the pages of Scripture but rather were cultivated over many years. These doctrines are from Scripture to be sure, but God's people have often formulated very specific ways of articulating that doctrine in order to accurately preserve what Scripture teaches and avoid error. This is true, for example, with the doctrine of the Trinity. Traditionally, we describe God as being one essence in three persons, yet that language (and even the term "trinity" itself) does not come from a chapter and verse in Scripture; it was developed later as a way to carefully avoid theological heresy in the realm of God's essence. Today, we accept this inherited way of describing God as orthodox and even insist upon the preservation of very specific phraseology. It would be the height of arrogance, not to mention naïve, for someone to simply reject that traditional doctrinal formulation out of hand and instead come up with something entirely different. While it is certainly possible that he could develop a description of what Scripture says about God that is equally accurate, there is little reason to reject traditional definitions, and someone who gives no thought to *why* God's people chose to articulate that doctrine in specific ways is bound to repeat the very heresies those church leaders were avoiding.

In other words, tradition is inevitable and valuable. Tradition is not infallible; often we will need to reject what we have inherited if we find that it does not fit within a biblical framework. Yet even a rejection of one tradition will mean that we are accepting another, and we must be always aware of what tradition(s) we are embracing and building upon in our current worship practice. We must remember that just as some traditions have been cultivated within crucibles of transcendent, biblical values, others were nurtured in an environment of paganism. Cultural forms, customs, and mores develop because of the imaginations out of which they grew, and we must evaluate those imaginations in order to judge the traditions themselves.

Changed from Glory into Glory

What this in-depth study of Christian worship has demonstrated is the inexorable link between worldview, belief, worship, and Christian living. In order to make disciples, churches should consider employing biblical liturgies that reenact the gospel of Jesus Christ and aesthetically embody values consistent with God's holiness. The primary way that churches can shape the inclinations and impact the behaviors of people in their churches is by influencing their habits, and one of the primary means they have to do this is through their corporate liturgies. Scripture-shaped gospel liturgies and reverent art forms will inform people's liturgies of life, which will in turn form them into mature disciples of Jesus Christ.

By reenacting what they are in Christ, Christian worshipers become what they are.

> Changed from glory into glory,
> till in heav'n we take our place,
> till we cast our crowns before Thee,
> lost in wonder, love, and praise.[9]

---

[9] Charles Wesley, "Love Divine, All Loves Excelling," 1747.

Study Guide for Part Six
People and Terms

aesthetics
affections
appetites
attraction
conservative
discipleship
dual citizens
effective principle
exiles
experience
flow liturgy
gospel-shaped liturgy
governing principle
Great Commission
habit
inclination
leitourgia
lex orandi, lex credendi
liturgy
Moralistic Therapeutic Deism
normative principle
passions
pluralism
pragmatism
progressive
reenactment
regulative principle
revival
revivalist liturgy
sanctification
secular culture
secular cultus
secular religion
tradition
traditional
worldview

Recommended Resources

Aniol, Scott. *By the Waters of Babylon: Worship in a Post-Christian Culture.* Grand Rapids: Kregel Ministry, 2015.

Castleman, Robbie F. *Story-Shaped Worship: Following Patterns from the Bible and*

History. Downers Grove, IL: InterVarsity Press, 2013.

Chapell, Bryan. *Christ-Centered Worship: Letting the Gospel Shape Our Practice*. Grand Rapids: Baker Academic, 2009.

Horton, Michael. *Ordinary: Sustainable Faith in a Radical, Restless World*. Grand Rapids: Zondervan, 2014.

Meyers, Jeffrey J. *The Lord's Service: The Grace of Covenant Renewal Worship*. Moscow, ID: Canon Press, 2003.

Smith, James K. A. *You Are What You Love: The Spiritual Power of Habit*. Grand Rapids: Brazos Press, 2016.

Questions for Discussion and Reflection
1. Explain the theo-logic of a gospel-shaped liturgy, including where examples are found in Scripture and in church history.
2. Discuss how corporate worship functions within Christ's commission to the church.
3. Explain ways in which worship can hinder Christian sanctification.
4. Discuss the ways in which the thesis of this book—liturgy forms our religion, and our religion forms our liturgy—was argued, supported, and illustrated throughout the liturgical story of the Christian faith.

Appendix 1
Planning a Gospel-Shaped Worship Service

If you want to employ a gospel-shape to your church's worship service, you can, of course, benefit from any of the historic liturgies outlined throughout this book. However, here is a brief summary of how I plan such services in a modern context.

As I've argued throughout the book, since worship itself is drawing near to communion with God through Christ in the Spirit by faith, the order of corporate worship should reflect this. Corporate worship that is shaped by the gospel reminds us weekly of how and why we can draw near in communion with God despite our sin, and it shapes us to live our lives in light of these truths.

Therefore, the order of corporate worship should follow the flow of the gospel. This is how Christians have structured their worship for hundreds of years, and I believe that we should continue this practice today. I also believe the structure should reflect worship in "spirit and truth," that is, corporate worship should be a dialogue in which God speaks to us, and then we speak back to him. Finally, worship is "the people's work," that is, the structure of worship should allow for regular, active participation of the congregation rather than a divide between "performer" and "spectators."

These are the governing principles that determine how I order worship services. Each week the hymns are different, the Scripture readings vary, and the sermon progresses expositionally through books of the Bible, but the "skeleton" of the service always remains the same. The basic structure of the service is the shape of the gospel:

1. Revelation: God reveals himself and calls us to worship.
2. Adoration: We recognize the greatness of God and praise him for it.
3. Confession: When we acknowledge the holiness of God, we also recognize our unworthiness to draw near to him because of our sin.
4. Propitiation: As Christians, we are assured of pardon through the sacrifice of Christ, which makes worship possible.
5. Proclamation: The Word of God is taught.
6. Dedication: We respond to the Word of God with consecration.
7. Supplication: We bring our requests before the Lord.
8. Communion: Celebration of free access to God because of Christ's death on our behalf.
9. Commission: God sends us into the world to serve him. Just as the service began with God's word, it ends with a word of blessing from him.

Changed from Glory into Glory

The service opens with a historic Christian greeting (also known as the "Salutation") that sets apart this as a gathering of Christians. The service actually begins, however, with God speaking to us. We do not come to worship of our own initiative, and we are not (contrary to pagan worship and some evangelical emphases as well) somehow "calling God down" or inviting him to join us. Rather, it is God who calls us to draw near to him, and thus the service begins with a scriptural call to worship.

When God reveals himself to us, two responses are inevitable. First, we respond with adoration and praise. This usually takes the form of a hymn, a prayer of praise, and a doxology. Then, we recognize our sin and unworthiness, and so we confess our sins to God. We responded this way when we first believed, and we should continue to do so daily. Thus, through a Scripture reading, a hymn, silent repentance, and a corporate prayer of confession, the congregation acknowledges our sin together before God. As Christians, we find forgiveness and pardon in Christ, and so the service continues with celebrating that forgiveness. Through a Scripture affirmation and a hymn of praise for Christ's sacrifice, we both rejoice in the gospel and proclaim it to any unbelievers who may be attending. Next, we are ready to hear God's instructions through the preaching of his Word. Our response is one of consecration and dedication. We then bring our requests for ourselves, our church, and the world to God in corporate prayer.

The climax of the service is Communion. Worship is drawing near to God in communion through Christ, and this is what the whole service has been progressing towards. Coming boldly to the Throne of Grace (Heb. 4:16) for supplication and eating at God's Table means that we are welcome and that we have open access to him, despite our sin. This is possible only through Christ's sacrifice on the cross, which is beautifully pictured in the Communion elements. Communion with God is the purpose of the gospel, and thus Communion is the climax of a worship service. I actually advocate weekly Communion, although our church does not at this time. The service concludes with a word from God in which he sends us into the world to obey him and share the gospel to unbelievers, along with a word of blessing.

The particular hymns, Scripture passages and other elements of the service that I choose are determined by their fit in three categories: First, I consider the church year. Our church follows the general Protestant church calendar including Advent, Epiphany, Lent,[1] Easter, Pentecost, Ascension, and Trinity Sunday. I use a lectionary as a starting point here, but I don't always follow it strictly if the assigned passages don't fit other objectives I have for the service. Second, I consider the function of the hymns or Scripture passages within the liturgy. I pay careful attention to choosing elements that

---

[1] Like the Protestant Reformers, I consider Lent as simply a time of preparation for celebrating Easter, not as a time in which we somehow "participate" in the sufferings of Christ.

fit the structure of Revelation, Adoration, Confession, Pardon, Proclamation, Dedication, Supplication, Communion, and Commission, and that also facilitate the dialogue between God and us in the service. Third, I consider the sermon passage and theme for the day. I choose hymns and Scripture passages that fit both the gospel shape and tie into the sermon text, which usually follows a *lectio continuo* progress through books of the Bible. Usually, I am able to create a service that connects all three of these categories so that through the course of the church's life, we are formed both by the gospel narrowly (in the weekly liturgy) *and* the "whole counsel of God" broadly (as the songs and texts connect with the *lectio continuo* preaching). This takes a lot of work and a good bit of time, but it is always very rewarding when it all comes together and, I believe, formative for our church.

Here are a few sample services to help give you an idea of what this might look in your context:

Example 1: Service without the Lord's Table

Revelation: God Making Himself Known to Us

Silent Prayer and Meditation

Prelude: "Guide Me, O Thou Great Jehovah"

Christian Greeting
   Leader: The Lord be with you.
   People: And also with you.

Scripture Reading: Isaiah 25:1–9
   Reader: The Word of the Lord.
   People: Thanks be to God.

Adoration: Exalting Our Glorious God

Hymn: Let Us, with a Gladsome Mind

Prayer of Praise

Gloria Patri

Changed from Glory into Glory

Confession: Lifting Contrite Hearts up to the Lord

Scripture Reading: Psalm 70:4–5

Hymn: Come, Ye Sinners

Silent Prayers of Repentance

Corporate Prayer of Confession

> Have mercy on me, O God,
> according to your steadfast love;
> according to your abundant mercy blot out my transgressions.
> Wash me thoroughly from my iniquity,
> and cleanse me from my sin!
> For I know my transgressions,
> and my sin is ever before me.
> Against you, you only, have I sinned
> and done what is evil in your sight,
> so that you may be justified in your words
> and blameless in your judgment.
> Behold, I was brought forth in iniquity,
> and in sin did my mother conceive me.
> Behold, you delight in truth in the inward being,
> and you teach me wisdom in the secret heart.
> Purge me with hyssop, and I shall be clean;
> wash me, and I shall be whiter than snow.
> Hide your face from my sins,
> and blot out all my iniquities.
> O Lord, open my lips,
> and my mouth will declare your praise.
> For you will not delight in sacrifice, or I would give it;
> you will not be pleased with a burnt offering.
> The sacrifices of God are a broken spirit;
> a broken and contrite heart, O God, you will not despise,
> through Jesus Christ, our Lord. Amen.
> *—from Psalm 51*

Planning a Gospel-Shaped Worship Service

Propitiation: God Declaring Forgiveness

Declaration of the Good News: 1 Thessalonians 5:9
    Leader: In Christ your sins are forgiven you!
    People: The Lord be praised!

Hymn: Sing Praise to God Who Reigns Above

Proclamation: God Speaking through His Word

Scripture Reading: 1 Thessalonians 5:23

Sermon: "What Is Sanctification?"

Dedication: Responding to the Word of God

Hymn: Take My Life and Let It Be Consecrated

Offertory Prayer

Offertory

Supplication: Praying for the Church & the World

Intercessory Prayer

Commission: God Sending Us Forth to Serve Him

Pastoral Welcome & Announcements

Hymn: Lord, Speak to Me, That I May Speak

Pastoral Charge and Benediction

Postlude: "Glory Be to God on High"

Changed from Glory into Glory

Example 2: Service with the Lord's Supper

Revelation: God Making Himself Known to Us

Silent Prayer and Meditation

Prelude: "My Inmost Heart Now Raises"

Christian Greeting
    Leader: The Lord be with you.
    People: And also with you.

Responsive Scripture Reading: Psalm 145:8–9, 14–21

> Leader: The Lord is gracious and merciful, slow to anger and abounding in steadfast love.
> **All: The Lord is good to all, and his mercy is over all that he has made.**
> The Lord upholds all who are falling and raises up all who are bowed down.
> **The eyes of all look to you, and you give them their food in due season.**
> You open your hand; you satisfy the desire of every living thing.
> **The Lord is righteous in all his ways and kind in all his works.**
> The Lord is near to all who call on him, to all who call on him in truth.
> **He fulfills the desire of those who fear him; he also hears their cry and saves them.**
> The Lord preserves all who love him, but all the wicked he will destroy.
> **My mouth will speak the praise of the Lord, and let all flesh bless his holy name forever and ever.**
>
> Reader: The Word of the Lord
> **People: Thanks be to God.**

Adoration: Exalting Our Glorious God

Hymn: O Worship the King

Prayer of Praise

Gloria Patri

Planning a Gospel-Shaped Worship Service

Confession: Lifting Contrite Hearts up to the Lord

Scripture Reading: Isaiah 55:1–5

Silent Prayers of Repentance

Corporate Prayer of Confession

> Almighty and merciful God,
> we have erred and strayed from your ways like lost sheep.
> We have followed too much
> the devices and desires of our own hearts.
> We have offended against your holy laws.
> We have left undone those things which we ought to have done;
> and we have done those things
> which we ought not to have done,
> and there is no good in us.
> O Lord, have mercy upon us.
> Spare those who confess their faults.
> Restore those who are penitent,
> according to your promise declared to the world
> in Christ Jesus, our Lord.
> And grant, O merciful God, for his sake,
> that we may live a holy, just, and humble life
> to the glory of your holy name.
> Amen.
> —*from The Book of Common Prayer*

Propitiation: Declaring God's Forgiveness

Declaration of the Good News: John 7:37–38
    Leader: In Christ your sins are forgiven you!
    People: The Lord be praised!

Hymn: I Heard the Voice of Jesus Say

Proclamation: God Speaking through His Word

Scripture Reading: 1 John 2:15–18

Sermon: "Love Not the World"

Changed from Glory into Glory

Dedication: Responding to the Word of God

Hymn: O Jesus, I Have Promised

Offertory Prayer

Offertory

Communion: Feasting with the Master

Declaration of Faith: Nicene Creed

Introduction and Welcome

Prayer of Thanksgiving
Words of Institution

The Acclamation
    Leader: Great is the mystery of our faith!
    People: Christ has died! Christ is risen!
    Christ will come again! Hallelujah!

Hymn: Praise God from Whom All Blessings Flow

Benevolence Offering

Commission: God Sending Us Forth to Serve Him

Pastoral Welcome & Announcements

Hymn: A Charge to Keep I Have

Pastoral Charge and Benediction

Postlude: "Blest Be the Tie that Binds"

Planning a Gospel-Shaped Worship Service

Example 3: Service Based on Isaiah 6

God Calls Us to Worship

Scripture Reading: Isaiah 6:1–4

We Praise God

Song: Holy, Holy Holy

Corporate Prayer of Praise

> We praise you, O God; we acclaim you as Lord;
> all creation worships you, the Father everlasting.
> To you all angels, all the powers of heaven,
> the cherubim and seraphim, sing in endless praise:
> Holy, holy, holy Lord, God of power and might,
> heaven and earth are full of your glory.
> The glorious company of apostles praise you.
> The noble fellowship of prophets praise you.
> The white-robed army of martyrs praise you.
> Throughout the world the holy church acclaims you:
> Father, of majesty unbounded;
> your true and only Son, worthy of all praise;
> the Holy Spirit, advocate and guide.
> You, Christ, are the King of glory,
> the eternal Son of the Father.
> When you took our flesh to set us free,
> you humbly chose the virgin's womb.
> You overcame the sting of death
> and opened the kingdom of heaven to all believers.
> You are seated at God's right hand in glory.
> We believe that you will come to be our judge.
> Come, then, Lord, and help your people,
> bought with the price of your own blood,
> and bring us with your saints
> to glory everlasting. Amen.
> —*based on the fourth-century Latin hymn Te Deum Laudamus*

Changed from Glory into Glory

God Calls Us to Confession

Scripture Reading: Isaiah 6:5

We Confess Our Sins

Song: When I Survey the Wondrous Cross

Silent Prayers of Repentance

Corporate Prayer of Confession

> Out of the depths I cry to you, O Lord!
> O Lord, hear my voice!
> Let your ears be attentive to the voice of my pleas for mercy!
>
> If you, O Lord, should mark iniquities,
> O Lord, who could stand?
> But with you there is forgiveness, that you may be feared.
> I wait for the Lord, my soul waits, and in his word I hope;
> my soul waits for the Lord
> more than watchmen for the morning,
> more than watchmen for the morning.
>
> We hope in the Lord!
> For with the Lord there is steadfast love,
> and with him is plentiful redemption.
> And he will redeem us from all our iniquities
> through Jesus Christ, our Lord. Amen.
> —*from Psalm 130*

God Declares Us Forgiven in Christ

Scripture Reading: Isaiah 6:6–7

We Thank God

Song: And Can It Be

Planning a Gospel-Shaped Worship Service

God Speaks to Us from His Word

Scripture Reading: Isaiah 6

Sermon

We Dedicate Ourselves to God

Scripture Reading: Isaiah 6:8

Song: Take My Life, and Let it be Consecrated

God Invites us to His Throne of Grace

Scripture Reading: Hebrews 4:16

We Bring our Supplications to God

Scripture Reading: Isaiah 6:11a

Intercessory Prayer

God Sends us into the World with His Blessing

Scripture Reading: Isaiah 6:9–13

Song: Christ for the World We Sing

Benediction

> The grace of the Lord Jesus Christ
> and the love of God
> and the fellowship of the Holy Spirit
> be with you all.
> Amen.

Appendix 2
Glossary[1]

absolution: pronouncement of forgiveness through the authority of the priest (Roman Catholic) or the gospel (Protestant).

Advent: the season that includes the four weeks leading up to Christmas, focusing on prophecies concerning the coming of Christ.

Agnus Dei: sung part of the mass ordinary from the Latin, "Lamb of God."

altar: structure on which sacrifices take place; in sacramental traditions, the table on which the Lord's Supper is celebrated.

altar call: introduced during nineteenth-century camp meetings and popularized by Charles Finney, an invitation for new converts or those wishing to rededicate themselves to Jesus Christ to come forward to kneel and pray.

anamnesis: the Greek word for "remembrance," as in "Do this in remembrance of me." It usually describes that portion of a eucharistic prayer in which God's works in creation and history, including Christ's death and resurrection, are recounted.

anaphora: a Greek word meaning "offering." It is used in the Eastern Church to designate the eucharistic prayer.

ante-communion: the first part of a service prior to the Lord's Supper, i.e., the Service of the Word.

anthems: choral music, usually sung by a trained choir.

antiphon: a sung response to Scripture.

Ascension: the celebration of Jesus's ascent into heaven, forty days after his resurrection.

Ash Wednesday: the first day of Lent.

---

[1] Adapted from White, *Protestant Worship*; Metzger, *History of the Liturgy: The Major Stages*; White, *Documents of Christian Worship*; Senn, *Introduction to Christian Liturgy*; Gibson and Earngey, *Reformation Worship*.

Ausbund: a collection of hymns used by some Anabaptists since the sixteenth century.

benediction: a blessing, usually from Scripture, upon the people.

breviary: the book containing songs and readings for the daily prayer services.

canon: Latin for "rule"; liturgically the main portion of the eucharistic prayer in the Lord's Supper.

canticles: poetry from Scripture, other than the psalms, often said or sung.

catechumens: those preparing to be baptized.

catholic: literally means "universal."

chancel: the area in the front of a church building designed for the use of the persons presiding.

Christmas: the twelve days between December 25 and January 6 celebrating Christ's birth.

collect: a prayer.

compline: the last of the daily prayer services performed in the late evening.

Credo: sung creed as part of the mass ordinary; usually a setting of the Nicene Creed.

cultus: a general term designating the forms and practices of worship for a particular religious community.

daily office: a cycle of daily services.

Deutsche Messe: Luther's German revision of the mass, published in 1526.

Didache: "The Teaching of the Twelve Apostles," a church order from the late first or early second century.

doxology: the conclusion of a prayer that expresses praise to God, usually the three persons of the Trinity.

Glossary

Easter: the fifty days between Easter Sunday and Pentecost celebrating Christ's resurrection.

elevation: the lifting of the consecrated bread and wine in the Lord's Supper after the Words of Institution.

epiclesis: a Greek word meaning "invocation." It usually refers to the section of the eucharistic prayer that calls upon the Holy Spirit to bless the elements of Communion.

Epiphany: January 6, the day commemorating the revelation of Christ, usually in the visit of the Magi.

Epistle: the Scripture read in a service from the New Testament epistles, Acts, or Revelation.

Eucharist: another name for the Lord's Supper, taken from the Greek term for "thanksgiving."

evensong: the evening daily prayer service, also called vespers.

excommunication: the excluding from communion with the church.

Formula Missae: Luther's first revision of the mass, published in Latin in 1523.

fraction: the act of breaking of the bread in Communion.

Gloria in excelsis: a musical part of the mass ordinary, beginning with the words, "Glory to God in the highest," from Luke 2, known as the Great Doxology.

Gloria Patri: The Lesser Doxology, "Glory be to the Father, and to the Son, and to the Holy Spirit, as it was in the beginning, is now, and will be forever."

Good Friday: the day commemorating Christ's death on the cross.

Gospel: the Scripture read in a service from the New Testament Gospels in public worship.

Gradual: a psalm of response following a Scripture reading.

Holy Week: the week between Palm Sunday and Easter Day.

homily: a sermon.

iconoclasm: the opposition of using images in worship.

introit: a sung entrance hymn or psalm at the beginning of a service.

koinonia: Greek for "fellowship" or "communion."

Kyrie: sung part of the mass ordinary from the Greek, "Lord, have mercy."

lauds: a morning service of prayer.

lectionary: a book prescribing readings for particular days in the year.

Lent: the forty-day penitential season, not including Sundays, leading up to Easter Day.

litany: a form of prayer in which a refrain is repeated by the congregation in response to a series of petitions or thanksgivings spoken by a leader.

liturgy: from the Latin, *leitourgia,* meaning "the people's work," used to describe the order and elements of worship.

matins: originally a nighttime service, but since the Reformation, a morning praise service.

Maundy Thursday: the day commemorating the Last Supper, from the "mandate" of Christ given at the supper to love one another.

Mennonites: Anabaptist descendants from followers of Menno Simons.

missal: the book containing the texts and rubrics for saying mass.

nave: the area of a church building usually occupied by the congregation.

offertory: the time in a service when the elements for the Lord's Table are offered and prepared, sometimes accompanied by the giving of alms.

ordinary: texts in worship that do not change including *Kyrie, Gloria, Credo, Sanctus,* and *Agnus Dei.*

ordo: a liturgical book from Rome containing rules and texts for celebrating the liturgy.

Glossary

Our Father: the model prayer Jesus taught his disciples, also called "The Lord's Prayer."

paraments: linens that adorn the sanctuary, usually in the color of the liturgical day or season.

Pater Noster: Latin for "our Father."

Pentecost: the fiftieth day after Easter, commemorating the coming of the Holy Spirit and birth of the church.

preface: the beginning section of the eucharistic prayer in which God is praised for his works, usually introduced by the *Sursum Corda* and concluding with the *Sanctus*.

prime: a daily service at the first hour of the day.

propers: texts in worship that change from date to date based on the liturgical calendar.

responsory: verse/refrain response said between a leader and congregation.

sacrament: ordinances of God that visibly picture a spiritual reality.

Salutation: formal liturgical greeting, usually beginning with "The Lord be with you."

Sanctus: sung part of the eucharistic prayer, "Holy, holy, holy."

Sursum Corda: Latin for "Up hearts," the introduction to the eucharistic prayer.

transubstantiation: doctrine that the substance (but not the accidents) of bread and wine become the body and blood of Christ in the eucharist; Roman Catholic doctrine formalized by Thomas Aquinas.

Trent, Council: counter-Reformation council for the reform of the Roman Catholic Church, convened between 1545 and 1563.

tridium: the three days of the passion week, Thursday, Friday, and Saturday.

Trisagion: Greek for "thrice holy," the Eastern version of the *Sanctus*.

Changed from Glory into Glory

Vatican Council II: Roman Catholic council from 1962–1965, the first significant revision of the liturgy since Trent, advocating for local practices and vernacular language.

vespers: the evening daily prayer service, also called evensong.

vestments: attire worn by clergy for the worship services.

Westminster Directory: Puritan document replacing the *Book of Common Prayer* in the Church of England from 1645 to 1660, now revered by some Presbyterians.

Words of Institution: words that recount Christ's institution of the Lord's Supper, either from the Gospels or 1 Corinthians 11.

Appendix 3
Timeline

B. C.[1]

1900	Call of Abraham; Egyptian pyramids
1700	Joseph in Egypt
1500	The Exodus, Sinai
1450	Israelite conquest of Canaan
1200	Trojan War
1050	David becomes king
1015	Solomon becomes king, temple built
975	The Kingdom divides into Israel (north) and Judah (south)
880	Elijah
800	Jonah
760	Homer writes *The Iliad* and *The Odyssey*
750	Founding of Rome
722	Assyria conquers Israel
690	Isaiah
630	Jeremiah
621	Reform under Josiah
586	Babylon destroys Jerusalem
538	Persia conquers Babylon
537	Cyrus allows exiles to return to Jerusalem
515	Second temple completed
510	Esther saves her people; founding of the Roman Republic
467	Ezra returns to Jerusalem and reforms Jewish worship
454	Nehemiah returns to Jerusalem and rebuilds its walls
380	Plato's *Republic*
397	Malachi
330	Alexander conquers Persia
277	Septuagint translated
170	Greeks capture Jerusalem and ransack the temple
165	Judas Maccabeus retakes Jerusalem and the temple
146	The Roman Empire conquers Greece
88	Anna begins prayer and fasting in the temple

---

[1] Some dates are approximate.

	64	Rome captures Jerusalem
	45	Julius Caesar becomes dictator of the Roman Empire
	44	Julius Caesar is assassinated
	27	Caesar Augustus (Octavius) becomes the first Emperor of Rome
	10	Herod rebuilds the temple
	5	Birth of Jesus
A. D.		
	30	Crucifixion of Jesus
	45	Beginning of the writing of Paul's letters
	50	Jerusalem Council
	60	Mark writes his Gospel
	63	Roman General Pompey captures Jerusalem
	67	Peter crucified
	70	Temple at Jerusalem destroyed
	96	John banished to Patmos
	96	Clement of Rome, writings
	100	Ignatius of Antioch, writings
	100	*Epistle of Barnabas*
	112	Letter of Pliny to Trajan
	120	*Didache*
	155	Polycarp, writings
	155	*Apology* of Justin Martyr
	200	Tertullian, writings
	200	Irenaeus, writings
	215	Clement of Alexandria, writings
	215	*Apostolic Tradition*
	230	*Didascalia Apostolorum*
	258	Cyprian of Carthage, writings
	270	Papyrus from Oxyrhynchos (Egypt) includes a hymn
	284	Diocletian divides Rome
	313	Edict of Milan
	325	Council of Nicaea
	330	Athanasius, writings
	350	*Testamentum Domini*
	350	Cyril of Jerusalem, *Catechetical Lectures*
	360	Canons of Laodicea
	363	Council of Laodicea
	370	*Divine Liturgy of St. James*

Timeline

374	Ambrose becomes bishop of Milan
375	Basil the Great, writings
375	*Apostolic Constitutions*
381	First Council of Constantinople
387	Augustine baptized by Ambrose in Milan
390	John Chrysostom, *On the Priesthood*
391	Theodosius declares Christianity the official religion of the Empire
397	Augustine becomes bishop of Hippo
400	*Divine Liturgy of St. John Chrysostom*
405	Jerome, *Vulgate*
431	Council of Ephesus
440	Leo the Great asserts primacy of Rome
451	Council of Chalcedon
476	The fall of Rome
510	Boethius, *De Musica*
540	Rule of St. Benedict
590	Gregory I, "the Great" becomes pope
622	Birth of Islam
680	Second Council of Constantinople
700	*Ordo Romanus Primus*
800	Charlemagne crowned by Leo III
1020	Pope Benedict VIII introduces the Creed into the liturgy
1054	Eastern and Western parts of the church split
1066	Battle of Hastings
1096	First Crusade
1198	Innocent III becomes pope; height of papal power
1204	Fourth Crusade, sack of Constantinople
1215	Magna Carta
1215	Fourth Lateran Council codifies transubstantiation
1224	Francis of Assisi, "Canticle of the Sun"
1232	Inquisition founded
1274	Thomas Aquinas, *Summa Theologica*
1320	Dante, *The Divine Comedy*
1323	William of Ockham, *Summa Logicae*
1347–1350	Great Plague; one quarter of Europe's population dies
1309–1377	"Babylonian Captivity of the Church"; popes exiled at Avignon
1382	John Wycliffe, English Bible translation
1440	Invention of the printing press

1415	John Hus, Bohemian reformer, executed
1447	Construction on Vatican begins
1453	Fall of Constantinople
1492	Columbus discovers America
1509	Henry VIII becomes King of England
1517	Martin Luther's 95 Theses
1522	Ulrich Zwingli, "Affair of the Sausages"
1523	Martin Bucer, *Grund und Ursach*
1524	*Achtiederbuch*
1527	Schleitheim Confession
1529	Marburg Colloquy
1534	Acts of Supremacy in England
1542	John Calvin, *Form of Church Prayers*
1543	Nicholas Copernicus, *On the Revolutions of the Celestial Spheres*
1549	Thomas Cranmer, *Book of Common Prayer*
1553	Mary I ("Bloody") becomes queen of England
1556	John Knox, *The Forme of Prayers*
1558	Elizabeth I becomes Queen of England
1559	Final edition of John Calvin's *Institutes of the Christian Religion*
1561	Second Helvetic Confession
1562	*Genevan Psalter* and Sternhold and Hopkins English Psalter
1545–1563	Council of Trent
1580	*Formula of Concord*
1588	Defeat of the Spanish Armada
1609	William Shakespeare, *Hamlet*
1611	King James Version of the Bible
1620	Mayflower at Plymouth
1630	Massachusetts Bay Colony
1636	Harvard College founded
1640	*Bay Psalm Book*
1644	Westminster *Directory for Public Worship*
1644	Rene Descartes, "I think, therefore I am."
1647	Johann Crüger, *Praxis pietatis melica*
1675	Philip Jacob, Spener, *Pia Desideria*, beginning of German Pietism
1678	John Bunyan, *The Pilgrim's Progress*
1687	Isaac Newton, *Mathematical Principles of Natural Philosophy*
1689	The Second London Baptist Confession
1696	Tate and Brady Psalter ("New Version")

Timeline

1707	Isaac Watts, *Hymns*
1719	Isaac Watts, *Psalms of David*
1727	Zinzendorf begins leadership of Moravians
1737	Jonathan Edwards, "A Faithful Narrative"
1738	John and Charles Wesley's conversion
1730–1740	American "Great Awakening"
1740	George Whitefield preaches in America
1741	G. F. Handel, "Messiah"
1746	Jonathan Edwards, *The Religious Affections*
1749	J. S. Bach, "Mass in B minor"
1769	Steam engine patented
1776	U. S. Declaration of Independence
1780	Sunday School movement
1781	Immanuel Kant, *Critique of Pure Reason*
1775–1783	American Revolutionary War
1791	Wolfgang Amadeus Mozart, "The Magic Flute"
1801	Cane Ridge camp meeting
1789–1799	French Revolution
1804	Napoleon Bonaparte becomes Emperor of France"
1810	Ludwig van Beethoven, Fifth Symphony
1830	Friedrich Schleiermacher, *Brief Outline for the Study of Theology*
1833	Oxford Movement
1835	Charles G. Finney, *Lectures on Revival*
1844	*Sacred Harp*
1847	Karl Marx, *Communist Manifesto*
1850	Stephen Foster, "Camptown Races"
1853	Thomas Hastings, *Dissertation on Musical Taste*
1859	Charles Darwin, *Origin of Species*
1860	*Hymns Ancient and Modern*
1861–1865	American Civil War
1875	Philip Bliss and Ira Sankey, *Gospel Hymns and Sacred Songs*
1876	Invention of the telephone
1883	Friedrich Nietzsche, *Thus Spoke Zarathustra*
1897	John Dewey, *My Pedagogic Creed*
1905	Sigmund Freud, *Three Essays on the Theory of Sexuality*
1906–1909	Azusa Street revival
1914–1918	World War I
1922	John Dewey, *Human Nature and Conduct*

1923	Arnold Schoenberg, "Suite for Piano"
1928	Invention of the television
1929	Stock market crash
1933	Adolf Hitler becomes dictator of Germany
1939–1945	World War II
1952	C. S. Lewis, *Mere Christianity*
1955	Start of the church growth movement
1957	Harold Ockenga coins "New Evangelicals"
1960	Jesus movement
1962–1965	Vatican Council II
1967	Bob Oldenburg's youth musical, *Good News*
1967	Jacques Derrida promotes "deconstruction"; beginning of Postmodernism
1973	Judson Cornwall, *Let Us Praise*
1989	Fall of the Berlin Wall and communism

Appendix 4
For Further Study

This is a select bibliography of books that will help the student of worship explore the details of this book in even greater detail.

Aniol, Scott, Kevin T. Bauder, David de Bruyn, Michael Riley, Ryan Martin, and Jason Parker. *A Conservative Christian Declaration*. Religious Affections Ministries, 2014.
Aniol, Scott. *By the Waters of Babylon: Worship in a Post-Christian Culture*. Grand Rapids: Kregel Ministry, 2015.
Aniol, Scott. *Worship in Song: A Biblical Approach to Music and Worship*. Winona Lake, IL: BMH Books, 2009.
Barrett, Michael. *The Beauty of Holiness: A Guide to Biblical Worship*. Greenville, SC: Ambassador-Emerald International, 2006.
Beale, G. K. *We Become What We Worship: A Biblical Theology of Idolatry*. Downers Grove: IVP Academic, 2008.
Begbie, Jeremy S. *Voicing Creations Praise: Towards a Theology of the Arts*. T. & T. Clark Publ, 1991.
Bradshaw, Paul F. *Early Christian Worship: A Basic Introduction to Ideas and Practice*. Collegeville, MN: Liturgical Press, 2010.
Bradshaw, Paul F. *Reconstructing Early Christian Worship*. Reprint edition. Collegeville, MN: Liturgical Press, 2011.
Bradshaw, Paul, ed. *The New Westminster Dictionary of Liturgy and Worship*. Louisville, KY: Westminster John Knox Press, 2003.
Bruyn, David de. *The Conservative Church*. Religious Affections Ministries, 2016.
Carson, D. A. *Christ and Culture Revisited*. Grand Rapids: Wm. B. Eerdmans, 2008.
Castleman, Robbie F. *Story-Shaped Worship: Following Patterns from the Bible and History*. Downers Grove, IL: InterVarsity Press, 2013.
Chapell, Bryan. *Christ-Centered Worship: Letting the Gospel Shape Our Practice*. Grand Rapids: Baker Academic, 2009.
Davies, Horton. *Worship and Theology in England*. Five vols. Grand Rapids: Wm. B. Eerdmans Publishing Company, 1996.
Dawn, Marva. *Reaching out Without Dumbing Down: A Theology of Worship for the Turn-of-the-Century Culture*. Grand Rapids: Wm. B. Eerdmans, 1995.
Dreher, Rod. *The Benedict Option: A Strategy for Christians in a Post-Christian Nation*. New York: Sentinel, 2017.

Ellis, Christopher J. *Gathering: A Spirituality and Theology of Worship in Free Church Tradition*. SCM Press, 2004.

Eskew, Harry. *Sing with Understanding: An Introduction to Christian Hymnology*. Second. Nashville: Genevox Music Group, 1995.

Faulkner, Quentin. *Wiser Than Despair: The Evolution of Ideas in the Relationship of Music and the Christian Church*. 2nd ed. Simpsonville, SC: Religious Affections Ministries, 2012.

Gordon, T. David. *Why Johnny Can't Sing Hymns: How Pop Culture Rewrote the Hymnal*. Phillipsburg, NJ: P & R Publishing Company, 2010.

Gray, Scotty. *Hermeneutics of Hymnody: A Comprehensive and Integrated Approach to Understanding Hymns*. Macon: Smyth & Helwys Publishing, 2015.

Hart, D. G., and John R. Muether. *With Reverence and Awe: Returning to the Basics of Reformed Worship*. Phillipsburg, NJ: Presbyterian & Reformed Publishing Company, 2002.

Hodges, Donald A. *A Concise Survey of Music Philosophy*. New York: Routledge, 2016.

Horton, Michael. *Ordinary: Sustainable Faith in a Radical, Restless World*. Grand Rapids: Zondervan, 2014.

Hustad, Donald P. *Jubilate II: Church Music in Worship and Renewal*. Wheaton: Hope Publishing Company, 1993.

Ingalls, Monique M. *Singing the Congregation: How Contemporary Worship Music Forms Evangelical Community*. New York: Oxford University Press, 2018.

Jasper, R. C. D., and G. J. Cuming. *Prayers of the Eucharist: Early and Reformed*. Edited by Paul F. Bradshaw and Maxwell E. Johnson. Fourth. Collegeville, MN: Liturgical Press Academic, 2019.

Johansson, Calvin M. *Discipling Music Ministry: Twenty-First Century Directions*. Peabody, MA: Hendrickson Publishers, 1992.

Lim, Swee Hong, and Lester Ruth. *Lovin' on Jesus: A Concise History of Contemporary Worship*. Nashville: Abingdon Press, 2017.

Lovelace, Austin C. *The Anatomy of Hymnody*. GIA Publications, 1965.

Makujina, John, and Calvin M. Johansson. *Measuring the Music: Another Look at the Contemporary Christian Music Debate*. Third Edition. Religious Affections Ministries, 2016.

Martin, Ralph P. *Worship in the Early Church*. Revised edition. Grand Rapids: Wm. B. Eerdmans, 1975.

Morgenthaler, Sally. *Worship Evangelism: Inviting Unbelievers Into the Presence of God*. Grand Rapids: Zondervan, 1999.

Munson, Paul, and Joshua Farris Drake. *Art and Music: A Student's Guide*. Wheaton: Crossway, 2014.

Further Study

Myers, Kenneth. *All God's Children and Blue Suede Shoes: Christians and Popular Culture*. Wheaton: Crossway Books, 1989.

Old, Hughes Oliphant. *The Reading and Preaching of the Scriptures in the Worship of the Christian Church,*. Seven vols. Grand Rapids: Wm. B. Eerdmans Publishing, 2010.

Old, Hughes Oliphant. *Worship: Reformed According to Scripture*. Revised and expanded. Louisville: Westminster John Knox Press, 2002.

Reynolds, William J, and David W. Music. *A Survey of Christian Hymnody*. Fifth Edition. Carol Stream, IL: Hope Publishing Company, 2010.

Ross, Allen P. *Recalling the Hope of Glory: Biblical Worship from the Garden to the New Creation*. Grand Rapids: Kregel, 2006.

Ryken, Leland. *The Liberated Imagination: Thinking Christianly About the Arts*. Eugene, OR: Wipf & Stock, 2005.

Senn, Frank C. *Introduction to Christian Liturgy*. Minneapolis: Fortress Press, 2012.

Smith, James K. A. *You Are What You Love: The Spiritual Power of Habit*. Grand Rapids: Brazos Press, 2016.

Spinks, Bryan D. *Do This in Remembrance of Me: The Eucharist from the Early Church to the Present Day*. London: SCM Press, 2013.

Stapert, Calvin R. *A New Song for an Old World: Musical Thought in the Early Church*. Grand Rapids: Wm. B. Eerdmans, 2006.

Thompson, Bard. *Liturgies of the Western Church*. St. Louis: Fortress Press, 1980.

Torrance, James. *Worship, Community, and the Triune God of Grace*. Downers Grove, IL: InterVarsity Press, 1996.

Tozer, A. W. *Worship: The Missing Jewel of the Evangelical Church*. Fort Lauderdale, FL: Christian Publications, Inc., 1961.

VanDrunen, David. *Living in God's Two Kingdoms: A Biblical Vision for Christianity and Culture*. Wheaton: Crossway, 2010.

Wainwright, Geoffrey, and Karen B. Westerfield Tucker, eds. *The Oxford History of Christian Worship*. Oxford: Oxford University Press, 2006.

Ward, Matthew. *Pure Worship: The Early English Baptist Distinctive*. Eugene, OR: Pickwick Publications, 2014.

Webber, Robert E., ed. *The Complete Library of Christian Worship*. Eight vols. Nashville: Star Song, 1994.

Westermeyer, Paul. *Te Deum: The Church and Music*. Minneapolis: Fortress Press, 1998.

White, James F. *A Brief History of Christian Worship*. Nashville: Abingdon Press, 1993.

White, James F. *Documents of Christian Worship: Descriptive and Interpretive Sources*. Louisville, KY: Westminster John Knox Press, 2007.

White, James F. *Protestant Worship: Traditions in Transition.* Louisville, KY: Westminster John Knox Press, 1989.

Index

Act of Uniformity, 235
Acts of Supremacy, 233, 254, 368
Advent, 176, 195, 206, 353, 360
Aestheticism, 273, 309
Aesthetics, 345, 349
Affair of the Sausages, 217, 368
Affections, 22, 68, 70, 71, 267, 268, 269, 270, 279, 313, 315, 338, 339, 343, 349
Age of Reason, 260, 267, 313, 324
Ainsworth, Henry, 247
Ambrose, 173, 195, 367
Ambrosian rite, 184
American Puritans, 247
Amish, 224
Anabaptists, 221, 222, 223, 224, 254, 360, 363
Andreae, Jakob, 214
Anglicanism, 289, 308
Anthropology, 27
Apollo, 268
Apollonian music, 269
Apostles' Creed, 151, 171, 195, 214, 219, 220, 226, 230, 231
Aquinas, Thomas, 189, 194, 202, 267, 338, 363, 368
Architecture, 58, 191, 192, 193, 345
Aristotle, 189, 202
Arminianism, 281
Art, 28, 29, 62, 71, 72, 165, 193, 199, 207, 210, 265, 268, 270, 271, 272, 317, 322, 345, 347
Arts, 28, 193, 270, 305, 306
Asbury, Francis, 284
Ascension, 176, 195, 206, 353, 360
Ascension Day, 176
Athanasian Creed, 214
Athanasius, 175, 366
Atonement, 26, 39, 42, 43, 44, 46, 47, 48, 49, 50, 60, 75, 81, 84, 85, 87, 88, 102, 104, 124, 125, 131, 132, 133, 140, 242, 311, 343

Augustine, 163, 174, 195, 229, 259, 267, 268, 337, 338, 367
Azusa Street revival, 294, 370
Baby boomers, 293
Baldiun, Friedrich, 215
Baptism, 99, 100, 106, 109, 118, 119, 120, 122, 123, 142, 147, 149, 150, 152, 162, 163, 172, 175, 176, 192, 195, 212, 213, 221, 222, 242, 243, 245, 289, 294, 300, 327
Baptism of the Holy Spirit, 294
Baptismal liturgy, 99
Baptists, 221, 241, 243, 244, 245, 246, 247, 283, 284, 299
Basil the Great, 167, 367
Basil's Feast Day, 180
Baxter, Richard, 249
Beauty, 35, 47, 68, 190, 194, 234, 270, 273, 274, 281, 306
Benedict VIII, 186, 367
Benediction, 170, 183, 206, 221, 226, 232, 237, 238, 240, 248, 331, 355, 357, 359
Beza, Theodore, 229
Blaurock, George, 221, 224
Bliss, Philip, 288, 370
Bloody Mary. *See* Mary I
Boleyn, Anne, 235
Book of Common Prayer,, 233, 280
Bourgeois, Louis, 229, 253
Brochmand, Jesper Rasmussen, 212
Bucer, Martin, 219, 224, 225, 226, 227, 228, 231, 234, 254, 368
Bullinger, Heinrich, 218, 220, 232, 254
Burkitt, Lemuel, 285
Burnt Offering, 48
Byzantine Church, 183
Calamy, Edmond, 242
Calvin, John, 82, 83, 96, 161, 214, 219, 224, 227, 228, 229, 230, 231, 232,

234, 235, 238, 239, 252, 253, 254, 268, 330, 338, 368, 374, 375
Campbell, Alexander, 286
Campbell, Thomas, 286
Catechumens, 149, 150, 167, 182, 361
Catherine of Aragon, 233, 234
Celestine I, 174
Celibacy, 188
Cerularius, Michael I, 184
Charles I, 186, 238
Charles V, 214, 226
Chauncy, Charles, 278, 279
Chemnitz, Martin, 214
Cherubim, 39, 46, 145, 169, 180, 358
Children, 45, 53, 81, 86, 100, 152, 173, 213, 223, 266, 285, 286, 322
Christmas, 176, 180, 195, 206, 219, 360, 361
Chrysostom, John, 176, 179, 180, 367
Church and state, 60, 241
Church discipline, 219, 222
Church Growth Movement, 293, 303, 305
Church of England, 233, 235, 236, 238, 240, 246, 254, 280, 289, 308, 364
Clement of Alexandria, 147, 149, 161, 267, 366
Clement of Rome, 147, 366
Collins, Hercules, 243
Communion with God, 38, 39, 43, 47, 48, 49, 93, 102, 106, 110, 127, 130, 134, 139, 336, 344, 351
Conscience, 113, 128, 204, 205, 213, 239, 311
Constantine, 162, 165, 166, 171, 179, 195
Continuationist theology, 295
Copernican Revolution, 259
Corporate worship, 15, 19, 29, 32, 47, 53, 60, 61, 63, 68, 97, 111, 112, 113, 118, 119, 121, 123, 125, 137, 141, 163, 165, 191, 193, 209, 211, 239, 286, 288, 307, 335, 336, 340, 342, 345, 350, 351
Cotton, John, 247
Council of Chalcedon, 179, 367

Council of Constantinople, 171, 195, 367
Council of Laodicea, 190, 367
Council of Nicaea, 171, 172, 195, 366
Council of Trent, 179, 186, 187, 369
Cranmer, Thomas, 199, 225, 226, 233, 234, 236, 254, 309, 368
Creation, 31, 33, 37, 90, 143, 267, 375
Crüger, Johann, 211, 369
Culture, 1, 27, 28, 29, 30, 31, 33, 34, 37, 44, 47, 51, 60, 61, 62, 86, 106, 115, 162, 165, 184, 187, 193, 194, 198, 209, 233, 251, 260, 261, 263, 264, 265, 266, 268, 269, 270, 271, 272, 273, 274, 275, 277, 284, 305, 306, 307, 311, 312, 313, 314, 319, 321, 322, 323, 324, 325, 326, 327, 329, 330, 333, 335, 342, 349
Cultus, 1, 30, 31, 33, 34, 37, 44, 46, 61, 86, 193, 198, 233, 311, 319, 323, 335, 342, 349, 361
Cybele, 95
Cyprian of Carthage, 156, 159, 366
Cyril of Jerusalem, 157, 367
Dancing, 62, 63, 64, 82, 83, 96, 161, 162
Dannhauer, Johann Konrad, 211
Darwin, Charles, 264, 265, 313, 370
Darwinism, 264, 323
Davenport, James, 278
Day of Atonement, 47, 50, 56, 88, 104, 140, 343
Day, John, 235
Deacons, 151, 170, 175, 180, 181, 182, 183, 185
Decalogue, 44
Decius, Nicolaus, 208
Deism, 264, 313, 349
Descartes, René, 259, 313, 369
Dewey, John, 265, 266, 370
Didache, 100, 147, 148, 150, 153, 154, 167, 196, 361, 366
Dionysian music, 269
Dionysus, 95, 96, 161, 268
Discipleship, 12, 336, 339, 340, 341, 345, 349

Index

Easter, 175, 176, 177, 180, 196, 206, 219, 353, 361, 362, 363
Eden, 37, 38, 46, 47
Edict of Milan, 165, 176, 196, 198, 366
Edward VI, 233
Edwards, Jonathan, 267, 268, 277, 278, 279, 284, 315, 337, 338, 369
Edwards, Sarah, 278
Effective principle, 290, 313, 329, 333, 349
Elizabeth I, 235, 254, 368
Emergent Church, 306
Emotion, 70, 266, 268, 269, 270, 273, 278, 279, 313, 326
Emotionalism, 278, 289, 309
Empiricism, 261, 262, 313, 323
English Civil War, 236
Enlightenment, 165, 260, 261, 263, 264, 266, 268, 269, 270, 272, 276, 277, 279, 287, 290, 306, 311, 313, 315, 320
Epiphany, 176, 180, 196, 353, 361
Episcopal Church, 289
Eucharist, 147, 150, 153, 155, 156, 158, 163, 168, 182, 183, 188, 189, 196, 197, 202, 205, 218, 235, 241, 255, 289, 299, 309, 362, 363, 374, 375
Eucharistic Prayer, 183, 187, 206, 226, 232, 238, 240
Evangelicalism, 302, 325
Exile, 64, 69, 76, 77, 78, 94, 95, 97, 172, 234, 235, 253, 264, 319, 320, 321, 322
Faber, Frederick, 289
Farel, William, 227
Fasting, 149, 150, 217, 280, 366
Fawcett, John, 244
Finney, Charles G., 284, 287, 294, 304, 315, 360, 370
First London Baptist Confession of Faith, 242
Flavius, Josephus, 96, 97, 103
Forgiveness, 13, 26, 43, 49, 60, 75, 102, 103, 105, 116, 125, 132, 135, 140, 141, 151, 155, 172, 187, 189, 237, 239, 311, 352, 359, 360
French Revolution, 260, 370
Gallican rite, 184

General Baptists, 242
Gerhardt, Paul, 210
German Mass, 204, 205
Gill, John, 244
Gnosticism, 267
Goudimel, Claude, 229
Graduals, 174, 185, 186, 196, 237, 362
Grain Offering, 49
Great Awakening, 247, 277, 278, 283, 284, 313, 369
Great Commission, 105, 107, 118, 143, 335, 336, 342, 349
Great Entrance, 182
Great Litany, 181
Grebel, Conrad, 221
Greco-Roman world, 95
Gregory I, 184, 185, 196, 367
Grossgebauer, Theophil, 211
Guilt Offering, 48
Habits, 28, 149, 156, 325, 336, 337, 338, 339, 341, 342, 344, 347
Half-Way Covenant, 276
Helwys, Thomas, 241, 242
Henotheism, 45
Henry II, 186
Henry VIII, 233, 254, 368
Heresy, 166, 173, 187, 188, 191, 205, 347
Herod the Great, 95, 96
Holy of Holies, 46, 47, 50, 56, 88, 298, 332
Holy Spirit, 11, 12, 13, 14, 47, 48, 58, 93, 99, 105, 109, 110, 112, 118, 120, 121, 122, 123, 134, 142, 143, 150, 151, 155, 157, 158, 159, 169, 171, 172, 173, 177, 181, 182, 183, 186, 190, 203, 204, 231, 236, 253, 277, 279, 294, 295, 296, 300, 301, 302, 335, 339, 341, 343, 358, 359, 361, 362, 363
Holy Week, 175, 196, 207, 362
Hubmaier, Balthasar, 221, 223, 224, 254
Hus, John, 276, 368
Hutterites, 222
Hymns, 69, 70, 102, 115, 117, 119, 120, 142, 147, 151, 153, 159, 160, 161, 173, 180, 183, 205, 209, 210, 224,

333

236, 238, 248, 252, 253, 280, 281, 282, 286, 352, 358, 362, 366
Iconoclasm, 218, 227, 362
Idolatry, 50, 55, 56, 73, 75, 76, 81, 88, 149, 235, 373
Ignatius, 147, 148, 161, 188, 366
Ignatius in Antioch, 147
Incarnation of Christ, 93
Industrial Revolution, 266, 312, 313
Infant baptism, 152, 221
Instruments, 61, 62, 64, 77, 82, 116, 160, 162, 211, 229, 262, 319, 336
Introit, 174, 185, 186, 196, 206, 236, 237, 331
Irenaeus, 149, 188, 366
Isis, 95
Islam, 45, 183, 367
James I, 238
James, William, 265
Judgment, 26, 28, 109, 129, 132, 135, 137, 140, 213, 354
Justin Martyr, 147, 148, 151, 153, 154, 196, 366
Keach, Benjamin, 245, 246
Keble, John, 289, 290
Kiffin, William, 243, 244
Kiss of Peace, 183
Knox, John, 148, 198, 227, 234, 235, 238, 239, 254, 255, 315, 368, 373, 375, 376
Kuyper, Abraham, 260
Lampe, John F., 282
Lateran Council, 189, 368
Layzell, Reg, 295
Legalism, 112
Leipzig Interim, 214
Lent, 175, 180, 196, 206, 207, 217, 353, 360, 362
Leo I, 175
Leo III, 186, 367
Leo IX, 184
Lewis, C. S., 266, 321, 338, 370
Little Entrance, 181
Liturgy of St. James, 145, 180, 367
Locke, John, 259
Lord's Day, 111

Lord's Day, 12, 148, 149, 153, 163, 196
Lord's Prayer, 157, 159, 183, 185, 206, 220, 221, 230, 231, 236, 237, 238, 239, 331, 363
Lord's Supper, 13, 102, 104, 106, 110, 111, 118, 119, 123, 143, 150, 153, 155, 163, 188, 190, 202, 218, 219, 220, 223, 225, 246, 247, 280, 285, 286, 288, 289, 309, 331, 332, 344, 346, 353, 355, 362, 363, 364
Ludwig, Nicholas, 276
Luther, Martin, 201, 202, 203, 204, 205, 206, 207, 208, 209, 210, 212, 213, 214, 217, 218, 219, 224, 226, 229, 231, 233, 234, 252, 253, 254, 330, 361, 362, 368
Lutheranism, 210, 211, 214, 215, 225, 275
Manz, Felix, 221, 224
Marburg Articles, 218
Marot, Clement, 229
Mary I, 234, 254, 368
Mass, 150, 184, 192, 202, 203, 204, 205, 208, 217, 225, 226, 234, 266, 308, 313, 360, 361, 362, 363
Materialism, 264
Meisner, Balthasar, 211, 215
Melanchthon, Philip, 214, 215, 224
Melchizedek, 41, 57, 89
Mennonites, 222, 224, 241, 363
Methodism, 280, 309, 313
Modernism, 306, 313
Monotheism, 45, 80, 82
Moody, D. L., 288
Moralistic Therapeutic Deism, 324
Mosaic Law, 47, 87
Mozarabic rite, 184
Music, 47, 57, 60, 61, 62, 64, 65, 70, 82, 87, 96, 115, 161, 162, 173, 174, 175, 190, 193, 201, 204, 207, 208, 211, 212, 218, 219, 224, 228, 229, 235, 252, 267, 268, 269, 270, 272, 273, 275, 281, 282, 283, 285, 288, 289, 290, 296, 298, 299, 301, 302, 303, 304, 305, 329, 330, 332, 345, 360

Index

Musicians, 61, 62, 210, 235, 274, 296, 301
Naturalism, 261, 262, 314, 323
Neale, John Mason, 289
Neumeister, Erdmann, 276
Newman, John Henry, 289
Newton, Isaac, 259, 369
Nicene Creed, 171, 183, 186, 196, 214, 236, 238, 357, 361
Nietzsche, Friedrich, 260, 268, 370
Ninety-Five Theses, 201, 368
Norcott, John, 243
Normative principle, 245, 252, 255, 256, 290, 314, 329, 349
Octavian, 95
Oecolampadius, Johannes, 219, 220
Offertory Prayer, 183, 355, 357
Origin, 189, 370
Ottoman Muslims, 183
Oxford Movement, 280, 289, 308, 314, 370
Ozmen, Agnes, 294
Palm Sunday, 175, 196, 207, 362
Parallelism, 66, 67, 88, 89
Parham, Charles, 294
Particular Baptists, 242, 284
Passover, 42, 43, 50, 52, 53, 74, 89, 93, 102, 103, 104, 111, 118, 142, 162, 172, 343
Peace Offering, 49
Peirce, John Sanders, 265
Pentecost, 104, 109, 110, 120, 131, 142, 176, 196, 206, 219, 353, 361, 363
Pentecostalism, 293, 294, 300, 301, 314
Perfectionism, 287, 294
Persecution, 127, 160, 165, 227, 234
Philosophy, 95, 189, 194, 203, 263, 264, 265, 267, 268, 288, 290, 302, 304, 307, 313, 314, 315, 327, 328, 330
Pietism, 275, 280, 281, 314, 369
Pliny the Younger, 147, 197
Pluralism, 265, 306, 314, 323, 325, 349
Poetry, 18, 37, 66, 67, 79, 209, 281, 361
Polycarp, 147, 148, 366
Polytheism, 45, 80, 82
Pop culture, 270, 287

Pragmatism, 265, 303, 314, 323, 326, 349
Praise and worship theology, 295
Prayer, 11, 12, 18, 19, 31, 47, 48, 59, 67, 84, 97, 98, 99, 100, 101, 102, 106, 111, 114, 118, 123, 152, 153, 154, 155, 156, 157, 158, 159, 160, 167, 168, 169, 170, 171, 174, 180, 181, 182, 183, 185, 186, 188, 189, 196, 204, 211, 213, 217, 218, 223, 228, 229, 230, 231, 234, 236, 237, 238, 239, 240, 242, 246, 247, 248, 270, 275, 276, 280, 284, 285, 289, 317, 322, 323, 344, 352, 360, 361, 362, 363, 364, 366
Prayer of the Faithful, 182
Preaching, 11, 12, 111, 114, 123, 141, 175, 205, 207, 217, 218, 219, 225, 229, 230, 245, 247, 277, 278, 280, 288, 304, 329, 330, 333, 336, 342, 352, 353
Presbyterians, 245, 246, 247, 364
Prophecy, 37, 95, 99, 120
Protestantism, 100, 187, 188, 217, 233, 234, 244, 251, 255, 259, 273, 288, 302, 307, 308, 315, 353, 360, 376
Public worship, 32
Purgatory, 188
Purification, 46, 79, 133
Puritans, 3, 235, 238, 239, 241, 245, 246, 247, 248, 255, 276, 283, 364
Radical Reformers, 222, 255
Rationalism, 274, 276
Reformation, 17, 165, 179, 187, 191, 192, 201, 217, 220, 221, 225, 227, 233, 235, 251, 252, 253, 255, 259, 267, 275, 290, 293, 302, 305, 306, 309, 311, 360, 363, 364
Regeneration, 47, 327
Regulative principle, 238, 239, 244, 245, 252, 253, 255, 256, 276, 290, 314, 329, 333, 349
Renaissance, 259, 263
Revivalism, 288, 289, 290, 291, 293, 304, 314
Robinson, John, 246

Robinson, Robert, 286
Rodeheaver, Homer, 288
Roman Catholicism, 187, 214, 226, 234, 235, 251, 289, 307, 308
Roman rite, 184, 186, 234
Romanticism, 268, 283, 314
Sabbath, 44, 49, 50, 53, 86, 89, 111, 113, 343
Sacerdotalism, 190, 192, 197
Sacramentalism, 190, 192, 197
Sanctification, 121, 202, 281, 287, 294, 339, 349, 350, 355
Sankey, Ira, 288, 370
Sarum rite, 184
Satan, 26, 85, 151, 239, 276, 282
Sattler, Michael, 221, 222
Schleiermacher, Friedrich, 273, 370
Schleitheim Confession, 222, 255, 368
Schumann, Robert, 345
Science, 233, 259, 260, 265, 270, 306
Scientific Revolution, 259, 314
Scripture reading, 97, 99, 111, 114, 155, 168, 218, 220, 240, 276, 352, 353, 354, 355, 356, 357, 358, 359, 362
Second Helvetic Confession, 220, 368
Second London Baptist Confession, 242, 369
Second Wave Charismatic Movement, 294
Secularism, 268, 273, 314, 324
Sedulius, Caelius, 209
Separatists, 241, 242, 248, 276
Septuagint, 29, 95, 142, 365
Service of the Table, 150, 152, 154, 158, 170, 175, 182, 187, 191, 197, 206, 220, 226, 231, 238, 240
Service of the Word, 150, 152, 154, 155, 158, 168, 170, 181, 182, 186, 191, 197, 205, 206, 220, 223, 226, 230, 231, 237, 240, 248, 360
Seymour, Jane, 233
Shema, 45, 89, 98
Sign of the cross, 149, 167
Simons, Menno, 222, 224, 363
Sin Offering, 48

Singing, 12, 60, 61, 62, 68, 69, 70, 71, 75, 86, 99, 114, 115, 123, 124, 139, 160, 161, 172, 173, 174, 176, 182, 183, 205, 207, 211, 212, 219, 224, 226, 228, 229, 230, 235, 241, 245, 246, 247, 248, 252, 253, 276, 280, 281, 282, 285, 286, 297, 301, 374
Smyth, John, 241
Sorge, Bob, 295
Spener, Philipp Jakob, 275
Spilsbury, John, 244
Stone, Barton, 286
Stryk, Johann Samuel, 275
Summers, Thomas O., 309
Sunday, Billy, 288
Swiss Brethren, 221, 222
Synagogue, 94, 96, 97, 111
Syncretism, 50, 52, 55, 73, 75, 78, 85, 89, 94, 101
Synod of Whitby, 172
Tabernacle, 41, 43, 46, 47, 48, 49, 52, 55, 56, 57, 58, 69, 75, 89, 93, 104, 112, 120, 129, 130, 131, 297, 298, 304
Taylor, Nathaniel, 287
Technology, 233, 266
Temple, 12, 41, 46, 49, 57, 58, 59, 62, 69, 73, 74, 75, 77, 78, 83, 89, 93, 94, 95, 96, 97, 99, 101, 102, 103, 104, 105, 111, 112, 122, 123, 125, 130, 131, 132, 134, 135, 140, 192, 297, 298, 319, 320, 365, 366
Ten Commandments, 44, 230, 231, 236, 237
Tertullian, 149, 151, 155, 159, 160, 162, 163, 192, 366
Theocracy, 60, 61, 89
Theodosius I, 165
Theology, 2, 3, 11, 15, 24, 25, 26, 27, 28, 30, 31, 32, 33, 34, 37, 41, 45, 46, 48, 53, 67, 71, 82, 83, 84, 85, 86, 106, 127, 129, 137, 165, 179, 184, 187, 189, 191, 192, 193, 201, 202, 205, 207, 212, 214, 217, 226, 231, 233, 235, 238, 242, 251, 256, 261, 264, 275, 279, 280, 281, 284, 289, 290, 293, 294, 295, 296, 297, 298, 299, 300,

Index

303, 304, 305, 306, 307, 311, 315, 324, 325, 326, 327, 328, 335, 336, 337, 338, 339, 342, 345
Trajan, 147, 366
Transubstantiation, 188, 189, 197, 202, 217, 218, 234, 363, 368
Trinity, 159, 183, 347, 361
Trinity Sunday, 206, 353
Trisagion Hymn, 182
Tucker, Bland, 153
Twain, Mark, 345
Tylor, Edward, 27, 265
Union with Christ, 106, 119, 189
Vatican II, 189, 308, 309, 314
Virgin birth, 93, 151, 157, 172, 311, 358
Voltaire, 259, 260
Von Zinzendorf, Nikolaus, 252, 281
Watts, Isaac, 247, 248, 255, 257, 281, 369
Wesley, Charles, 280
Wesley, John, 252, 280, 282, 283, 284

Westminster Confession of Faith, 239, 242
Whitefield, George, 247, 278, 284, 314, 369
William of Ockham, 194, 368
Winkworth, Catherine, 253
Wittenberg Concord, 224
Words of Institution, 158, 169, 171, 183, 187, 197, 206, 221, 223, 226, 231, 237, 238, 240, 248, 357, 361, 364
Worldview, 2, 11, 21, 22, 23, 24, 25, 26, 27, 28, 29, 30, 31, 33, 34, 37, 45, 53, 68, 85, 86, 106, 165, 193, 233, 251, 261, 262, 263, 264, 266, 270, 272, 311, 320, 321, 324, 327, 335, 337, 338, 339, 340, 347, 349
Youth ministry, 293
Zwingli, Ulrich, 217, 218, 219, 220, 221, 222, 224, 226, 227, 228, 230, 232, 252, 255, 368

Scripture Index

Old Testament

Genesis
- 1:1–2 ... 225
- 1:2 ... 97, 98
- 1:27 ... 10
- 2:3 ... 66
- 2:8 ... 115
- 2:15 ... 21
- 2:18 ... 292
- 3:8 ... 22, 115
- 3:15 ... 23, 73
- 3:23–24 ... 115
- 3:24 ... 23
- 4:3–8 ... 23
- 4:4 ... 24
- 6:1–4 ... 60
- 8:20–21 ... 24
- 11:21 ... 60
- 12:1 ... 24
- 12:3 ... 25, 82
- 12:7 ... 24
- 14:18 ... 25
- 15:5 ... 25
- 15:18 ... 25
- 17:5 ... 25
- 22:1–14 ... 24
- 22:1–19 ... 25
- 26:24–25 ... 24
- 28:18 ... 24
- 31:27 ... 42

Exodus
- 3:5 ... 26
- 3:14 ... 25
- 3:18 ... 26
- 4:14 ... 8
- 4:4–17 ... 32
- 5:3 ... 26
- 6:2–3 ... 59
- 12:14 ... 35, 296
- 15:20 ... 44
- 19:5 ... 26
- 19:17 ... 115
- 20:1–17 ... 27
- 20:8–9 ... 35
- 20:24–26 ... 31
- 23:14–17 ... 32
- 24:1 ... 26
- 24:7 ... 26
- 25:8–9 ... 29, 60
- 25:10–22 ... 30
- 25:13–14 ... 38
- 25:18–22 ... 30
- 25:23–30 ... 30
- 25:31–40 ... 30
- 27:1–8 ... 30
- 27:8 ... 29
- 29:45 ... 97
- 29:38–42 ... 32
- 30:1–10 ... 30
- 30:7–8 ... 32
- 30:17–21 ... 30
- 31:1–5 ... 97
- 31:1–11 ... 30
- 31:12–17 ... 36
- 32:4–6 ... 34
- 32:6 ... 34
- 32:17 ... 34
- 35:30–35 ... 97
- 37:1–9 ... 30
- 37:10–16 ... 30
- 37:17–24 ... 30
- 37:25–29 ... 30
- 38:1–8 ... 30
- 40:35 ... 31
- 40:38 ... 31

Leviticus
- 4:1–5 ... 31
- 5:15–6 ... 31
- 6:8–13 ... 31
- 6:24–30 ... 31
- 7:1–6 ... 31
- 7:11–36 ... 32
- 9:5 ... 27
- 10:1–3 ... 34
- 18:5 ... 22

Numbers

3:7–8	22
4:23–24	22
4:26	22
7:89	31
8:4	29
8:26	22
10:2	43
11:17	79
18:5–6	22
21:17–18	42
28:2–8	32
28:11–15	32

Deuteronomy

4:19	22
4:24	110
5:4–21	27
6:1–3	28
6:4–5	28
6:4–9	77
6:6–9	29
9:16	34
12:2–8	33, 61
34:9	79

Joshua

13:1	37
18:1	37
24:2	24

Judges

5:1	8
6:34	79
13:25	79

1 Samuel

4:3	37
4:11	37
6:1	37
6:13–15	38
11:15	37
16:13–14	79
18:6	42
22:9–23	37

2 Samuel

1:18–27	42
6:16	45
7:6–7	22
23:2	97

1 Kings

1:39–40	42
4:30	53
6:23–28	30
6:29	30
7:1	40
8:27	29
9:10	40
11:38	53
12:25–33	53
13:33–34	53
14:22–24	54
16:24	80
18:1	62
18:12	79
18:18	62
18:36-37	63

2 Kings

17:7–8	57
21:1–18	54

1 Chronicles

9:25–27	90
13:1	38
13:8	42
15:2	38
15:13	38
15:15	38
15:17	42
15:22	43
22:6–8	39
23:2–5	39
28:19	39
29:18	8

2 Chronicles

3:1	25, 39
3:3	40, 90
3:6–7	40
4:1–5	40
4:7–22	40
5:12	42
5:12–13	40
5:64	0
6:1–11	40
6:6	39
7:1–7	41
15:12–14	43

16:9	8
20:28	42
29:11	80

Ezra
1:1–11	57
1:4	90
3:10	57
6:18	57
7:1–10	57

Nehemiah
2:1–10	57
6:10	90
8:2–3	57
9:20	97

Job
1:6	60
33:4	97

Psalms
13:2	8
19:1	21
42:4	90
55:17	133
78:60–61	37
78:67–68	37
90:2	61
104:30	97
110:4	25
118:1–4	42
121:4	63
149:1	44
149:3	44
149:5	44
149:6–7	44
150:1	44
150:4	44, 182
150:6	44

Proverbs
2:10	8
4:23	9
16:1	8

Ecclesiastes
1:9	3

Isaiah
6:1–4	309
6:1–8	xi
6:1–13	54
6:5	310
6:6–7	310
6:8	311
6:9–13	311
6:11	311
7:14	73
11:2	79
25:1–9	305
29:13	58
42:1	79
43:6–7	21, 115
43:7	22
48:16	79
51:11	2
55:1–5	307
61:1	79

Jeremiah
7:11	74
15:16	8
25:30	42
29:4–7	277
30:3	57
31:4	44
48:33	42
52:21	40

Ezekiel
6:9	8
9:3	31, 58
10:18	31, 58
11:23	31, 58
14:3	8

Daniel
1:2	90
3:18	56
6:10	56, 133
10:12	8

Hosea
6:6	58

Micah
4:1–2	84

Haggai
2:5	31, 97

Zechariah
12:10	83

Malachi
1:6–7	58

1:10 58	1:13–14 58

Scripture Index

New Testament

Matthew
- 1:23 73
- 3:13–17 78
- 3:15 79
- 3:17 79
- 11:28 204
- 12:4 90
- 14:23–24 79
- 15:8 74
- 15:22 148
- 17:15 148
- 18:15–18 191
- 18:15–20 299
- 18:19–20 84
- 18:20 110
- 19:13–15 79
- 20:30 148
- 21:12–17 73
- 21:14 74
- 22:36–40 28
- 22:37–39 8
- 26:17–20 81
- 26:17–30 95
- 26:26 81
- 26:26–28 81
- 26:27 174
- 26:27–28 81
- 26:30 .... 81, 92, 212
- 26:36–46 79
- 28:19 .... 95, 127, 289
- 28:19–20 289

Mark
- 1:35 133
- 1:9–11 78
- 2:26 90
- 2:27 296
- 6:46 133
- 11:15–19 74
- 14:12–17 81
- 14:12–26 95
- 14:22 81
- 14:22–24 81
- 14:26 .... 81, 92, 212
- 16:14 84

Luke
- 1:1–4 99
- 1:46–55 94
- 1:68–79 93
- 2:14 .... 94, 148
- 2:29–32 94
- 2:41–50 73
- 2:49 73
- 3:21 79
- 3:21–22 78
- 4:16–30 74
- 4:31 74
- 4:38 74
- 4:44 74
- 5:16 79
- 6:4 90
- 6:12 79
- 9:28 79
- 15:21 192
- 19:1 192
- 19:45–48 74
- 22:19 81
- 22:20 81
- 22:7–16 81
- 22:7–39 95
- 24:46–47 84

John
- 1:1 106
- 1:14 73
- 1:29 83
- 1:29–34 78
- 2:13–22 73
- 2:19–21 74
- 2:21 83
- 3:12 24
- 3:16 204
- 4:7–26 80
- 4:9 192
- 4:22 80
- 4:24 259
- 5:14 74
- 6:47–63 190

6:48	83	8:4	98
6:59	74	8:26	213
7:7	275	8:27	213
7:14	74	8:32	192
7:37–38	308	10:14	117
8:2	74	11:36	225
8:12	83	12:2	293
10:23	74	12:5	99
13:1	82	15:5	x
15:1	11	15:5–6	91
16:8	98	15:6	x
16:13	99	15:16	98
16:13–14	88		
17:6	79		
17:20	79		
18:28	82		
19:31	82		
20:21	84		

1 Corinthians
2:12–13	99
2:16	293
3:16	89
5:7	82, 83
10:11	21
10:16–17	88
10:31	xi, 115
11:2–34	299
11:16	299
11:20	95
11:20-29	190
11:24	88, 128
11:25	88
11:28–34	96
12:7	99
12:12	99
12:13	87, 99
14:12	99
14:26	xi, 92, 93, 185
14:26–33	96
15:20	83
15:52	83
16:2	95

Acts
1:1	87
1:5	87
1:8	87
1:16	99
2:4	98
2:41	83, 87, 96
2:42	87, 91, 92, 96, 128
4:25	99
7:44	29
8:21	8
9:17	98
10:3	133
15:1	90
16:25	133
17:28	165
20:7	88
20:27	x

2 Corinthians
2:4	8
3:3	8
3:18	293
4:4	12, 275
5:7	113
5:17	289
6:16	89
8:1–5	95
9:7	8

Romans
1:19–20	61, 226
1:20	10
1:21	226
1:28	293
2:6	13
2:29	98
3:23	115
5:5	98
6:17–18	289

Scripture Index

Galatians
- 1:4 275
- 2:10 95
- 5:22 98
- 5:22–23 99

Ephesians
- 1:1–11 93
- 1:3–14 x
- 2:2 .... 99, 275
- 2:6 276
- 2:18 110
- 2:20–22 89
- 3:16 98
- 4:6 225
- 4:13 .... 99, 292
- 4:17 293
- 5:19 .... 92, 93, 99, 182

Philippians
- 2:5–11 93
- 2:12–13 .... 100, 293
- 3:17 299
- 3:19 .... 230, 291
- 3:20 276

Colossians
- 1:15–20 93
- 1:16 225
- 1:17 .... 165, 225
- 2:22 90
- 3:12 230
- 3:16 .... 92, 99, 179

1 Thessalonians
- 1:9–10 290
- 5:9 306
- 5:23 306

1 Timothy
- 1:15 204
- 2:1 92
- 2:1–2 278
- 3:15 99
- 3:16 93
- 4:7 292
- 4:13 91
- 5:3 95
- 5:17–18 95
- 6:50 293

2 Timothy
- 2:2 299
- 3:8 293
- 3:16–17 .... 91, 99
- 4:2 91

Titus
- 1:15 293
- 3:5 98

Hebrews
- 1:1–3 93
- 1:2–3 83
- 1:3 36
- 2:17 83
- 4:12 8
- 4:16 .... 103, 304, 311
- 7:17 25
- 7:21 25
- 7:25 .... 83, 103
- 8:5 29
- 10:1 116
- 10:20 116
- 10:21 90
- 10:25 x
- 10:24–25 88
- 11:1 225
- 11:3 225
- 11:4 24
- 11:6 104
- 11:8 225
- 12:14 292
- 12:18 106
- 12:18–29 .... 106, 108, 110, 111
- 12:22 276
- 12:22–24 .... 162, 255
- 12:28 111

James
- 4:4 11
- 5:13 92

1 Peter
- 1:2 98
- 1:15 13
- 1:16 289
- 1:18 13
- 2:12 13
- 2:13–18 278
- 2:21–25 93
- 3:13 226

2 Peter
- 1:19–21 99
- 1:21 .... 88, 99, 293

1 John
- 2:1 204
- 2:15–18 308
- 2:25 11
- 4:9 192

Jude
- 1:1 24
- 1:12 95

Revelation
- 1:10 124
- 4:8 100
- 4:9 101
- 4:11 101
- 5:12 101
- 5:13 101
- 7:4 83
- 14:8 275
- 14:16 275
- 21:3 83
- 21:22 84